No Condition Is Permanent

No Condition Is Permanent

THE SOCIAL DYNAMICS OF AGRARIAN CHANGE IN SUB-SAHARAN AFRICA

Sara Berry

THE UNIVERSITY OF WISCONSIN PRESS

The University of Wisconsin Press
114 North Murray Street
Madison, Wisconsin 53715

3 Henrietta Street
London WC2E 8LU, England

5 4 3 2 1

Printed in the United States of America

Library of Congress Cataloging-in-Publication Data
Berry, Sara.
No condition is permanent : the social dynamics of agrarian change in sub-Saharan Africa / Sara Berry.
272 p. cm.
Includes bibliographical references and index.
ISBN 0-299-13930-1 ISBN 0-299-13934-4
1. Agriculture—Economic aspects—Africa, Sub-Saharan.
2. Rural development—Africa, Sub-Saharan. 3. Agriculture and state—Africa, Sub-Saharan. I. Title.
HD2117.B46 1993
338.1′0967—dc20 93-7102

Dedicated to
the African Studies Community
at Boston University
1975–1991
with gratitude and affection

Contents

Illustrations

MAPS

FIGURE

Tables

Acknowledgments

THIS STUDY grew out of a review essay, "The food crisis and agrarian change in Africa," which I wrote for the Joint Committee on African Studies of the Social Science Research Council and the American Council of Learned Societies. I am grateful to the members of the committee and to numerous reviewers who read and commented on drafts of that essay for stimulating me to broaden my understanding of agrarian change and rural development in Africa, and to think about my previous work on western Nigeria in comparative perspective.

My research and writing were supported by a Noyes Fellowship at the Bunting Institute, Radcliffe College, in 1984–85, and a John Simon Memorial Guggenheim Fellowship in 1989. At the Bunting Institute, I had the opportunity to pursue my own research without interruption, while benefiting from the knowledge and friendship of the extraordinarily diverse and talented group of women who made up that year's group of Fellows. The Guggenheim Fellowship enabled me to take a year's leave from Boston University to write full time.

In carrying out research for this study, I relied heavily on the patience and expertise of Gretchen Walsh and David Webster, curators of the Africana collection at the Mugar Library, Boston University, and am very grateful for their help. I also received unfailingly courteous and informed assistance from staff members at the Tozzer Library at Harvard, the Dewey Social Science Library at MIT, and the Melville Herskovits Africana Library at Northwestern.

In writing this book, I have drawn on many years of reading, observing, and teaching about processes of rural economic and social change, and I cannot begin to name all of the people who have influenced and encouraged my thinking in one way or another. For some time, however, I have been fortunate to work especially closely with Jane Guyer, Gillian Hart, and Pauline Peters. Their insights and encouragement have been crucial to my efforts to explore new evidence and rethink prevailing ideas about agrarian change in Africa and elsewhere, although they are in no way responsible for the use I have made of their teachings. My sixteen years at Boston University were enriched and enlivened, personally and professionally, by my colleagues and students in African Studies, to whom this book is affectionately dedicated.

No Condition Is Permanent

Chapter One

Introduction

SINCE THE EARLY 1970s, most African economies have experienced a dramatic deterioration of their capacity to maintain or expand production and provide for the basic needs of the majority of their citizens. Efforts to explain and alleviate the economic crisis have spawned an extensive literature. Confronted with an apparently "seamless web of political, technical and structural constraints which are a product of colonial surplus extraction strategies, misguided development plans and priorities of African states since independence, and faulty advice from many expatriate planning advisors" (Eicher, 1982:157), scholars have struggled to disentangle it, debating the relative importance of various causal factors and the possibilities of effective intervention. (See Berry, 1984; Shipton, 1990; Delgado & Mellor, 1984; Commins et al., 1986; Jones, 1988; and Peters, 1988 for reviews.)

This book is intended as a contribution both to African agrarian history and to debates over the role of agriculture in Africa's recent economic crises. It presents a comparative study of changing patterns of resource access and resource use in several local agrarian systems during and after the colonial period. Specifically, it traces the effects of commercialization and political centralization on the conditions under which African farmers gained access to productive resources, and the ways in which resource access influenced patterns of resource use. The analysis rests on the premise that understanding resource access and resource use is not simply a matter of tracing rational actors' responses to relative factor prices and rules governing the definition of property rights or the nature and enforcement of contracts. Farmers' access to and uses of the means of production have also been shaped by the mobilization and exercise of power and the terms in which rights and obligations are defined. To study changing conditions of access is also to consider the history of legal and political processes, social relations, and culturally constructed understandings which influence patterns of authority and obligation, the division of labor and output, and the meaning of exchange.

Any attempt to understand African agrarian change in the context of wider social processes is complicated by the conceptual and methodological diversity of the literature—particularly the conceptual differences between analyses of African agriculture by economists and other quantitatively oriented social scientists, on one hand, and by historians and anthropologists on the other. Anthropologists and historians have been engaged in increasingly self-conscious debates over how to describe and understand African societies and social processes. These debates focus on both the nature and extent of cultural diversity within sub-Saharan Africa, and the question of how far particular unities or diversities among African cultures have been constructed by outsiders rather than by Africans themselves. Some maintain that "sub-Saharan Africa is characterized by a fundamental cultural unity" (Kopytoff, 1987:10), while others stress the enormous diversity of African languages and cultures. Africanist scholars have also questioned the conceptual typologies established by their predecessors. Houndtounji (1976) and Mudimbe (1988) have alerted us to the inventions of Africa which pervade scholarly literature, while others have argued that contemporary ethnic identities were created by European missionaries, officials, and scholars (e.g., Vail, 1989:11ff; Ranger, 1983:247–52), or even that some frequently described events in African history were figments of outsiders' interested imaginations (Cobbing, 1988:509 and passim; Fisher, 1982:559 and passim; see also, Rosberg and Nottingham, 1967:321ff.).[1] As Feierman (1990:38) points out, it is difficult for anthropologists to write about other cultures without reification or condescension—yet "the problem of otherness is not easily solved, for the subject matter of anthropology is cultural difference." Historians of Africa face the same dilemma.

Recent historical and anthropological literature has been especially critical of the structuralist and jural paradigms which informed both the classic British ethnographies of the late colonial period and much of the Marxist literature of the 1960s and early 1970s.[2] These critiques have been accompanied by a growing tendency to portray African cultures and institutions as fluid and ambiguous, subject to multiple interpretations and frequent redefinition in the course of daily practice (see, inter alia, Moore, 1986; Comaroff and Comaroff, 1991; Jones, 1988; Peters, 1988; Cooper, 1990; Comaroff, 1980; Feierman, 1990; Kopytoff, 1987).

In contrast, the literature on African economic development is dominated by writers who believe in universal models of behavior and social process, and the importance of verifying and applying them through quantitative analysis. On the whole, studies of African economic development have made scant use of the extensive historical, ethnographic, and sociological literature on local agrarian systems in Africa, because it consists of culturally specific case studies, based primarily on qualitative evidence, which do not lend themselves readily to quantitative methods of aggregation and analysis. However, reliable quantitative data on agricultural and economic processes in Africa are not easy to find. Neither colonial regimes nor independent African governments have had the resources to undertake much systematic collection of economic data, and the quality of available aggregate statistics is notoriously poor, especially for agriculture (Berry, 1984:61–63; World Bank, 1984:90, Eele, 1989:431).

Beginning in the late colonial period, when—in the name of economic development—governments stepped up their efforts to regulate African farmers' productive activities, officials and scholars carried out numerous surveys at the micro level, designed to generate more quantitative evidence on agricultural performance. Initially, most surveys focused on issues of farm management and producers' response to economic stimuli, such as changes in price or technical knowledge.[3] By the end of the first decade after independence, farm-management surveys had been widely criticized for studying farms in isolation from their immediate economic and ecological contexts and for focusing too narrowly on input-output relations. In the 1970s, economists and agronomists shifted their efforts to farming-systems research, seeking to understand farm practices in terms of "the 'total' environment in which the farming family operates . . . [including] technical and human elements" (Norman and Baker, 1986:40–41).[4]

As part of their quest for accurate information on local agricultural practices and socioeconomic conditions, farming-systems researchers have continually modified their methods of data collection and analysis. In general, the search for realism has proceeded on two fronts: the identification of relevant units of analysis and the documentation of change. Initially, most researchers assumed that rural economies in Africa were made up of local variants of generic institutional categories: households, villages, agroecological zones.[5] More recent studies have taken explicit account of the complexity of rural institutions in Africa. In doing so, however, researchers often assume that what's needed is to identify those clearly bounded, homogeneous social entities which carry out the function of resource allocation in the local setting. In a survey of households in an irrigated rice-farming project in the Gambia, for example, the authors "subdivided [large compounds] into subunits of decision-making and management of production and consumer affairs" (Von Braun et al., 1989:108). Following the francophone tradition, agriculture has also been depicted as a "hierarchy of systems," ranging from biological systems of individual plants to regional systems of ecological, economic, and administrative interaction (Fresco, 1986:42–47).

Economists have also expressed concern over the short time frame of much farming-systems research. "Although targetting is a key element in FSR, neither the concepts nor the procedures take sufficient account of the fact that farming systems are in constant flux: the 'target' is not static, but continuously on the move" (Maxwell, 1986:65). However, suggestions for making farming-systems research more dynamic stop short of any fundamental reconceptualization. Thus, Maxwell recommends that researchers estimate likely changes in ecological and socioeconomic parameters "over the next 10–15 years," and calculate their expected impact on inputs, outputs and on-farm activities, but he does not question either the range of variables or the units of analysis employed in most farming-systems research.

In this study, I will argue that the implicit adherence of economists and policy analysts to structuralist concepts of rural societies and institutions—while understandable in terms of their interest in quantitative analysis—has also limited their ability to describe and explain processes of agrarian change. Generalizations about agricultural practices and performance in Africa are problematic not only because reliable quantitative evidence is scarce, but also because the data available rest on misleading or overly restrictive assumptions about the social organization of rural economic activity. Farming-systems researchers emphasize the importance of studying production and exchange in specific social contexts, but usually do so on the assumption that African societies are composed of stable institutions which perform various functions in consistent ways. However, if economic activity is embedded in multidimensional social processes (Peters, 1987:181ff.), questions raised by historians and anthropologists about the fluidity and ambiguity of African cultures are also relevant to the study of economic processes in Africa. In particular, there is no reason to assume that farms, economic "decision-making units," and farming systems are any less fluid than other African social institutions.

The following examination of changes in farmers' access to productive resources and patterns of resource use rests on the premise that African cultures and institutions are fluid, dynamic, and ambiguous. In elaborating this assumption, I attempt both to illustrate ways in which students of economic development and change might make use of the richly detailed monographic literature on local agrarian systems, and to work through some of the conceptual implications of the dynamic and ambiguous character of social institutions and boundaries for understanding rural and agricultural change.

The rest of this chapter outlines my approach in three steps. In the next section I describe the design of the study and explain the criteria I used in defining the overall framework of the comparative analysis and in selecting specific cases for comparison. This is followed by a brief overview of how my theoretical approach compares with prevailing paradigms in the literature on African rural development. Finally, I present a synopsis of the main historical argument of the book, which concerns the changing conditions of African farmers' access to land, labor, and capital, and the impact of those conditions on production and agrarian structure in the four case study areas.

THE DESIGN OF THE STUDY

Since a central objective of this study is to compare local variations in processes of agrarian change, I have limited my discussion to the twentieth century, when most rural areas in Africa were influenced by the common experiences of colonial and postcolonial rule, and of increasing involvement in commercial activity.[6] All four of the case study areas are located in former British colonies, and all are in relatively high rainfall areas. Thus, I have deliberately set aside questions of the impact on agricultural production of (1) different European powers' strategies of colonial domination in Africa and (2) varying degrees of aridity and environmental stress, in order to focus on the effects

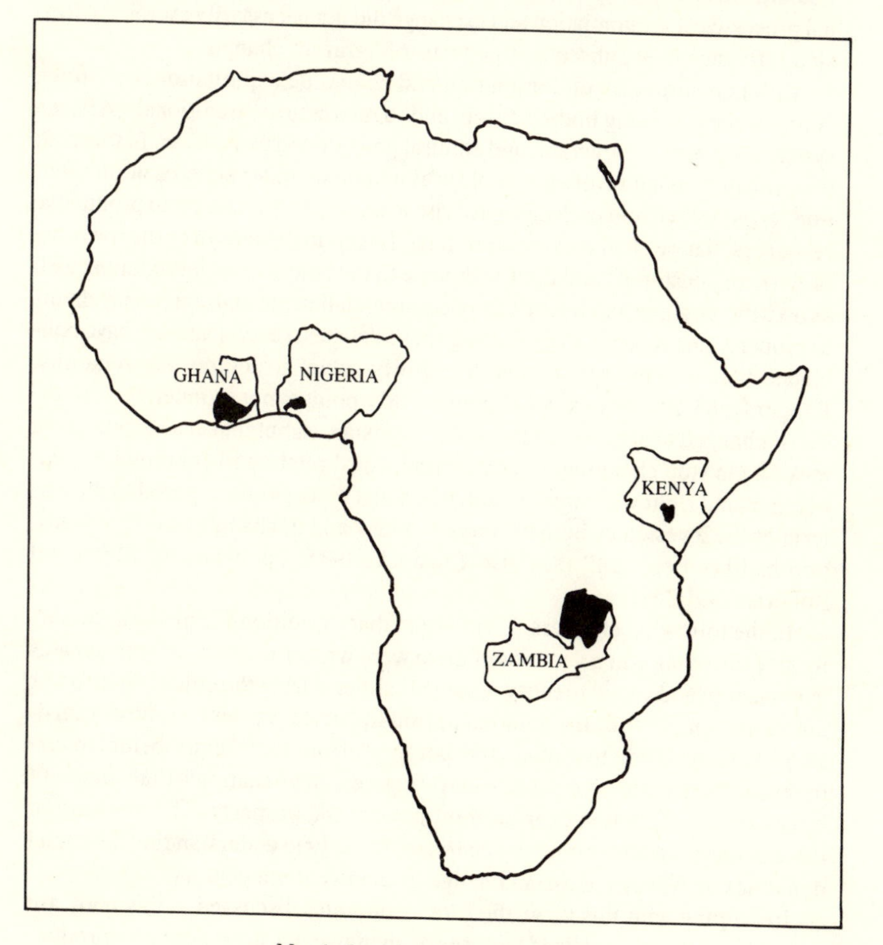

Map 1. Location of case study areas

of commercialization and political centralization under different local configurations of power, production, and culture.

Initially, I selected the four cases to represent different patterns of local incorporation into colonial (later national) and global political economies. Accordingly, the cases include two rural economies which experienced long periods of expanding peasant production for the world market (the cocoa-farming areas of southern Ghana and southwestern Nigeria), a settler economy (central Kenya), and a rural labor reserve (northeastern Zambia). In the course of exploring and comparing the agrarian histories of these four rural economies, however, I've come to the conclusion that the way in which a particular rural area was incorporated into the colonial economy and/or into global processes of accumulation and exchange did not necessarily exercise a decisive influence over subsequent patterns of agrarian change.

Colonial strategies of domination and economic exploitation were often contradictory, seeking both to co-opt and to restructure "traditional" African systems of power, production, and cultural practice and expression. In this context, the increasing involvement of rural people in wider spheres of domination, exploitation, and exchange gave rise to struggles over access to productive resources. These struggles were, in turn, linked to debates over the meaning of African "customs" and their relevance to the colonial social order, as well as over the meaning and legitimacy of commercialization and competing claims to property and power.[7] In examining these debates, several authors have concluded that colonial rule tended to rigidify social structures and relations. Ranger (1983:251) writes, for example, "My point is not so much that 'traditions' changed to accommodate new circumstances but that at a certain point they had to stop changing; once the 'traditions' relating to community identity and land right were written down in court records and exposed to the criteria of the invested customary model, a new and unchanging body of tradition had been created" (see also Chanock, 1985:esp. chap. 10; Mann and Roberts, 1991:22).

In the following chapters, I will argue that "traditions" did not necessarily stop changing when versions of them were written down, nor were debates over custom and social identity resolved, either during the colonial period or afterward. In general, the colonial period in Africa was less a time of transition—from isolation to global incorporation, from social equilibrium to turbulence, from collective solidarity to fragmented alienation—than an era of intensified contestation over custom, power, and property. The intensity of these contests and their ongoing character are keys to understanding the social dynamics of African agrarian change in the twentieth century.

In keeping with this view, the rural economies discussed in this book are defined in terms of localized patterns of change in farmers' access to productive resources and patterns of resource use, rather than according to territorial boundaries. In fact, the spatial and social boundaries of each rural economy have fluctuated over time, both because the locus of cultivation of particular crops or crop combinations has shifted, and because farmers' access to productive resources hinged, in part, on struggles over the demarcation of political and social jurisdictions. For example, in southern Ghana and southwestern Nigeria, the physical boundaries of the cocoa economies shifted over time as new areas were opened up for cocoa planting or yields in older areas declined. The spread of cocoa production also gave rise to the formation of new communities, as farmers migrated into sparsely inhabited forest areas to plant the new crop. In the process, people often asserted claims to land and cocoa farms on the basis of their membership or status in descent groups or communities, or secured them in the process of negotiating new social relationships. In general, the spread of cocoa engendered or intensified struggles over the demarcation of jurisdictions and structures of authority, as well as over property rights per se.

Similarly, in central Kenya, colonial officials both sanctioned European settlers' appropriation of land and attempted to impose fixed administrative boundaries on highly fluid and mobile communities (Ambler, 1987: chaps. 2, 7). In practice, the boundaries of both "native reserves" and administrative districts were redrawn repeatedly, as African farmers contested the legitimacy of European settlers' appropriations of land and struggled over the definition and acquisition of rights to land within areas reserved for African use. Since independence, both property rights and political spheres of influence have remained contested and flexible—despite registration of land titles and the stabilization of administrative boundaries. In northeastern Zambia, struggles between officials and rural dwellers centered on the control of settlement patterns rather than of land rights, but these struggles also revolved around interpretations of the structure of "traditional" authority and jurisdictions.

The flexible definition of agrarian localities employed in this study not only reflects the historical realities of changing patterns of cultivation and contested social boundaries, but also makes the most of available sources. Since the main aims of this study are comparative and synthetic, the book is based primarily on secondary sources. Monographs on local patterns of agrarian change often focus on one or a few villages, or on particular crops or types of enterprises within diversified agrarian systems. In assembling material for the book, I have tried to canvass the most informative works on aspects of agrarian change within each region, even if this has meant using evidence from geographically scattered communities whose local histories diverge in some respects. Thus, for Ghana, I draw primarily on studies of cocoa farming in various parts of Asante and Brong-Ahafo, but also refer to research by Polly Hill, Gareth Austin, Inez Sutton, and others who worked in areas south of Asante. In central Kenya, I focus on the heart of the former Kikuyu Reserve (now Kiambu, Murang'a,

Nyeri and Kirinyaga Districts) but also cite studies conducted in Embu and Mbeere which offer valuable insights into some of the central themes of the book. For northeastern Zambia, I make extensive use of Audrey Richards' and William Watson's classic studies of Bemba and Mambwe communities and subsequent research in the same areas (e.g., Harries-Jones and Chiwale, 1962; Moore and Vaughan, 1987; Pottier, 1988) but also refer to Kay's work on Ushi and on recent studies of the effects of agricultural commercialization in Serenje and Mpika Districts. For western Nigeria, I rely primarily on my own previous research, which focused at different times on individual villages in the rural hinterlands of Ibadan, Ife, and Ondo, and also traced people's movements among rural communities within and outside the cocoa belt, and between rural and urban areas.

Understanding Agrarian Change: The Theoretical Locus of the Book

Much of the literature on agrarian change and the recent agricultural crises in Africa is informed by theoretical frameworks which explain agricultural change either in terms of rational actors' responses to market incentives and rules governing property rights and contracts, or in terms of structural imperatives which emanate from the world capitalist system. I undertook a lengthy review of this literature several years ago (Berry, 1984) which I will not recapitulate here. Instead, in this section I offer a brief schematic review of the way in which dominant paradigms of economic analysis have informed debate over the causes of agrarian change in Africa, and indicate how my assumptions differ from those paradigms.

According to neoclassical theory, economic progress springs from the forces of market competition. Economic agents (firms, households, individuals, etc.) seek to maximize their profits (or utility) by economizing on scarce resources and/or developing new methods of production which enable them to compete more effectively in available markets. Technological leadership can lead to monopoly power, but such power is usually considered temporary, likely to decline as competitors imitate technological advances, thereby bidding away monopoly profits and reproducing competitive conditions. Within this framework, the only legitimate role for power—that is, one which enhances economic efficiency—is an economically neutral one. Rather than seeking to amass capital or to corner markets, the state is presumed to regulate market conduct in the interests of the whole society and to provide social goods which are not profitable to produce privately. Politics, law, and adjudication complement production, investment, and exchange, but are not considered integral to processes of resource allocation or economic progress.

In postulating the separation of economic and political processes, neoclassical theory ignores a contradiction at the heart of the idea of a competitive market: namely, that because competitive markets are hazardous ones, firms (or other economic agents) may seek market power in order to protect themselves. In the framework of rational expectations analysis, this strategy is ruled out—or regarded as deviant and temporary. Instead, agents are presumed to react to uncertainty in an individual manner: they recalculate the profitability of alternative activities in terms of probability distributions rather than fixed values, and those with a subjective aversion to risk will adjust their activities to trade off higher means for lower variance in expected costs and returns. Economic agents are also assumed to act individually to overcome information asymmetries or to minimize potential losses from moral hazard or adverse selection. The idea that producers might systematically seek to deal with these problems by combining forces—with one another or with other powerful agents—is played down, presumably because it would invalidate the whole idea that competition is the motor of economic progress.

For example, in the recent literature on factor markets in developing rural economies, it is argued that contracts and institutions adjust so as to reduce the transaction costs associated with asymmetries in information, moving the economy towards Pareto efficiency by approximating the results of perfect competition.[8] As Bardhan (1980, 1989) has pointed out, however, interlinked contracts which bypass some market imperfections usually rest on, or create, others. Bardhan also questions the common neoclassical assumption that government intervention is otiose: "Even when the market outcome is inefficient (as in the case of externalities), people will supposedly get together and negotiate their way to efficiency under private property rights. This view I find simply incredible" (Bardhan, 1989:14). In general, as Stiglitz (1989:23) reminds us, the rational actions of even well-informed peasants are no guarantee of "Pareto efficiency" in resource allocation. However, even self-critical neoclassical economists have not developed a systematic explanation of how power interacts with production and exchange to shape processes of economic growth or differentiation over time.[9]

Marxist economics provides a fundamental critique of the neoclassical idea that competition reproduces the conditions for its own existence and that power can therefore be treated as exogenous to economic processes. According to Marxist theory, commercialization generates differential rewards, leading to the division of producers into owners and nonowners of the means of production, and creating the conditions for capitalist accumulation based on the exploitation of alienated labor. As production expands, rising wages induce profit-seeking capitalists to substitute capital for labor in the process of production. This reproduces surplus labor, which keeps wages down and profits up. In Marxist theories of capitalist development, power is treated not as exogenous, but rather as subordinate to processes of capitalist accumulation. Because they control the resources on which production depends, capitalists are in a position to exercise hegemony vis-à-vis the state. Accordingly, the power of the state is used to write and enforce laws which legitimize and facilitate capitalist expansion—by, for example, upholding private property and the sanctity of contracts—and the ideological resources of the state are mobilized to mystify the exploited classes, thus forestalling any tendency for them to combine against their exploiters.[10]

In both neoclassical and Marxist theory, culture—like power—is treated as exogenous or subordinate to economic systems and processes. The neoclassical argument that competition insures efficient resource allocation rests on the assumption that people's preferences are completely independent of the process by which resources are allocated among alternative uses. The possibility that preferences are shaped by production is largely ignored, perhaps because it too would invalidate the concept of Pareto efficiency. Marxist economics addresses this possibility, but largely in terms of the way dominant classes use ideology to mask exploitation and manufacture wants, or the way class struggle transforms consciousness. Most Marxist literature glosses over the difference between culture and the way people draw on cultural categories in constructing ideology and consciousness (Comaroff and Comaroff, 1987:205). In sum, neoclassical theory places culture on a par with the supernatural—standing outside the possibility of rational explanation—while in Marxist theory, culture is subordinated to material conditions.

Implicit in neoclassical and Marxist treatments of power and culture as exogenous or subordinate to economic forces is the assumption that power and culture operate through individuals' enforced or voluntary adherence to rules (or norms) which are unambiguous and which tend to endure for long periods of time. For the most part, jural rules are assumed to be clearly formulated and consistently enforced, and to play a hegemonic role in processes of social and economic change. In both Marxist theory and the "new institutional" neoclassical economics, for example, rules of private property serve to promote economic growth. Recently, Bardhan (1989:237) has suggested that in emphasizing "the role of interlinked, often personalized transactions between economic agents . . . the economic literature has only caught up with the relevant literature in economic anthropology." However, neither he nor most other contributors to the literature on interlinked transactions mentions the work of anthropologists who emphasize the fluidity of institutions or the multiple and contested nature of meanings associated with exchanges of goods or claims on productive resources. (For an exception in the economic literature, see Hart, 1991.)

Economists who have noted the fact of negotiability in African economic life tend to assume that its effects on economic efficiency and progress are negative. Carol Lancaster (1990:36) argues, for example, that "perhaps the most important obstacle to private investment and growth in Africa is that everything is open to negotiation." However, she goes on to relate negotiation to the standard World Bank argument that African economic decline is due in large part to African governments' failure to manage their economies effectively. "Rules and regulations are frequently implemented by government officials in an arbitrary and capricious fashion. Above all, investors require predictability on the part of their host governments. This is not present for them in much of Africa and so they go elsewhere" (1990:36).

My point is a more general one. Negotiability is not just an inconvenience for foreign investors, but a pervasive feature of social and economic processes which calls for reconceptualization rather than conditionality. In rethinking African agrarian change, we need to begin with historical and anthropological literature which represents law as social process, transactions as subject to multiple meanings, and exchange as open-ended and multidimensional rather than single-stranded and definitive.

In this study, I have tried to develop such a reconceptualization from a detailed comparison of several historical cases. Such an inductive approach, while methodologically cumbersome, is justified in this case by the need to examine critically the degree to which the assumptions underlying standard paradigms of economic change accurately reflect African historical realities.[11] For example, the neoclassical argument that institutions substitute for imperfect or missing markets doesn't apply very well to African rural societies in which market activity is ubiquitous *and* social institutions play important roles in the organization of economic activity.[12]

My analysis is based on the assumption that culture, power, and material resources are of equal importance, acting in mutually constitutive ways to shape the course of economic and social change. In economic (as in other forms of human activity) people are continually engaged in efforts both to influence and to understand the circumstances under which they produce, invest, exchange, and consume goods and services. Producers, for example, seek to bring power to bear on acquiring and using the means of production, on gaining access to income and wealth, and on increasing (or maintaining) their capacity to produce or earn income in the future. They also think about what they are doing and what they are up against. Thus, people are continually reformulating (or reaffirming) their preferences, strategies, and understandings on the basis of their experience—both at and beyond specific "points" of production, consumption, or exchange. Culture and politics neither imitate nor distort economic activity: all three are interrelated dimensions of social processes.[13]

During the colonial period, struggles over access to economic opportunities and the means of production centered on the definition and exercise of rights to resources and output. Accordingly, these struggles were linked to debates provoked by the process of colonial conquest and domination over relations of authority and ideas of legitimacy at all levels of social interaction. Such debates drew on established lexicons, but also imparted new meanings to them. Thus, while ideas and practices relating to property, power, and legitimacy were specific to the cultural milieux in which struggles over resources were taking place, the process of colonial conquest and domination subjected local cultural practices to similar forces of change.

For example, the connotations of terms interpreted by colonial officials to mean "tenant" varied from one locality to another. In Ghana, for example, *abusa* laborers were sharecroppers, working a plot of land in exchange for one-third of the crop, while in central Kenya, *ahoi* were more like clients, who grazed livestock and cleared plots for their wives to cultivate in proximity to their patron. However, in both colonies, increasing demand for agricultural land provoked multifaceted debates among European officials, settlers (in Kenya), and African farmers—debates which both promoted the increasing commercialization of transactions in land-use rights and linked the definition of property rights to issues of social identity and political relations.[14] Similarly, varied local practices with respect to the division of labor and output in agricultural production were subjected to common pressures from increasing agricultural commercialization, while the results of those pressures were played out in terms of culturally specific debates over age and gender roles, kinship and community relations, and changing conceptualizations of people's relations to the environment and one another.

If rules, transactions and values are ambiguous and negotiable, then economic activity cannot necessarily be explained in terms of decisive choices or efforts to gain exclusive control over goods and resources. If access to resources and opportunities depends on one's ability to negotiate, people may be more interested in keeping options open than cutting them off, and in strengthening their ability to participate in and influence negotiations rather than acquiring exclusive control over resources and severing connections which are not immediately profitable. As we will see in the following chapters, the literature on African rural economic life is filled with examples of farmers who prefer not to register their land rights, even though it is legally and administratively feasible to do so; employers who don't dismiss redundant or unproductive workers; laborers who work without pay, though hiring-out is an option; lenders who do not charge interest, and borrowers who pay back more than they owe. Such behaviors are not simply the results of backwardness or altruism. Rather, I will argue, they reflect people's efforts to keep their options open and to mobilize potential allies and supporters.

In many African societies, a person's status and influence depend directly on his or her ability to mobilize a following. If access to resources depends on the influence one brings to bear in negotiations over property rights, production, or exchange, and influence is enhanced by having followers, then it is not necessarily advantageous to exclude people from social networks, even if these networks also serve as channels of access to resources or frameworks for organizing production and accumulation. Redundant workers and multiple claims on property reflect systematic efforts to exercise influence in ongoing struggles over access to resources.

In the same vein, open-ended claims and unresolved transactions leave room for negotiation and maneuver. The point may be illustrated with an episode described by a visitor to the Asante capital of Kumasi in the early nineteenth century. A wealthy state official named Tando, returning from a royal mission to the coast, passed through Wassa and took the opportunity to settle a long-standing dispute between the local chiefs and the court at Kumasi. When he reached Kumasi and reported his achievement to the king, however, he was fined and demoted for "spoiling a palaver which [the king] and his great men meant to sleep a long time" (Bowdich, 1819, quoted in Robinson and Smith, 1979:179). Like inclusive strategies of social organization, indecision may enhance, rather than hinder, the pursuit of wealth and power.

In the following chapters, I will explore the implications of negotiable, ambiguous rules and transactions for African farmers' strategies of resource management and accumulation. In general, I will argue that ambiguity gave rise both to exclusive and to inclusive strategies of social mobilization and resource control, and that changes in both economic practices and social relationships reflected tension between these two tendencies. In addition, since access to resources depended, in part, on the ability to negotiate successfully, people tended to invest in the means of negotiation as well as the means of production per se. In the African economies discussed in this book, this meant in practice that agricultural surplus was used in part to establish or strengthen the social identities and relationships through which people entered or influenced negotiations over access and control of resources.

As will be demonstrated in the following chapters, both these tendencies are evident in farmers' strategies of resource management and use. However, their impact on agricultural performance also depended on a number of other factors—including cropping patterns, cultural understandings, and specific conjectures of economic, social, and political conditions—which varied from one locality to another. In general, the agrarian crises in Africa were not a uniform and inevitable consequence of colonial domination and capitalist penetration, "bad policy," or innate features of African culture. Instead, agrarian change has been shaped by the way power, economy, and culture have come together at particular times and places. To illustrate, I'll outline the main historical argument of the book and indicate how it will be developed and documented.

The Argument in Brief

Since precolonial times, African farmers have gained access to productive resources both through market transactions and through social relationships. During the colonial period, African farmers became increasingly involved in market exchanges—albeit at very different rates in different localities—but this did not necessarily diminish the importance of social networks as channels of access to productive resources. As increasing amounts of cash flowed into rural economies, and/or farmers' incomes rose, transactions in material goods and claims on productive resources became increasingly commercialized. However, commercialized transactions were not automatically divested of multiple meanings or separated from social relations or the definition and exercise of authority.

Colonial regimes promoted and engaged in the exploitation of Africa's economic resources, but they also sought to maintain order and exercise control over Africans' conduct. In doing so, they tried to incorporate "customary" systems of law and authority into the apparatus of colonial administration, as well as to reorganize "traditional" polities according to Western conceptions of administrative stability and efficiency. Often the result was to provoke or prolong debate over the legitimate interpretation of customary rules and the demarcation of traditional political jurisdictions and hierarchies (see chapter 2). As agricultural production for the market increased, the resulting struggles over access to land, labor, and capital fed into and intensified ongoing debates over the meaning of customary rules and structures of authority.

Since colonial officials relied primarily on varied, often conflicting local testimonies for information about customary rules and practices, such debates were rarely resolved in a definitive manner. Instead, Africans' ability to exercise influence within the colonial order was linked to their continued participation in debates over the meaning and application of custom. The ability to participate and/or influence the course of debate depended, in turn, on a person's social identity or status as well as his or her command over material wealth. Thus, people were encouraged to invest in reaffirming or strengthening social ties which served as means to debate. Such investments tended, in turn, to reinforce the importance of social relations as mechanisms of access to productive resources.

Social relations continued to provide significant channels for negotiating access to resources, even after African countries gained independence from colonial rule. Most African governments and political opposition movements sought to mobilize popular support by appealing to sectional identities of various kinds. Thus, social identity and status became important as channels of access to the state, as well as to local resources. In recent years, the uncertainties of weather, world markets, and contemporary politics have encouraged farmers to diversify their income-generating activities and channels of access to resources and opportunities. Both sectional politics and socioeconomic diversification in the face of uncertainty have further reinforced the proliferation of social networks and their continued importance as channels of access to productive resources and economic opportunities (see chapter 3).

In the four agrarian localities discussed below, farmers gained access to land, labor, and various forms of agricultural capital through social networks as well as through impersonal commercial transactions. However, over the course of the twentieth century, changes in conditions of access to land and land-based forms of capital (such as cleared fields or tree crops) followed a different trajectory from conditions of access to labor and working capital. (These points are documented in detail in chapters 5 and 6.) Specifically, access to land continued to be mediated through membership in various social networks, while access to labor has become increasingly individualized.

In the case of land and land-based forms of fixed agricultural capital, the commercialization of transactions in particular rights (to plant annual or permanent crops, to hunt or gather, to alienate land or improvements on it) did not result in the consolidation of rights into private property—that is, exclusive control over land either by individuals or by corporate groups. For example, rights to plant or cultivate tree crops were often rented or sold independently of the land they stood on. In addition, tree crops themselves were subjected to increasing numbers of claims over time, through inheritance, labor arrangements, or the farmer's accumulation of clients. Thus, the definition of property rights has been shaped by ongoing debates over social identities and relationships. To gain or defend access to rural landed property, it has been necessary for people to participate actively in the politics of rural groups which either hold various rights over land or serve as forums for the mediation of disputed claims. Such groups include not only those of ancient lineage, such as descent groups, villages, traditional ritual communities, or chiefdoms, but also many of recent origin, including recently constituted religious or ritual associations, patronage networks, political parties, cooperatives, and rural settlements created by the state.

In the case of labor and working capital derived from the earnings of rural household members, patterns of access have followed a different trajectory. Increased agricultural production for the market usually led to increased demand for agricultural labor, while the growth of opportunities for off-farm employment tended to reduce the supply. Both contributed to an upward drift in the real price of farm labor, though the upward movement was frequently constrained by the low level of returns to agricultural production. Rising labor costs served, in turn, to limit the commercialization of agricultural employment. Low and uncertain returns to agricultural production meant that many farmers lacked the working capital to hire in labor. As rural household members became increasingly involved in off-farm activities (school, wage employment, trade, etc.), many farmers have had to rely increasingly on their own labor. Continued participation in family and other social networks is no longer a guarantee of continued access to agricultural labor.

Changing conditions of access to the means of production have influenced patterns of agricultural growth and distribution. In general, these effects have varied across local farming systems, depending on how land and labor are combined in the process of production; how markets for agricultural commodities and opportunities for off-farm income earning have changed over time; and how the terms of debate over relations of authority and obligation and over the division of labor and output have been renegotiated over time.

Among the four agrarian regions covered in this book, there were two major patterns of agricultural growth and changing agrarian structure. In the cocoa economies of West Africa, farmers negotiated access to land for cocoa cultivation through descent groups and, in Ghana, through stools. Members of the lineage or stool which controlled a given area of land enjoyed a presumptive right to use portions of that land for any type of cultivation; in practice, however, as areas became extensively planted in cocoa, some people were unable to exercise such rights and had to seek land elsewhere. In addition, "strangers" to the group in question could negotiate rights to plant permanent crops in exchange for payments of money, produce, or sometimes labor, and acknowledgement of the "owners'" continued rights over the land.

Cocoa farmers in both Ghana and Nigeria also relied heavily on family and other dependent forms of labor for establishing new cocoa farms. By drawing on the unpaid labor of kin and other social subordinates, many people were able to establish cocoa farms without prior access to working capital. Once cocoa farms matured, they usually produced enough revenue to cover the cost of using hired labor for weeding and harvesting, and farmers tended to substitute hired for family labor. (Major exceptions occurred when cocoa prices fell to unusually low levels or farms were subjected to severe attacks of pests or diseases.) Thus, the spread of cocoa cultivation gave rise to widespread use of hired labor in small-scale farming.

Cocoa also enjoyed long periods of relatively favorable market conditions. Real prices were buoyant throughout the first thirty years of the century, except for sharp declines during World War I and the depression of 1919–20, and again from the end of the Second World War to the mid-1960s. During these periods, many farmers in Ghana and Nigeria were able to derive modest profits from cocoa production and invest in establishing additional farms. Even during the prolonged slump of the 1930s and early forties, cocoa cultivation remained a relatively attractive economic activity, and plantings actually increased in some areas. Because of the long-term growth of cocoa planting and production, the "life cycles" of cocoa farms were continually repeated, creating renewed demand for family labor to help in establishing and tending immature farms. The demand for dependent labor also rose in periods when returns were too low to pay hired workers.

The long-term growth of cocoa output and rural incomes stimulated the growth of rural markets for other commodities. Thus, cocoa farmers were able to mobilize the unpaid labor of their social subordinates in exchange for future assistance in helping wives, offspring, and junior kin to establish farms or other income-earning enterprises of their own. By the same token, farm workers enjoyed fairly widespread opportunities for modest upward mobility. The result was a kind of contra-Leninist pattern of agricultural development, in which the commercialization of agricultural labor relations was not accompanied by increasing differentiation between farm owners and farm workers, but rather by considerable socioeconomic mobility within and beyond the agricultural sector.

In farming systems where annual crops played a dominant role in agricultural production for the market, small-scale farms did not have the same tendency as cocoa farms to become self-financing over time. Returns to annual crop production were often too low or unreliable to cover the cost of using hired labor on a regular basis. Hence, labor hiring has been limited to farmers with large holdings or steady access to off-farm income. In northeastern Zambia, the number of such farmers was limited in the colonial period by British policies designed to discourage growth of agricultural markets in the northeast and by general rural poverty since independence, especially after the decline of the copper industry in the mid-1970s. In central Kenya, production of annual crops for sale grew steadily during the colonial period and continued to rise after independence. However, pressure on rural land limited the growth of large farms in the colonial period and has resulted in substantial subdivision of holdings since independence. Farmers in Central Province have cultivated tree crops at various times (wattle in the 1930s and early 1940s, coffee and tea in the 1960s and early 1970s), but growth of production has been limited by changing market conditions and by the subdivision of holdings since the late 1960s. Thus, tree crops have never attained the dominant position in the agricultural systems of Central Province that cocoa did in Ghana and Nigeria, and overall patterns of agricultural change have been shaped by the predominance of annual crops in local agricultural production and sale.

In central Kenya and northeastern Zambia, agricultural employment has been much less commercialized than was the case in the cocoa economies of West Africa. Paradoxically, however, these economies have experienced a more pronounced tendency towards differentiation. In central Kenya, land shortages have given rise to unequal patterns of access, reflected in rising numbers of landless households (Collier and Lal, 1980:28) and extremely small holdings (Livingstone, 1986:161–64), and in increasing restrictions on women's access to land. In both central Kenya and northeastern Zambia, differential access to nonagricultural sources of income has widened the gap between prosperous rural households, who can afford to hire in farm labor, and the poorer majority of farmers, who rely on their own labor or that of their immediate dependents. Both poor and prosperous rural households engage in off-farm or nonagricultural employment, but for the poor this serves only to supplement farm proceeds which fall short of minimal consumption needs, rather than to generate resources for accumulation and upward mobility. In northeastern Zambia, even cooperative work groups are increasingly characterized by nonreciprocal exchanges of labor for food between impoverished and relatively prosperous individuals.

Similar patterns may be observed in Ghana and in Nigeria in the 1970s and 1980s, when the terms of trade shifted in favor of food crops relative to cocoa. In all three cases, the predominance of annual crop production for sale has been associated with a tendency towards socioeconomic differentiation without commercialization of agricultural employment—a pattern of rural development which also departs from the standard Leninist model, but in a different way from that of the cocoa economies of West Africa.

Outline of the Book

In the ensuing chapters, this argument will be elaborated as follows. Chapters 2 and 3 consider the role played by colonial and postcolonial states in shaping the conditions under which African farmers gain access to productive resources. The discussion emphasizes the contradictory interests underlying official strategies of governance and of agricultural policy, and suggests that state intervention has been intrusive rather than hegemonic in its effects on agricultural performance. Chapter 4 provides outline histories of agrarian change in the four case study areas as background for the remaining chapters, in which specific topics are analyzed using comparative evidence from all four cases.

Chapters 5 and 6 trace changes in farmers' access to land and labor respectively, while chapters 7 and 8 examine the implications of changing conditions of access for patterns of resource use and agricultural performance. In chapter 7, I focus primarily on patterns of investment out of farm income, arguing that farmers' investments in social relationships have helped to prolong debate over social identities and rights to resources, keeping social networks fluid and open-ended. As a result, rural institutions often operate as arenas of negotiation and struggle, rather than as closed corporate units of accumulation and resource management. In chapter 8, I explore the implications of this argument for changing patterns of agricultural production and rural income-generating activities, with particular emphasis on changes in techniques of agricultural production and on African farmers' ability to cope with the growing instability of economic and political conditions in the last fifteen to twenty years.

Chapter Two

Hegemony on a Shoestring

Indirect Rule and Farmers' Access to Resources

WITH THE IMPOSITION of colonial rule, the pace of agricultural commercialization accelerated in Africa. Farmers sold more of their output and took up the cultivation of new crops expressly for local or overseas markets. Rural dwellers spent more on consumer and capital goods, and transactions in rights to land, labor, and credit became increasingly monetized. Markets for agricultural commodities expanded, stimulated by growing European demand for African exports, by the development of colonial towns and the growth of wage employment, and by colonial administrators' insistence that taxes be paid in cash. By the time of independence, it was becoming increasingly difficult to find rural areas in which people were not engaged in market transactions (Hill, 1969:392–94).

Commercialization, together with colonial regimes' exactions of taxes, labor, and provisions, increased Africans' demand for land and labor, and intensified their efforts to appropriate a share of the increased flow of income from cash crops and wage employment. Competition over land, labor, and income gave rise, in turn, to struggles over the terms on which people gained access to productive resources and/or controlled both income and processes of production and exchange. In this chapter, I will look at the ways in which colonial regimes influenced the structure of opportunities and constraints facing rural producers, and the course of struggles over access to productive resources.

African farmers' access to productive resources was affected not only by government policies aimed directly at regulating rural economic activity, but also by colonial regimes' overall strategies of surplus appropriation and social control. Administrators' efforts to collect taxes, keep order, and mediate disputes shaped the legal and institutional conditions under which farmers sought access to land and labor, whether or not they were explicitly designed for that purpose. Thus, the effects of land and labor laws, or of efforts by agricultural officers to introduce new methods of cultivation and animal husbandry, must be understood in the context of colonial processes of governance in general.

Recent literature on the colonial state in Africa has attempted to move beyond the dominant liberal and Marxist paradigms of the 1960s and 1970s. These paradigms, articulated in part as reactions against the laudatory or apologetic historiography of the colonial era, depicted colonial states as external agents, seeking to govern or exploit African societies according to the interests and political philosophies of European powers. The liberal or neoclassical paradigm portrayed the state as an arbiter of conflicting interest groups, existing outside the social and economic system, and capable of impartial intervention to advance the "public interest," while Marxist writers played a series of variations on the theme of the state as an executive committee of the metropolitan (or local settler) bourgeoisie. (For reviews of some of this literature, see Lonsdale, 1981; and Kitching, 1985.)

More recently, several authors have tried to unpack these arguments—to look at the state as a complex institution made up of individuals and interest groups with diverse links to the societies they seek to govern (e.g., Bates, 1983; Jessop, 1977, 1982; Chazan et al., 1988; Berman, 1990). Lonsdale and Berman (1979; Berman and Lonsdale, 1980) argued, for example, that the colonial state in Kenya was drawn into increasingly coercive patterns of labor control through officials' efforts to cope with the contradictions of capitalist accumulation in a colonial context. Others have suggested that the state plays several roles, serving as an agent of capitalist or other class interests, as an arbiter of social conflict, and as an arena within which social groups struggle to advance their interests through alliances with elements in the state apparatus (Joseph, 1984; Beinart et al., 1986; Chazan et al., 1988).

Scholars' interest in disaggregating the state, conceptually speaking, has intersected with a growing interest among students of political economy and social history in the role of culture in shaping social and economic processes. Colonial rule and capitalist accumulation generated conflicts of interest, among Europeans and Africans as well as between them. The outcome of those conflicts was shaped not only by the material and political sources which different groups could marshal in support of their interests, but also by the terms in which people understood their interests and expressed them (Peters, 1988; Carney, 1988; Carney and Watts, 1990). Historians such as Beinart (1984), Anderson (1984), and Vaughan (1987) have shown how major events such as famine or soil erosion become foci of multiple explanations which, in turn, shaped people's responses to the events themselves. Similarly, Peters (1984), Comaroff (1980), and other anthropologists have explored the role of struggles over meaning in shaping government policies and interactions between colonized peoples and colonial regimes. In particular, a growing body of literature has shown that "customary" laws were not static perpetuations of precolonial norms, but new systems of law and adjudication based on colonial administrators' interpretation of African tradition (Colson, 1971; Moore, 1975, 1986; Ranger, 1983; Chanock, 1985; Snyder, 1981).

The present discussion is intended as a contribution to ongoing efforts to draw these strands of argument together. In this chapter, I will look at the early decades of British colonial rule in Africa, when administrators struggled to establish effective control with extremely limited resources. Scarcity of money and manpower not only obliged administrators to practice "indirect rule," but also limited their ability to direct the course of political and social change. In effect, I will argue, colonial regimes were unable to impose either English laws and institutions or their own version of "traditional" African ones onto indigenous societies. Colonial "inventions" of African tradition served not so much to define the shape of the colonial social order as to provoke a series of debates over the meaning and application of tradition, which in turn shaped struggles over authority and access to resources.

The chapter is organized in four sections. The first presents my general argument about the impact of colonial rule on conditions of access to agricultural resources. The second describes the kinds of debate which arose under indirect rule over the meaning and uses of "custom," while the third and fourth illustrate their implications for the organization of native administration, and the limits of colonial authorities' control over rural economic and social life. Because of the time period covered, African countries are referred to by their colonial names.

HEGEMONY ON A SHOESTRING: THE ARGUMENT

As they moved to assert military and political control over most of sub-Saharan Africa, colonial administrators faced from the outset a continual struggle to make ends meet. As self-declared rulers of the African continent, Europeans assumed responsibility for governing extensive territories inhabited by scattered and diverse peoples—a vast and potentially expensive project. The British Exchequer was, however, reluctant to subsidize either the recurrent or the capital costs of colonial administration (Frankel, 1938; Pim, 1940, 1948; Hailey, 1957:1307ff.; Hopkins, 1973:190–91). Partly because of financial stringency, the number of European personnel posted to colonial administrations was limited, and officials were expected to raise enough revenue from their colonies to cover the costs of administering them. However confidently administrators might share Earl Grey's conviction that "the surest test for the soundness of measures for the improvement of an uncivilised people is that they should be self-sufficient" (quoted in Pim, 1948:226), the daily struggle to wrest revenue, labor, and provisions from reluctant, hostile, or scattered subjects was not an easy one (Asiegbu, 1984:chaps. 3–5, 8, 10, 11; Munro, 1975:36ff.; cf. Weiskel, 1975:esp. chaps. 2, 4, 6).[1]

To live within their means, officials worked both to raise revenue and to keep down the costs of maintaining order and running the day-to-day business of administration. One obvious way to cut costs was to use Africans both as employees and as local agents of colonial rule. African clerks and chiefs were cheaper than European personnel; also, by integrating existing local authorities and social systems into the structure of colonial government, officials hoped to minimize the disruptive effects of colonial rule (Hailey, 1957:133ff.,528). In other words, for reasons of financial and administrative expediency, most colonial regimes in Africa practiced indirect rule, whether or not they had articulated it as their philosophy of imperial governance.

Although colonial administrators did evolve an elaborate set of principles and institutions for formalizing the conception and practice of indirect rule, in fact they not only failed to preserve (or restore) stable systems of traditional social order, but actually promoted instability in local structures of authority and in conditions of access to productive resources. My argument differs from those of authors who have suggested that European "inventions" of African tradition served to rigidify jural norms and practices, and hence social structures, in Africa.[2] Colonial officials certainly tried to govern according to fixed rules and procedures which were based on what they imagined to be the stable political and jural systems of the African past, but they rarely exercised enough effective control to accomplish exactly what they set out to do.

This was so for several reasons. First, colonial administrators' own economic and political interests often had contradictory implications for their strategies of exploitation and control. Second, contrary to British expectations, African societies were not divided into neatly bounded, mutually exclusive, stable cultural and political systems; they were dynamic, changing communities, whose boundaries were fluid and ambiguous and whose members were often engaged in multiple contests for power and resources. Finally, officials' efforts to learn about indigenous societies in order to build on them frequently elicited conflicting testimony about the nature of "native law and custom." I shall elaborate each of these points in turn.

The Contradictions of Colonial Interest in African Agriculture

The financial viability of a colonial regime was likely to be both threatened and enhanced by successful African participation in cash cropping and wage employment. Whether or not a particular episode of conquest was motivated by the desire to promote European capitalist interests in Africa, once colonial rule was established, officials counted on European enterprise to generate taxable income and wealth. Trading firms, concessionaires, mining companies, and European settlers were all expected to increase the volume of commercial activity and hence the flow of taxable income generated by the colonial economy. European profits depended, in turn, on ready access to cheap African labor—farm workers and mineworkers, porters and dockhands, and producers of commodities for export or for the direct provisioning of Europeans in Africa. Africans were, in turn, more likely to offer their labor cheaply if they were hard-pressed to meet their own needs independently of trade with or employment by Europeans. In short, African prosperity threatened the profits of European enterprise on African soil.

However, Africans also paid taxes and bought European goods, and their ability to do so increased with their incomes. Thus, colonial regimes walked a tightrope between encouraging Africans to become involved in labor and commodity markets, and attempting to prevent them from becoming economically independent enough to ignore the opportunities afforded by European-controlled markets and jobs. Officials did not want to stifle the flow of African labor, produce, and tax revenue on which the fiscal and economic health of the colony depended, but they were equally anxious to minimize the cost of African labor and produce, and to limit Africans' ability to influence the terms of exchange.

Colonial administrators' ambivalence towards African agricultural growth and commercialization was expressed differently in different colonies, depending on the particular local configuration of economic activities and interests. In settler economies, such as Kenya, officials faced conflicting pressures to encourage increased African production for sale in order to generate taxable income, supply the home market, and keep down wage costs, and to suppress it in order to force out labor and protect European farmers from African competition. Officials advocated the creation of African reserves both to limit Africans' access to land and augment the flow of labor to European farms, and to "protect" Africans from dispossession or excessive exploitation. On the issue of labor recruitment, they shifted their strategies, first using African headmen as recruiters in order to forestall the abuses of commercial recruiters and then using professional recruiters or even acting as recruiters themselves when popular discontent threatened to undermine the authority of headmen and hence their effectiveness as agents of indirect rule (Lonsdale and Berman, 1979:502–3; Clayton and Savage, 1974:63).

In Northern Rhodesia, large tracts of land were cleared for settlers, but so few ever arrived that their labor needs were insignificant, and colonial authorities never faced the issue of restricting African cultivation in order to generate labor supplies. Instead, they wrestled with the issue of settlement patterns. For administrative purposes, it was convenient to have people concentrated in large settlements under the effective control of powerful chiefs, and officials of the British South Africa Company and, later, the colonial administration waged a series of unsuccessful campaigns to prevent the dispersal of

Bemba settlements. However, concentrated settlements soon led to deforestation and soil erosion. No sooner had the colonial administration moved people into newly demarcated Native Reserves in the 1930s, than the resulting overcrowding led to visible signs of environmental degradation, and villagers had to be resettled within a few years (Allan, 1965:109ff.).

In West Africa there were no settlers to speak of, and colonies prospered from the rapid expansion of tree crops and other forms of agricultural production for export. However, officials worried that in their rush to produce for export, farmers would neglect food crops; that African methods of production resulted in poor-quality produce which brought low prices in Europe; and that European traders' efforts to protect themselves against African competition would provoke disturbances that might threaten the smooth flow of trade (Hopkins, 1973:212ff.). Here, too, official policy towards agriculture and commerce wavered between encouraging export crop production and African commerce and limiting it, as administrators struggled to balance competing interests and manage the contradictions of agricultural development.[3]

The Dynamics of African Political Economies

For much of the colonial era, many Europeans assumed that African communities consisted of mutually exclusive sociocultural units—tribes, villages, kin groups—whose customs and structures had not changed very much over time. Officials could see, of course, that there was conflict among Africans at the time of colonial conquest, but they assumed they could restore order by reconstituting what they believed to have been the "closed, corporate, consensual systems" of the past (Ranger, 1983:249). Accordingly, colonial administrators set out to discover the boundaries and customs of "traditional" communities and the "original" relations between them, in order to use tradition as the basis for their own administrative structures and practices.

In attempting to construct stable, workable administrative systems in Africa, officials sometimes sought to preserve traditional structures of authority, sometimes to reorganize or completely recreate them. In Northern Nigeria, colonial officials found a system of Muslim emirates, complete with written legal codes, courts, and administrative structures, which were almost ideally suited to their purposes. Also, since a majority of the Fulani aristocracy agreed to accept British overrule in exchange for confirmation of their own authority, the process of conquest was brief and relatively smooth. However, few other systems of local government proved as comprehensive or congenial to British notions of administrative efficiency (Perham, 1938:43ff.; Hailey, 1957:416–17). Most African chiefs kept no tax rolls or law books; few made any attempt to separate either the principles or the practices of adjudication from those of politics or diplomacy; and many were vague about the exact boundaries of their domains. In decentralized societies, such as those of central Kenya or southeastern Nigeria, where colonial administrators were unable to find strong chiefs or hierarchical systems of authority, they created them.

In more centralized polities, chiefs who resisted or challenged colonial domination were deposed, and their governments sometimes reorganized as well, to prevent renewed dissent. For example, the British deliberately weakened Asante hegemony after 1896 by signing separate treaties with chiefs and communities formerly subordinate to Kumase and disregarding Kumase's claims to "customary" overlordship (Dunn and Robertson, 1973:13; Lewin, 1978:207). In western Nigeria, where Yoruba states had been engaged in a series of battles and shifting alliances for most of the nineteenth century, British officials insisted on assigning them to positions in a fixed hierarchy under the supreme authority of the Alafin of Oyo, despite the fact that since the 1850s, Ibadan had been stronger than Oyo, and Ibadan's principal opponent (the Ekitiparapo, or Ekiti-Ijesha alliance) was quite independent of Oyo (S. Johnson, 1921:532ff.; Atanda, 1973:99–101; Akintoye, 1971:chap.3).

In the early years of colonial conquest and "pacification," officials dealt with each area ad hoc, responding pragmatically, sometimes ruthlessly, to local conditions in their efforts to establish control and mobilize resources. By the end of the First World War, however, official thinking was converging towards a standard "mental map of an Africa comprised of neatly bounded, homogeneous tribes" (Ambler, 1987:32) and an increasingly uniform conception of their own imperial mission and how best to realize it. Lugard's *The Dual Mandate in Tropical Africa* (1923) laid out the philosophy of indirect rule, and during the next twenty years, officials labored to replicate a common system of native administration across the map of colonial Africa. In 1929, the Secretary for Native Affairs in Northern Rhodesia noted with satisfaction that, when the Colonial Office took over administration of the colony in 1924, "'the tribes were in a very disorganised state', but since then a tribal organization had been 'created'" (quoted in Chanock, 1985:112).

In fact, precolonial communities were neither static nor internally cohesive. In central Kenya during the nineteenth century, "men and women throughout the region moved in a complex world of overlapping, layered and shifting associations," formed through migration, marriage, trade and blood brotherhood (Ambler, 1987:32). "As agricultural settlement steadily expanded, the patterns of [social] identity were continually recast by the evolving relations among communities" (Ambler, 1987:35). Nor were fluid, overlapping, or contested social boundaries and lines of authority peculiar to acephalous polities such as those of the Kikuyu, Igbo, or Tiv. Even as British missionaries moved into Northern Rhodesia, followed in 1895 by agents of the British South Africa Company, a major realignment was taking place among Bemba chieftaincies. As Roberts (1973) has shown in detail, the "strength" of Bemba chiefs and the cohesiveness of the tribe under the central authority of the Chitimukulu, which so impressed early British observers, rested not on any institutionalized system of central authority, but rather on a particular conjuncture of historical circumstances. In the 1860s and 1870s, shifting alliances and conflicts among neighboring peoples combined with a realignment of long-distance trade patterns to reward Bemba skills at ivory hunting and slave raiding without bringing dissident groups into their territory (Roberts, 1973:198–99). This led to a temporary consolidation of Bemba power within the region, but also promoted competition among Bemba chiefs. By the 1880s, the power of the Chitimukulu was declining, and several smaller chieftaincies switched their allegiance to the increasingly powerful Mwamba (Roberts, 1973:211–14; Werbner, 1967: 29ff.). With the establishment of company control in 1895, large fortified Bemba settlements dispersed, leaving much room for the subsequent debate over which chiefs had traditional claims to authority over whom.

In Asante, since the eighteenth century, successive Asantehenes had manipulated the allocation of rights over land and people in order to consolidate and extend the power of Kumase (McCaskie, 1980:196ff., 1984:171; Tordoff, 1965: 7–9). In 1889, Yaa Kyaa secured the throne of Kumase for her son, Agyeman Prempe I, by promising his supporters to restore to them all the land and subjects "who had been sold, pawned, confiscated or otherwise alienated" from their ancestors by previous Asantehenes (McCaskie, 1984:182–83). After more than a century of confiscation and redistribution by several Asantehenes, Yaa Kyaa's promises left much room for debate over who was entitled to what. Similarly, in western Nigeria, much of the nineteenth century was taken up by warfare, migration, and shifting alliances among Yoruba states which generated multiple, conflicting precedents for demarcating "traditional" social boundaries and chiefly jurisdictions.

In general, colonial regimes imposed themselves on societies already engaged in struggles over power and the terms on which it was exercised. By announcing their intention to uphold "traditional" norms and structures of authority, colonial officials were, in effect, declaring their intention to build colonial rule on a foundation of conflict and change. The result was "a blizzard of claims and counterclaims" to rights over land and people, which served as "a mechanism for generating factional struggle" rather than eliminating it (Dunn and Robertson, 1973:73).

The Search for Tradition

The debates and tensions provoked by European efforts to construct stable governing structures on top of volatile African social realities were exacerbated by colonial administrators' methods of implementing indirect rule. To build colonial administration on a foundation of "native law and custom," officials needed information about traditional systems of law and authority. But few African societies, apart from those with established traditions of Islamic scholarship, possessed written bodies of legal and historical knowledge from which such information might be drawn. Officials had therefore to rely on travelers' accounts (sketchy and dated, at best) and oral testimony.

Oral evidence was gathered informally at first; later, it was gathered more systematically by official commissions of inquiry and by professional anthropologists hired by colonial regimes for the purpose (Hailey, 1957:54–56; further discussion follows). But the search for oral tradition was fraught with difficulties. Like scholars who collect oral history, colonial administrators who set out to gather information on local laws and customs were told multiple, often conflicting stories. Whichever version of customary rights and practices an official chose to believe, people were sure to challenge it—both because the past was in fact complex and changing, and because Africans took advantage of officials' interest in tradition to offer evidence favorable to their own interests.

When tensions rose over a particular aspect of colonial policy, the Colonial Office convened commissions of inquiry, both to investigate immediate grievances and to amass information about local customs. Though the work of these commissions contributed to the emergence of an official orthodoxy concerning "native law and custom," the evidence they collected was often full of varied and conflicting testimony. For example, in Southern Nigeria and the Gold Coast, after recurring protests both from influential Britons opposed to commercial concessionaires and from Africans who objected to the proposed enactment of a Crown Lands Ordinance for these territories, the Colonial Office convened the West African Lands Committee in 1912, to consider the "laws in force" concerning "the conditions under which rights over land or the produce thereof many be transferred," and whether those laws needed amending (West African Lands Committee, 1916b:2). Perhaps unintentionally, the committee's draft report (which was never published) summed up the colonial administrator's dilemma. In principle, "natives have rights under their own laws and customs," and, for the courts to protect them, "the appropriate custom or law must be brought to the knowledge of the court." In practice, however, the testimony offered to the courts "is often very unsatisfactory and untrustworthy" (West African Lands Committee, 1916b:2).[4]

Partly because they often received confusing or contradictory evidence on traditional norms and practices, administrators searched for common rules by which to interpret customary practices and apply them to the business of governance. In the 1920s, colonial regimes began to employ professional anthropologists to help them discover the rules and practices of traditional African cultures. Anthropologists such as Rattray, Meek, and Gluckman assumed that traditional African societies were well-ordered, self-reproducing systems, whose natural evolution had been disrupted by the trauma of colonial conquest. Their self-assigned mission was to discover or reconstruct these "original" systems through fieldwork and then persuade colonial authorities to restore them, in order to put African societies back on a normal, evolutionary path towards civilization (Kuklick, 1979:50). Rattray, for example, declared that the "true Ashanti" was to be found among elderly people in remote forest settlements, isolated from the corrupting influences of commerce and colonial politics, where social interaction was still ordered according to traditional religious precepts (McCaskie, 1983:187–89). From his investigation of the Aba women's war in Nigeria in 1929, Meek concluded that colonial rule had weakened the religious basis of traditional law and order, undermining "what was before a well-ordered community," and threatening to replace it with "a disorganized rabble of self seeking individualists" (quoted in Chanock, 1985:26). Gluckman (1941, 1965) portrayed the Lozi kingdom as a coherent, self-contained system, in which economic, political, social, and religious practices complemented and reinforced one another in harmonious and well-ordered fashion.

By the 1920s, the study and interpretation of African custom was becoming institutionalized as part of the routine activity of colonial administration. In the Gold Coast, district officers were "obliged to take examinations in native custom, although apparently they were not required to pass them" (Kuklick, 1979:51). In general, anthropological research served to reinforce the official view of African societies as clearly bounded and coherently organized (Crook, 1986:89–90; Kimble, 1963:486). To be sure, some administrators were well aware that tradition could be invented as well as recalled. "After a review of fifty years' disputes" in the coastal Ghanaian stool of Ada, one official commented sarcastically that the Adas' "knowledge of ancient traditions is, in fact, small, but the manufacture of new ones has been raised by them to the status of a rural industry" (quoted in Sutton, 1984:42–43). Indeed, some saw distinct advantages in the confusion: in Ahafo, one official pointed out in 1930 that "as a result of the system of indirect rule in vogue it is extremely unlikely that any riot or disturbance should be directed against Government authorities. What disturbances occur are invariably in the nature of 'faction fights'" (quoted in Dunn and Robertson, 1973:87).

Multiple and conflicting testimonies were more likely to be dismissed as evidence of Africans' venality or obtuseness, however, than examined for the possibility that the homogeneous systems of primordial law and culture which officials had painstakingly pieced together to serve as the basis of the colonial order may never have existed in the first place. In Brong-Ahafo, "it was the conventional wisdom of the administration, apt to be produced without noticeable irony after the recital of the most baroque confusions, that in unravelling disputes about traditional issues, one must 'always be governed by well established Akan custom'" (Dunn and Robertson, 1973:169).

In short, colonial rule affected conditions of access to land and labor through the interplay of administrators' ambivalence towards African farmers' prosperity, their efforts to govern through indigenous rules and authorities, and ongoing debates over the meaning of "native law and custom." As agricultural commercialization and labor migration gave rise to disputes over the means of production, officials insisted on resolving them in terms of "native law and custom." Their insistence served, in turn, to reinforce existing linkages between farmers' access to resources, their positions in local structures of power, and their ability to win arguments over customary rules and practices. Ongoing struggles over power and the interpretation of tradition were incorporated into the rules and procedures through which officials sought to "cope with the contradictions" and "crises of accumulation" which accompanied colonial rule (Lonsdale and Berman, 1979:487; Berman and Lonsdale, 1980:37). Struggles over the meaning of traditional rules and structures of authority shaped struggles over resources, and vice versa (Peters, 1984:29–30).

In general, the effect of indirect rule was neither to freeze African societies into precolonial molds, nor to restructure them in accordance with British inventions of African tradition, but to generate unresolvable debates over the interpretation of tradition and its meaning for colonial governance and economic activity. As Watson (1976:181) remarked of the Lungu in northeastern Zambia, "in a sense, the British policy of indirect rule preserved the Lungu political system, complete with all its conflicts." In seeking to maintain social and administrative stability by building on tradition, officials wove instability—in the form of changing relations of authority and conflicting interpretations of rules—into the fabric of colonial administration.

The Interpretation of Custom: Rules and Social Identities

In their respective attempts to enhance the power and exploit the resources of colonial regimes, Europeans and Africans debated both the nature of customary rules and the demarcation of social groups to which they should apply. For European officials, the second question arose because they assumed that Africans belonged to distinct, mutually exclusive groups, each with its own set of rules and institutions for enforcing them. Whether or how a particular rule should apply to a given individual depended on the group to which that person belonged. For example, the right to cultivate land or the obligation to pay tribute for doing so was held to depend on the social origin of the person in question. The rights and obligations of "strangers" were commonly held to be different from those of indigenes, and much effort was devoted accordingly to determining who was a stranger by classifying people according to descent group, or "tribal" affiliation. How "the law" was applied followed from the decision as to who a person was.

In the Gold Coast, for example, by endorsing the view that a chief's right to collect cocoa rents depended on the social origin of the farmer, the colonial authorities helped to intensify disputes over boundaries between stools and over the designation of "paramount" and subordinate chiefs (Austin, 1988:75–77). In Kenya and Northern Rhodesia, where African reserves were demarcated on tribal lines, rights to land and labor were similarly linked to social identity. Officials often sought to determine people's "tribal" identity in order to decide which rules to enforce. Since "the boundaries of ethnicity were themselves [often] vague and fluctuating . . . finding and applying the customary law . . . was difficult" (Chanock, 1985:174; see also Sorrenson, 1967:37–38).

For Africans, the interpretation of rules also depended on who was involved, but for different reasons. In most precolonial African societies, status and wealth depended on accumulating dependents or followers. "Strangers" were welcomed—as wives, clients, "blood brothers," settlers, or disciples—because they enhanced the prestige and often the labor force of the head of a household, kin group, or community. Access to land and labor thus followed from negotiations over a person's relationship to other individuals or groups. Negotiations could take a long time. Payment of bridewealth, for example, sometimes took years: an adult son might still be paying part of his mother's bridewealth after his own sons were eligible for marriage and/or his mother had died (Glazier, 1985:135). In the event of divorce or separation, the disposition of a couple's children and property depended not on whether or not the couple were married, but on how married they were at the time of separation—which depended in turn on the interpretation of transactions and other events in the history of their relationship (see also Comaroff, 1980:172).

As commercialization led to new demands for land and labor, Africans increased their efforts to negotiate new relationships in order to gain access to additional productive resources. In Akan, Yoruba, and Kikuyu societies, marriage gave men various claims on the labor of their wives, while women (and, in matrilineal Akan communities, men) gained the right to cultivate land belonging to their spouses' lineage. In central Kenya in the nineteenth century, people participated in rituals of "blood brotherhood" in order to augment the portfolio of kinlike relationships through which they could organize trade or seek refuge in other communities in times of famine or disease (Ambler, 1987:82–84, 134–35).

As cocoa farming spread in southern Ghana and Nigeria during and after the 1890s, would-be farmers sought access to suitable uncultivated forest land by negotiating with heads of local families or chieftaincies. Often they acquired rights to plant tree crops or even rights to the land itself in exchange for money, labor services, and/or annual "gifts" of produce or cash, which served to acknowledge the continued authority of local leaders. Similar processes occurred in Kenya, where migrants (*ahoi*) "begged" permission to settle and farm in a new area. *Ahoi* might work for local elders or marry into their families in order to get established. As they accumulated herds and formed their own domestic establishments, they advanced to full membership in the *mbari*, or settlement, of their hosts (T. Kanogo, 1987:26). Also, in Northern Rhodesia, access to land or labor followed from a decision to marry or join a new community (A. Richards, 1939:254, 256; Watson, 1958:19–20).

In general, then, people tended to negotiate access to land and labor in the process of joining a new household or community. Negotiations often included transfers of goods or money in exchange for rights of access or control, but the meanings of such transfers were not fixed—as colonial officials assumed them to be. For example, the sale of land or other assets did not necessarily extinguish the rights of the seller: in central Kenya, land sold in exchange for cash might be reclaimed by the seller or his kin on the grounds that custom dictated that land belonged to the "family" or that sales were redeemable (Sorrenson, 1967:40; J. Fisher, 1954?:195). Similarly, in both Ghana and Nigeria, purchasers of cocoa farms might be held responsible for paying tribute (or rent) to the landholders who had given the original farm owner permission to plant permanent crops in the first place (Berry, 1975:103; Hill, 1963:157). In both cases, terms of access were negotiable, and the outcome in any particular transaction depended on the history of relations between the persons involved and the way they were interpreted at the time of land acquisition. As Chief Kinyanjui told the Kenya Land Commission, when questioned about his role in an old land dispute, "I do not remember what I said before the District Commissioner eight years ago. Tell me who summoned me to give evidence. What I said depends on whose witness I was" (Kenya Land Commission, 1934b:282).

In short, administrators sought information on traditional social structures and identities in order to know how to apply customary rules in governing colonial peoples, while African colonial subjects renegotiated rules and social identities in order to cope with or take advantage of colonial rule and commercialization. Together they debated the nature of linkages between customary law and social identity. But the debates remained unresolved, partly because European officials were struggling with conflicting evidence about social processes which they misunderstood, and partly because Africans' efforts to take advantage of the colonial economic and political order led them to keep redefining the rules and institutions on which colonial officials predicated their strategies of governance. Whatever conclusions officials reached about the content of customary laws or the boundaries of traditional societies were either challenged by Africans offering a different version of tradition, or outpaced by changing social and economic practices. Both processes tended to keep the debates going, rather than give rise to a new set of fixed rules or social relations.

THE ORGANIZATION AND REORGANIZATION OF NATIVE ADMINISTRATION

After World War I, colonial regimes across Africa moved to codify customary law and formalize the structures of indirect rule, in keeping with the general trend towards rationalization and professionalization of the colonial service (Young, 1988:48ff.). Chieftaincies—often reorganized in accordance with British ideas of administrative efficiency—were legally constituted as "native authorities." Chiefs were empowered (and required) to raise revenue, spend money on public facilities such as roads, latrines, and clinics, and adjudicate cases according to customary law—all under the supervision of British officials, who also had the power to appoint and depose chiefs themselves. In principle, British officials sought to create permanent structures for the consistent and disinterested enforcement of fixed rules. In practice, both the structures and the boundaries of native administrations were periodically readjusted—in some cases practically up to the eve of independence.

For example, in the Gold Coast, native authorities were not even fully established until 1944, less than a decade before they were abolished altogether. From the nineteenth century, British officials had found it expedient to negotiate with Akan stools as semiautonomous states, rather than subsume them under the formal apparatus of indirect rule. This did not stop the British from working actively to undermine the power of Asante, first by military attack and, in 1896, by negotiating a series of treaties with neighboring states which placed them on an equal footing with Kumase in the eyes of the colonial regime.

During the early decades of colonial rule, as the spread of cocoa raised the value of land and the volume of litigation over access to it, chiefs maneuvered to maximize their revenues from cocoa "rents" and judicial fees and fines by asserting claim to land and subjects which the British had allocated to other jurisdictions, and by reinterpreting customary rules concerning their prerogatives. Citizens and aspiring candidates for chiefly office responded with a flood of protests and destoolment proceedings, which kept administrators busy and led to periodic adjustments of stool boundaries and hierarchies. One of the most dramatic cases was the decision, in 1935, to restore Kumase hegemony over a number of neighboring stools, in response to prolonged agitation by Kumase chiefs and their supporters. Their interest in reviving apparently anachronistic jurisdictional claims was not lessened by the fact that, since the British occupation, the land in question had been extensively planted in cocoa and increased in value many times over. "With the restoration of the Ashanti

Confederacy in 1935 reasonably clear . . . titles to land in return for regular payments gave way to a massive Kumasi *Reconquista*" (Dunn and Robertson, 1973:53).

In western Nigeria, early treaties between colonial agents and Yoruba chiefs were supplanted, after 1916, by the designation of Yoruba *obas* as native authorities. The colonial regime also attempted to establish hierarchies of superior and subordinate chiefs, both within preexisting Yoruba states and between them. Since Yoruba states had been engaged for much of the nineteenth century in a series of struggles over hegemony, "tradition" offered a poor guide for demarcating these hierarchies. As in the Gold Coast, Yoruba communities regularly questioned their assigned status vis-à-vis their neighbors. Administrators were confronted with countless petitions from communities seeking autonomy from a neighboring chief, or from groups of people within a town or state seeking to depose a chief in the hopes of enthroning a successor who would be more favorable to their interests. During the 1930s, District Officers prepared a series of "Organization and Re-organization Reports," in which fresh batches of local testimony were presented to support administrators' decisions to preserve or redraw boundaries between communities and to define or redefine hierarchical relations among their chiefs.[5]

In the settler colonies, the formal demarcation of social boundaries was guided by issues of land appropriation as well as local administration. In Kenya, where administrators had to contend with the absence of "any Chief who could command the respect accorded to the Kabaka of Uganda" or any "ready-made organization which could be converted into an administrative machine,"[6] British officials often appointed headmen on the basis of their willingness to collaborate with colonial authorities rather than any traditional claims to power (Tignor, 1976:45–46). Local Native Councils were created in 1925, modeled on Kikuyu *kiama* (councils of elders), but drawn from administrative districts designated by the colonial administration and comprised of individuals selected or approved by District Officers. In practice, spheres of authority were not clearly defined, and the councils and the Native Tribunals (customary courts) functioned more as arenas of struggle over control of land, revenue, jobs, and influence than as guardians of Kikuyu custom (Kitching, 1980:198; Glazier, 1985:82ff.).

Native Reserves were not formally demarcated until 1926, largely because settlers objected to being cut off from potential access to land within them (Sorrenson, 1967:19). Once established, however, the reserves were organized on tribal lines, thus linking land rights firmly to social identity and provoking prolonged debate over the relative weight of "tribal," "family," and individual rights (Sorrenson, 1967:24, 29–31; Kenya Land Commission, 1934b:35, 43, 60). Within the reserves, migration and changing economic opportunities led to new demands for access to land, which intensified debate over "which communit[ies]" had the right to allocate use rights to individuals. (See the discussion near the end of the first section of chapter 4.)

In Northern Rhodesia, British officials waged a series of unsuccessful campaigns to control settlement patterns and shape Bemba chieftaincies to the needs of orderly administration. When agents of the British South Africa Company first moved into the new protectorate in the late 1890s, they were favorably impressed with the apparent power of Bemba chiefs, who presided over large fortified settlements, and even worried that they might have a tendency to abuse their power. *Pax Britannica* obviated the need for such encampments, however, and people lost no time in dispersing themselves over the countryside, in order to practice their extensive system of *citemene* agriculture. Company officials were afraid the dispersal of the population would erode the authority of Bemba chiefs, making them useless as agents of company rule. In 1907, the company banned the practice of *citemene* and forcibly rounded people up into villages, "but the famine which followed led to a change of mind" (Hellen, 1968:203; see also Kay, 1964b:248). Colonial officials who succeeded the company pursued similar ends with less draconian means, but their efforts to establish a minimum size for Bemba villages were no more successful. When admonished that their authority would dwindle if they permitted their "subjects" to scatter, Bemba chiefs blandly countered that "the greater the number of villages, the greater the prestige of the chief" (Ranger, 1971:27).

When indirect rule was formally established in 1929, four out of thirty-odd Bemba chiefs were designated native authorities; the rest were relegated to "subordinate" status. Elsewhere in the colony, chieftaincies were created outright. In both cases, colonial restructuring provoked numerous disputes over chiefly ranking, prerogatives, jurisdictions, and succession (Meebelo, 1971:195–219). As in other colonies, efforts by the Colonial Office to implement "national self-determination on a tribal level" resulted in African complaints about the rankings of native authorities, and British complaints about Africans' "failure" to follow custom (Gann, 1963:230). Native administrators were reorganized periodically, up to the eve of independence.

In short, British efforts to build stable systems of native administration on customary foundations had the effect of maintaining fluid, flexible social boundaries and structures of authority. In practice, British officials' efforts to impose fixed rules in the name of tradition served to "institutionalize" struggle and debate over the meaning of customary rules and structures of authority—an outcome which is reflected in their own continual readjustment of the formal institutions of native administration.

CONTESTED CUSTOM: THE LIMITS OF COLONIAL CONTROL

In constructing the edifice of colonial administration on contested foundations, the practice of indirect rule both expressed and exacerbated the problematic basis of colonial authority in Africa. Strategies employed by colonial officials to pursue the contradictory objectives of exploitation and social order with limited material resources created new sources of confusion over what constituted legitimate rules and who had the right to enforce them. In this respect, the exercise of authority by colonial officials aggravated the ungovernability of colonial societies.

This point is vividly demonstrated in Inez Sutton's (1984) study of colonial rule in Ada, a small community on the southeast coast of Ghana. In the early twentieth century, the inhabitants of Ada were divided into nine groups of clans of varied ethnic origins. The stool rotated among three clans, one Krobo and two Akan, while control over the community's principal economic resource (the salt flats of the lagoon) was shared by the stoolholder and the most important priest, who came from another Krobo clan. During the colonial period, the collection of salt (and hence most of the state's tax revenue) was frequently interrupted, either by disagreements between the stool and the chief priest, or by vacancies in one or both offices which were often prolonged by disputes among the clans over the choice of a successor. Neither colonial administrators nor the courts were eager to decide these issues, "but preferred to let such disputes be settled by traditional means" (Sutton, 1984:54). These produced only temporary solutions: "in 1943 [for example] . . . a 'declaration of native custom' by the Ada State Council" was considered by the Provincial Commissioner to have "enough support to be binding," but he "soon realized that this complacency was premature" (58).

By the 1940s, "many of the Ada state institutions, both traditional and recent, [were] unworkable" (Sutton, 1984:59). Taxes were rarely collected; most people refused to serve on the Ada Finance Board or participate in the deliberations of the State Council, and those who did reached few decisions. On occasion, "resolutions were passed by the council, but the people were not informed, and council members who signed resolutions later opposed them" (Sutton, 1984:59). Sutton concludes that in Ada and elsewhere in British colonial Africa, officials' efforts to build imperial rule on a customary base "opened opportunities for actions to be heard in both systems, leading to virtually unending disputes, and paralysis in the workings of the state" (Sutton, 1984:62).

Sutton's tale of political and administrative chaos in Ada provides a graphic illustration of tendencies at work throughout our four case study areas. In the cocoa economies of Ghana and Nigeria, struggles over the income generated by the crop gave rise to endless jurisdictional wrangles among chiefs, citizens, and rival lineages. In northeastern Zambia, representatives of the British South Africa Company who first visited the area in the 1890s were favorably impressed by the large, fortified villages and authoritarian style of Bemba chiefs, and their successors were correspondingly dismayed when these villages began to break up under the aegis of *pax Britannica*. Subsequent efforts to round people up and bolster the authority of the chiefs met with limited success, but were profoundly disruptive of people's lives, inhibiting the growth of agricultural production and contributing to rural unrest in the late colonial period (see the discussion in section 2 of chapter 4).

In central Kenya, the ineffectiveness of colonial authorities' early efforts to reduce tensions between Africans and European settlers over land rights and labor recruitment led to the imposition in the 1920s of a pass law and the decision to demarcate Native Reserves.[7] Like the consolidation of rural settlements in Northern Rhodesia, this proved to be a protracted process. As we have seen, formal demarcation of most reserves was delayed until 1926 because of complaints from the settler community that they would be debarred from expanding into areas reserved for Africans' use (Sorrenson, 1967:19). When the boundaries were finally laid down, protests came mainly from Africans. The ensuing series of official enquiries culminated in the Kenya Land Commission, which collected several volumes of evidence in 1933, including petitions from over nine hundred Kikuyu families and individuals concerning land claims in Central Province (Kenya Land Commission, 1934b:258–376). The commission declined to address individual African grievances, opting instead to accommodate Kikuyu grievances by adjusting the boundaries of the "tribal" reserve.

In Sorrenson's trenchant phrasing, "the 'final solution' of the Kikuyu-European land conflict was seen in tribal terms" (Sorrenson, 1967:24). Administrators did indeed cling to their belief in the primacy of tribes and tribal tenure, but the "solution" turned out to be anything but final. Within a few years, the colonial government decided to open up additional blocks of land to displaced squatters, but to exercise close control over the way they used the land, in order to forestall problems of overgrazing and soil erosion, which were already serious in some of the African reserves. The controls greatly angered Kikuyu settlers (some of them displaced for the third or fourth time), as did the government's refusal to grant them full *githaka* rights to land allocated them in the settlements. The resulting tensions contributed directly to the Mau Mau uprising of the early 1950s (Throup, 1988:132–33; Kanogo, 1987:116, 120; Sorrenson, 1967:83–84).

CONCLUSION

Colonial efforts to exercise hegemony on a shoestring did not block the commercialization of agricultural production and resource mobilization in Africa, but did shape the way in which rights of access to land and labor were defined and transacted, and the way people used resources to establish and defend rights of access. Under indirect rule, colonial regimes incorporated ongoing struggles over power and social identity into the structure of colonial administration, and elicited conflicting testimonies from their African subjects concerning the meaning of "native law and custom." As a result, property rights and labor relations were neither transformed according to the English model nor frozen in anachronistic "communal" forms, but instead became subjects of perpetual contest. Under indirect rule, British officials sought to make rights of access contingent on people's social identity. At the same time, Africans sought to negotiate new social identities in order to take advantage of commercial or political opportunities. The combined result was a series of ongoing debates about how rules of access were linked to social identity and vice versa.

My conclusions differ from those of scholars who have argued that by codifying customary law and using fixed rules to adjudicate disputes, colonial governments incorporated custom, transforming it from a flexible idiom of dispute to an instrument of authoritarian rule. According to this view, power was transferred from traditional communities to appointed chiefs and their literate clerks, and fixed rules, based on British inventions of African tradition, replaced the flexible, negotiable arrangements of the past. In turn "legalisation led to a freezing of rural status and stratification, henceforth defined and not negotiated" (Chanock, 1985:47; see also Ranger, 1983:254ff.).[8]

The literature on customary law and dispute settlement does not entirely support this interpretation. Writing of Zambia, Chanock himself points out that the effects of commercialization on social relations were contradictory. People ignored traditional obligations to kin in order to save money for other uses, and at the same time intensified the exploitation of family labor in order to expand production for the market: "Conflicts about what was and what was not customary were intense" (Chanock, 1985:236). Such conflicts underlay many of the cases heard in customary courts, where they were argued from multiple perspectives. In the courts of Bemba chiefs, Richards observed in the mid-1930s that "the composition of the court varied according to the issue discussed" (A. Richards, 1971:111). Infractions of regulations imposed by the colonial regime (such as sanitation laws or tax liabilities) were frequently heard only by the chief and court clerk, but disputes over land, marriage, chiefly succession, or protocol attracted large, varying groups of participants, who debated each case at length (Richards, 1971:112–13, 116–20; see also Perham, 1936:21–24).

Forty years later, Canter (1978:264–68) studied disputing processes in a Lenje chieftaincy near Lusaka. He found that while local court proceedings were brief, formal, and authoritarian, enforcement of court rulings was left to informal negotiations between the parties involved (Canter, 1978:268). Moreover, a large number of disputes were heard in family or village moots, where attendance was open, and there were no limits to the number of issues which might be raised, the number of people who might speak, or the length of time they might discuss a case (Canter, 1978:264–67). From observations in a rural district near Chipata, Van Donge (1985:69) concluded that "life in Mwase Lundazi was not so much shaped by 'development policies' and their intended and unintended consequences as by arbitration sessions, which were chaired by the chief, in which land and headmanships were discussed and by local court sittings which mostly dealt with disputes between co-wives" (see also Bond, 1987:182ff.).

Often, there was also confusion over which laws applied in what contexts. In Ada, "it was not a question merely of 'two systems of jurisprudence . . .'—African and English—but of English law and many African systems" (Sutton, 1984:47). It was unclear, for example, whether a case on appeal from a Native to a Superior Court was to be heard according to English or customary law and, if the latter, whether English judges were qualified to hear it. There were also endless possibilities for reopening cases on the grounds that previous rulings had misinterpreted customary law, or for moving cases back and forth between courts and informal moots for the same reason. In the process, rules were continually reinterpreted in an ongoing dialogue which was influenced by multiple interests and ideas, rather than dominated by any single view. As Moore (forthcoming:10) writes of local courts in Tanzania today, "not only has much of the British-designed structure of the courts been inherited, but so have many of the resistances to it and circumventions of it. That dynamic combination *is* the African institution."

The continual renegotiation of rights of access and control which occurred under indirect rule affected both the significance of market transactions and farmers' strategies of investment. Much of the literature on the nature of African property rights and their implications for economic development postulates a universal dichotomy between individual and communal rights, and then deduces behavior from the supposed logic of whichever system appears, from available evidence, to have gained the upper hand in a particular colonial context (Feder and Noronha, 1987:154–58; cf. Collier and Lal, 1986:130–32). In fact, individual and community rights frequently coexisted, and more than one community might claim rights to a particular resource. Structures of access to productive resources involved "bundles of rights" (Gluckman, 1965) and bundles of right-holders. The way in which a particular resource was managed depended on relations among right-holders as well as on the jural content of the rights they held.

Under indirect rule, membership in a community came to be considered the primary basis for claiming rights to productive resources. Hence the delineation and exercise of property rights became enmeshed in conflicting testimony over community boundaries and structures. Indirect rule affected the management of resources not by preserving communal property rights, with their attendant problem of "free riders" (people who misuse resources because they cannot be held accountable for conserving them), but by assigning property rights to social groups whose structures were subject to perennial contest.

African farmers' management of productive resources depended on the course of debates among multiple claimants to rights of access and control. Farmers didn't squander their patrimony because they figured they could get away with it, but they did often find it advisable to invest part of any available surplus in the means of contesting access to resources, leaving less for investment in directly productive capital. As rural commercialization spread under the aegis of indirect rule, Africans found that they could use wealth to promote interpretations of custom which might strengthen their own claims to productive resources. People invested in the means of access to productive resources—including social identities or forms of status through which they could claim rights to productive resources—as well as in the means of production per se.

Chapter Three

Inconclusive Encounters

Farmers and States in the Era of Planned Development

INTRODUCTION

RURAL DEVELOPMENT PROGRAMS in Africa rarely work the way they are supposed to. Since independence, international agencies and African governments have initiated hundreds of programs designed to accelerate agricultural growth and/or raise rural living standards. With a few exceptions (World Bank, 1989), the achievements of rural development policies and projects have fallen short of expectations or turned out opposite to what was intended. Agricultural price controls produced parallel markets, rather than cheap urban food supplies or higher revenues for the state. Crop subsidies and price supports have usually led to increased sales, but not necessarily to higher output. In the long run, subsidized prices may even have reduced output, by tempting farmers to sell off stocks normally kept for seed. Legislation designed to facilitate investment by giving farmers secure title to their land has been more likely to create a market in title deeds than an appreciable increase in the rate of farm investment. Multipurpose development projects have generated as much conflict over access to new resources as increases in productivity, while cooperatives, village development committees, and the like have failed to "capture" the peasantry.

In recent years, a substantial literature has appeared that seeks to explain "what went wrong." A full review of the literature is beyond the scope of this chapter, but I will comment on a few aspects of it, in order to clarify the argument which follows. Three commonly cited views are (1) that policy has little effect on rural economic activity, because peasants have managed to escape government control; (2) that development policies are economically inappropriate, because politicians are more concerned with staying in power than with promoting economic growth; and (3) that colonial rule left Africa with a legacy of neopatrimonial rule which undermines effective government and aggravates underdevelopment. I will examine each of these arguments in turn.

Goran Hyden is a leading exponent of the view that African peasants remain "uncaptured" by the state. He attributes the limited impact of state policies on rural economic activity to the cohesiveness of traditional society (Hyden, 1980:18–19 and passim; 1983:196–98). Secure in a traditional "economy of affection," Tanzanian peasants have little need of markets or the state, and remain uncaptured by the latter, despite forcible villagization of most of the rural population in the mid-1970s. Hyden was one of the first to point out how limited the impact of state policies has been in rural Africa, but his vision of peasant communities as harmoniously self-sufficient is strikingly at odds with others' reports that rural poverty and inequality—not to mention increased tension, even violence, within rural communities and families—often follow in the wake of increased state intervention (C. Jones, 1986:110; Carney, 1988:340; Carney and Watts, 1990:224ff.; Pottier, 1988:117ff.). Also, the implication that peasants are uncaptured because they want to be underestimates African farmers' eagerness to improve their access to market opportunities, and overestimates their ability to control their economic circumstances.

The second argument is widely associated with the work of Robert Bates (1981, 1983), who has attributed many of the failures of rural development policy in Africa to the fact that, as members of the state apparatus, politicians and civil servants are more concerned with staying in office than with promoting economic development. Officials choose to spend money on rural development projects, Bates argues, rather than offer farmers higher prices because access to projects can be rationed, allowing officials to reap political benefits from them, whereas prices benefit all farmers, and cannot therefore be turned to political advantage by those who administer them. Also, higher food prices hurt urban consumers, who are likely to be more politically active and influential than peasant producers scattered across the countryside.

Like Hyden's notion of the uncaptured peasantry, Bates' argument is suggestive, but does not tell the whole story. Officials certainly try to protect their jobs, but it is not clear that expensive, wasteful projects help them to do that—or that offering farmers higher prices leads to increased agricultural production (rather than sales) or investment (Ghai and Smith, 1987:chap. 5; Colclough, 1985:27–30; Bequele, 1983:235ff.). Indeed, if outlays on unproductive development schemes divert funds from more productive uses, they tend to reduce the incomes of everyone—state officials and their clients included. Also, just as Hyden implies that peasants have the power to realize their desire for autonomy from the state, Bates' analysis suggests that officials' preferences determine the course of political and economic change. Such a view overlooks the limits on governmental ability to control economic change. High levels of government spending on amenities are, in part, an implicit acknowledgment of African governments' dependence on popular support (Young, 1988:59).

A third type of explanation for the weak or perverse effects of rural development policies in Africa emphasizes the role of particular political structures in shaping both government policies and their consequences. Several recent studies have described African regimes as neopatrimonial—characterized by personalistic rule and authoritarian tactics (Sandbrook, 1986:321). Leaders treat public offices as prebends, to be allocated to key supporters in exchange for personal and political loyalty (Joseph, 1987:esp. chap. 5; Young, 1988: 57–58), and corruption has become a way of life—necessary to stay in power or get things done (Turner, 1978:173–75). In effect, it is argued, African governments are unable to use their power for anything other than repressing dissent and supporting a class of unproductive retainers.

Such descriptions of neopatrimonialism accord closely with the style and practice of government in countries such as Zaire or Guinea in the later years of Sekou Toure's rule, but are hardly ubiquitous in sub-Saharan Africa (Chazan et al., 1988:173–75). Events of the 1980s suggest that trade liberalization is neither a sufficient condition for accelerated development in Africa, nor more likely to be implemented by democratic than by authoritarian regimes. Many African governments moved, in the 1980s, to devalue their currencies and reduce controls on foreign trade, but it is not at all clear that such measures promoted development (Havnevik, 1987:18 and passim; Helleiner, 1986:73–74). Since independence, several countries (Côte d'Ivoire, Cameroon, Malawi) have experienced substantial rates of economic growth under authoritarian governments, and corruption has not been confined to autocratic regimes—as illustrated by the experience of Ghana and Nigeria under civilian rule.

In sum, much of the literature explains the poor performance of rural development policy in Africa as a logical consequence of either the rationality of a particular class of actors (politicians, bureaucrats, or peasants) or the structure of particular institutions (traditional communities, contemporary states). Both interpretations tend to ignore the interplay between individual action and institutional structure, and both imply that rural development programs have definitive consequences which can be clearly labeled successes or failures. In contrast, many case studies of what actually goes on in development projects or rural communities describe a series of inconclusive encounters among farmers, government officials, project staff, and local authorities, in which the objectives of a project or program are neither achieved nor resisted in a consistent fashion, and its effects on rural economic performance are often contradictory or unclear (Thiele, 1986:passim; Van Donge, 1985:69; Pottier, 1985:119–20, 1988:chap.5; Konings, 1986:128ff; see the concluding discussion in this chapter). Government actions—legislation, rural institution building, revenue collection, expenditures, and so on—do affect rural economies, often in disruptive ways. But the rural consequences of state intervention are neither determined by nor limited to the stated aims of rural development policy. The presence of the state in rural communities is palpable, but unpredictable.

The combination of intrusive, authoritarian styles of government and the relatively limited ability of most African states to control actual patterns of resource allocation can be traced, in part, to governments' increasing efforts to manage rural production in the name of conservation and development. Such efforts predate independence. As Young (1988:55–56) has pointed out, once decolonization was underway in the 1950s, both colonial officials and nationalist politicians seized on economic development as a legitimizing objective for their respective efforts to control the terms of Africa's independence. But colonial regimes began to be concerned with development long before they thought seriously of decolonization. Lugard's *The Dual Mandate in Tropical Africa*, which affirmed colonial governments' responsibility for managing colonial economies for the benefit of Africans as well as Europeans, was first published in 1922. What Lugard and his contemporaries understood by development for the benefit of Africans was primarily the conservation of Africa's natural resources for future generations—if necessary, by holding down current levels of African production and wealth (Young, 1988:50–51).

In the early years of British colonial rule, official measures to prevent the misuse of natural resources were largely preventative—demarcating Forest Reserves, where Africans were not allowed to farm or graze livestock, and taking steps to protect Africans' access to land and natural resources from the commercial ambitions of Europeans. In British West Africa, this took the form of denying or limiting concessions to European firms, as in the celebrated case of the application by Lever Bros. for palm oil concessions in Nigeria (Phillips, 1989:97–100). In Kenya and, to some extent, in Northern Rhodesia, the demarcation of Native Reserves represented an effort to accommodate both European settlers and African farmers. By the late 1920s, however, some officials were beginning to advocate a more interventionist approach to the conservation and management of natural resources. During the next two decades, the early emphasis on laissez-faire gave way increasingly to policies which involved direct efforts by the state to regulate or direct Africans' patterns of land use.

The rise of state interventionism was partly a response to emerging evidence of environmental problems: soil erosion, overgrazing, deforestation, and diseases of animals and plants.[1] The fact that environmental degradation was most acute in areas where colonial authorities had crowded Africans into Native Reserves was largely overlooked (Ranger, 1971:18–19). Most administrators blamed environmental degradation on the destructive effects of African husbandry (a view strongly seconded by European settlers) and also on the sudden intrusion of Western commerce and individualism in societies which, in their view, had not yet evolved values and institutions capable of managing these powerful forces for change. For both reasons, it was felt, colonial authorities must intensify their efforts to protect the African environment from destructive forms of exploitation. Beginning in the late 1920s, officials began to do this. They curtailed Africans' access to land, prohibited them from growing certain crops (coffee in Kenya) or using traditional methods of cultivation (*citemene* in Northern Rhodesia), slaughtered their livestock (Kenya), and uprooted diseased trees (Gold Coast)—all in the name of conservation and disease control.

During the global depression of the 1930s, financial stringencies and shortages of staff prevented colonial regimes from intervening actively to regulate Africans' land use or methods of cultivation. Such constraints remained in force during World War II. In West Africa, the Marketing Board actually destroyed stocks of cocoa for want of shipping, while in Kenya, the opening of new areas for African settlement was delayed, in part, because of wartime shortages of staff and funds (Sorrenson, 1967:58ff.).

However, official debate over appropriate policy towards agriculture and land use continued, and the case for state control of peasant production was expanded. This occurred for a couple of reasons. On one hand, the contradictions of indirect rule—reflected in the inability of colonial regimes to solve the Kikuyu land problem, create stable rural settlements in northeastern Zambia, or settle disputed claims to tribute or rent in the cocoa economies of West Africa—led officials to argue for more comprehensive and centrally controlled approaches to these problems (see, e.g., Throup, 1988:69ff.; Beinart, 1984: 75,78). In addition, the depression provoked a fundamental rethinking in Britain of the government's role in maintaining national economic stability. By the 1940s, Keynesian economics had so far penetrated the Colonial Office that deficit spending was no longer unthinkable, and there was even talk of a Marshall Plan for the colonies.

As funds and manpower became available after 1945, colonial regimes hastened to make up for lost time. Using the authority given them under the Colonial Development and Welfare Act of 1940, officials increased spending on development schemes and conservation works, and mapped out ambitious blueprints for improved African farming. However, the assumption of increased state responsibility for promoting the development of African economies was not accompanied by any fundamental change in administrators' understanding of African social realities. For the most part, they continued to approach the tasks of conservation and development within the ideological framework of indirect rule. In particular, they assumed that economic development was contingent on putting African societies back onto the path of normal evolutionary development, from which they had been dislodged by the trauma of colonial conquest and commercial exploitation. In short, colonial regimes emerged from World War II ready to resume the work of "modernizing Native Administrations" (Crook, 1986:83–85).

Accordingly, the increased level of state intervention in agricultural production and trade tended to reinforce incentives for Africans to seek access to the colonial state in the name of traditional social identity or status. Development spending increased the stakes in competition for access to the state but did not change the structure of that competition or lessen the tensions and ambiguities surrounding the interpretation of tradition for political and jural purposes. With independence, the struggles intensified as Africans competed for control of the state as well as access to it. These struggles, in turn, shaped economic policies as well as political conflict, contributing to the unevenness of development and the inconclusive authoritarianism of farmer-state relations in much of contemporary Africa. As I will argue in more detail below, during the "second colonial occupation" and since independence, the presence of the state in rural economies has been intrusive rather than hegemonic.

The chapter is organized as follows. The section beginning on page 48 describes the rise of both popular and official enthusiasm for planned economic development under African self-rule from the 1930s to independence, and discusses some of the ways in which struggles for power after 1945 shaped government strategies of resource allocation and social control after independence. The section beginning on page 53 outlines the major directions of government strategies for economic development and political control since the early 1960s and the effects of state actions on conditions of access to productive resources in rural areas. The concluding section elaborates the argument that postcolonial governments have been more successful in disrupting than in directing rural economic activity, using examples from Kenya, Tanzania, and Nigeria.

STATE AND ECONOMY IN THE LATE COLONIAL PERIOD

During the 1930s, colonial officials struggled to cope with the economic and financial crises resulting from the global depression, amid growing uncertainty and concern over the future of the environment. In eastern and southern Africa, settlers' need for cheap labor, their fears of competition from successful African farmers, and officials' growing concern with overpopulation and environmental degradation combined to "raise soil erosion to a subject of 'Imperial importance.'" By the end of the decade, there was widespread support among colonial officials for "large-scale solutions to what were viewed as large-scale problems" (Anderson, 1984:342), and administrators were poised to take direct control of an increasing range of economic activities, from farmers' cultivation methods to the marketing of export crops. Action was postponed during the war, due to shortages of money and manpower, but after 1945 the pace of government activity increased. In turn, "the 'second colonial occupation' . . . with its 'do-good' justification for meddling in African agriculture, heightened political consciousness by giving African families something to complain about" (Anderson, 1984:321).

In Kenya, settlers joined officials in a rising chorus of complaints about the destructiveness of African farming (Anderson, 1984:323–24; Throup, 1988:64–65; Heyer and Waweru, 1976:120–21). To forestall what was seen as an imminent threat of overgrazing, the administration undertook forcible culling of Africans' herds. They began in 1929, with livestock which belonged to squatters on European estates, moving on to the reserves in the late 1930s (Kanogo, 1987:46–48; Throup, 1988:65; Swainson, 1980:30). Africans were also forbidden to plant export crops, except for wattle and cotton (Heyer and Waweru, 1976:116). In 1937, a new Resident Native Labourers' Ordinance made the squatters' right to reside on a European estate conditional on their working for the landowner and raised the required amount of labor from 180 to 240 (later 270) days per annum. The ordinance also placed squatters fully under the authority of settler-controlled District Councils in the Rift Valley, giving settlers a free hand to enforce the harsh terms of employment laid down in the ordinance (Kanogo, 1987:97–100).

Squatters who refused to abide by the harsh terms of the ordinance were obliged to move. In theory, displaced squatters were entitled to settle in the reserves. In practice, however, Kikuyu who returned to Central Province often found that there was no land available, while those who sought access to land in reserves earmarked for other tribes were not always welcomed (Sorrenson, 1967:82; Bullock, 1974:69; Throup, 1988:112). Officials tried to relieve tension by opening new areas for settlement but felt obliged to impose strict controls on land use, in the interest of conservation and increased productivity. Like the government's use of compulsory labor to combat erosion by constructing terraces, efforts to control African settlers' uses of land only aggravated long-standing grievances over their expropriation by Europeans. By the late 1940s, rural discontent erupted in strikes, demonstrations, and the Mau Mau oathing campaign (Kanogo, 1987:112ff.; Throup, 1988:chaps.6, 7; Sorrenson, 1967:83–84).

In northeastern Rhodesia, officials of the British South Africa Company and, later, the colonial government imposed controls on African settlement patterns, both to gain administrative leverage and to prevent deforestation and improve agricultural practices. As described in chapter 2, company and, later, colonial officials made periodic efforts to prevent the dispersal of Bemba villages, in order to shore up the authority of Bemba chiefs and enhance their effectiveness as agents of colonial rule. On the agricultural front, Europeans took a dim view of the "wasteful" and "destructive" practice of *citemene* cultivation (Richards, 1958:310; see also Moore and Vaughan, 1987:526–27).

By the 1930s, agricultural officers had discovered that crop yields in *citemene* gardens were three times those obtained under traditional hoe cultivation (Baldwin, 1966:26), but they worried that *citemene* could not be sustained if population density increased. This was, indeed, occurring—principally through further state-directed resettlement of Africans on reserves created in the east and far north of the colony in 1930. These reserves were quickly overcrowded and began to show signs of deforestation. To relieve population pressure and facilitate "*citemene* control," land was added to the reserves, and villages were moved again (Wood and Shula, 1987:277; Allan, 1965:447–52).

Not surprisingly, repeated forced relocations left a legacy of anticolonial resentment. In the 1940s and 1950s, the rural areas of Northern Province provided fertile ground for nationalist party organizers, some of whom were migrant laborers returning from periods of employment on the Copperbelt or in Southern Rhodesia (Rasmussen, 1974:43 and passim; Bates, 1976:chap.4). In the late 1950s, Allan reported that the *citemene* control scheme had not prevented degeneration of the forests in the Mambwe areas—in part because it provoked political repercussions. "Resistance to control assumed a political and emotional content, which was intensified after the creation of the Central African Federation, and defiance of Native Authority regulations became a vehicle for the expression of political discontent" (Allan, 1965:135).

In West Africa, government efforts to improve production were limited to lectures on crop husbandry by a few agricultural officers and, in the 1930s, the establishment of cooperative cocoa-processing and marketing societies. Official exhortations, which usually urged farmers to adopt laborious solutions to apparently minor problems, were largely ignored (Green and Hymer, 1965:300, 307–10), and membership in the government-sponsored cooperatives was never more than a small fraction of the cocoa-farming population (Young et al., 1981:183). The first significant state intervention into the West African cocoa economies was directed towards marketing rather than production. During the late 1920s, European trading firms began to merge, ostensibly to protect themselves against fluctuations in world market conditions (Bauer, 1963:107–8; Hancock, 1942:207–10). As the depression deepened, officials effectively abandoned their earlier insistence on maintaining a competitive export marketing system and condoned the mergers. However, African farmers and traders saw the mergers as a direct threat to their own profits. In 1931, producers "held up" a substantial proportion of the Gold Coast crop for several weeks. In 1937, farmers and African traders organized an even more effective boycott, which threatened to spread to Nigeria as well (Miles, 1978:160; Southall, 1978:206ff.; Austin, 1988:72). Thoroughly alarmed, the Colonial Office convened a commission of enquiry. The Nowell Commission's recommendation—that government take over the marketing of major export crops for all of British West Africa—was implemented in 1939. The Marketing

Boards were retained through the war and became important fiscal agencies in the 1950s (Helleiner, 1966:159–84; Hopkins, 1973:286–88; Bauer, 1963: 294ff.).

Conservationist concerns also surfaced in West Africa in the late 1930s, although the issue was not soil erosion, but the spread of swollen-shoot disease. Swollen shoot devastated much of the cocoa in eastern Ghana during the 1930s and by the 1940s, it appeared to threaten the entire West African crop. To avert disaster, the Department of Agriculture launched a campaign to cut down diseased trees—just as the colonial regime in Kenya destroyed Africans' livestock to avert the effects of overgrazing. Cutting out was much more extensive in Ghana than in Nigeria and provoked a more vigorous response. As in Kenya, the destruction of farmers' capital in the name of conservation did much to rally rural support for the anticolonial cause (Crook, 1986:95–96; Austin, 1964:59ff.; see also Throup, 1988:106–8).

Government "meddling" into African agriculture met with protests, evasion, and outright resistance, even in the 1930s. However, this did not immediately shake officials' commitment to the empire or weaken their faith in indirect rule. Rather than scrap the creaky machinery of native administration, officials worked after 1945 to rebuild and retune it, in an effort to increase the efficiency of local administration and promote the "natural" evolution of tribal societies towards modern nation-states. In the Gold Coast, where colonial authorities had never formally established Native Treasuries or appropriated the right to appoint chiefs, government was obliged to create the full apparatus of indirect rule in order to modernize it! "Under the 1944 Ordinances, the government at last regularized the appointment of chiefs, established Treasuries with regular tax income (thus dramatically increasing the revenue of the NAs) and rationalized the system of Native Courts" (Crook, 1986:84; see also Hailey, 1957:470ff.). Eight years later, the native authorities were scrapped in favor of elected local government councils, as the British hastily prepared for decolonization (Crook, 1986:84ff.).

In the early years of colonial rule in Kenya, administrators had created chiefs and headmen in order to coopt them; by 1945, they worried that the resulting erosion of "communal feeling" had jeopardized prospects for agricultural improvement. After reviewing evidence on the growing scarcity of arable land in South Nyeri, Humphrey warned that "individualism is running riot and . . . is being carried so far that the future is fraught with danger." The remedy, he felt, lay in social as well as environmental conservation. "We have to make the Kikuyu himself realize that [agricultural] advancement involves his assuming once again a fair share of communal responsibilities" (Kenya, 1945:21). Two of his colleagues went further, urging that "government should recognize and use as far as possible the indigenous institutions" which, they assumed, were waiting untarnished in the wings, "ready to be called into activity" to manage the adoption of farm plans and improved methods of cultivation (Kenya, 1945:63–64).

In keeping with their rhetorical commitment to "encourag[e] the development of the African 'along his own lines'" (Crook, 1986:74), colonial officials continued to invoke "traditional" precedents as the basis for administrative practice. In doing so, they helped to prolong unresolved debates over customary rules and jurisdictions. The contradictions of the "second colonial occupation" were epitomized by officials' ambivalence towards Africans who had received Western schooling. Literate Africans were clearly necessary, both to the colonial administration itself and to the dissemination of technological improvements based on Western scientific research, but their ability to debate the merits of colonial rule in terms of Western moral and political philosophy was unnerving. European officials deplored Africans' neglect of "traditional education" in favor of "a travesty of our Western schooling" (Kenya, 1945:39), even as they hired African graduates of mission schools to serve as clerks, technical assistants, and administrative functionaries.[2] In fact, Western-educated Africans wielded a good deal of power by virtue of their ability to communicate in two cultures. Native Court clerks—hired in principle simply to record customary court proceedings—in fact acted as interpreters between litigants, elders, and the colonial state, and exercised considerable influence over the interpretation of customary law and the settlement of disputes (Asante, 1975: 37–38).

Debates over the appropriate roles of indigenous and Western "traditions" in the process of African "modernization" shaped both popular responses to state intervention and the structure of political competition in Africa's emerging nationalist movements. At first, colonial officials assumed they could rely on native authorities both to assist in implementing state programs for conservation and development and to counterbalance the demands of Western-educated nationalists for what European officials felt would be premature independence. However, colonial administrators overestimated conflicts of interest between chiefs and people, and between Western-educated Africans and traditional authorities. Many chiefs earned their livelihoods in the same way as their subjects: when colonial authorities attempted to curtail production or destroy agricultural capital, chiefs and elders were as likely to join in the resistance as to help suppress it. In the Gold Coast, some chiefs supported the cocoa holdups, and others joined the mass of ordinary farmers in resisting the government's swollen-shoot campaign (Crook, 1986:99–100). In Kenya, the Agriculture Department embarked on large-scale terracing with compulsory labor while prohibiting African cultivation of profitable crops (coffee, tea, pyrethrum). Chiefs and headmen who dragged their heels in mobilizing labor were often dismissed; their younger, better-educated replacements became targets of popular hostility, in turn (Throup, 1988:chap.7). In Northern Rhodesia, chiefs and headmen were no more receptive than commoners to official exhortations to abandon *citemene*—although they were sometimes better-placed to enter market gardening, by virtue of their "traditional" rights to tribute labor (Richards, 1958:311).

In the same vein, popular support for nationalist parties was rarely sharply divided between Western-educated and illiterate people, or between peasants and professionals. Aspiring politicians campaigned both by appealing to sectional loyalties and by touting their qualifications as graduates or businessmen to lead the government of an independent nation, or to represent the interests of their kin and neighbors to national authorities.[3] Ordinary people sought access to well-paid jobs, loans, amenities, and contracts both by pressing for favors from their kin or clansmen in government and by investing in market enterprises and schooling for their children.

Because aspiring politicians and their constituents both pursued wealth and power through multiple channels, one of the striking features of political parties in the 1950s and early 1960s was their mutability. In western Nigeria alone, although the Action Group had emerged as the dominant regional party by 1951, its history was marked by shifting internal conflicts and alliances as well as by changing ties to other regional parties (Dudley, 1982:62–67; Mackintosh et al., 1966:chap.13; Williams, 1980:77–78). In western Nigeria and in Ghana opposition parties were weakened by the repressive tactics of ruling regimes and by politicians' tendency to switch parties in order to preserve their access to the state. In Kenya's and Zambia's one-party states, opposition was internal by definition, and individual members of the ruling elite rotated in and out of office with almost predictable regularity.

For most rural dwellers, nationalist parties provided an institutional framework through which to pursue local interests. This has remained true with respect to government institutions in general, under single-party or even military rule (Rasmussen, 1974:47; Sklar, 1963:chap.10; Apter, 1963:chap.12; Dunn and Robertson, 1973:chap.8; Chazan, 1983:96–97; Barkan, 1984:86; Baylies and Szeftel, 1984:172–73; Oyediran, 1973:passim). Neither resistance to colonial rule nor competition for control of independent governments led people to identify permanently and exclusively with any one social group or political organization. Instead, people continued to seek access to resources and opportunities through multiple channels, diversifying their memberships in political groups and other social networks, and shifting allegiances whenever the fortunes of one group took a turn for the worse.

RISKY BUSINESS: THE POLITICAL ECONOMY OF ACCESS AFTER INDEPENDENCE

Since independence, the impact of the state on farmers' access to productive resources has been shaped both by the structure of political competition and by government efforts to accelerate the pace of economic development. Once the Europeans had left, competition among Africans for control of national governments was no longer muted by political rivals' common interest in getting rid of their colonial masters. Party conflict became increasingly turbulent and bitter in the years immediately following the end of colonial rule. The intensity of the conflict was heightened by the rapidly growing size of the public sector, which increased the resources politicians could use to court supporters, and enlarged opportunities for personal gain through access to political power.

Independent African governments were even more inclined than their colonial predecessors to take an active role in managing economic activity. Popular expectations of postindependence prosperity were high, and it was politically expedient for elected officials to take visible steps to promote economic development. On this point "there was a convergence of interests on the part of the colonial official class and nationalist forces" (Young, 1988:55). There was also convergence between the desire of African regimes to stay in power and the views of development economists, liberal and Marxist alike, who held that development depended on central planning and a "big push" by the state.[4] Encouraged by colonial precedents and contemporary economic precepts, African regimes launched ambitious programs of investment and economic planning.

In western Nigeria, for example, the regional budget tripled during the first few years of self-government, and marketing board surpluses were channeled to party coffers, fueling competition for power at both regional and national levels (Helleiner, 1966:177; Coker Commission, 1962:passim; Brown, 1966: 29ff.). The structure of conflict within the region was complex. In addition to rivalries between individual leaders and conflict among economic, religious, and subethnic factions, there were deep divisions over how to ally with extraregional parties in order to share in national power. In 1963, the regional party (Action Group) split between a majority who wanted to ally with the other southern party (NCNC) to prevent northern control of the federal government, and a substantial minority who thought it expedient to cast their lot with the ruling Northern People's Congress. By 1965, electoral contests within the region had degenerated into pitched battles, prefiguring the explosive sectional conflict for control of the federal government which brought about a military coup, followed by civil war, within seven years of independence (Post and Vickers, 1973:chap.10; Dudley, 1982:67–73).

Party conflict was less overtly explosive in Ghana than in Nigeria, partly because the ruling Convention People's Party did not represent an ethnically defined constituency, and Nkrumah was able to discredit the Asante-based National Liberation Movement (NLM) as "tribalist," thus gaining ideological legitimacy for his often ruthless suppression of the opposition (Rathbone, 1978:147–48). The CPP's position was undermined, however, by Nkrumah's lavish spending on poorly conceived development projects and an increasingly large and elaborate state apparatus. Disenchanted with corruption, waste, and the increasing authoritarianism of Nkrumah's reign, Ghanaians raised few objections when he was ousted by the military in 1966.

In Kenya and Zambia, the electoral process has remained in effect, but opposition parties were eliminated within a few years of independence, and civilian heads of state survived in part by deftly playing sectional factions off against one another within the framework of one-party rule (Bates, 1989: 112–14; Tordoff and Scott, 1974:151–54). Whether overt or muffled under a mantle of single-party or military rule, political conflict in postcolonial Africa has been widespread, intense, and potentially explosive. Struggles for power within and beyond the state absorbed substantial amounts of government revenue and served, in the long run, to undermine the process of planned economic development which helped to inspire them in the first place.

The economic crises which beset sub-Saharan Africa in the 1970s and 1980s were hardly anticipated at the time of independence. Although the postwar boom in African export prices came to an end in the mid-1950s, and countries such as Ghana rapidly accumulated unmanageable levels of foreign debt, on the whole the prosperity of the 1950s continued through the first decade of independence. In Zambia, copper earnings rose 260 percent between 1965 and 1974, leading to a surge in imports and government revenues and a similar rate of growth in GDP (Daniel, 1979:7). In Kenya, agricultural output grew (though at a declining rate) from 1966 to 1978, while growth of manufacturing output accelerated, and real GDP rose steadily at more than 5 percent per annum (Ikiara and Killick, 1981:5). With a diversified and relatively commercialized agricultural sector, Nigeria enjoyed steady rates of growth of income, foreign exchange earnings, and government revenues, which helped to sustain the economy through the civil war (Aboyade and Ayida, 1971:28; Rimmer, 1978:147ff.).

Prosperity and rising government revenue made it relatively easy for newly independent African governments to finance ambitious programs of bureaucratic expansion and economic development. Spending rose rapidly, as governments increased employment and stepped up the pace of investment in infrastructure and development projects, and of outlays for schools and other amenities. During the 1960s, civil service employment in Africa grew at an average annual rate of 7 percent. In 1970, "60% of wage earners were government employees," and ten years later, wages and salaries accounted for half of all government outlays (Chazan et al., 1988:52). As political tensions mounted, governments also increased the size of their security forces: Africa's share of world arms imports rose from less than 5 percent to almost 20 percent during the 1970s. Escalating levels of government spending also meant rapidly rising demand for imports—both from government agencies and from wage and salary earners whose incomes originated in the public sector. Spending on imports soon outstripped export earnings, and governments were obliged to borrow abroad or intervene directly in the domestic economy, in order to promote exports, curtail imports, and/or ration foreign exchange. Efforts to relieve domestic shortages through import substitution often added to total outlays of foreign exchange and public funds, further increasing domestic and foreign debt (Seers, 1963:171–72; Seidman, 1974:605–7; Nixson, 1982:45–46; see also Table 1).

In addition to higher levels of government spending and employment, the early years of independence were also marked by an extraordinary proliferation of new laws, programs, and public (or semipublic) institutions in the name of promoting economic development and fostering national unity. Governments enacted laws to regulate investment, trade, and prices, to institute land reform, to provide loans, subsidies and incentives to foreign and domestic investors, and to give nationals preferential access to jobs and assets in the domestic economy. They also created hundreds of new institutions, ranging from cooperative societies, settlement schemes, and village administrations to public enterprises,

Table 1. Government budgets: surpluses and deficits (−)

Year	Ghana (cedis, mil)	Kenya (shillings, mil)	Nigeria (naira, mil)	Zambia (kwacha, mil)
1960	—	-245	—	—
1965	-94	-393	-78	24
1970	-50	-376	-119	23
1971	-88	-335	36	-194
1972	-161	-782	37	-176
1973	-187	-696	404	-266
1974	-196	-558	1,478	64
1975	-401	-1,259	—	-341
1976	-736	-1,558	-1,130	-270
1977	-1,057	-1,020	1,135	-261
1978	-1,897	-871	2,122	-325
1979	-1,800	-2,411	2,871	-241
1980	-1,808	-1,122	9,184	-568
1981	-4,707	-3,897	2,055	-450
1982	-4,848	-4,462	—	-668
1983	-4,933	-1,597	—	-327
1984	-4,843	-2,710	-2,900	-414
1985	-7,579	-3,775	-1,999	-1,051
1986	299	-5,586	-2,774	—
1987	4,059	-9,841	-9,702	-2,692
1988	3,900	-5,526	—	-2,911
1989	—	-6,574	—	-2,757

Source: International Monetary Fund, *International Financial Statistics.* Washington, DC: IMF.

parastatals, marketing boards, development banks, and a host of new bureaucratic agencies. The proliferation of institutions and government controls transcended ideological and economic differences among African nations. Parastatals multiplied as rapidly in Nigeria and Côte d'Ivoire as in Ghana and Tanzania (Chazan et al., 1988:53). Export marketing boards were ubiquitous: by 1980, governments in thirty-three out of forty countries also controlled domestic marketing of one or more agricultural staples (USDA, 1981:127).

In rural areas, African governments established dozens of new institutions designed both to facilitate state and party control over rural communities and to assist, induce, or coerce farmers into raising agricultural output and productivity. Often, this was done at the behest of governments or international donor agencies, whose projects placed considerable demands on the time and resources of local administrators (Morss, 1984:466–67). The process of institution building not only increased the size of the state apparatus in rural communities, but also continued the restructuring of local jurisdictions and administrative systems which, as we have seen, had begun under colonial rule. In all four of our case study areas, the proliferation of state institutions in rural areas multiplied potential channels through which bureaucrats and farmers sought access to each other's resources.

In Ghana, the Nkrumah regime expanded farmers' cooperatives, established state farms and settlement schemes, and created a rural wing of the party—the United Ghana Farmers' Cooperative Council—to oversee rural political activity and help mobilize the cocoa surplus for the national government. In 1961, the UGFCC was made sole buyer of the cocoa crop, and the cooperatives were disbanded, to be replaced by workers' brigades (Beckman, 1978:101–2; Young et al., 1981:185–86). Subsequent regimes dismantled many of Nkrumah's institutions but added their own. In addition to reviving the farmers' cooperative societies, efforts were made both to provide government support for private ventures, such as the heavily subsidized, mechanized rice-farming schemes in the north (Shepherd, 1981:172ff.; Konings, 1986:163–65), and to establish new state farms and irrigation schemes (Beckman, 1981:148; Konings, 1986:256ff.).

In western Nigeria, rural development schemes appeared in rapid succession, often lingering as institutional structures even after state funding had been withdrawn. For example, after a prominent Yoruba politician paid a brief visit to Israel in 1961, the regional government spent £6.4 million to establish thirteen farm settlements modeled on Israeli *moshavim* (Roider, 1970:24, 121–22). By 1967, it was clear that the settlements had failed either to promote agricultural development or to provide jobs for unemployed school dropouts (Roider, 1968:114, 120; Wells, 1974:249ff.; Forrest, 1981:234–37). State funding was subsequently withdrawn, but the buildings remained, to be occupied eventually by retired soldiers and other state clients who hoped to convert the empty structures into a base from which to gain access to state resources.[5] In the cocoa-growing areas, cooperatives, cocoa-replanting schemes, agricultural development projects, and large private farms owned by ex-military officers and even multinational corporations (e.g., Texagri) have followed one another in rapid succession, serving as channels for the dissemination of state subsidies and patronage (Forrest, 1981:239ff., and forthcoming).

In addition to the multiplicity of development schemes, local governments in Nigeria were reorganized repeatedly after independence, partly as a result of sectional conflict for control of the federal government. Both civilian and military regimes engaged in repeated rounds of state creation in order to defuse political tension by catering to sectional constituencies' demands for direct pipelines to federal resources (Dudley, 1982:106–10; Berry, 1985:39–40; Yahaya, 1978:201ff.). In 1963, the Midwest was separated from the Western Region and, in 1966, following a second military coup, Nigeria's four regions were split into twelve states. The Western Region remained intact at that time, but in 1976 it was divided into three states: Ogun, Oyo, and Ondo (Yahaya, 1978: 219). With each reorganization, substantial amounts of state revenue were devoted to the construction of new state capitals.

On the local level, jurisdictional restructuring was, if anything, more frequent and contested than under colonial rule. As political conflict escalated in 1964 and 1965, new jurisdictions were created to woo local areas to the governing party (Berry, 1985:174–75; Guyer, 1991:10). After the military took power in 1966, elected local government councils were abolished and replaced by "sole native authorities" appointed by the military governors of the states. The return to civilian rule in 1979 was preceded by a return to elected local authorities in 1976, together with a proliferation of local administrative structures—Town Planning Authorities, Land Allocation Boards, and so forth. During the 1980s, the structure of local governments was reorganized four more times (Guyer, 1991:7–8).

In Kenya, the colonial system of local government councils was retained after independence, with some modifications (Kitching, 1980:198; Mulasa, 1970:238–39). In addition, an elaborate network of local development agencies was created to foster national consciousness and increase central control over local political activities, as well as to mobilize resources for development. The government established Community Development Committees and encouraged the formation of a parallel system of self-help groups (*harambee*), which mobilized communal labor for local projects. Marketing Boards and Farmers' Associations, which in the colonial period had operated mainly for the benefit of European farmers, were now expanded to include African farmers as well. African farmers sold coffee to local cooperative societies, which served as agents for the Marketing Board until 1966, when the government reorganized the cooperative system to increase central control over the finances of the primary societies and enforce national agricultural policies (Lamb, 1974:111). The Kenya Tea Development Authority, established in 1961, encouraged African farmers to plant tea and then struggled to limit the dissemination of stumps and control the quality of the crop (Lamb and Muller, 1982: 32–33; Steeves, 1976:51ff., 1978:127ff.). The government also established or supported an array of rural development ventures, including parastatals, settlement schemes (notably the politically charged schemes for transferring former European farms to Africans), Special Rural Development Programmes (1970), and in the 1980s, contract-farming schemes (Heyer, 1981:114–15; Holmquist, 1970:207; Hansen and Marcussen, 1982:21–27; Lamb and Muller, 1982: passim; Ayako et al., 1989:passim).

In Zambia, the Kaunda regime continued the colonial policy of "regrouping" villages into large, stable units to facilitate administrative and political control in the name of promoting development (see below, p. 000). They also created a series of new institutions designed to promote rural development by extending the apparatus of the state into every village. "By the mid-1970s, Zambia had attempted to encourage cooperatives alongside family farms, state farms alongside private commercial estates, and small-scale, self-help social service schemes alongside heavily capitalized 'intensive development' schemes" (Bratton, 1980a:29). The government abolished local administrative structures inherited from colonial days, replacing them with elected Rural Councils and a set of Provincial and District Development Committees. These proved ineffective, owing to excessive centralization and inadequate funding, and in 1969 they were themselves replaced with Development and Productivity Committees which extended to the ward and village levels (Bratton, 1980b:35–40; 1980a:205).

In 1973, a single-party state was set up, with a system of party organs paralleling the development committees at all levels (Gertzel et al., 1984:intro.; Bratton, 1980a:36). Agricultural marketing was centralized under the National Agricultural Marketing Board (NAMBOARD); rural cooperatives were set up to dispense credit from the Credit Organization of Zambia; and Intensive Development Zones were created to concentrate technical and financial services in areas with good development potential (Gertzel, 1980:248ff.). When one scheme proved ineffective, new ones were created, sometimes alongside the discredited institution. In 1970, the bankrupt Credit Organization of Zambia was replaced by the Agricultural Finance Corporation (Elliott, 1983:170). The Intensive Development Zones had mixed results, but remained in place until 1975 (Gertzel, 1980:254–57). Crops were marketed through both cooperatives and NAMBOARD, with no clear demarcation of their respective spheres of authority. Despite ministerial criticism and presidential promises to improve crop marketing, the inefficient dual marketing system was retained (Good, 1986:259–64). In general, the instability of government policies and institutions added to the uncertainty of rural economic life—leading one observer to conclude that "the problems surrounding government intervention in farming have more to do with a general loss of direction than entanglement in class formation" (Van Donge, 1982:105–6).

In an effort to explain why African governments engaged in so much rural institution building to so little apparent effect, several scholars suggest that the proliferation of government controls and institutions in postcolonial Africa served politicians and bureaucrats in their pursuit of power and personal gain, even though it hindered national economic development (Bates, 1981:113ff.; Sandbrook, 1986:326–27; Callaghy, 1988:82–84, 87). Development projects, parastatals, and village administrations have done more to extend state influence into every corner of society than to effect increases in output or standards of living for the masses (Bratton, 1980a,b:251ff.; Hyden et al., 1970:60; Watts, 1986:15–18; Heyer, 1981:12–13). Such institutions work in the interests of bureaucrats rather than farmers: they give officials control over jobs, loans, and contracts with which to reward supporters, punish rivals, or simply to line their own pockets (Bates, 1981:113–18; Sandbrook, 1986:326).

Such arguments are persuasive but incomplete. To write off the postcolonial proliferation of government institutions and controls as merely a misguided effort to consolidate state power or further the personal ambitions of African politicians is to underestimate both the perspicacity of African leaders and the complexity of their task. Like their colonial predecessors, African regimes have tried to sustain as well as exploit the economic base from which they draw their revenues, and to contain conflict and keep order as well as enforce their own rules and unseat opponents.[6] But African politicians and bureaucrats are also members of their societies, who look to the rural population for votes or clients as well as for cheap labor and produce. African elites have, of course, been anxious to stay in power, but not so naive as to think they could do so without resources. Once in office, politicians and bureaucrats set out both to create conditions for increased output and investment and to monopolize access to them. Strategies of development included direct state regulation of prices, trade, education, and other services; investment in infrastructure; and the proliferation of state agencies to manage productive activity directly. At the same time, officials used their knowledge of government affairs and the prerogatives of office to monopolize access to state jobs, contracts, loans, and licenses for themselves and their political clients.

In these circumstances, the creation of a particular project or regulatory agency may occur as part of an individual's or faction's bid for power and wealth, but the proliferation of regulations and institutions in the aggregate is more an unintended consequence of the process of competition itself. For example, competition among state officials for clients and prestige tends to limit the power wielded by any individual or faction. Would-be patrons have an interest both in exercising exclusive control over state resources and in using them to include more people among their clients and supporters. For potential supporters, this creates the opportunity to move from one patron to another in order to advance their own position, which obliges would-be patrons to compete for clients. Competition for clients and supporters can inhibit development by channeling scarce state resources into relatively unproductive uses (bribes, padded budgets, redundant facilities or personnel) and/or hampering the effective implementation of government policies. In addition to the costs of administrative reorganization designed to placate sectional interest groups, such as the creation of new states in Nigeria, project budgets are often inflated to provide jobs, contracts, or kickbacks to officials and their supporters.[7]

But political competition does not act only to channel government revenues to nonproductive or poorly managed ventures; it can also tie up state revenues so that they cannot be used to cope with economic shocks, such as poor harvests, world price fluctuations, and shortages of key imports. In 1985, for example, Zambia was unable to import enough jute bags and diesel fuel to handle the bumper maize crop, in part because necessary foreign exchange was diverted to other uses at the last minute (Good, 1986:268). Similarly, during the oil recession of the early 1980s, government employees in some Nigerian states were sometimes simply not paid (Falola and Ihonvbere, 1985:116).

In the 1970s and 1980s, African economies were subjected to a series of external shocks which dramatized their vulnerability and further undermined the already limited ability of African governments to protect the livelihoods of their citizens. Since the early 1970s, world markets for Africa's principal exports have become increasingly volatile (Wheeler, 1984:6; Maizels, 1987: 538), and changes in weather have added to the uncertainty. In many African countries, not only crop yields on rain-fed land, but also irrigated agriculture, fishing, power, and transportation depend on rain-fed rivers and lakes. In Ghana, the drought of 1983–84 caused "an unprecedented fall in the level of the Volta river and hence of the Volta Dam lake . . . [As a result] the Volta Dam power station's output was cut back to 5 percent of its normal level, the VALCO aluminum smelter . . . was closed, [and] power rationing was introduced in Ghanaian cities" (Derrick, 1984:286; see also Glantz, 1987:passim). Since 1968, several major droughts have combined with mounting balance of payments deficits to produce severe fluctuations in imports. Because most African economies are heavily dependent on imports of basic commodities such as fuel, fertilizer, and spare parts for vehicles, variations in export earnings or the terms of trade lead, in turn, to multiplied fluctuations in aggregate levels of output, income, and employment (Helleiner, 1986a:150).

Rising indebtedness and politically indissoluble commitments to projects and expenditure programs have made it difficult for African governments to protect their citizens from exogenous shocks. In addition, governments themselves have added to the uncertainty of conditions under which ordinary Africans live and work by frequent reorganizations of government institutions and changes of policy, as well as frequent delays in government deliveries of inputs, payment for crops, provision of transport services, and so on. In Zambia, for example, Pottier (1988:40–42) describes how cutbacks in the staff of the International Red Locust Control center in Mbala eliminated a key source of steady employment for several hundred people. In northern Ghana, urban growth and state subsidies for basic foodstuffs combined with government promotion of mechanized rice farming to divert local food supplies from rural into urban markets, increasing rural communities' vulnerability to famine (Shepherd, 1981:184–86). Frequent shifts in policies and programs also result from financial crises, brought on by economic fluctuations to which financially overextended regimes are highly vulnerable. Sudden declines in revenue have obliged African governments to lay people off, ration or ban key imports, abandon projects in mid-stream, or simply fail to pay salaries of state employees. As government resources—or the fortunes and influence of particular officials—rose and fell, the supply of public services and returns to state clients fluctuated too (Chazan, 1983).

For most Africans, economic security is guaranteed neither by access to the state nor by autonomy from it. Many people seek to activate ties to the state when there are gains to be made from it, and to escape when state resources dwindle or political opponents gain the upper hand. To remain flexible and diversify their options, people straddle the public and private sectors—either by working simultaneously in government jobs and farming or other forms of self-employment, or by moving back and forth between public and private sector jobs over time. Such employment patterns have been described in Kenya (Cowen and Murage, 1972:39; Swainson, 1980:174; Cowen and Kinyanjui, 1977:15), Zambia (Baylies and Szeftel, 1984:70–71), Nigeria (Berry, 1985: 260–61), and Ghana (K. Hart, 1973:66–67; Chazan and Pellow, 1986:167–72), among senior bureaucrats and politicians as well as lower-level state employees and ordinary citizens (Swainson, 1987:147ff.; Anyang' Nyang'o, 1987:221ff.). Faced with declining perquisites, salary freezes, or the threat of retrenchment, civil servants have invested in the private sector, at home or abroad. "Even Houphouet-Boigny admitted to having stashed billions of francs CFA in Switzerland on the grounds that 'any intelligent politician does so'" (Sandbrook, 1986:329). In Nigeria, neither secondary school dropouts nor university graduates were under any illusions in the late 1970s about the levels of pay and perquisites to be expected in government employment, but many still planned to start their careers by working in a state or federal ministry. As one of my informants explained, it is good to work in government for a while so that, "after you go out, you know where to lay your hand on things" (Berry, 1985:177). As food prices rose in the 1970s and 1980s, many bureaucrats turned to farming (Forrest, forthcoming; Bratton, 1980a:264–65; Shepherd, 1981: 173–74; Goody, 1980:passim, Hinga and Heyer, 1976:222; Okoth-Ogendo, 1981:335).

Similarly, people outside the state have attempted both to cultivate potential patrons within it and to evade official demands or restrictions on trade and investment. Individuals moved in and out of public employment over the course of their careers; money flowed between state employees and private producers and traders, both legally and illegally. People have also endeavored to diversify their networks within the state, to avoid being stuck to the coattails of a politician who fell out of favor. For both state officials and private citizens, economic success hinged on the ability to maintain contacts both inside and outside the state, and to move quickly from one enterprise, occupation, or patron to another (Leonard, 1991:82–86, 95–100; Van Donge, 1982:94ff., 103; Berry, 1985:176–77; Pottier, 1988:chaps.3, 7).

The efforts of citizens and bureaucrats to diversify their options by multiplying clientage networks and straddling the public and private sectors have, in turn, complicated the task of controlling resource flows and the terms on which transactions take place. The more governments tried to cope with economic decline and instability by imposing additional controls on resource allocation and the terms of exchange, the more individuals (including government officials) sought to enrich or protect themselves, both by evading controls and by gaining preferential access to rationed resources. In the process, an increasing range of economic activities has gone "underground," and public as well as private resources flow between the official and the underground, or "parallel," economy through myriad channels (MacGaffey, 1987:112–17; MacGaffey et al., 1991:passim; Chazan, 1983:194ff.; Clough, 1985:33–34; Forrest, forthcoming; Kitching, 1980:180–81; Saul, 1986:143, 1987:78–79). Such uncharted resource flows make it difficult for governments to measure (let alone control) economic activity, and virtually oblige civil servants to enter the parallel economy in order to make ends meet.

In the long run, then, postcolonial governments' pursuit of economic development and national unity has helped to promote competition and uncertainty over conditions of access to productive resources—among state agencies and personnel as well as private citizens. People have responded by intensifying their efforts to exploit *and* to evade government controls, by straddling the public and private sectors, and by proliferating their memberships in social networks. The resulting ease with which resources flow between official, unofficial, and illegal enterprises and income-generating activities has, in turn, rendered controls virtually unworkable. In many respects the proliferation of development programs and rural institutions after independence paralleled the institutional confusion fostered by indirect rule. In most contemporary African societies, the allocation of state resources and the enforcement of state directives are, to say the least, negotiable, and ordinary Africans invest as much (if not more) time and money in the means of access and maneuvering as in the means of production.

AN UNGOVERNABLE COUNTRYSIDE?

Since the late colonial period, governments' willingness to intervene in farmers' activities has tended to outstrip their ability to control or direct the course of rural economic change. Hyden's argument that African peasants remained "uncaptured" by the state understates the degree to which rural people's livelihoods have been disrupted or undermined by government actions, ranging from unsuccessful efforts to maintain basic infrastructure to widespread corruption and harassment. But the counterargument—that, far from remaining autonomous, African peasants have been impoverished by their governments' excessive and ill-conceived controls on prices and production—tends to overestimate bureaucrats' ability to enforce their own directives. In the 1960s and 1970s, for example, official prices in many countries tended to discourage agricultural production and investment, but so few goods changed hands at official prices that it is not clear just how they affected patterns of production and trade.

Parallel market transactions are only one of numerous ways in which Africans have evaded or resisted the exactions of the state. Recent scholarship has drawn attention to episodes of organized, collective peasant resistance to direct assaults by colonial or postcolonial states on their property or labor.[8] In addition to organized protest and insurgency, however, African farmers have engaged in innumerable forms of "everyday resistance," from holding crops off the market or refusing to cultivate according to official instructions, to "feigning illness, sabotage, flight and banditry" (Isaacman, 1990:32). Such activities have exercised a persistent, sometimes cumulative effect on the impact of particular state interventions and the course of rural economic change.

Taken together, the contradictions of state interests in African agriculture, their strategies of governance, and the diversity of farmers' responses have meant that the overall effect of state intervention on rural economic life has been intrusive and disruptive rather than hegemonic. Farmers have not been able to escape the presence of the state, nor have they necessarily wanted to: gaining access to resources and opportunities often means working through as well as around the system. But "the system" is far from monolithic. Individuals and agencies struggle for influence and resources within the state as well as outside it, and outcomes are not fully determined by any single set of interests. Instead, rural economies and societies appear as a shifting kaleidoscope of conflicts, alliances, and maneuvers, in which it is difficult to discern who is in control.

Even as highly centralized and bureaucratic a government as Tanzania's may exercise only tenuous control over resource allocation and the implementation of policies at the local level. During the heyday of *ujamaa*, for example, villagers in Dodoma not only took part in the official village administration, but also established parallel committees ("apparently modelled on" those of the formal village administration) to handle matters of importance which the government had not provided for—such as making rain. During the unusually long dry season of 1981, the rain committee decided to engage a rainmaker and "called upon [party] Cell leaders to ensure that homesteads in their Cells paid their contributions." When the cadres protested that their job was modernization, not magic, the committee spokesman demurred. "It was no use for Cell leaders to carry out only duties connected with collective work on the Village farm, he said, for if no rain fell, this work would be wasted" (Thiele, 1986:547).

Like *ujamaa* villages in Tanzania, Village Productivity Committees in Zambia and various local government agencies in Ghana, Nigeria, and Kenya have all provided channels through which rural dwellers can pursue access to the state, and through which the state attempts to regulate rural economic and political activity. But they have rarely functioned smoothly in either direction. In a recent paper, Guyer (1991:2–3) points out that vigorous popular opposition discouraged both colonial governments and their successors from attempting to collect significant amounts of revenue through direct taxation. In western Nigeria, local governments rely on subsidies from state and federal treasuries, or try to collect fees for services rendered. One result is that construction and maintenance of local infrastructure—bridges, roads, culverts, piped water supplies—tend to be financed either through private subscriptions or inside connections. Contributions are often inadequate to complete the job, and many such efforts at locally organized self-help come to naught (Guyer, 1991:11–12; Berry, 1985:187–88). In Kenya, *harambee* (self-help) groups have been supported more consistently by the state and provide a channel for modest degrees of local influence over the deployment of government resources (Holmquist, 1984:passim). Even here, however, farmer-state interactions operate through multiple institutional and informal channels (Lamb, 1974:chap.6), and the impact of the state on local resource access is not clearly aligned with a single set of class interests. As we will see in chapter 5, nowhere is this more apparent than in the case of land tenure.

For the most part, then, development schemes and projects do not achieve their intended objectives, even when they are deliberately designed to be participatory and/or culturally specific. State intervention in rural areas touches off dynamic processes which affect the consequences of state actions and limit the degree to which officials control actual patterns of resource allocation. In addition, the fact that government objectives are themselves often contradictory or inconsistent leads farmers to expect that government policies will be transitory and hence to use them as channels of access to state resources in the short run, rather than as aids to long-term development. In the process, rural dwellers often "straddle" formal and informal institutions in an effort to diversify their options and maintain flexibility in the face of uncertain opportunities and constraints.

The result is neither effective state control of the countryside nor an uncaptured peasantry, but rather multiple linkages between farmers and states which affect patterns of resource allocation and agricultural performance partly by encouraging mobility and diversification of networks and income sources. As Van Donge (1985:69) found in eastern Zambia, "life in Mwase Lundazi was not so much shaped by 'development policies' and their intended and unintended consequences as by arbitration sessions, which were chaired by the chief, in which land and headmanships were discussed and by local court sittings which mostly dealt with disputes between co-wives." In such contexts, access has remained negotiable, resources mobile, and peasant agriculture surprisingly resilient in the face of economic and environmental crises. The impact of state policies and power on conditions of access to rural land and labor does not depend solely on the interest of politicians and bureaucrats, but on specific histories of debate and interaction among farmers, traders, headmen, officials, and their relatives and associates.

Chapter Four

Commercialization, Cultivation, and Capital Formation

Agrarian Change in Four Localities

IN THIS CHAPTER, I outline the principal changes in agricultural production and rural economic life which have occurred since the time of colonial conquest in the four localities covered in this study. In all four areas, rural dwellers became increasingly involved in market activity, although the pace and extent of commercialization varied a great deal among them. In the forest regions of south central Ghana and southwestern Nigeria, farmers began to cultivate cocoa and other crops for export before the turn of the century. The resulting growth of rural markets for labor and commodities drew nearly all rural households into some form of commercial activity and attracted large numbers of migrants from poorer regions as well. In central Kenya, trade with the coast began only a few decades before the British conquest, but agricultural production for the market increased rapidly after 1900, as the colonial economy expanded. Many Africans also worked for European settlers—as squatters or wage laborers—and for the colonial state. In northeastern Zambia, there was never more than a handful of settlers and very little growth in agricultural production for the market until after independence. However, thousands of Africans migrated to work for wages in the mines and towns of South Africa, Southern Rhodesia, Katanga and, after 1928, the Copperbelt in Zambia itself. As workers brought or sent part of their earnings to their rural relatives, rural cash incomes and expenditures rose gradually, although at a much slower rate than in the other case study areas.

The following pages describe periods of expansion and contraction in local and regional markets for agricultural commodities, and trace changes in cropping patterns, agricultural trade, and rural household members' involvement in off-farm employment. This chapter sets the stage for subsequent discussions of farmers' access to land and labor, and their effects on agricultural performance. For convenience of exposition, the two West African cocoa economies are discussed together, followed by separate sections on central Kenya and northeastern Zambia.

THE COCOA ECONOMIES OF NIGERIA AND GHANA

In southern Ghana and southwestern Nigeria, commercial activity predated colonial conquest by centuries. Both the rulers of large states (the Asante and Oyo empires) and the chiefs and citizens of smaller communities within and beside them bought and sold goods in local markets and through regional trading networks, some of which were linked to trans-Atlantic and trans-Saharan commerce. With the decline of the Atlantic slave trade in the latter part of the nineteenth century, both African and European traders turned their attention to agricultural and forest products.[1] From the 1840s, palm oil and kernels were exported in increasing quantities from the ports of Ghana and Nigeria. In the 1890s, there was a boom in exports of wild rubber: in Ghana, exports grew from 1.5 million to over 4 million pounds between 1885 and 1895; in Nigeria, from a mere 56 pounds in 1893 to over 5 million pounds two years later (Dumett, 1971:91; Arhin, 1972:34; Berry, 1975:29). The boom collapsed after 1900 as suddenly as it had begun, from a combination of overtapping and increased competition from Malaysia, and farmers turned their attention to more profitable crops (Dumett, 1971:100).

As world markets recovered from the long depression of the late nineteenth century, demand for tropical crops increased, creating new opportunities for the export of West African produce. Prospects were sufficiently favorable to convince the British government to invest in building railways to link what were expected to be important export producing areas to the major ports. In Ghana, a rail line was constructed in 1903 from Sekondi to Kumasi, to service the gold mining industry. In Nigeria, the British pushed a railway all the way through to Kano by 1911, in the expectation that Northern Nigeria would become a major source of raw cotton for British textile mills (Hogendorn, 1978:18–21). In both cases, however, the economic consequences of railway construction diverged from official expectations. Ghanaian gold reserves proved expensive to exploit, and the growth of production was limited (Killick, 1978:6); in Nigeria vigorous efforts by the British Cotton Growing Association to promote their crop produced meager results. However, exports of cocoa (and, in Northern Nigeria, groundnuts) grew apace, requiring rapid expansion of railway services and providing ample revenues for colonial governments and merchant firms alike. By the 1920s, governments and farmers were both constructing feeder roads to facilitate the evacuation of cocoa from areas remote from the railway (Hill, 1963:247; Berry, 1975:80).

Like agriculture and mining, road and railway construction also required substantial amounts of labor. In western Nigeria, colonial rule put an end to decades of warfare among the Yoruba states, releasing large numbers of men from military activity. Men from Ilesha, Oyo, and Ilorin headed south in search of income and adventure. In 1899, over 10,000 Nigerians were employed on construction of the Lagos-Ibadan railway (Oyemakinde, 1974:306), and many

Map 2. Cocoa farming areas of Ghana

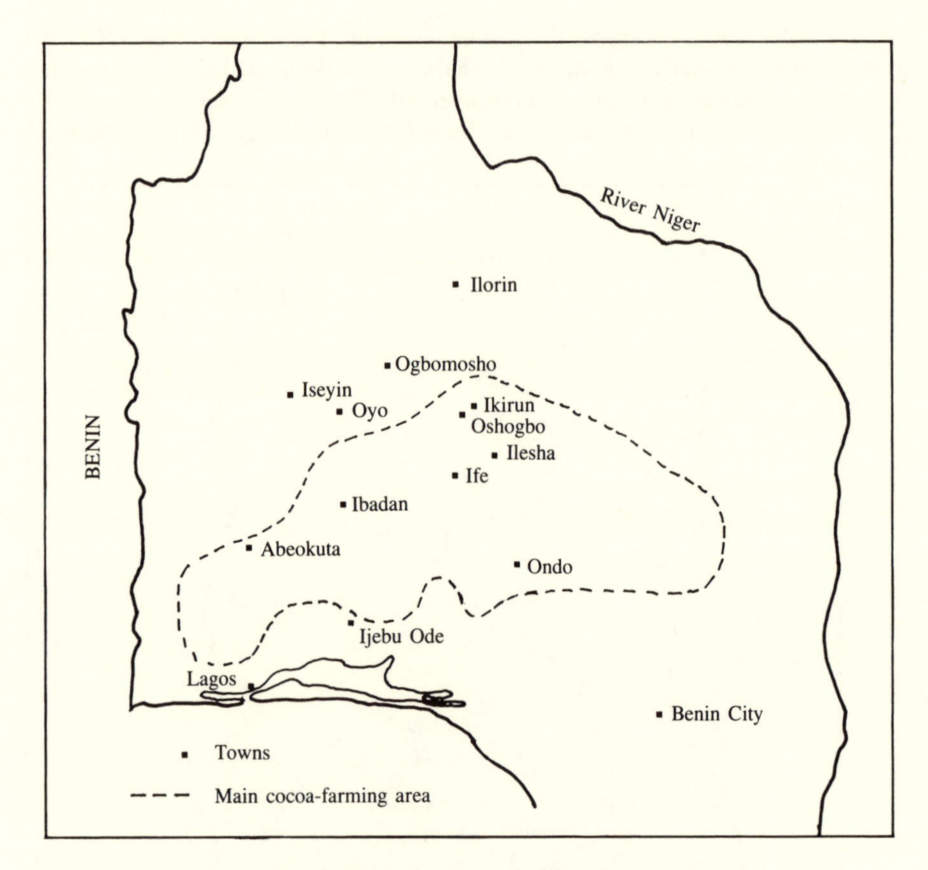

Map 3. Cocoa farming areas of Nigeria

others found work in Lagos or other towns as porters, dockhands, or petty traders (Berry, 1975:67ff.; Agiri, 1972:46; cf. Peel, 1983:147ff.). Some migrants settled permanently in the city, but most returned eventually to their home towns, to marry and establish farms or other enterprises with their savings.

In Asante and neighboring states, British annexation did not lead to the demobilization of precolonial armies on the same scale as in western Nigeria. Moreover, cocoa cultivation grew much more rapidly in Ghana than in Nigeria, so that southern Ghanaians did not set out in large numbers to seek wage employment, as was the case in Nigeria. To build the Gold Coast Railway, labor was recruited in the northern territories and beyond (Thomas, 1973:82). In 1901, thousands of Nigerians were reported to be working on the

Gold Coast Railway (Agiri, 1972:168; Oyemakinde, 1974:305), and as late as 1922, the District Officer in Ife reported that "large numbers of the youngmen go and work on the Gold Coast" (Oyo Province, 1922).

The growth of agricultural production for export was facilitated not only by the development of transportation, but also by the introduction of new American crops, such as cocoa and coffee, which were brought to West Africa in the late nineteenth century by traders and returned slaves, via the islands of Sao Tome and Fernando Po (Hill, 1963:172; Berry, 1975:40). By 1910, Ghana was the world's largest exporter of cocoa, followed by Brazil and Nigeria (Kay, 1972:410; Hopkins, 1973:216). Ghanaian exports rose tenfold between 1910 and 1926 (Kay, 1972:337). In Nigeria, production grew more slowly at first and then jumped from 5,000 tons in 1914 to 30,000 in 1922 and to over 100,000 by the late 1930s (Berry, 1975:221). In Ghana, cocoa cultivation began in the southeast and spread to Asante and Brong-Ahafo shortly after 1900. Production in Brong-Ahafo increased following the construction of roads to Goaso, Wenchi, and Sunyani in the early 1920s and again in the late 1930s and 1940s, after much of the crop in Eastern Region was destroyed by swollen-shoot disease (Konings, 1986:62ff.). In Nigeria, cocoa production was concentrated in areas served by the railroad (Egba,[2] Ijebu, Ibadan, and parts of Ilesha) until the 1920s, when road construction opened up large areas of Ife and Ondo (Berry, 1975:82; see figure 1).

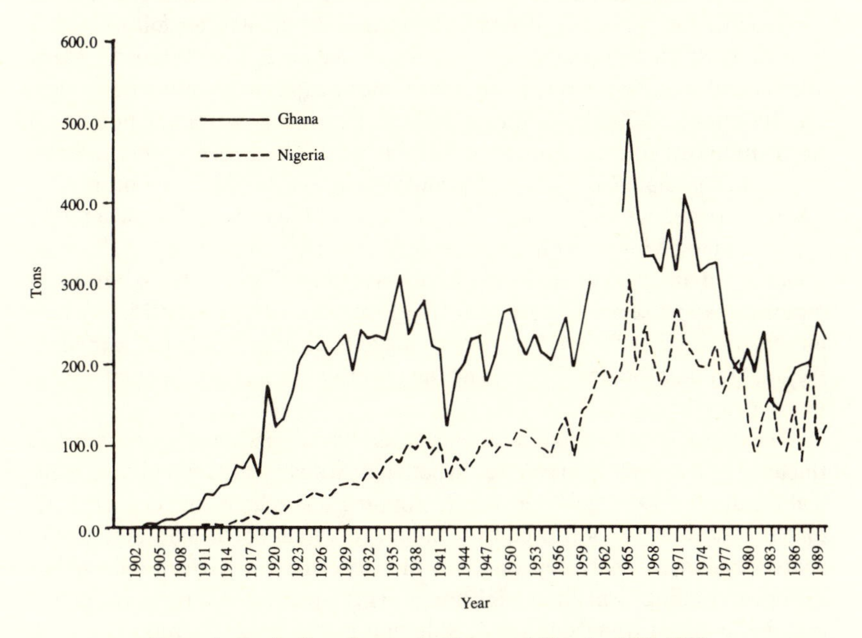

Figure 1. Production of cocoa in Ghana and Nigeria, 1902–1989

Before the First World War, the terms of trade generally moved in favor of West African exports, and farmers' incomes rose with the spread of cocoa production, aided in part by competition among the numerous European trading firms which handled the import/export trade. In 1915–16, "13 large and 23 smaller expatriate firms were . . . exporting 89 percent of [cocoa] shipments to the United Kingdom" (Southall, 1978:197). Rising farm incomes, together with the growth of towns and the increased flow of cash income to rural areas also stimulated demand for foodstuffs and other consumption goods.[3] Demand for food crops, in particular, tended to outrun locally produced supplies. By the 1950s, cocoa farmers in western Nigeria purchased between half and three quarters of the calories they consumed (W. O. Jones, 1972:60). In savannah areas adjacent to the cocoa belt, farmers began to increase food crop production for "export" to the cocoa-farming areas and towns (Anthony et al., 1979:138–39). In western Nigeria, "exports" of foodstuffs from Ilorin and northern Oyo Provinces increased steadily during the 1920s (Berry, 1975:169). Similarly, in Ghana the expansion of cocoa farming gave rise to the growth of specialized food production and trade in Suhum, Atebubu, and Ejura (Schwimmer, 1976:130; Arhin, 1979:chap. 6; Benneh, 1973:107).

Agricultural growth also created opportunities for Africans to invest in trade and transport. Many of the people who migrated from Yoruba towns in the interior to Lagos, Ibadan, or the Gold Coast traded in both local and imported commodities or worked as porters or dockhands. Migrants often followed their fellow townsmen in choosing their destination and occupation "abroad." Many Yoruba traders in Kumasi came from the same or adjacent home towns in Nigeria (Sudarkasa, 1979:153ff.; Eades, 1979:169), while a substantial number of Ijesha migrants sold cloth in other Yoruba towns (Peel, 1983:148ff.). Some traders accumulated significant amounts of capital. In 1922, one prominent trader in Ibadan was reported to own "a fleet" of motor vehicles and a repair garage and to be investing in large cement-block houses, while "an illiterate trader at Iseyin" who owned three Reos was competing with the government motor transport service to Ibadan (Oyo Province, 1922). By 1925, "fifteen motors owned by Africans" were entering and leaving Oyo daily for Ibadan, Iseyin, Ogbomosho, and Ilorin, and the government service shut down (Oyo Province, 1925).

The rate of growth of agricultural exports and farmers' and traders' incomes fluctuated, of course, with changes in both global and local economic and political conditions. During World War I, shipping was scarce, and exports fluctuated. The war was followed by a boom, in which cocoa sales and prices soared, and then a sharp depression, which forced many African and smaller European trading firms into bankruptcy. Trade recovered during the 1920s, and the terms of trade improved, although not to prewar levels (Hopkins, 1973:180–84). However, the global depression of the 1930s ushered in a period of unprecedentedly low prices and purchasing power, which persisted through the Second World War. In some areas cocoa planting ceased entirely; elsewhere it continued, chiefly because returns to most other crops also fell, and income-earning opportunities in trade and wage employment declined even further (Berry, 1975:84). In Ghana the effects of declining trade were compounded by the appearance of swollen-shoot disease. In the older cocoa-growing areas of the Eastern Region, output fell by about 60 percent from the late 1930s to the late '40s—enough to offset the gains from new planting in parts of Ashanti and Brong-Ahafo. As a result, total Ghanaian output remained constant from 1925 until the late 1950s (Kay, 1972:336–37; Birmingham et al., 1966:241). In Nigeria, by contrast, road construction ushered in a sharp increase in cocoa plantings in the late 1920s, which continued throughout the depression (Berry, 1975:81–82).

After 1945, world commodity prices rose rapidly, buoyed by pent-up American demand, European economic recovery, and government stockpiling during the Korean War. In both Ghana and Nigeria, rising prices spurred extensive new plantings of cocoa, which came into bearing during the 1950s and early 1960s. Encouraged by agricultural officials, farmers also began to use chemical sprays to control insect and disease attack and, beginning in the 1950s, new hybrid varieties of cocoa which matured in only three to four years, instead of seven years or more for the older varieties. All these developments contributed to rising output.[4]

Increased planting after 1945 was accompanied by new waves of migration into previously undeveloped areas, such as western Ahafo and southeastern Ife (Adomako-Sarfoh, 1974:134; Konings, 1986:62–64; Berry, 1975:67–71; Olusanya et al., 1978:passim). Most of the new farms were planted by migrant farmers who moved from older cocoa regions, where land was no longer available or yields were falling, or from savannah areas which were too dry for cocoa. In Ghana, farmers from the Eastern Region migrated into undeveloped parts of Ashanti and Brong-Ahafo in the late 1940s, following new roads cut by timber companies, which began large-scale operations in Ahafo in 1948. They were followed in the 1950s by farmers from older cocoa-growing areas in Brong and Ashanti, and by former traders and artisans seeking to participate in the booming cocoa sector. "The influx of migrant farmers . . . contributed considerably to the remarkable increase in the population of Ahafo"—from 23,000 in 1948 to nearly 82,000 in 1960 (Konings, 1986:64). Migrants also moved into the western districts of Wassa and Sefwi during the 1950s and 1960s (Arhin, 1985:vi-viii, 6). Similarly, in Nigeria, beginning in the late 1940s, thousands of farmers moved from Yoruba-speaking communities in the savannah into Ilesha, Ife, and Ondo to plant cocoa (Berry, 1975:69–70; see also Agboola et al., 1978).

Control over cocoa income was influenced by the organization of marketing as well as by relations of production. Before World War II, the export of cocoa and other commodities from Ghana and Nigeria was handled largely by expatriate trading firms, although occasionally African merchants managed to sell directly to foreign buyers.[5] The trading firms relied, in turn, on a large network of African buyers—over 38,000 in 1938—who purchased cocoa from hundreds of thousands of farmers, collecting it at major buying centers, for shipment to the ports (Miles, 1978:161).[6]

Both officials and farmers regarded African produce traders with mixed feelings. African traders were disparaged as greedy middlemen, who profited at the expense of farmers and European merchants (Beer, 1976:228ff.; Miles, 1978:161ff.). Merchants could not, however, dispense with their services in collecting produce from thousands of small growers (Southall, 1978:197ff.), while, for farmers, "cocoa brokers" provided both marketing services and loans—usually in the form of crop advances. If farmers organized to press traders for higher prices, they risked losing their primary source of credit. A significant minority of cocoa farmers operated on both sides of the market, buying cocoa and reselling it to "brokers" or agents of European firms, as well as growing it (Konings, 1986:70; Berry, 1985:91).

In the early years of colonial rule, officials worked to foster competition among produce traders, going so far as to provide government transport services to enable small African traders to enter the market. However they did nothing to prevent the series of mergers among European firms which began in the late 1920s and early 1930s, as merchants struggled to survive worsening conditions in the world economy. To African farmers and traders alike, collusion among European firms was seen as a primary cause of the declining cocoa price (Miles, 1978:157; Beer, 1976:227). However, the multiple and conflicting interests of African farmers, traders, and farmer-traders made it difficult to organize collective action against the European firms.

For example, farmers' cooperative societies—assiduously promoted by colonial officials to "protect" farmers from middlemen and improve the quality of cocoa exports—were in practice dominated by farmer-traders and attracted relatively few members. Before 1945, cooperatives handled less than 5 percent of the crop, in both Ghana and Nigeria (Beer, 1976:24; Young et al., 1981:178–83). African farmers and traders also attempted to hold cocoa off the market to force up the price. Cocoa "holdups," as they were called, occurred more often and to greater effect in Ghana than in Nigeria. The most successful was the Gold Coast cocoa holdup of 1937–38 when, between late November 1937 and mid-February 1938, firms managed to purchase only about 2,200 tons of cocoa in Ghana—less than 1 percent of the average crop in each of the previous three years (Howard, 1976:479).

The success of the 1937 holdup in Ghana has been attributed to the fact that African traders played a major role in organizing and financing it (Southall, 1978:206–9), but this interpretation is not entirely convincing. Some traders profited handsomely during the holdup at farmers' expense, buying cocoa at very low prices from farmers who had run out of cash, then selling it at inflated prices after the boycott ended (Austin, 1988:90). Nor is there reason to believe that African traders would have been more likely to boycott firms in Ghana than in Nigeria, where efforts to organize holdups foundered, in 1937 and earlier, on competition among African traders and between traders and farmers (Beer, 1976:21–22).

One factor which may help to explain the greater frequency and effectiveness of holdups in Ghana is the different positions of Akan and Yoruba chiefs in their respective cocoa economies. In both countries, most chiefs were also farmers and, as individuals, shared farmers' interest in higher producer prices. In Ghana, however, chiefs also received substantial amounts of tribute from strangers who grew cocoa on land belonging to their stools—whereas Yoruba chiefs profited from cocoa only to the extent that they grew or traded it for themselves, or received *isakole* on their family lands.[7] In principle, then, Akan chiefs had a larger stake in farmers' obtaining higher prices for their crops.

In practice, as several recent studies have suggested, chiefs did play an important part in the cocoa holdups in Ghana. To be sure, some opposed the holdups or succumbed to pressure from the colonial administration to enforce government policy against combinations in restraint of trade (Miles, 1978:168; Austin, 1988:81; cf. Mikell, 1983:44).[8] But other chiefs supported the holdups, or were believed to have done so (Austin, 1988: 81–82, 86), and chiefs who opposed them came under pressure to change their stance. Nana Ofori Atta's celebrated opposition to the cocoa holdup of 1930–31 "was quickly followed by the most serious political crisis of his long reign, when in 1932 all his divisional chiefs were destooled—and he himself only narrowly escaped." Apparently sobered by the experience, he emerged in 1937 "as . . . undisputed spokesman" for a coalition of farmers and chiefs "against the government and the firms" (Miles, 1978:168).

Austin (1988:87–88) concludes that, as farmers and rentiers in their own right, chiefs were inclined to be sympathetic towards the farmers, while their control over land (backed by the colonial state) gave them the authority to ensure compliance with the boycotts. But control over land and cocoa rents was a two-edged sword. Popular pressure for destoolments proliferated in the colonial period, fueled by grievances over the amount of rent collected from cocoa farmers and by chiefs' insistence on treating cocoa tribute as personal income rather than as revenue for the stool (Grier, 1987:36–37). Under indirect rule, the colonial regime was prepared to uphold the authority of legitimate chiefs, but legitimacy ultimately depended on popularity. Thus colonial officials also recognized a number of locally initiated destoolments, even when—as in Akim Abuakwa in 1932—part of the popular case against the chiefs was that the latter had sided with the European trading firms against the farmers (Miles, 1978:168).

As these examples suggest, a chief's willingness to support farmers' demands for higher prices could, paradoxically, serve to strengthen his claim to legitimacy in the eyes of the colonial regime. Like cocoa brokers who both supported the holdup and speculated against its termination, chiefs also had multiple, sometimes conflicting interests in the price of cocoa. Under both colonial and postcolonial rule, chiefs were more likely to retain their titles by maneuvering adroitly among competing interest groups than by taking a strong stand on one side or the other.

In 1938, the Nowell Commission (appointed by the British crown to investigate the cocoa holdup) recommended that the colonial regime regulate cocoa marketing to protect farmers' welfare and avoid further disturbances. When war broke out in Europe in 1939, ships were diverted to the war effort, and West African farmers were threatened with unsold crops. To forestall unrest, the government took direct control of export marketing.[9] After 1945, the marketing boards were retained, ostensibly to stabilize producer prices and, it was hoped, producer politics. In practice, as world market prices rose steadily for the next ten years and new plantings soared, the marketing board became a convenient tool for channeling a substantial share of rising export earnings into government hands (Beer, 1976:16; Helleiner, 1964:584–88; Austin, 1964:341; Killick, 1978:119).

So much new cocoa was planted in the late 1940s and 1950s, that cocoa output in both countries remained high long after the world price turned down in 1955. In Ghana the volume of exports reached a peak in 1965; then leveled off for a decade before beginning to decline (Tabatabai, 1988:717). In Nigeria, cocoa exports grew until the early 1970s and then fluctuated widely, but showed no clear trend until they began to decline in the early 1980s (see Figure 1). The fact that output remained buoyant for so long in the face of declining world prices and (especially in Ghana) high rates of government surplus extraction reflects the limited role of cocoa prices in determining levels of current output.[10] In both Ghana and Nigeria, production began to decline when the trees planted after 1945 passed the peak of their bearing years. Output was also adversely affected by the decline in farmers' incomes, which reduced their ability to purchase insecticides, and by severe shortages of labor (Tabatabai, 1988:721–24; Berry, 1985:88).

Ironically, the labor shortages which contributed to the decline of cocoa output and farmers' incomes in both countries occurred under diametrically opposed macroeconomic conditions. In Ghana real incomes fell precipitously in the 1970s, diverting sahelian migrant laborers to the booming economies of Nigeria and Côte d'Ivoire and driving two million Ghanaians to emigrate in search of better opportunities (Tabatabai, 1988:715–17). At the same time, the oil boom in Nigeria drew farmers and farm workers to seek quick gains in the buoyantly volatile trade and service sectors, leaving Nigerian cocoa farmers almost as hard-pressed by labor scarcity and inflation as their counterparts in Ghana's severely depressed economy (Berry, 1985:88).

Observers of trends in economic policy and agricultural performance in Ghana and Nigeria have debated the political consequences of agricultural stagnation and declining terms of trade for cocoa farmers in particular. Despite the obvious clash of interests between farmers and independent governments over the cocoa price, farmers did not emerge as a major political bloc in independent Ghana or Nigeria. In Ghana, the NLM was the only party which tried to turn cocoa farmers' discontent into a national opposition movement, and its success was limited—partly because the party was open to the charge of Ashanti chauvinism, and Nkrumah exploited this to devastating effect (Austin, 1964:342). No other political party in Ghana has identified as closely with farmers' interests. Like all Ghanaians, cocoa farmers pursued access to the state through sectional as well as occupational ties, and this tended to compromise their ability to advance their interests as farmers with the state. In Ahafo, for example, disputes over cocoa revenues between pro-Ashanti chiefs led by the Mimhene and an anti-Ashanti faction led by the Kukuomhene opened the door for Nkrumah to take direct control of all land in Ahafo, pending settlement of the chiefs' wrangles (Konings, 1986:69; Dunn and Robertson, 1973:228).

Similarly, in Nigeria, although cocoa revenues fed regional government and party coffers in the 1950s and 1960s, party conflict in the Western Region never crystallized around farmers' opposition to the state. In the 1950s and 1960s, for example, both the Action Group and its rivals (the National Council of Nigeria and the Cameroons and, later, the Nigerian National Democratic Party) drew support from cocoa farmers (Beer, 1976:chap.5; Oyediran, 1973: 74ff.). The most serious protest by cocoa farmers occurred in 1968–69, under military rule, when government levies to support the war against Biafra, coming at the end of a decade of falling cocoa prices, sparked rebellion in some of the older cocoa-growing areas. At the time, some observers heralded the Agbekoya protests as the beginning of a full-scale peasant movement, but this did not happen. The rebellion subsided within a few months as the government reduced taxes and raised the price of cocoa, and disputes developed among the farmers' leaders (Beer, 1976:chap. 8; Berry, 1985:88).

By the 1970s, farmers were too busy scrambling for a share of the oil wealth in Nigeria or escaping the worst effects of economic decline in Ghana to have time or energy to invest in expanding or upgrading their cocoa farms, let alone organizing collectively to raise the price of cocoa or improve the terms on which they took part in the wider economy. In the 1980s, as the oil recession got underway in Nigeria and the economic depression deepened in Ghana, increasing numbers of people began to grow food crops—something both governments had tried unsuccessfully to accomplish in the 1970s through rural development programs.

CENTRAL KENYA

In the mid-1890s, the Imperial British East Africa Company moved through what was to become Kenya, establishing a series of fortified posts in order to guarantee British access to Uganda and the headwaters of the Nile. In 1895, Britain declared a protectorate over the territory between Uganda and the coast and began to build a railway from Mombasa to Kisumu. The imposition of British protection coincided with a period of drought, disease, and scarcity between 1897 and 1901, which drove many people into the highlands around Mt. Kenya in search of food (Ambler, 1987:130ff.). British soldiers and officials found it difficult to procure adequate supplies of food and firewood, and almost impossible to mobilize enough local labor for railway construction. Accordingly, they resorted to forced requisitioning of provisions, imported labor from India, and concluded that if the area were ever to pay for the railway and support a colonial administration, European settlers would have to be brought in to generate taxable income (Mungeam, 1966:77ff.; Sorrenson, 1968:41–42).

By 1901, the drought had ended, rinderpest and smallpox had abated, and people had began to return to the lowlands. They were followed almost immediately by the first European settlers, and soon found themselves dislodged or excluded from arable and pasture land, streams, and salt licks to which they had enjoyed access in the past. In addition, the Europeans demanded African labor, resorting to coercive methods of recruitment when voluntary supplies fell short (Clayton and Savage, 1974:29–30, 37, 44; Presley, 1986:95).

Migrants who returned from the highlands after the famine also found a growing market for agricultural and livestock products in colonial towns and on the more successful European estates. Between 1904 and 1914, African farmers (in what would later become Central Province) sold increasing amounts of maize, beans, and potatoes (Overton, 1988:118). To expand production for the market, Africans needed land and labor too—a fact which deepened their resentment over European expropriation and diluted their interest in working for Europeans. Frustrated in their search for cheap labor, European settlers demanded that the government help to force it out (Sorrenson, 1968:151ff.; Clayton and Savage, 1974:128–30; Lonsdale and Berman, 1979:passim). Officials sympathized with the settlers but were not prepared to suppress African commercial activity altogether. If the government obliged settlers by limiting Africans' opportunities to produce for the market, they risked losing revenue and foreign exchange. In 1910, Africans paid 40 percent of government revenue from taxes and duties; in 1913, African produce accounted for three-fourths of Kenyan export earnings (Lonsdale and Berman, 1979:497).

As Europeans flooded into what is now Central Province (see Map 4), land prices rose, and speculators profited. One farm of 145 acres changed hands five times between 1907 and 1911, its price rising from Rs 9,000 to Rs 44,500 in the process (Kenya Land Commission, 1934b:323). Accordingly many settlers moved further west, into the Rift Valley, in search of more and cheaper land (see Map 5). The Rift Valley was occupied at the time mainly by transhumant Maasai, who offered little resistance to European settlement, but who

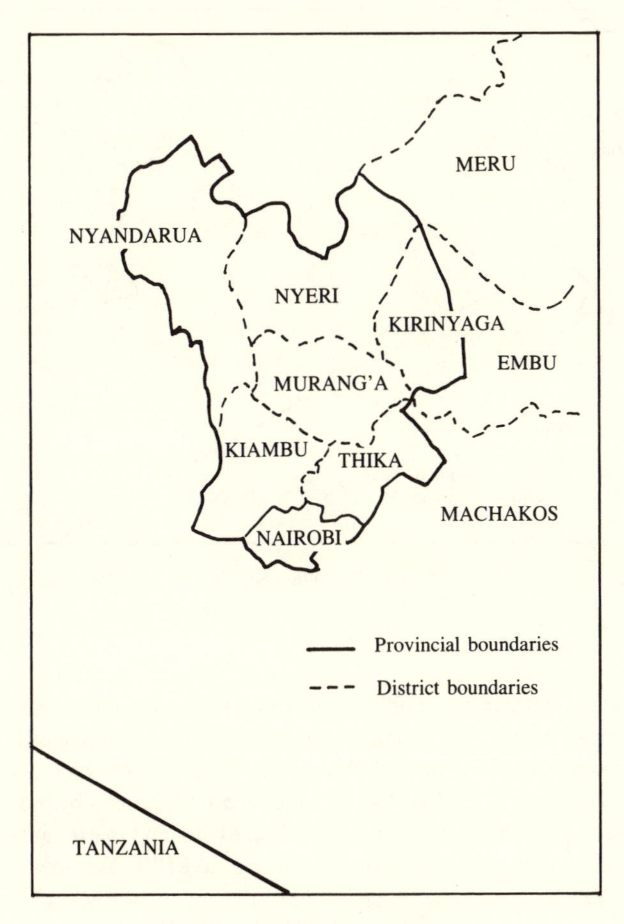

Map 4. Central Province, Kenya

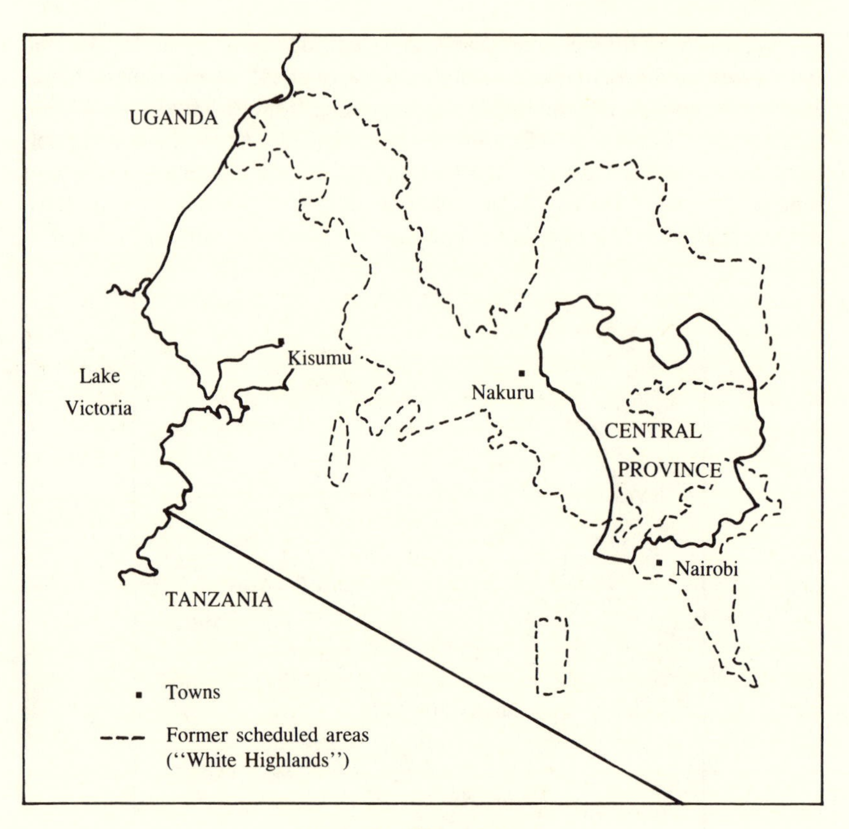

Map 5. The White Highlands

were also too scattered and mobile to provide a viable supply of labor for European farms. Consequently, when Kikuyu (who had been displaced by the first European settlers in Kiambu and Murang'a, or who simply wanted more land) also began to move to the Rift Valley,[11] they were welcomed by the European settlers, who gave them almost unlimited access to land in exchange for relatively small amounts of labor time (Kanogo, 1987:19; Wambaa and King, 1975:196–97).

At first, many squatters prospered. Most families had five or six acres under crops and sold their surplus to their employers (Kanogo, 1987:20–23). Others accumulated substantial herds of livestock. According to a contemporary observer, "squatters with the really big herds didn't have to do any work at all; they just kept their ears to the ground and when they heard that pasture was better in, say, Visoi, they would just pull their stock out . . . and move" (Wambaa and King, 1975:199). During the 1920s, relations between squatters and European landowners began to deteriorate. Faced with rising competition from successful African farmers and stockowners, Europeans began to restrict the size of squatters' herds and to demand more labor from them. Kikuyu squatters, who saw themselves as permanent colonists in the Rift Valley, resented the settlers' insistence that they were only tenants, subject to eviction at the settlers' discretion (Kanogo, 1987:26). As the settlers raised their demands, squatters began "to resist settler authority by leaving the farms, squatting illegally, staging strikes characterised by a refusal to perform tasks allotted to them, and engaging in other acts of sabotage, like maiming settler cattle and setting fire to settler crops" (Kanogo, 1987:50).

Meanwhile, Kikuyu who remained in Central Province also became increasingly involved in the market economy.[12] They worked for wages on settler estates or in towns and produced increasing amounts of foodstuffs for the colony's growing internal market. The principal cash crops were white maize, beans, and European potatoes, and some farmers also grew bananas and vegetables for sale. Sales of foodstuffs continued to rise after 1930, and African farmers also began to grow wattle (Cowen, 1978:74). By the 1940s, the increased availability of maize from other parts of Kenya (where land was more abundant and/or better suited to oxen and ploughs) allowed farmers in Central Province to concentrate on potatoes and vegetables, which brought higher returns per acre of cultivated land. As population growth and increased agricultural production put pressure on land in the Kikuyu Reserve, fallow periods declined (Kenya, 1945:25; Fisher, 1954?:257).

Together with Kikuyu migration to the Rift Valley, the growth of African agricultural production for the market in Central Province reduced the numbers of Kikuyu willing to work on European estates. European settlers complained constantly of the scarcity of labor. In 1912, the Native Labour Commission recommended that in order to increase and stabilize the supply of labor to European estates, Africans should be separated from non-Africans, territorially and administratively; their movements should be controlled; and their opportunities to earn income independently of working for Europeans should be curtailed (Clayton and Savage, 1974:61).[13] Little action was taken during the war, but in 1918, under renewed pressure from settlers, the colonial authorities promulgated a series of measures designed to control the squatter population and regulate conditions of employment. Taxes were raised to force Africans into the labor market, and compulsory labor levies were imposed. Beginning in 1919, Africans were required to carry identity papers (worn, humiliatingly, in a metal cylinder hung around the neck on a thong) and were permitted to live outside their "tribal" areas only if gainfully employed (Kanogo, 1987:37ff.; Clayton and Savage, 1974:131–34). To further protect the settler economy, the government also prohibited Africans from cultivating coffee, tea, or pyrethrum. Formal demarcation of tribal reserves was, however, delayed until 1926, because of opposition from settlers who objected to being permanently excluded from access to land in the reserves (Sorrenson, 1967:19).

In Central Province, sales of African agricultural produce rose rapidly in the early 1920s and then leveled off (Heyer, 1975, cited in Swainson, 1980:34). Within the Kikuyu Reserve, the rural population was already fairly differentiated in terms of levels of agricultural wealth as well as relations of production. Chiefs and headmen accumulated followers and livestock. Expansion depended on access to land, however, which was blocked in Central Province by European settlers and the government Forest Reserves. Stock owners were forced to limit their herds or seek new ways to benefit from the European presence. In Nyeri, some prosperous men sent their sons to the Christian missions to learn new skills (Cowen, 1972:40). Others moved their herds to the Rift Valley, entrusting them to the care of relatives who had settled there as squatters (Kitching, 1980:223).

Increasing numbers of Kikuyu were also drawn into wage employment, as laborers in towns or on European estates, and used their earnings to purchase livestock, pay bridewealth, or hire in labor to expand agricultural production for the market. Many women who lived within walking distance of European farms worked there as daily laborers during the coffee harvest, often under abusive conditions (Presley, 1986:197ff.). Increasingly, men and women also hired out to prosperous African farmers within the reserves. By the late 1930s, demand for African labor had outrun local supplies, and farms in Kiambu and Nyeri had begun to attract migrants from Embu, Meru, and Ndia (Cowen and Murage, 1972:43).

After 1918, some of the young men who had attended mission schools during the war returned to the reserves, hoping to find employment and establish homesteads. Known as *athomi* (readers), they used their mission training to take up employment as artisans and clerks, accumulating savings which they later invested in farms. They were also called upon to represent their kinsmen's interests before the Native Tribunals, established in 1913 by the colonial regime to adjudicate disputes among Africans according to customary law (Phillips, 1944:9–11, 230). When a family won a land case, the *muthomi* who had represented them before the Native Tribunal was often rewarded with a piece of the land (Cowen and Murage, 1972:52; Cowen, 1978:74; cf. Njonjo, 1977:48ff.). In this way, some *athomi* acquired sizable holdings on which they established commercial farms, using savings from nonagricultural employment to purchase improved inputs and especially to hire in labor. They grew maize, English potatoes, and vegetables for urban markets, and were among the first Africans to plant wattle and produce bark for the tanning industry (Cowen, 1978:74).

In the late 1920s, with the tacit backing of the government, some settlers in the "White Highlands" confiscated and slaughtered large numbers of squatters' livestock. Kikuyu called it *kifagio* ("broom" in Swahili) "to imply the 'sweeping away' of squatter stock. . . . No compensation was paid for the eliminated stock." The destocking campaign reduced squatters' livestock "from an average of several hundred per labourer to about five per family" (Kanogo, 1987:46). To escape further assaults on their herds, some squatters moved their remaining animals back into the reserve. At the same time, drought led to the evacuation of large numbers of stock from Machakos and the northern frontier, "the vast bulk of which went into Kikuyuland" (Kitching, 1980:222). Officials steered incoming herds toward Ndeiya, a semiarid area in the southwest corner of the reserve, where the government prohibited cultivation in order to provide as much grazing land as possible. The Kikuyu who settled there were not pure pastoralists, however, and this restriction caused them much hardship. The ensuing tensions foreshadowed the conflicts over land access and use which developed in the settlement schemes of the 1940s, and contributed directly to the Mau Mau oathing campaign (Bullock, 1974:93–94; Throup, 1988:chap.6; Kanogo, 1987:116ff.; Furedi, 1989:81–83).

Kifagio did not save European settlers from the depression. European farmers suffered from both falling prices and increased competition from African farmers, whose costs were lower and whose numbers rose as workers were laid off by European estates and by the government. As the European agricultural sector contracted, Africans' sales of agricultural commodities increased. The quantity of beans and potatoes sold in the Kiambu, Nyeri, and Fort Hall districts doubled between 1934 and 1938, while sales of dry bark wattle jumped from 900 tons in 1929 to over 10,000 tons in 1933 and 16,000 tons in 1937 (Kitching, 1980: 64, 68). Wattle—a crop grown mostly on large farms before the early 1930s—was taken up by peasant farmers when processing firms switched from green to dry bark. To cut costs, Forestal, the principal manufacturer of tannin from wattle bark, began to purchase dry bark, which was lower in quality but much cheaper to produce than the green bark sold by European estates and by *athomi*, who had invested in wattle in the late 1920s. The ensuing expansion of wattle plantings by smallholders undercut the profits of the *athomi* as well as those of European growers.[14]

The growth of African agricultural sales accelerated during the war as the government temporarily tabled the problems of Kikuyu land grievances and squatter resettlement to concentrate on promoting food-crop production in support of the war effort (Kitching, 1980:68–70). Sales by African farmers may actually have been stimulated by marketing controls, which were instituted in the late 1930s (over the objections of the Coffee Board) to protect European maize growers from African competition. The Maize Control Board established quotas for European farmers and a dual pricing system. These measures led to the emergence of parallel markets, in which Africans' sales flourished (Kitching, 1980:180–81; Heyer and Waweru, 1976:323).

Wartime supply problems also distracted Kenyan officials from a new crisis which engulfed the squatter economy in the late 1930s. Under the Resident Native Labour Ordinance of 1937, landowners were authorized to eliminate squatters' herds completely and to demand as much as 270 days of labor per man per year in exchange for cultivation rights. In addition, responsibility for local government in the Rift Valley was formally transferred to the settler-dominated District Councils, giving European settlers a free hand in implementing the Ordinance (Kanogo, 1987:97). Squatters who refused to "reattest" their contracts under the new terms were evicted. Some returned to the reserves, where their presence added to the conflict over land rights; others made their way to new settlement schemes laid out by the government, where tension soon developed over officials' efforts to regulate land use in the name of conservation and improved African farming.

Coming after decades of land appropriation by Europeans, forced relocation of Africans, and tightening controls on squatters, government efforts to control Africans' land use in the reserves were deeply resented. In areas which were opened to African settlement in the 1940s, in order to absorb some of the overflow from the crowded reserves, the government refused to grant settlers "customary" occupancy rights, referring to them as *ahoi* (Sorrenson, 1967:83). Officials limited the amount of land each settler could use for cultivation and grazing, and imposed numerous restrictions on methods of cultivation. At Olenguruone, after several years of mounting tension between Kikuyu settlers and officials, the settlers were evicted and their crops and homes destroyed (Throup, 1988:chap. 6; Sorrenson, 1967:84).

At about the same time, headmen in the reserves were ordered to mobilize "communal labor" to construct terraces to prevent soil erosion.[15] Those who proved reluctant to alienate their people by enforcing these orders were dismissed and replaced by educated men who supported the government's goals of soil conservation and agricultural improvement. In 1947, the Kenya African Union (KAU) picked up on popular opposition to forced terracing and the chiefs who enforced it. With encouragement from local KAU activists, women boycotted communal labor, bringing the whole enterprise to a virtual halt, and violent disturbances broke out when a chief had KAU leaders tried for illegal political activities and sentenced to hard labor (Throup, 1988:150–56). The disturbances were suppressed, but popular anger towards the colonial regime and its African agents continued to simmer, increasing people's receptivity to the Mau Mau oathing campaign which followed (Kanogo, 1987:116–20).

During the Mau Mau rebellion, thousands of people, mostly Kikuyu, were detained for subversive activity, and over a million others were rounded up in villages to "protect" them from the freedom fighters and facilitate government control (Sorrenson, 1967:103, 110; Mukaru Ng'ang'a, 1977:369ff.). British officials relied on a core of Kikuyu "loyalists" to help police the countryside, rewarding them with loans, licenses to trade, and permission to plant coffee (Sorrenson, 1967:41; Mukaru Ng'ang'a, 1977:366). Loyalists also played a key role in the initial registration of land titles, a measure which, though designed to assuage long-standing Kikuyu grievances over land as well as create a basis for agricultural improvement, was in fact forcibly imposed on the rural population. The establishment of fortified villages during the emergency "paved the way for consolidating all the land in the Kikuyu country" (Sorrenson, 1967:112), and the government seized the opportunity in 1955 to "strike while the iron is hot" (Sorrenson, 1967:113). Most of the land in Central Province was registered before people were released from the villages. Loyalists, who were under no such restraints, were first in line for registration, and some managed to retain their holdings even after the initial titles were "corrected" in response to the protests of former detainees (Mukaru Ng'ang'a, 1978:163; 1977:377). However, the subsequent proliferation of unrecorded transfers of land and the mounting political tension over the whole issue of land ownership suggest that their gains were only temporary (Sorrenson, 1967:211; Okoth-Ogendo, 1976:177; see also ch. 5 below).

In addition to the consolidation of landholdings and registration of titles, colonial officials launched an ambitious program of agricultural improvement in 1954, known as the Swynnerton Plan. The program was designed to create a new class of "progressive" farmers, who would both contribute to economic development by producing commercial crops with improved techniques and exercise a stabilizing influence in rural politics. Although predicated on the notion that private property was a necessary condition for increased agricultural productivity, the plan's approach to agricultural modernization was anything but laissez-faire. The government supplied credit and inputs, while farmers were required to obtain licenses to grow coffee and obliged to join government-sponsored cooperative societies in order to sell it. To qualify for these services, farmers were supposed to manage their farms according to detailed plans drawn up by agricultural officials (Smith, 1976:131; De Wilde, 1967, vol. 2:17–18).

From the late 1950s to the mid-1970s, production and sales from small farms in Central Province grew dramatically (Kitching, 1980:318). How far this growth is attributable to the policies implemented under the Swynnerton Plan is, however, a subject of debate (House and Killick, 1981:51–53). Even in Central Province, only a minority of farmers participated in the "agricultural revolution" of the 1950s and 1960s (see table 2).

Table 2. The importance of export crops on small farms

A. Smallholders growing selected crops, Central Province (%)

	1960	1974	1976–77	1977–78	1978–79
Coffee	16.3	45.1	24	28	20
Tea	2.9	17.7	15	16	17
Hybrid maize	—	66.6	97	80	61

B. Sales by adult-equivalent income group, Kenya (shillings)

	0–249	250–499	500–999	1000–1499	1500–2499	>2500
Export crops	9	27	54	54	98	78
Food crops	20	37	73	178	299	309
Milk	12	11	35	53	146	164
Livestock	28	38	57	72	-19	10

Sources: A. 1960, 1974: Livingstone, 1986:170; 1976–77 and 1978–79: Kenya, 1982:111, 116. (Note that the sampling frame for the Integrated Rural Surveys changed in 1976 from smallholders to rural households.) B. Livingstone, 1986:318.

An observer who was sympathetic to the aims of the Swynnerton Plan commented in the mid-1960s that "the progress that has undeniably been made has, as yet, left untouched the great majority of African farmers and pastoralists who still . . . produce little more than what is required for their bare subsistence" (De Wilde, 1967:31). In the mid-1970s, official surveys showed that commercial crops such as coffee and tea were grown by only a minority of rural households, and that there was considerable inequality among rural households in terms of income and farm sales (Livingstone, 1986:304–7, 318; see also Kitching, 1980:328). In a careful statistical analysis of rural income distribution in two Nyeri locations, Cowen (1974) found that the proportion of households in middle-income categories increased between 1965 and 1971, but his sample was limited to the minority of rural households who sold milk and/or tea. Elsewhere, Cowen also demonstrated the emergence of a permanent category of landless or near-landless households, whose members depended almost entirely on wage employment for their livelihood (Cowen and Murage, 1972:49–57; Cowen, 1972:52ff.).

Landless households were not the only ones who relied on off-farm sources of income. "Straddling," which had been practiced by some rural households in Central Province since the 1910s, became the norm after independence. By the mid-1970s, rural households throughout Kenya were estimated to derive one-third of their incomes, on the average, from nonfarm sources; in Central Province, the proportion was one-half (Collier and Lal, 1984:1014;

see also Kenya, 1982:79). As in earlier periods, straddling meant different things to households in different income categories. For the relatively well-to-do, off-farm income probably helped to finance agricultural improvements (Collier and Lal, 1986:262–65; Haugerud, 1981b:14,17–21, 1984:chap. 7; Kitching, 1980:362–63). For poorer households, however, straddling was part of a continual struggle to make ends meet. In 1974, the proportion of household income derived from farm surplus was lower for the poorest rural households than for households in all other income categories (see table 5).[16]

Growing evidence of unequal development led to much official soul-searching in the 1970s. Much-publicized studies by the ILO (1972) and individual scholars (Leys, 1974; Leonard, 1977; Heyer and Waweru, 1976) were accompanied by changes in government policy designed to generate more egalitarian patterns of rural income and growth by equalizing access to productive resources within smallholder agriculture. In practice, this meant equalizing access to resources—farm inputs, credit, infrastructure and amenities—provided by the state (Heyer and Waweru, 1976:205–16; Killick and House, 1983:53–58). Official controls continued to proliferate, despite the government's rhetorical commitment to capitalism (see, e.g., Bates, 1989:chaps. 4, 5).

Within Central Province, many people had already been excluded from access to land, either through adjudication or because they subsequently sold land to pay off their debts (Okoth-Ogendo, 1976:178; Collier and Lal, 1980:28–29; Mbithi and Barnes, 1975:27,45–47). In the years following land registration, some of these people again moved out of Central Province—just as their forebears had done in the wake of European settlement after 1903—seeking land in other parts of Kenya where supplies were not so tight. Their quest was shaped but not controlled by government efforts to check rural impoverishment and control the distribution as well as the rate of growth of agricultural income. The history of this new generation of "squatters" has yet to be written.

Over the course of the twentieth century, the growth of commercial farming and high rates of seasonal and longer-term labor migration out of Central Province combined to increase the proportion of agricultural production carried out by women. In 1945, Humphrey commented that in their husbands' absence, many Kikuyu women were obliged to clear land as well as cultivate it. He also felt that they were spending more time than in the past collecting firewood and carrying goods to market, adding sentimentally that the sight of women "returning heavily laden from Karatina, 18 miles away" suggested that "something is radically wrong somewhere" (Kenya, 1945:52). In the early 1950s, Kikuyu women complained to Fisher (1954?:266) that their workload had increased because most of their children were in school. In the 1970s, many women routinely performed farm tasks previously handled by men and children, and some worked such long hours that they had no time to socialize

(Abbott, 1974; see also Stamp, 1975–76:29). Faced with intense pressure on their own time and energy, Kikuyu women introduced several labor-saving changes in cropping and food-consumption patterns, including the substitution of white maize for traditional varieties and the adoption of quicker-cooking varieties of arrowroot and vegetables (Mackenzie, 1986:285).

Agricultural commercialization, together with increased migration and off-farm employment, also affected the organization of labor within rural households. As rural household members became increasingly mobile, the division of labor by gender "has become blurred" (Barnes, 1984:60). With many adult men employed away from home, women assumed more responsibility for managing farms as well as working them. This often led to tension—reflected, for example, in the contradictory testimony of the woman who told Fisher (1954?:273) that "a woman can plant whatever she likes in her gardens, but some men tell their wives they must plant a certain crop in a certain garden. . . . If she does not he may beat her." When husbands were absent for much of the farming season, tension was likely to focus on the disposition of the output (Fisher, 1954?:273ff.; Mackenzie, 1986:419). In the 1960s, when the Cooperative Union's insistence on buying coffee only from heads of households (usually men) led women to switch their labor from coffee to food crops, the union backed down, permitting husbands and wives to open joint accounts in order to increase supply (Mackenzie, 1986:419–20). Struggles also focused on women's access to land, as we shall see in chapter 5.

In general, the small-scale farming sector appears to have absorbed a growing rural labor force during the 1960s and 1970s, through continued subdivision of family holdings, rather than the creation of a growing class of landless agricultural laborers. Cultivation of tea and coffee raised returns per hectare in the 1960s, and many farmers appear to have achieved very high yields on plots of less than 0.5 hectare through intensive methods of cultivation (Livingstone, 1986:161ff.; see also Haugerud, 1983:72–77, 1984:356; Brokensha and Glazier, 1973:190). By the 1980s, however, there was growing evidence of landlessness in Central Province and increasing out-migration to more marginal areas (Livingstone, 1986:182ff.; Alila et al., 1985:11).

NORTHEASTERN ZAMBIA

Like central Kenya, northeastern Zambia was "pacified" and administered by a chartered company (the British South Africa Company) before it was taken over by the Colonial Office in 1924. Both the company and the Colonial Office hoped to follow the Kenyan example and attract European settlers. The British South Africa Company sold some land to individual buyers, mainly in the vicinity of Abercorn (now Mbala) and Fort Jameson (now Mansa), but sales were few and far between. When the Colonial Office took over administration of the territory in 1924, the first governor evacuated Africans from large areas, but the anticipated influx of settlers never materialized (Vail, 1983:244–45; Palmer, 1973, vol. 1:57). By 1931, there were only about 4,000 Europeans in Northern Rhodesia outside the Copperbelt, most of them concentrated along the railway in the south (Gann, 1963:442). Those who did settle in the north were too few to create a local market for African labor and too isolated to produce for distant urban markets. The Copperbelt, which opened in the late 1920s, purchased food supplies from European and African farmers in the south, while the northeast supplied cheap migrant labor.

Much of the literature on the political and economic history of Zambia attributes the underdevelopment of the northeast to its importance as a labor reserve for the mines and cities of colonial southern Africa (Cliffe, 1978:329–30; Turok, 1979:130ff.; ILO, 1981:5). By 1900, the British South Africa Company had imposed a hut tax and a tax on iron, and had also banned the manufacture of salt and the sale of ivory in order to promote labor migration as a source of taxable income (Vail, 1983:225–26). In the early 1900s, migrants from the northeast began to seek work in Katanga, Southern Rhodesia and South Africa; later, many went to the Copperbelt (Meebelo, 1986:6–7; Roberts, 1976:chap. 10). Recruitment methods were harsh, and officials waged

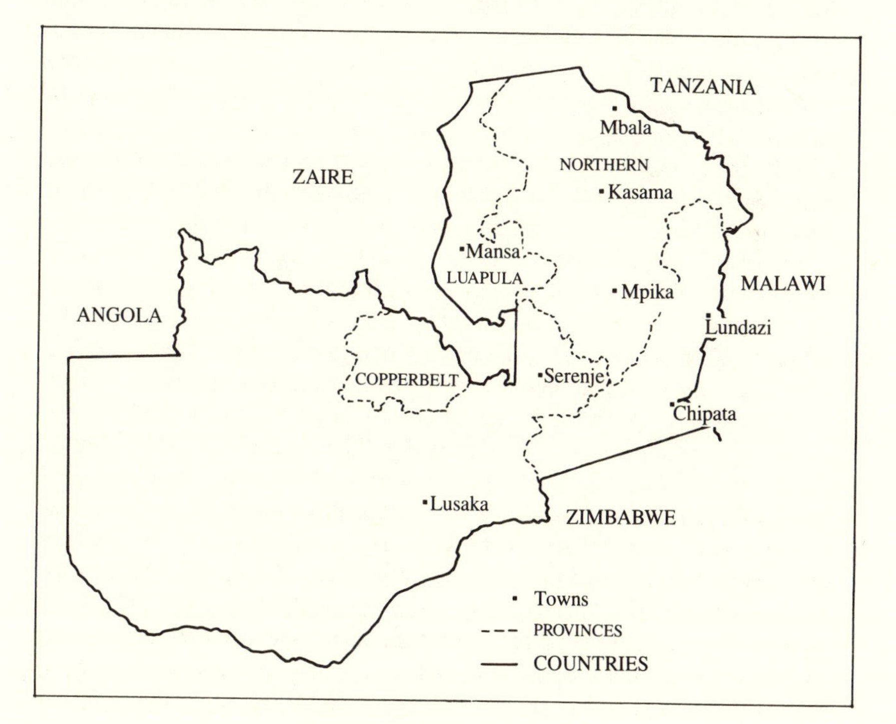

Map 6. Northeastern Zambia

a continual struggle against workers' efforts to evade controls (Van Onselen, 1976:chap. 8; Vail, 1983:225).

As copper production expanded in the 1930s, the flow of migrant labor increased, despite the absence of transportation. People traveled hundreds of miles by bicycle or on foot to work in the Copperbelt, often remaining there several years before undertaking the arduous journey home (A. Richards, 1939:397). By the late 1950s, transportation facilities had improved, and workers traveled back and forth more often (A. Richards, 1958:309). However, little effort was made to develop rural roads or encourage the marketing of agricultural produce. In the 1950s, officials described agricultural policy for Northern Province as one of "care and maintenance" (Makings, 1966:225). In 1960, only 5 percent of total cash income in five Ushi villages came from agricultural sales (Kay, 1964c:20). As late as 1962, women in a Bemba village walked sixty miles headloading groundnuts and cassava to exchange for dried fish, which were rumored to be temporarily in abundance near the Chambeshi River (Harries-Jones and Chiwale, 1962:63, n3).

While the colonial government did little to promote commerce or agricultural development in the northeast, it does not follow that its presence was not felt in the region. The issue of labor recruitment posed a dilemma for colonial authorities in Northern Rhodesia, just as the commercialization of African agriculture did for officials in central Kenya. In Kenya, colonial authorities wanted both to promote African agricultural production for the market in order to enlarge the tax base and to curb it in order to ensure a plentiful supply of cheap labor for European settlers and the colonial regime itself. In northeastern Zambia, officials were also keen to augment the flow of taxable remittances from migrant workers and not at all interested in the commercialization of African agriculture. However, colonial regimes had to maintain order, as well as raise revenue and mobilize labor. In northeastern Zambia, where wealth and power consisted largely in "rights over the services of others" (Richards, 1939:211), European labor recruitment threatened to undermine the authority of chiefs and hence the underpinnings of indirect rule.

At the same time that they were deliberately neglecting commercial and agricultural development in the northeast, officials in Northern Rhodesia were struggling to create effective structures of political and administrative control by building on indigenous authorities and institutions. Their task was complicated not only by confusion over the nature of customary rules and institutions, but also by the fact that most people in northeastern Zambia lived in tiny, scattered settlements and moved frequently, often splitting up villages in the process. After British "pacification," even the large, fortified Bemba villages (where people had gathered for protection during the turbulent times of the late nineteenth century) began to disperse—much to the dismay of Company officials, who had taken large villages and ruthless chiefs as evidence that traditional Bemba polities were strong, stable, centralized, and hierarchical. Fearing that a scattered, mobile population would be difficult to tax and administer and that dispersal would erode the authority of chiefs on whom they sought to build their own administration, company and, later, colonial officials tried repeatedly to stop dispersal and concentrate the rural population in large villages.

The official view that dispersal of the population tended to undermine chiefs' authority has been widely accepted by scholars (Ranger, 1971:26; Kay, 1967:43). Yet there is considerable evidence that dispersed settlements predated British conquest and that neither the Bemba nor other peoples of the region had a long history of political centralization (Werbner, 1967:passim; Roberts, 1973:17, 305–7). The large villages and powerful Bemba chiefs of the late nineteenth century were temporary consequences of a particular configuration of historical circumstances, rather than an inherent feature of traditional political processes (Werbner, 1967:31; Roberts, 1973:212–14, 305ff.). In fact, large, fortified villages were the exception rather than the rule (Kay, 1967:9), and those which existed at the time of British conquest broke up soon afterwards.

Villages moved and split up for both agricultural and social reasons. Under prevailing methods of shifting cultivation (described on pp. 000–000), people moved periodically to make new fields in areas of uncut woodland. Wealth and prestige depended on "rights over the services of others, whether slaves, relatives, fellow villagers, or subjects" (Richards, 1939:211), rather than on control over particular territories. For individual Bemba, residence was "a matter of individual choice" (Richards, 1959:172), and chiefs were in no position to prevent people from moving or renegotiating political and social allegiances. Effective authority was more likely to be manifested through a chief's ability to mobilize tribute labor when needed or to exercise influence over the appointment of new headmen than by his presiding over a large, permanent village. In the 1930s, local chiefs assured the District Commissioner at Fort Rosebery that "the greater the number of villages, the greater the prestige of the chief" (quoted in Ranger, 1971:27).

British officials' efforts to reorganize the rural population into large, permanent villages were ultimately unsuccessful, but profoundly disruptive nonetheless. Both agricultural production and social structures in the region were predicated on frequent changes of residence and village memberships. Thus, government efforts to consolidate and stabilize rural settlements actually disrupted people's access to land and labor and injected new uncertainties into agricultural systems where food security was already tenuous.[17]

Measures to reorganize rural settlements were launched by the British South Africa Company as early as 1905. In Ushi, for example, company officials demarcated boundaries between "chiefs' areas" and then set out to consolidate small chieftaincies into larger units. Since chiefs' domains had not previously been defined in territorial terms, demarcation led to boundary disputes "which have continued, more or less peacefully, to the present day" (Kay, 1964b:245). By 1917, the number of Ushi chiefs had been reduced from twenty-seven to eighteen,[18] and by the 1940s, to ten (Kay, 1964b:247).

The British South Africa Company consolidated villages as well as chiefdoms. In 1906, Native Commissioners throughout the region were instructed to amalgamate small settlements into larger ones. Farm camps (*mitenda*) were declared illegal. When an Ushi chief complained that his people were building them anyway, the Native Commissioner "lent him Messengers to burn them, which he did, and brought the people before me" (quoted in Kay, 1964b:245). Between 1906 and 1908, the number of Ushi settlements was reduced from 436 to 190 (Kay, 1964b:247). Elsewhere, comparable consolidations took place: the number of villages declined from 282 to 74 in Kasama District, from 560 to 77 in Luwinga District, and from 70 to 5 in Chief Kopa's Area, Mpika District (Kay, 1967:10).

In the wake of village consolidation, the adjacent woodland was soon cut down to make *citemene* fields. To prevent deforestation, the company also outlawed *citemene* cultivation in 1908, "but the famine which followed soon led to a change of mind" (Hellen, 1968:203). However, the company continued to consolidate settlements. In 1910, following an outbreak of sleeping sickness, the company evacuated the entire Luapula Valley, herding people into large villages on the adjacent plateau. A contemporary observer hoped that "I shall not witness such misery again. More people died of hunger and hardship than died of the sleeping sickness" (quoted in Kay, 1964b:248). Famine recurred in 1917 and 1918, following wartime conscription of African laborers (who were used to headload supplies for hundreds of miles from the railway to the border with German Tanganyika, in a manner reminiscent of the notorious Carrier Corps in Kenya). In 1918, the area was also struck by influenza. Between 1905 and 1917, the population of Ushi is estimated to have declined by 4,000, or 17 percent (Kay, 1964b:248).

When the Colonial Office took over the government of Northern Rhodesia, indirect rule was formally introduced. Statutory changes included the consolidation of "traditional" political authority into the hands of a few "paramount" chiefs, and the demarcation of African Reserves.[19] Both measures created difficulties. Chiefs who resented being relegated to "subordinate" status tried to regain their influence by manipulating colonial administrators' understanding of traditional rights of succession and the legitimacy of chiefly titles. "In a sense, the British policy of indirect rule preserved the Lungu political system, complete with all its conflicts" (Watson, 1976:181). In the case of land policy, the areas set aside as Native Reserves quickly proved inadequate, under prevailing methods of cultivation, to support the population assigned to them. Within a few years, the government was obliged to open new areas to African settlement. In keeping with contemporary concerns over environmental degradation, officials took the occasion to enforce changes in Africans' methods of cultivation. However, as in Kenya, official efforts to control farmers' activities did more to promote opposition to colonial rule than to transform agricultural practices (see above, pages 49–50).

In general, "unauthorized" village dispersals continued in the face of even the most stringent controls. In a study of ten Bisa villages carried out in 1963, Kapferer found that all but one of them had moved to their present locations *after* 1944, having "experienced a considerable degree of mobility" before that. "The people of Namasulwa village, for example, had moved nine times in 55 years" (Kapferer, 1967:7). By the 1930s, officials themselves were divided on the merits of dispersal. Some wanted to preserve large villages for administrative convenience, but others opposed them as unhygienic, "untraditional," and conducive to popular unrest (Kay, 1967:13–14). Agronomists discovered that *citemene* fields produced much higher yields than could be obtained under any other available method of cultivation—making it unlikely that farmers would readily abandon them (Svads, 1983:264). In an effort to reconcile the contradictory needs of efficient administration and viable agriculture, the administration proposed in 1932 to replace existing controls with a "taxpayer" rule, under which any headman who could muster a following of fifteen adult males could found a new village. This rule was honored mainly in the breach: in fact, villages moved and reorganized freely after 1932, although the taxpayer rule remained in effect until the late 1940s (Kapferer, 1967:7).

However, officials remained uneasy over the mobility of the rural population. After independence, the Zambian government rejected the conservatism of indirect rule and set out to transform the structures of rural administration into effective instruments of economic development and central political control. The government stripped chiefs of their judicial functions and created an elaborate infrastructure of party branches, district and village administrations, farmers' cooperatives and development committees (Tordoff, 1980:passim; Bratton, 1980a:215; Quick, 1978:passim). To facilitate these changes, they also instituted a program of village regroupment, which was strikingly reminiscent of colonial practices of village consolidation (Bratton, 1980b:125ff.; Bwalya, 1979:passim; Kay, 1967:10–12).

Colonial officials' preoccupation with creating (or discovering) stable, bounded African polities was paralleled by colonial ecologists' preoccupation with taxonomy. The dynamics of African cultivation practices were as baffling to European observers as the fluidity of African cultural boundaries and relations of authority. In a characteristically lucid expression of prevailing assumptions, the ecologist Trapnell (1953:34) described the precolonial history of the northeast as "a chaotic tale of immigration and raids and disruption and intermingling of races." Because of these upheavals, African systems of cultivation "are still changing . . . , former staples even disappearing, and new ones taking precedence over them . . . while curious hybrid agricultural systems . . . have evolved in intermediate zones of contact between tribes of different cultures. A full state of equilibrium has yet to be attained and a straightforward classification of agricultural systems is consequently not easy to present" (Trapnell, 1953:34).

In fact, farmers in northeastern Zambia practiced a variety of cropping patterns and methods of cultivation.[20] Except where forced relocation led to actual overcrowding (e.g., in the Native Reserves), labor rather than land was often the "scarce" factor of production, and farmers' ability to mobilize and control labor determined both levels of output and methods of cultivation. Most farmers aimed to cultivate several fields at a time. The "full complement of gardens" needed to ensure adequate food supplies for a rural household included fields at different stages of a single system of rotational fallow, as well as fields under different systems of cultivation (Kay, 1964a:35).

In most of Northern Province, farmers practiced some form of *citemene* cultivation. Trees or branches were cut, stacked in circles to a height of two to three feet, and burned. The resulting ash bed enhanced soil fertility, while the intense heat of the burn sterilized the soil, effectively inhibiting the growth of weeds (Svads, 1983:260–61). During the first year, millet was the main crop sown, together with some cassava, maize, perennial sorghum, and vegetables. Thereafter, farmers followed one of a variety of crop rotations for several years and then left the trees to regenerate—a process which might take fifteen to twenty years. Because of the large amount of wood used in preparing fields and the long regeneration period, *citemene* is an extremely extensive system of cultivation.[21] In northeastern Zambia, *citemene* was associated with very low population densities: 3.9 persons per square mile, according to Richards (1958:305).

Farmers also practiced hoe cultivation and composting, both on separate fields and at various stages in crop rotations on *citemene* fields. Village gardens were made by mounding earth over sod or cut vegetation, cultivated with hoes, and left fallow for only a few years. But mounds were also made on *citemene* fields, during the third or fourth year of cultivation, for beans and annual sorghum, and millet might be planted on old mounds which were spread flat for the purpose (Trapnell, 1953:48). Farmers also extended the harvest season by planting early millet plots or cultivated several varieties of millet with different maturation periods. In some Mambwe villages in the north, most fields were hoed and composted (Trapnell, 1953:57,110; Pottier, 1988:168). In comparison to *citemene*, mound cultivation produced lower yields and promoted weed growth, thus requiring extra labor during the growing season. Fields were abandoned after a few years, not because of soil exhaustion but because weeds became too numerous to cope with.

Between the early days of colonial rule and the introduction of hybrid maize in the late 1970s, the major changes in agricultural practices in northeastern Zambia consisted of alterations in the mix of existing activities rather than the introduction of new crops or methods of cultivation. In particular, there was a gradual shift from *citemene* to composting as the principal method of cultivation, and a tendency to substitute cassava and/or maize for millet as the principal staple (Stromgaard, 1985:45).[22] Through much of the region, *citemene* did not disappear, even after the introduction of ploughs (Svads, 1983:250–51; Stolen, 1983:346–47), and millet continues to be grown as a secondary crop, increasingly for the market rather than for home consumption. The introduction of hybrid maize in the mid-1970s, followed by oxen and ploughs in the early 1980s, was the first major exogenous innovation to be introduced to local agriculture.

Several scholars have attributed the long-term decline of *citemene* and farmers' increasing reliance on cassava to the effects of labor migration—particularly the absence of many adult men, whose labor was needed to cut trees for new *citemene* fields (Richards, 1939:316; Allan, 1965:156–58; ILO, 1981: 81–84; Geisler et al., 1985:12). Recently, this thesis has been criticized on several grounds. Moore and Vaughan (1986:525) point out that Richards observed shortages of millet in villages with very different ratios of men to women among the adult residents. Women whose husbands had migrated could get new *citemene* fields cut by their kinsmen or by brewing beer for a work party. Also, by the 1950s, many women were accompanying their husbands to the Copperbelt, so that migration had a greater effect on the total size than on the gender composition of the rural labor force (Pottier, 1988:81–82; Richards, 1958:309–10; Moore and Vaughan, 1986:528). Finally, Richards and other contemporary observers may have underestimated the contribution which women's kitchen gardens made to total food supplies (Moore and Vaughan, 1987:534–35).

Pottier also notes that the contrast between the rural prosperity which Watson observed in Mambwe villages in the mid-1950s and Richards' portrayal of hunger and poverty in Bemba villages in the 1930s may have had more to do with differences in overall economic conditions than in kinship relations. He does not, however, discuss Richards' observation that when she revisited the Bemba area in 1957, "the diet seemed to me to be definitely worse" than it had been in the early 1930s (Richards, 1958:310). Pottier's own restudy of the Mambwe in the late 1970s looks at the effects of the sharp decline in labor migration which followed the collapse of the world copper price after 1974. The decline in labor migration was not followed by a revival of *citemene* cultivation, although other older practices, such as brideservice, did revive (Pottier, 1988:13). In general, Pottier's findings cast doubt on earlier explanations of how labor migration affected agricultural practices, but they do not preclude the likelihood that its effects were disruptive.

As we have seen, people in northeastern Zambia lived in small, scattered villages, which moved and/or broke up every few years. In 1963, the national census estimated that the average Zambian village contained seventy-five people, and the majority of rural settlements were well below average size (Kay, 1967:26ff.). In such settlements, the departure of even a few adults could create a critical shortage of agricultural labor. The ethnographic literature stresses that men who aspired to found their own villages could not do so unless they could recruit a sufficient following. Village headmen had, in other words, to strike a balance between the requirements of extensive cultivation, which militated against large permanent settlements, and the risk that even a few defections might so reduce the social and economic resources of a village that it would break up altogether.

The inherent uncertainties of social and agricultural life under such conditions are vividly described in Richards' writings on the Bemba. "The founding of a new village is a hazardous affair which they approach in an experimental frame of mind after taking omens and praying to ancestral spirits" (Richards, 1958:307). People "are reluctant to pin themselves down to one site which might prove to be unlucky, either agriculturally or socially" (Richards, 1958:308). Agricultural production on poor soils was clearly a risky business: "The failure of crops planted in the village mounds is not uncommon, in the first-year beds especially," and people spoke of "trying the soil" as a routine activity (Richards, 1939:283–84). Even routine changes of residence could provoke tension and ambivalence, as illustrated by the awkward position of the young Bemba husband whose tenuous authority over his wife in the house of his mother-in-law was a subject for general amusement (Richards, 1939: 126). A viable village, like a viable marriage, took time and skill to build. The "slow forging of human ties, and the establishment of common interests and a sense of security among the inhabitants . . . may take a year or more to complete" (Richards, 1939:238). An aspiring headman might spend considerable periods residing in temporary quarters ("grass houses," or *mitanda*) or moving from one place to another, testing the social climate and courting potential followers, before he was in a position to establish a village (Richards, 1958:307–8; Harries-Jones and Chiwale, 1962:14).

By providing a powerful inducement for large numbers of young adults to leave the rural areas, labor migration added significantly to the unpredictability of agricultural labor supplies and the potential for villages to break up. Especially in the early years, transportation was poorly developed, and individual employment histories varied, making it difficult to predict when a migrant worker might return. In addition, colonial authorities' repeated efforts to relocate people tended to interrupt labor supplies and farmers' access to their fields. The combined effect of colonial administrative methods and labor migration on the rural areas of the northeast was not simply to extract surplus—through taxation, underinvestment, and the exploitation of cheap labor—but also to increase the unpredictability of access to food supplies and the means of agricultural production.

The actual effects of resettlement and labor migration on agricultural production are difficult to trace. With few markets and little official interest in local agriculture, statistics on agricultural production in the colonial period are even scarcer for northeastern Zambia than for central Kenya or the cocoa economies of West Africa. However, it is likely that the disruptive effects of forced resettlement and large-scale labor migration took their toll on total agricultural output. Under *citemene* cultivation, at any given time farmers have a good deal of capital (literally, in this case, congealed labor) tied up in cultivated fields, and stand to lose part of their investment if they are forced to abandon a field before the crop rotation cycle is completed. In the absence of other disruptions, villages moved within fairly limited areas to enable farmers to retain access to established fields while making new ones in uncut woodland (Richards, 1939:278). When villages split up for nonagricultural reasons—illness, quarrels or the death of the headman—people often suffered economic losses. Labor out-migration, or the arbitrary relocation of villages by the state, would have increased the likelihood of such losses, just as imposed bans on village dispersal would raise the costs of establishing new *citemene* fields. Thus, disruptions of farmers' access to land and labor may have precipitated the replacement of *citemene* with hoe cultivation (which is easier to start and stop on short notice), even before agricultural production for the market began to grow.

Despite the government's interest in preserving the northeast as a labor reserve, the pace of rural commercialization increased after 1945.[23] Even in the 1930s, there were some local sales of foodstuffs and cut trees, especially in the vicinity of administrative centers such as Kasama (Richards, 1939:325–26). By the 1940s, increased demand for beer (for recreation and working capital) enabled some women to brew beer for sale, and created a market for millet (Richards, 1958:310; Hedlund and Lundahl, 1983). In some areas, Trapnell (1953:36) complained, cassava had become the staple and millet "has been reduced to the status of a beer crop" (see also Kay, 1962:32–33).

Commercialization was facilitated by improvements in transportation. In 1947, there were "flourishing markets on the Great North Road" (Kay, 1962: 32). Ten years later, Richards reported that bicycles had replaced headloading since the 1930s, and that a few chiefs and prosperous ex-migrants had even invested in trucks and were engaged in commercial market gardening (Richards, 1958:311–12). In the mid-1950s, Watson found that Mambwe villagers had money to spend on clothing, household goods, improved housing, and investment in ploughs, cattle, and tools (Watson, 1958:220).

In the years immediately following independence, the Zambian government set out both to rectify the injustices of colonial policy and to create an institutional apparatus for mobilizing the rural population politically and economically. On the one hand, it was widely believed that if African farmers were given access to agricultural inputs and services on the same terms as the colonial government had supplied them to European farmers, then agricultural output would grow, and rural income distribution would become more egalitarian (Wood and Shula, 1987:288). At the same time, the government and the United National Independence Party (UNIP) sought to mobilize the rural population behind the aims of the national government, in order to consolidate their political power as well as facilitate state management of the economy.

As described in chapter 3, both political consolidation and economic development gave rise to extensive rural institution building. To extend the benefits of a guaranteed market, formerly provided to European growers by the colonial Maize Control Board, to the whole country, the government created NAMBOARD—a "monolithic nationwide agricultural marketing and input supply organization" (Wood and Shula, 1987:288–89). It also introduced geographically uniform prices for officially marketed crops and expanded agricultural extension and rural credit services (Wood and Shula, 1987:289). At the same time, the government created a series of local administrative structures—Provincial and District Development Committees in 1966, Village and Ward Productivity Committees in 1971—which were charged, among other things, with conducting a nationwide campaign of village regroupment to concentrate the rural population into large villages to facilitate administrative control and the provision of rural amenities and economic services (Bratton, 1980b:125ff.).

The effects of national policies on agricultural production and rural incomes have been uneven. Price policies "proved erratic," and NAMBOARD's marketing services were not efficiently run (Wood and Shula, 1987:291). The Credit Organization of Zambia failed financially in 1970, and the cooperative movement was also plagued with financial and administrative problems (Johns, 1980:115; Quick, 1978:chap. 9). Uniform pricing encouraged the production of maize in remote areas from which cotton and groundnuts would have been cheaper to transport (De Wilde, 1984:68). By the early 1970s, emphasis had shifted towards concentrating rural development efforts in a few selected areas—an approach which prevailed into the 1980s, through a series of projects and programs.[24]

Efforts at rural institution building were equally problematic. By the late 1970s, the system of provincial and district Development Committees had not succeeded in reaching the rural population, and even the Village Productivity Committees had "not transformed villages into . . . 'effective production units' " (Bratton, 1980a:221). Village regroupment was particularly unsuccessful.

Some villagers regrouped at first but lost interest when promised amenities and services failed to materialize (Bratton, 1980b:138–39). Others refused to abandon established farms or favorable locations (Pottier, 1988:163), or simply failed to follow through on projected plans to relocate. In Serenje District, it was reported that "of over eighty village regrouping schemes that were planned, none had yet got off the ground" (Bwalya, 1979:92). After attending a meeting of the Nansala Village Productivity Committee, at which everyone expressed enthusiasm for regroupment, Bwalya asked the chairman of the newly created Regroupment Steering Committee what would happen next. He "just laughed and said quite amicably: 'It won't work, we only wanted the meeting to finish quickly'" (Bwalya, 1979:97).

In short, government institution building and policy initiatives had done little to raise agricultural output or strengthen the rural sector by the time the collapse of the world copper price in 1974 plunged the Zambian economy into a prolonged recession. The ensuing declines in foreign exchange earnings and government revenues were exacerbated by the war in Zimbabwe and by Zambia's own heavy investment in developing alternative transportation routes to the sea. Agricultural marketing and input supply services deteriorated; real crop prices stagnated. By 1980, Zambia—once a net exporter of maize—was importing half of the nation's domestic consumption (Wood and Shula, 1987:299).

In the northeast, the crisis appears to have facilitated the spread of hybrid maize and ox-plough cultivation in the early 1980s. The development of new transportation routes in response to Rhodesia's Unilateral Declaration of Independence, benefited the northeast. The Great North Road was paved in 1970, and the Tanzam railway opened five years later, creating significant new possibilities for commercial agriculture in Northern Province. Also, with the decline of employment opportunities in the Copperbelt, younger men and women remained in the rural areas. For the first time in decades, the net outflow of rural labor was reversed (Pottier, 1988:chap.3; Milimo, 1983:321).

As the Zambian government's financial and administrative problems mounted, the supply of services to farmers became increasingly unpredictable, even for the well endowed and well connected. In general, economic and political developments of the 1970s and 1980s reinforced the decline of *citemene*, increased reliance on cassava, and increased the number of rural households eking out a bare subsistence by juggling several marginal sources of income. By the 1980s, the convergence of interests between "emergent farmers" and rural bureaucrats, which Bratton (1980b:118ff.) discerned in the mid-1970s, had been shaken by economic decline and uncertainty. Among ordinary peasants, "the position of the emergent farmer is not the source of much envy. . . . In the eyes of many peasants, joining the 'emergent' farmers . . . was synonymous with taking unnecessary risks. The pattern of interaction between emergent farmers, field-based civil servants, and higher-ranking politicians was too rife with uncertainty and contradiction to appeal to outsiders" (Pottier, 1988:107; see also Van Donge, 1982:passim, 1985:68–69). Rural differentiation was associated more with unequal access to the private sector than with unequal access to the state.

CONCLUSION

As these historical sketches suggest, agricultural commercialization was not a uniform process across sub-Saharan Africa. Both the pace of increased agricultural production for sale and the terms on which Africans participated in colonial and postcolonial economies varied dramatically—from the cocoa economies of West Africa, where thousands of farmers experienced long periods of relatively favorable market conditions and varying gains in income, to central Kenya, where African farmers faced more volatile markets and direct demands on their land and labor from European settlers, and to northeastern Zambia, where colonial officials deliberately neglected local agriculture to stimulate a cheap supply of labor for the mines.

Despite major differences in the timing and structure of rural commercialization, the political and economic changes of the colonial period touched off new struggles among Africans over access to land and labor and the division of agricultural output. The following chapters compare the histories of those struggles and their impact on agricultural performance in these four rural economies. In all four cases, farmers' access to land and labor were shaped by the structure of regional economic opportunities and by the ways in which people sought to influence their access to economic opportunities and resources and debated their rights to do so. Conditions of access, in turn, affected the use of resources—for production and investment—in both agricultural and nonagricultural activities.

Chapter Five

Access to Land

Property Rights as Social Process

SO FAR, I have argued that while colonial and postcolonial states set the stage for struggles over access to productive resources, governments' actions neither determined nor controlled their outcomes. On the whole, state intervention into rural economies and societies has been intrusive rather than hegemonic. Both indirect rule and subsequent competition for power among African elites fostered debates over the legitimacy of competing claims to power which turned on multiple interpretations of history. In the long run, it was the process of debate, rather than any particular interpretation, which shaped the actual exercise of power at all levels of society and its impact on conditions of access to resources in rural areas.

In this chapter and the next, I will trace the course of struggles over access to land and labor in the four rural economies described in Chapter 4. I will argue that while access to land and labor were both influenced by processes of commercialization and political centralization and by farmers' membership in local social networks, the actual course of negotiations over transactions in land and the terms of agricultural employment followed different trajectories over time. Specifically, while access to land has remained linked to membership in social networks, farmers' ability to mobilize labor through such networks has declined. Consequently, for the great majority of African farmers, access to labor has been more vulnerable to the unevenness of commercialization and the constraints of poverty than access to land. This, in turn, helps to explain why, despite widespread poverty and underemployment, the agrarian question in Africa turns on scarcity of labor rather than land (Mkandawire, 1989:20).

In the following pages, I elaborate this argument with reference to the four rural economies discussed in this book. After a brief review of some recent literature on the conceptualization of rural land rights in Africa, I describe changing conditions of access to land in the four case study areas. I then discuss the implications of multiple rights for contemporary debates over land policy in Africa and for the effectiveness of African governments' efforts to promote agricultural development by nationalizing or privatizing the ownership of rural land.

CONCEPTUAL ISSUES

Recent literature on African systems of land tenure has stressed two main lines of argument. Some scholars believe that property rights exercise a determining influence on patterns of resource allocation and the course of economic development. Bates puts the case with characteristic lucidity. Defining property rights as "the power to limit the ability of other persons to enjoy the benefits to be secured from the use and enjoyment of a material good," he asserts that "to alter property rights is to redefine social relationships" (Bates, 1989: 28). This view underlies much debate over the relative merits of individual and communal ownership. If ownership is interpreted to mean exclusive control over all rights to a piece of land or other fixed assets, then whoever owns property exercises definitive control over how it is used. Critics of communal ownership often assume that communities are either internally anarchic, so that communal ownership leads to uncontrolled free riding by individual members, or monolithically egalitarian, in which case all returns to land use are equally shared, so there is no incentive for individuals to invest in land-augmenting improvements. Thus, it is argued, communal tenure leads to wasteful patterns of land use and underinvestment in land improvements. By implication, freehold tenure is a necessary condition for the optimal allocation of productive resources (Feder and Noronha, 1987:144–46; Collier, 1983:158).

In a variant of this approach, Feder and Noronha (1987:159ff.), among others, point out that under customary systems of African tenure, property rights are *not* clearly defined or consistently enforced. Consequently, they argue, land rights are insecure, and farmers are correspondingly reluctant to invest in agricultural improvements. Some proponents of this view advocate registering titles to land in order to promote agricultural development, while others favor nationalization to permit governments to allocate land rights in accordance with national priorities.[1] Both groups recognize that property rights in Africa are often ambiguous and contested, but they interpret this to mean that agricultural underdevelopment is due to the *absence* of the legal and political conditions assumed in their definition of property rights. In effect, they argue that African governments should create conditions in which property rights determine patterns of resource allocation, so that their model will suffice as a basis for policy formulation.

Other authors emphasize the transformative effects of political and economic change on property rights, rather than vice versa. In a seminal paper,

Elizabeth Colson (1971:196) pointed out that "customary law" in Africa was not traditional, but rather a creation of colonial rule. Under indirect rule, colonial authorities sought "to enforce long-established custom rather than current opinion. Common official stereotypes about African customary land law thus came to be used by colonial officials in assessing the legality of current decisions, and so came to be incorporated in 'customary' systems of tenure" (Colson, 1971:196). However, in the long run, the effects of agricultural commercialization and urban growth proved stronger than the conservative policies of colonial officials. Land was steadily converted "to economic use," despite officials' and traditional authorities' "encouragement [for] the development of communal holdings" (Colson, 1971:211). This tendency was furthest advanced in colonies such as Nigeria, where urban and agricultural development "provided the impetus for the development of more precise definition of rights" and descent groups were transformed into "economic corporations dealing in land" (Colson, 1971:211).

The idea that customary law was created under colonial rule has gained wide acceptance. According to Chanock, colonial administrators not only "recognize[d] local custom" (Colson, 1971:193) but also codified it, imposing rigid rules and an individualist ethos on formerly fluid, communal, and egalitarian societies (Chanock, 1985:46–47). Legalism, in turn, laid the foundation for a pattern of collaboration between colonial officials and senior African men, which transformed traditional African polities from "lost and lamented social solidarit[ies]" into rigid, hierarchical and authoritarian systems (Chanock, 1985:239; see also, Ranger, 1983:254–59). In a recent paper, Chanock (1991: 80ff.) extended this argument to the postcolonial period, suggesting that African governments have kept alive the colonial myth of communalism in order to justify increased state control. In the same vein, Goody (1980:140), Okoth-Ogendo (1976:180–82), Bassett (1992), and others point out that members of contemporary ruling classes often seek to extend their own rights in land by manipulating informal tenure arrangements and customary court procedures. Thus, customary law has been used to reinforce state hegemony in the name of universal entitlement, while ordinary Africans have been relegated "to a form of legal rightlessness in land" (Chanock, 1991:82).

Chanock's conclusion reflects his methodology. Persuaded of "the power of discourses to shape reality" (Chanock, 1991:62), he based his interpretation on the writings of government officials and anthropologists, rather than records of actual land transactions and disputes. Official policy and local practices often differ, however, and it is not clear that either colonial or independent African governments have been able effectively to control the conditions under which farmers gain access to land or the ways they use it. In practice, as I shall argue in more detail below, land-tenure rules have remained ambiguous, and rights in land are subject to ongoing reinterpretation.

The significance of ambiguous land rights for agrarian change in Africa is not so much that land rights are insecure and that land use, therefore, is inefficient, but that people's access to land depends on their participation in processes of interpretation and adjudication, as well as on their ability to pay. Rising land values and intensified patterns of land use have certainly fostered the emergence of exclusive forms of control over land. However, to muster sufficient authority to exercise and enforce exclusive land rights, African landholders seek, inter alia, to expand the number of their supporters. Authority, in other words, rests partly on inclusionary strategies which are undermined when authority is used for exclusionary ends. Because of these contradictory pressures, claims on land have tended to multiply over time.

As a result, the commercialization of land transactions has not led to the consolidation of land rights into forms of exclusive individual or corporate control comparable to Western notions of private property. Instead, people's ability to exercise claims to land remains closely linked to membership in social networks and participation in both formal and informal political processes. Membership in social networks does not guarantee anyone access to land, but it does tend to blur the impact of legally sanctioned processes of exclusion. Even land which has been formally registered or sold to an individual tends, in practice, to remain subject to multiple claims, and the power of landholders (including governments) over access to land is less than absolute.

WHO OWNS THE LAND?

In precolonial times, Africans' rights to use land and other natural resources were usually contingent on their membership in social groups and/or their allegiance to traditional authorities (Berry, 1988:4, 13; 1988b:62–67). This does not mean that every member of a descent group or community enjoyed access to land on equal terms, or that land use was communally controlled. For group members who held equal entitlements to land in principle, the exercise of those rights in practice often led to negotiation, conflict, and the intervention of local authorities. For outsiders, access to land depended on negotiating membership in the group or acknowledging the authority of its leaders. The actual exercise of rights was liable to change as a result of changes in the political structure of the group or in its relations with outsiders, quite apart from any change in patterns of land use per se.

In the nineteenth century, the Asantehene and chiefs of Kumasi regularly reallocated rights over land and people in order to consolidate their power, weaken their opponents, and strengthen the defenses of the state against outsiders (McCaskie, 1980:passim; 1984:171–72; Kyerematen, 1971:18). In central Kenya, relations of allegiance and access to land were frequently renegotiated as people moved and formed new alliances in order to cope with drought, disease, or political crises (Ambler, 1987:36ff.). In northeastern Zambia, access to land was contingent on allegiance to chiefs or headmen (Richards, 1939:250ff.; Watson, 1958:94–96), while in southwestern Nigeria access followed changes in patterns of settlement due to warfare, migration, or trade (Berry, 1975:91). In general, rights to land were contested and/or renegotiated in the course of changing patterns of settlement and structures of authority, and the security of tenure was linked to the overall security of social and political life.

In promulgating a legal framework for governing their newly acquired domains, most colonial regimes asserted some form of state control over land. In all of our cases, officials proposed to declare that vacant land belonged to the Crown—opening the way for immediate alienation to European settlers in Kenya and Northern Rhodesia, and awakening fears of a similar outcome in Ghana and southern Nigeria. Crown Lands Ordinances were enacted in Kenya in 1902 and in Northern Rhodesia in 1928. In the Gold Coast and later in Southern Nigeria, colonial authorities made several attempts to place unused land and forest areas under the protection of the Crown. Each time, their efforts were greeted with vociferous local opposition, and in the absence of pressure from European settlers to secure their rights to land, officials backed down. Forest reserves *were* demarcated and contested by local farmers, but no Crown Lands Ordinance was ever passed in either the Gold Coast or Southern Nigeria.

Although the success of their efforts varied, Africans in Kenya, Nigeria, and the Gold Coast protested Crown Lands legislation in similar terms. In all three colonies, Africans rebutted colonial authorities' claims to jurisdiction over vacant land by denying that vacant land existed. In the words of the Gold Coast Aborigines' Rights Protection Society,[2] "all land was owned," whether or not it was currently in use, and therefore unavailable for appropriation by the Crown or anyone else.

If all land was owned, colonial officials wanted to know: "owned by whom?" The answer was not immediately obvious. In the southern parts of the Gold Coast, commercial transactions in rights to land were common enough in the late nineteenth century that Governor Maxwell proposed, in 1897, to recognize the existence of individual ownership and the fact of land sales (Asante, 1975:33). In practice, British jurists were inclined to agree. For example, in 1907, the Chief Justice of the colony ruled that land which had been developed (by plantings tree crops, erecting buildings, etc.) by an individual could be attached and sold to pay off that person's debts to another party (Asante, 1975:41–42; Grier, 1987:33–34). The judge's ruling appeared to establish a strong precedent for applying British property laws in the colony. It also placed the opponents of Crown Lands legislation on dangerous ground, because it linked proof of ownership to effective occupation and left open the question of the status of "unoccupied" land. To bolster their claim that all land was owned, spokesmen for the Aborigines' Rights Protection Society insisted that land belonged to the "community" (Crook, 1986:89)—whether or not it was currently occupied.

Similar arguments were put forward in Southern Nigeria when rumors of impending Crown Lands legislation resurfaced in 1910. Asked by the governor to prepare a report on Yoruba customs, a committee of Lagosians headed by Henry Carr affirmed that "every piece of land, cultivated or uncultivated, including forests, has an owner" (Hopkins, 1969:85). Several years later, the West African Lands Committee endorsed this view. Quoting the words of a Yoruba chief "that land belongs to a vast family, of which many are dead, few are living, and countless numbers are yet unborn," the committee concluded that, in Africa, land is "God-given" and "cannot be alienated" (West African Lands Committee, 1916b:31–32).

The doctrine of community ownership gained currency across British colonial Africa, in part because it dovetailed with the emerging ideology of indirect rule. Testifying before the West African Lands Committee, C. W. Alexander, the Commissioner of Lands in Southern Nigeria, stressed the political importance of upholding "pure native tenure." If individual Africans acquired freehold rights to land, he warned, this would weaken the authority of chiefs and undermine indirect rule (West African Lands Committee, 1916a:Q.3554; see also, Chanock, 1991:64). The committee agreed, declaring that land tenure was the foundation of native rule: "together they stand or fall" (West African Lands Committee, 1916b:3).

As indirect rule evolved from a successful compromise in Northern Nigeria to a blanket prescription for British rule in most of colonial Africa, officials articulated an increasingly confident and uniform understanding of "pure native tenure." In ruling on a Kenyan land case in 1919, Chief Justice Maxwell declared with "absolute certainty" that "the theory of individual ownership of land is absolutely foreign to the mind of any African until he has begun to absorb the ideas of an alien civilization" (Kenya Land Commission, 1934b:32). Occasionally an official document sounded a note of realism. In 1947, a review of land disputes in Adansi (Gold Coast) concluded that because Native Court judgments "turned on questions of historical fact . . . rather than Court decisions on legal principles, . . . it has not proved possible to abstract . . . any general principles of Akan land tenure" from court records (Matson, 1947, quoted in Kyerematen, 1971:36). Such cautionary tales did not, however, stem the tide of official efforts to codify "native law and custom."

By linking land ownership to community membership, however, administrators opened a Pandora's box. As Crook has pointed out, "the irresoluble ambiguity in th[e] doctrine [of community ownership] was—*which* community?" The answer depended on "vexed questions of historical precedent and jurisdictional claims" (Crook, 1986:89) which, as we saw in chapter 2, were difficult if not impossible to resolve in the context of indirect rule. Thus, the effects of agricultural commercialization on rural land tenure became closely linked to ongoing debates over the interpretation of "native law and custom."

COMMERCIALIZATION AND THE PROLIFERATION OF CLAIMS TO RURAL LAND

The growth of agricultural production for sale both generated new demand for land and shaped people's strategies for gaining access to it. In the process of expanding agricultural output or switching to commercial crops, farmers both intensified patterns of land use and brought new land under cultivation. Agricultural sales, in turn, generated new flows of cash which farmers could use to gain access to rights in land. Rising farm incomes also became a focus of competing claims. Conflict over rights to control land use were intensified by the rising value of such control. In the process, payments for access to land tended both to increase in value and to become monetized.

In southern Ghana, companies of migrant farmers bought sizeable tracts of land from chiefs in Akim Abuakwa, subdividing them into individual plots for purposes of cultivation (Hill, 1963:48). Alarmed at the pace of rural commercialization in Akim Abuakwa, officials determined to forestall the process elsewhere and persuaded chiefs in Asante and Brong-Ahafo to prohibit the sale of land in their domains. However, they endorsed the chiefs' right to demand tribute from "strangers" who sought permission to cultivate land belonging to the stool (Grier, 1987:36; Asante, 1975:35; Austin, 1987:262). Invoking an established practice whereby Akan chiefs were entitled to one-third (*abusa*) of any gold or other valuable items collected from the territory of their stools, chiefs in Asante and neighboring states demanded one-third of the cocoa crop as tribute from stranger farmers.[3] In Ahafo, chiefs received "rent" (*nto*) in cash, the amount being subject to periodic renegotiation. In parts of Ahafo, *nto* was eventually replaced by *abusa* payments; in Wassa and Sefwi, where cocoa was not planted extensively until the 1950s, it was still in effect twenty years later (Konings, 1986:67; Kotey et al., 1973:175; Arhin, 1985:19).

In western Nigeria, where land was controlled by lineages rather than chiefs, farmers made an initial gift (*isagi*) to the person or lineage representative who "showed" them land for farming. They also presented the landholding lineage with a small amount of produce (*isakole*) each year at harvest time, to acknowledge their continued jurisdiction over the land. As cocoa planting spread, both *isagi* and *isakole* increased in value and took the form of payments in cash or marketable crops (Berry, 1975:105–7). For cocoa growers, *isakole* was commonly set at a fixed amount of cocoa per farmer, regardless of the size of his/her farm. In other words, *isakole* continued to function as a form of tribute rather than as an economic rent (Berry, 1975:108ff.).

In northeastern Zambia, where cash cropping was virtually nonexistent before the 1950s, farmers did not pay for access to cultivation rights, but Bemba chiefs collected tribute in labor (*umulasa*) from their followers. Collection of *umulasa* was encouraged by colonial officials, who felt it would reinforce the unity of villages and increase the frequency of people's contacts with their chiefs (Richards, 1939:262–66). It was abolished only after 1945, to conform to the standards of the Geneva Convention on Forced Labor (Richards, 1958:311).

In central Kenya, the commercialization of land transactions was complicated by the presence of European settlers. At first, settlers acquired land from the Crown, obtaining freehold titles or English-style leaseholds (which could be bought and sold). In principle, land allocations to Europeans were made "with due regard to African interests," but in practice little was done either to ascertain the nature of Africans' rights to land or to ensure that those displaced by European settlers received compensation (Sorrenson, 1967:18). By 1907, a thriving market had emerged in land titles held by Europeans. Prices in Central Province rose dramatically in the next few years (Lonsdale and Berman, 1979:499; Kenya Land Commission, 1934b:323), and newly arrived European settlers moved on to the Rift Valley, where land was cheaper and more abundant.

In Central Province, Kikuyu who found themselves displaced by settlers or barred from land to which they'd had access in the past, began to complain to the government (Sorrenson, 1967:19ff.). The colonial regime, which had staked its economic future as well as its reputation on encouraging European settlement, consistently rebuffed Kikuyu efforts to reclaim land from settlers, admitting only that Africans displaced by settlers should receive some form of compensation. This, in turn, raised the question of who was entitled to compensation under "native law and custom." Answers reflected emerging patterns of competition over land and authority within African societies, as well as continued debates between Kikuyu and the government over the land alienated to European settlers.

The first systematic inquiry into customary Kikuyu land tenure was carried out in 1911 by M. W. H. Beech, the district officer for Kiambu. Beech produced a list of 300 holdings (*ithaka*), with well-defined boundaries, which the Kikuyu "owners" said they had purchased from the previous inhabitants.[4] Beech's report laid the groundwork for a complex series of debates over the meaning of *githaka* rights and the legitimacy of land transactions among Africans. European settlers and officials sympathetic to their interest were inclined to discredit Kikuyu claims to have bought land in the past, accusing them of imitating Western ideas in order to justify retroactive demands for compensation or the outright return of their land (Sorrenson, 1967:7–8, 21; Kenya Land Commission, 1934b:34, 57–61). These doubts were reinforced by the emerging official orthodoxy of community ownership. In the case cited above, Chief Justice Maxwell dismissed Chief Kioi's complaint against two men who were cultivating land which Kioi claimed to have bought from Chief Kinyanjui, on the grounds that individual ownership was "absolutely foreign to the mind of any African" who had not been tainted by foreign influences (Clough, 1990:50–51).

As the Kioi case suggests, colonial officials not only insisted that customary ownership was vested in the community, but also assumed that community ownership precluded the possibility of sale (Sorrenson, 1967:29ff.; Kenya, 1934:57–61). Official antagonism to land sales and the individualization of Africans' land rights derived both from their wish to protect settlers' titles and from their fear that individualism and differentiation within African communities would prove to be socially disruptive (Sorrenson, 1967:32–33, 56–59). By the late 1920s, apprehensive over the rising number of landless Africans in Kiambu, which they attributed to "the rapid changes in native custom with regard to the purchase of land," colonial officials advocated a complete ban on land transactions among Africans (Clough, 1990:70).

Kikuyus concurred in opposing the permanent alienation of their land to settlers. By the 1920s, grievances over land had generated a groundswell of anticolonial sentiment, on which politically ambitious Kikuyu sought to capitalize (Clough, 1990:63, 90, 101ff., 159ff.). But opinions were divided over the interpretation of custom. In petitioning the Kenya Lands Commission for the return of land taken by settlers, witnesses in Kiambu claimed that sales of land were traditional, antedating the colonial era by many years (Sorrenson, 1967:20; Kenya Land Commission, 1934b:175ff., 258–376). However, they also maintained that in permitting Europeans to settle on their land, they had never intended to relinquish their own rights to it—even when they had accepted payment from the settlers (Sorrenson, 1967:20; Kenya Land Commission, 1934b:129, 132, 284). Such ambivalence helped to convince colonial officials and European settlers alike that Kikuyu testimony was opportunistic and could be disregarded when it proved inconvenient.

While officials dug in behind the comforting orthodoxy of traditional communalism, the pace of rural commercialization continued unabated, especially in Kiambu. During the 1910s and 1920s, land pressure in Nyeri and Fort Hall Districts was somewhat relieved by emigration, as people left to seek more land in the White Highlands or in other reserves, or to work for wages in Nairobi or Mombasa. People also left Kiambu, but the pull of the Nairobi market brought many people into the district as well, and commercial payments for land increased in frequency and value (Sorrenson, 1967:40; Kenya Land Commission, 1934b:57ff.; Cowen, 1972:62). In the early 1930s, a number of farmers in Kiambu lost land through foreclosure (Clough, 1990:70).

To reconcile these events with the doctrine of community ownership, officials seized on the idea that under customary law, sales of land were redeemable and, therefore, did not eliminate collective rights in land (Sorrenson, 1967:7–8). But even this comforting notion could not blind them completely to the accumulating evidence that Africans were selling land. In 1929, the Committee on Kikuyu Land Tenure accepted the Kikuyu claim that land sales had occurred before the arrival of settlers, and observed that outright sales were now the principal form of land transaction in Kiambu (Kenya Land Commission, 1934b:57; Clough, 1990:68–69). Five years later, the Kenya Land Commission (1934b:34) rejected these conclusions, arguing that Kikuyus' claims to have purchased land in precolonial times reflected their perception of the value of land to Europeans and their "natural desire to get something for nothing." In 1941, the District Commissioner for Kiambu lamented that "hundreds, possibly even thousands of acres have changed hands by 'irredeemable sale' during the past ten or fifteen years" (quoted in Phillips, 1944:59).

Meanwhile, after Native Tribunals were established in 1913,[5] Africans' struggles over rights to land moved into the courts. In Nyeri District alone, the number of land cases doubled, from 190 in 1924 to 389 in 1929 (Cowen, 1972:62, 67; see also Cowen, 1978:74; Sorrenson: 1967:39; Njonjo, 1977:44ff.; Mukaru Ng'ang'a, 1978:38). Chiefs received frequent presents from litigants, in appreciation for their role in presiding over the Native Tribunals or as witnesses. Since records were kept of court proceedings, *athomi* also played an important role as mediators or witnesses, often receiving a share of the land if the suit they supported was successful (Cowen, 1972:41). For both chiefs and *athomi*, therefore, litigation served as a means of accumulating land or wealth, some of which was reinvested in further litigation (Sorrenson, 1967:40; Cowen, 1972:62; Njonjo, 1977:44ff.). In 1945, an official inquiry reported that "powerful and influential Africans were abusing their position in order to acquire for themselves large 'estates' at the expense of the more helpless, improvident, or simple-minded members of the community; and there is a strong suspicion that tribunal members have often backed the interests of the new privileged class and have even joined in the 'racket' themselves" (Phillips, 1944:285).

The Politics of Access to Land: Chiefs and Strangers

As payments for land rights increased in frequency and value and patterns of land use intensified, the number of potential claimants to rural land increased. Claims to land were based on social identity and status, as well as evidence of purchase or rights of first clearance. Under Indirect Rule, customary rules were subject to multiple interpretation, and land disputes could be heard in more than one arena; thus, competing claims coexisted for long periods of time.

In all four of our case study areas, farmers had moved periodically to open up new land for cultivation long before the colonial conquest, but rates of rural migration increased under colonial rule. Migrant farmers were considered "strangers" in a political sense—subject to the authority of local chiefs or elders. In southern Ghana, even migrants who bought land were expected to pay tribute to the local chief, just like "tenant" farmers in Asante and Brong Ahafo. In southwestern Nigeria, lineage heads also collected tribute from nonlineage members, retaining control over the land itself, although tree crops were considered to belong to the farmers who planted them. In Kenya, Kikuyu who opened up new areas for grazing and cultivation in the nineteenth century offered land and protection to latecomers who, in turn, accepted the authority of the original settler (Cowen and Murage, 1972:51; Kanogo, 1987:11, 26). In all three areas, migrants sometimes married into a landholding family, thus acquiring land rights through affinal ties as well as their own efforts (Okali, 1983a:47; C. Clark, 1980:361–62). Similarly, among the mobile rural population of northeastern Zambia, farmers gained access to land in the process of relocation, through marriage, in forming or joining new villages, or when selecting a headman.

As production expanded and transactions in land rights became more frequent, migrant farmers were increasingly referred to as "tenants," and payments of tribute as "rent." However, access to land remained a political as well as an economic issue. "Tenants" were not simply unattached economic agents, but were also subject to the authority of their "landlords." Payments of "rent" carried tributary connotations, serving to acknowledge and therefore ratify landholders' continued jurisdiction over land and its occupants (Benneh, 1970:52–53; Berry, 1975:101ff.; 1988a:6; Francis, 1984:21; Arhin, 1985:19ff.). Increased demand for land raised the cost of gaining access to it and sharpened distinctions between "locals" and "strangers." At the same time, debate intensified over how such distinctions should be drawn.

In Ghana, stool-holders' demands for tribute linked the spread of cocoa farming to chieftaincy politics. Since the eighteenth century, Asantehenes had used the transfer of rights over land and people as a mechanism for consolidating their power and undercutting the autonomy of subordinate states (McCaskie, 1980:passim). By the late nineteenth century, attempts to resolve jurisdictional disputes on the basis of tradition usually foundered on a welter of overlapping claims. Colonial officials added to the confusion through their own efforts to define or restructure traditional polities. In Ahafo, for example, the government's decision to "restore" the Ashanti Confederacy in 1935 brought "streams of competing bailiffs from Kumase" (Dunn and Robertson, 1973:53), who claimed territorial jurisdiction and demanded tribute from Ahafo farmers in the names of various Kumasi chiefs (see also Konings, 1986:53). In Asante itself, gifts of land from former Asantehenes to chiefs "have been one of the principal causes of boundary litigation" since the early colonial period (Kyerematen, 1971:18).

Similar disputes occurred in other stools. In 1945, a group of migrants from Bekwai, who were farming in Adankranja, threatened to secede from the Ashanti Union in protest against the Asantehene's ruling (in customary court) that they owed allegiance to the Adankranjahene, rather than to the chief of Bekwai (Kyerematen, 1971:21). In Odumasi, "as cash cropping and land control became more lucrative, competing claims of the Bosomtwi and Antepim stools increased in number, and they tried to have inconsistencies in traditional law settled to their own advantage" (Mikell, 1983:39). "In an effort to extend their control over land, relatively minor and small towns litigated over their position within the traditional state and argued their right to control proceeds from resources within their unit" (Mikell, 1983:42).

In addition to the growing volume of litigation over land rights, the sometimes blatant efforts of chiefs to turn customary authority into profit gave rise to political conflict. By the 1930s, commercialization had proceeded to such a degree that people were losing cocoa farms through foreclosure. However, the collection of cocoa tribute continued unabated (Austin, 1987:271, 1988:69; Dunn and Robertson, 1973:57; Konings, 1986:71). In principle, "citizens" of a stool were exempt from paying tribute for cultivation rights, but if rival stools claimed jurisdiction over the same land, they could be forced to pay anyway. Chiefs also had a penchant for treating cocoa rents as their personal income, rather than public revenue belonging to the stool, and for selling land or levying their subjects to raise money for litigation (Kyerematen, 1971:59–69; Mikell, 1989:88ff.; Benneh, 1970:47; Busia, 1951:44–45). Such practices occasioned widespread discontent and contributed directly to the increasing number of destoolments in the 1920s and 1930s (Grier, 1987:36–37; see also Sutton, 1984:42).

In Nigeria, jurisdictional disputes among neighboring communities and chiefs were less closely linked to the control of rights in land. Because cocoa cultivation spread more slowly in Nigeria than in Ghana, and because most people accepted the principle that land belonged to lineages rather than states, there was little speculative demand for land of the kind which Hill (1963: 183–85) has described in Ghana. Cocoa "rents" accrued to lineages rather than to chiefs, and hence did not become a central focus of struggle over chiefly succession or jurisdiction as they did in Ghana (Hailey, 1957:856). Nevertheless, access to land did carry political overtones in Nigeria. In Ibadan, hunters who had used their knowledge of the forest to "show" land to early cocoa farmers, accumulated large numbers of "tenants" in the process and later competed for lineage and chieftaincy titles on the strength of their prestige as "landlords" (Berry, 1975:116ff.). In the late 1940s, the Ooni and chiefs of Ife used their influence in the customary courts to force hundreds of local farmers of Oyo origin to pay *isakole* to Ife families, on the grounds that they were "strangers" to Ife (see page 124).

In short, the spread of cocoa cultivation in West Africa led to the multiplication, rather than the consolidation, of claims to rural land—both through the spread of tenancy and because the definition of a "tenant" hinged on issues of descent and/or "citizenship" as well as land use. In Ghana, when rival stools claimed jurisdiction over the same land, farmers sometimes changed their "citizenship" to avoid having to pay "two landlords" (Austin, 1987:268–69). Cases of double jeopardy also occurred in Nigeria. In Ife, some migrant farmers complained in the early 1970s that they paid *isakole* twice—sometimes to two local lineages, both of which claimed the land on which the migrants had planted cocoa, and sometimes to a lineage and to the Ooni of Ife, who not infrequently asserted control over disputed land "to avoid trouble among my people" (Berry 1975:123).

In central Kenya, access to land within the Native Reserves was also linked to the politics of indirect rule. There were no chiefs in precolonial Kikuyuland comparable to those of Asante or the Yoruba city-states, but Kikuyu "big men" who impressed the British with their chiefly potential took advantage of the period of colonial conquest to acquire large tracts of land (Tignor, 1976:49–50; Kenya Land Commission, 1934b:224ff.; Sorrenson, 1967:44–45). Africans who were literate in Swahili or English also began to use their skills to acquire land. "Mission boys" (*athomi*) were among the first farmers in Central Province to take up commercial cultivation of "European" crops such as white maize, English potatoes, and wattle. Growing competition over land led to increased litigation which, in turn, reinforced the importance of literacy as a condition of access. With the establishment of Native Tribunals, *athomi* began to assist their relatives and neighbors in land disputes, receiving part of the land in return if the suit was successful (Cowen, 1978:74). By the 1920s, chiefs who had not sent their sons to school were likely to find themselves at a disadvantage in land disputes with those who had (Njonjo, 1977:54; Sorrenson, 1967:45–47).

Struggles over land rights spilled over into local politics. Beginning in 1919, the Kikuyu Association (whose members were mainly chiefs and *athomi*) made repeated requests to the government to register Africans' titles to land. These requests were refused on the grounds that they were not in accordance with customary law: *githaka* rights were interpreted as rights of occupancy rather than ownership (Clough, 1990:68). Not all Kikuyu leaders favored registration, however. Harry Thuku attacked the Kikuyu Association, accusing them of collaborating with the British to enrich themselves at the expense of their kin and compatriots. Thuku's threat to the chiefs was quashed by the government, which arrested and deported him in 1922, but debate over the meaning of customary land rights continued. The Kikuyu Association continued to press for registration of titles but, having learned a political lesson from Thuku's popularity, also sought to broaden their appeal to ordinary Kikuyus. In 1923, the association petitioned the government to grant land to the Kikuyu people "as a whole"—an appeal which contributed to the government's decision, three years later, to override settlers' objections and gazette the Kikuyu Reserve (Clough, 1990:109). It also helped to lay the groundwork for the Kenya Land Commission's recommendation that Kikuyu grievances be laid to rest by adding blocks of land to the reserve. As Sorrenson put it, "the 'final solution' to the Kikuyu-European land conflict was seen in tribal terms" (1967:24).

Formal demarcation of the Kikuyu Reserve neither satisfied Kikuyu grievances over the land they had lost to European settlers, nor resolved debates over which "customary" rules of tenure should be applied to land within the reserve. In implementing the Kenya Land Commission's recommendation to enlarge the Kikuyu Reserve, the government took the opportunity to "straighten" its boundaries. In the process, they subtracted some blocks of land from the reserve, and added others. Both kinds of adjustments proved controversial. Land added to the reserve was allocated to "the tribe," which was supposed to regulate individuals' access to it in accordance with "customary" principles. In fact, no "tribal" mechanism existed for doing this (Sorrenson, 1967:9), and access to the blocks of land added to the reserve was immediately disputed. At the same time, the government incurred fresh anger from people who were evicted from parcels of land taken away from the reserve in order to straighten the boundaries (Sorrenson, 1967:23–26). Thus, far from alleviating political tensions among the Kikuyu or among Kikuyus and Europeans, official efforts to resolve the land question served to aggravate these tensions.

In northeastern Zambia, the economic context was different, but the politics of dispute reflected a similar dynamic. From the early days of British South Africa Company rule, officials hoped to attract European settlers, and in the mid-1920s, they went so far as to evict Africans from large tracts of land in order to make room for them (Vail, 1983:244). However, a settler colony never materialized: those who did take up land were so few and scattered that their presence did not become the major focus of political and racial tension in Zambia that it did in Kenya (Palmer, 1973:56, 59). Africans were moved into reserves after 1929 not to make way for Europeans, but as one more phase in the administration's ongoing effort to consolidate and stabilize rural settlements (see above, pages 91–93; see also Meebelo, 1971:102ff.; Kay, 1967:10ff.).

In this context, tension between European officials and African farmers focused not on land ownership, but on Africans' right to change their place of residence at frequent intervals and to renegotiate their relations with chiefs and headmen when they did. Land remained abundant in most areas throughout the colonial period. Unlike the Kikuyu "squatters," migrant laborers from northeastern Rhodesia had little difficulty in gaining access to land when they returned to their home areas, even after a long absence (Watson, 1958: 221ff.). As late as 1959, Kay reported that, in Ushi, disputes over "abandoned land" or the disposition of gardens in the event of death or divorce were settled informally by local chiefs. "Since no money or compensation is involved, there is no need to go to the Native Court" (1964a:31).[6]

In most areas actually occupied by Africans, the viability of agriculture depended on farmers' ability to organize their own movements. People gained access to land in the process of negotiating terms of allegiance to headmen and chiefs. "Bemba rights to the use of land are part of a reciprocal series of obligations between subject and chief" (Richards, 1939:266). Relocation represented changes in political allegiance and disrupted administrative continuity. Competition for land did intensify in the reserves near Chipata and Mbala, where Africans were moved into areas too small to accommodate their extensive methods of cultivation (Allan, 1965:446ff.; Ranger, 1971:19ff.). But even here, the point at issue was not land rights per se, but administrators' efforts to control *citemene* cultivation (see above, page 92). At bottom, settlement and rights to land were issues of political control rather than productive capacity.

Access to Land and the Politics of Domestic Groups

Struggles over access to land took place within and between domestic groups, as well as chiefdoms and rural communities. Since "community" ownership was frequently interpreted in practice as family ownership, access to land was influenced by debates over the meaning of "customary" conjugal and kinship relations. Such debates sometimes dealt explicitly with land; more often, they dealt with issues of divorce, inheritance, or the organization of family labor.

Intrafamilial debates over rights to land turned on two central issues: descent and the investment of labor in land improvements. Where control over land was vested in descent groups, kinship became a basis for claiming rights to land, and differences in status within a kin group served to create differential land rights among its members. In all of our case study areas, families or descent groups did exercise control over land, apart from or in addition to the rights of chiefs and headmen. In Ghana, citizens of a stool held land through their membership in a descent group, and strangers sometimes acquired land as a family group (Hill, 1963:chap.3). In western Nigeria, as we've seen, land rights were controlled entirely by lineages. As the Bale of Ibadan explained to the West African Lands Committee in 1913, "I, as Bale, have no lands; I have my family lands only. I have no control over lands except to settle disputes" (West African Lands Committee, 1916b:202). As colonial officials became convinced that "native tenure" was uniform across Africa, West African cases were cited as precedents in Kenyan courts, and one can see how officials in Kenya came to believe that *githaka* rights (held by *mbari*) coexisted with "tribal" tenure (Sorrenson, 1967:19–20).

The fact that land was held by a descent group did not mean that all members of the group had access to it on equal terms. In Kenya and in patrilineal societies in Zambia and Ghana, wives were entitled to cultivate land controlled by their husbands' lineages, but could not alienate or inherit it.[7] Women could usually claim access to land controlled by their own descent groups, although if they lived with their husbands' kin, this might not have much practical relevance. Even as daughters, however, their rights were subordinate to those of the family as a whole. In patrilineal societies, sales or bequests to daughters were likely to be resisted for fear that the land would eventually pass out of lineage control (Mackenzie, 1986:380ff., 402; Bukh, 1979:54–56; Hill, 1963: 116–17; Mikell, 1984:209–11). Even in matrilineal (or cognatic) descent systems, where many women farmed land belonging to their own descent groups and husbands obtained land through their wives, women's rights to alienate land were circumscribed by those of the descent group. Thus, in Ghana, cocoa farms which women established for themselves tended to pass into the control of their lineages over time (Mikell, 1984:206–11, 1985:23–27). Men's rights to dispose of land through mortgage, sale, gift, or bequest were also subject to the interests of the lineage, but senior men especially exercised more authority within descent groups than women or junior men, and hence exercised greater influence over transactions in family land.

Commercialization affected the definition and exercise of family land rights in several ways. In effect, as land values rose in areas of expanding agricultural production for the market, competition over land intensified among individuals and groups, as well as among individuals. Competition between the claims of individuals and of groups became explicit in disputes over inheritance or in negotiations over compensation for the labor of family members which was invested in developing a farm or other jointly held asset.

Under "customary" rules of inheritance, individually acquired property usually passed to the control of the deceased person's relatives as a group. In Ghana, an "individual's right to the use of his land terminated on his death. His self-acquired farmland became vested in his family" (Benneh, 1970:48). Usually, a single heir was designated by the decedent's matrikin (*abusua*), but he was expected to serve as a trustee for the family (Hill, 1963:113). Thus, inheritance created a "drift toward family property over time" (Hill, 1963:115). Similarly, under the Yoruba system of inheritance *per stirpes*, farms become the joint property of the owner's children (Berry, 1975:182; Lloyd, 1962:296ff.). In both countries, property could be transferred to a single heir by gift or written will, but ambiguities remained. Even an outright purchase or written bequest did not eliminate the possibility that the buyer's (or heir's) right to sell, mortgage, or bequeath a farm could be successfully challenged in the name of continued family interest (Okali, 1983a:142; Berry, 1988a:5).

In keeping with the precepts of indirect rule and "community" ownership, customary courts favored claims based on family rights over those of individuals. As litigation over land increased in Central Province during the 1920s, for example, *athomi* and *athamaki* (heads of *mbari*) increasingly phrased their claims in terms of *mbari* rights (Njonjo, 1977:44; Cowen, 1972:62). By 1932, nearly all the Kikuyu claims presented to the Kenya Land Commission were submitted in the name of *mbari* (Kenya Land Commission, 1934b:258–376). To be sure, elders and *athomi* used their authority within their *mbari* to squeeze out low status members of the group, such as *ahoi* and *ndungata* (Njonjo, 1977:46; Fisher, 1954?:207). In the early 1950s, Fisher (1954?:207) commented that the "rights of *ahoi* are never rigidly defined," so that *ahoi* were often vulnerable when land pressure increased. Also, since an *mbari* tends to grow over time, "from a nuclear family (polygamous or otherwise) to . . . a sub-clan" (Sorrenson, 1967:10), the principle of *mbari* rights does not preclude the proliferation of claims on land over time. In general, Kikuyu landholders expect to divide land among their sons, whose interests accordingly limit fathers' rights to alienate land on their own.

Claims to inherit cultivated land or tree crops were also affected by the organization of farm labor. In Ghana, farmers' wives and children argued that by assisting on a husband's or parent's farm over a period of time, they had earned the right to inherit at least a portion of it (Okali, 1983a:96–97). Such claims were not always successful in court, but they could strengthen an individual's position within the family. Thus, a farmer could bequeath his farm to his wife and children or give it to them while he was alive, but he was more likely to get the consent of his matrikin to such a transfer if his wife and/or children had contributed to the "capital required for working the farm" (Kyerematen, 1971:41).

From her study of local court records in Ghana, Okali (1983a:128) concluded that kinship creates a presumption of multiple interests in property, regardless of which individual(s) in a family actually developed it.[8] However, the specification of individuals' claims was subject to debate. Polly Hill (1963: 118) noted that on cocoa farms being replanted after devastation by swollen-shoot disease, farmers often "prefer not to clarify their relationship to a farm over which they have assumed effective charge—presuming that any requests for clarification which they might put to their relatives would raise questions which had better lie latent." Twenty years later, Okali (1983a:142) found that "direct exchange claims between relatives, including wives, offspring and matrikin, which are not immediately reciprocated, [are] insecure," and concluded that relations among kin were especially "subject to tension and strain and frequently lead to open conflict" (Okali, 1983a:20). In the same vein, Francis (1981:210) wrote that in the small Ijesa town of Ibokun, "the contractual relations of tenancy were regarded as more secure than the reciprocal norms of kinship." In central Kenya, despite widespread opposition to bequeathing land to women, some men have gone out of their way to allocate farmland to individual daughters, in recognition of their contributions to family income and resources (Mackenzie, 1986:399–400).

Many Courts, Many Verdicts

One important source of proliferating claims on land was the multiplicity of judicial systems under indirect rule. Most colonial regimes established High Courts which judged some cases according to English law, but also heard appeals from the customary courts. Since there was widespread confusion over which courts exercised jurisdiction over what cases, according to which legal system, appeals were frequent, and rulings often inconclusive (Chanock, 1985:210ff.; Sutton, 1984:44–47; Kyerematen, 1971:103–4). In general, "it was not a question merely of two systems of jurisprudence and two conceptions of justice—African and English—but of English law and many African legal systems" (Sutton, 1984:47; see also Adewoye, 1977:185ff.; Kyerematen, 1971: 103–4; Richards, 1971:111; Chanock, 1985:117ff.).

Moreover, cases which were taken to court did not necessarily fall under the "rule of law." In western Nigeria, litigants in customary courts have often invoked personal ties to the presiding chiefs, or employed the services of letter-writers (*awon babaogun* or "champions-at-law"—literally, "fathers of battle") to intercede for them in courts where English-trained lawyers were prohibited (Adewoye, 1977:11, 185–87). Western education and British influence often led some customary court judges in western Nigeria to base their rulings on documented jural norms, but "the processes by which facts-in-law were produced before the courts did not change, and on this level litigation remained as manipulable as ever. . . . Thus the necessity of recruiting support in litigation survived the march of legal rationality" (Francis, 1981:221).

The multiplicity of judicial venues helped to keep boundaries and land rights open to renegotiation, even when land was mortgaged or sold. Mikell's (1983:39) comment on an official ruling in a 1929 dispute between a Brong and an Asante stool—that "the conflict was not settled, merely postponed"—applies to the majority of both chieftaincy and land disputes (Dunn and Robertson, 1973:225ff.; Kyerematen, 1971:78; Sutton, 1984:42; Crook, 1986:89; Berry, 1985:chap.7). The fact that judgments often turned on the interpretation of an earlier ruling by a colonial official did not mean that rules were any more fixed under colonial rule than in precolonial times. Written rulings were not free from ambiguity and could always be challenged if a new witness claimed that an earlier ruling had been based on a misinterpretation of tradition (Kyerematen, 1971:53ff.). A defendant or the court might reverse its own earlier position on matters of ownership and tribute (Kyerematen, 1971:90, 95).

Even English law was invoked and ignored by the same litigant, with respect to the same case, on different occasions (Kyerematen, 1971:77). Since family interests in land were multigenerational, it was impossible to render final judgments, and many court decisions were simply not enforced (Kyerematen, 1971:78, 95; cf. Canter, 1978:268–69).

Disputing processes also varied from one level of the court system to another. In western Nigeria, higher courts tended to make rulings based on legal norms, whereas lower courts sometimes deliberately obscured rules in order to negotiate a compromise or reiterate an ethical norm, such as respect for seniority (Francis, 1981:chap. 8). In Ibokun, cases were brought frequently against tenants for arrears of *isakole* because, as strangers to the local community, the tenants had little alternative but to acknowledge their subordinate status by paying. Tenants were also favored as witnesses in land disputes between locals because, as strangers, they could not be expected to know the original owner of the land (Francis, 1981:205). In such cases, strangers' testimony was confined to statements of recent practice—to whom they had paid *isakole*, for example—and could be used by local families to support a variety of jurisdictional claims. Serious questions about a tenant's liability to pay *isakole* arose only when there was doubt over whether or not the tenant was a stranger (Francis, 1981:194; see also Berry, 1975:111ff.).

Finally, many disputes over land and other fixed assets were handled outside of government-mandated or supervised courts in what Sally Moore (1986:275) calls "'life-term' social arena(s)" which "permit the reopening and renegotiation of issues after a period of time" (see also Canter, 1978:257–67; Francis, 1981:115; Arhin, 1985:28–33). As a result, rights to land remained open-ended and negotiable. As Van Donge put it for Zambia's Southern Province, farmers operate in "a fragmented legal arena. People shifted disputes from chief's arbitration to local courts, to State prosecuting agents. They resorted also to informal sanctions, like sending cattle through or setting fire to crops just before the harvest" (1985:71).

In general, then, informal processes of adjudication fostered the multiplication of rights in land. As Moore wrote of the Chagga, land-use patterns changed in the process of agricultural commercialization without any explicit revision of "customary" land law. "This was so because, unlike the higher levels of our own judicial system, the local courts on Kilimanjaro (and even more so, the new informal agencies of disputes settlement) have not been structured as factories for producing and specifying the scope of rules" (Moore, 1986:318). Similarly, in our case study areas, even when transactions in land rights have become thoroughly commercialized, they have remained tied to social identities, and claims on particular pieces of land have proliferated over time, rather than converging towards private ownership.

MULTIPLE RIGHTS AND SOCIAL PRACTICES: SOME CONSEQUENCES OF AMBIGUITY

The Ambiguities of Land Concentration

Because of the proliferation and negotiability of rights to land, the accumulation of large landholdings has often proved inconclusive in the long run. Some scholars have argued that in the context of rising competition and litigation over land rights in the 1930s and 1940s, "customary" claims were used to mask individual accumulation. Chanock (1991:64) suggests, for example, that with the backing of colonial authorities, chiefs in Zambia were able to manipulate the ajudication of land disputes to their own advantage: "It was a field into which African rulers at all levels could fruitfully insert their own definitions of their 'customary' powers." But open rules of succession militated against the creation of chiefly estates. In Ghana, "it was difficult for a chiefly family to convert the resources of the colonially-recognized Stool into hereditary landed property because of . . . the large number of shifting matrilineal segments from which the chief might be drawn" (Crook, 1986:92). In western Nigeria, chiefs' powers over land were political rather than proprietary. Chiefs settled disputes, but had no right to alienate land or even collect *isakole*, except on land belonging to their own families. Even in East and Central Africa, the authority of chiefs and headmen was far from absolute. In Zambia, "exactly what the rights of chiefs were was a constant matter of dispute, resolved in varying ways in different territories and often left unclear" (Chanock, 1991:64). Despite administrative attempts to codify customary law, access to land remained linked in practice to the structure of customary authority which, in the context of indirect rule, was under continual negotiation.

The commercialization of transactions in land rights opened another potential avenue of land accumulation, and some observers have argued that as population growth and the spread of cash cropping created land scarcity, farmers' holdings became increasingly unequal. In 1951–52, a massive survey of Yoruba cocoa farms showed that the top 10 percent of the farming households in their sample held 41 percent of the land, while the bottom 55 percent held only 19 percent (Galletti et al., 1956:150). By 1968, a survey of farm families in Ife Division concluded that "just under 48% of the land is in the hands of 22 per cent of the families, while at the other end of the scale 41 per cent of the families hold only 17 per cent of the land" (Van den Driesen, 1971:51). However, the significance of these findings is unclear. Galletti et al. used different definitions of land "holding" at different points in their study, which makes it difficult to interpret their data (Berry, 1975:178). In general, Galletti et al. and Van den Driesen write as if Yoruba farming households were stable social units with corporate authority over property and farm management—assumptions which have been questioned in subsequent research (Berry, 1985:70;

Guyer and Idowu, 1991:263ff.). Finally, both ignore the fact that rights in farmland have tended to proliferate in the long run, through inheritance and multiple patterns of land use. At any given point in time, individual and lineage claims to land may vary widely, but it remains unclear—in both western Nigeria and in Ghana—how far such claims endure over time or whether they are converging towards exclusive rights of ownership (see also Konings, 1986: 68–70; A. F. Robertson, 1987:77; Migot-Adholla et al., 1990b:16).

In Kenya, struggles over land in the Kikuyu Reserve are generally said to have benefited the rich and powerful at the expense of the poor. In 1941, the District Commissioner of Kiambu opined "that hundreds, perhaps even thousands of acres have changed hands by 'irredeemable sale' during the past 15 or 16 years, and that most of this has gone into the hands of a very few people, including Chiefs, Tribunal Elders and the educated minority." His views have been widely quoted (Furedi, 1989:141; Njonjo, 1977:44ff.; Sorrenson, 1967:40). Since the 1920s, chiefs, *athomi*, and other influential or wealthy individuals have been charged with using the courts to extend their own landholdings by advocating for their descent groups. In Mbeere, "the regular invocation of custom by the government . . . appears as a convenient metaphor for the ultimate administrative value on [*sic*] control and stability. At the same time, the varied local interpretation and use of custom would enjoy official sanction while masking self-interested land acquisition by chiefs and other functionaries" (Glazier, 1985:207; see also Bates, 1989:39; Kitching, 1980: 284, 291–96; Njonjo, 1977:44).

However, it was not always clear just what was being accumulated. Njonjo (1977:44) notes that chiefs who took advantage of official uncertainty during the early years of colonial rule to stake out large landholdings in the name of custom were not always successful in retaining them. Moreover, large landholdings did not necessarily serve as springboards to the accumulation of capital. The dominant position of large African farms in wattle growing declined after 1935 when Forestal—the largest manufacturer of tannin in Kenya—began to buy cheaper dry bark from small-scale growers (Cowen, 1978:93). To protect large-scale growers, the colonial government introduced marketing controls, but petty traders—especially women who bought smallholders' bark and headloaded it directly from their farms to central markets—were able to circumvent them (Cowen, 1978:195). Cowen concludes that small-scale peasant agriculture expanded during the 1930s, competing successfully with larger farms owned by both Africans and Europeans.

More generally, it is not clear how far competition over land led to the emergence of a permanent "landed gentry" in the Kikuyu Reserve (Sorrenson, 1967:80; Bates, 1989:39)—and how far to a state of heightened tension, in which struggles over conflicting claims to land and multiple interpretations of "customary" rights moved from the courts to the arena of political conflict and, eventually, to guerrilla warfare. Struggles over land tended to strengthen descent groups, as well as to heighten tension and inequality within them (Glazier, 1985:28; Cowen, 1978:74; Mackenzie, 1989:104–6). Thus, Sorrenson (1967:27) argued (contrary to the prevailing official view) that "Kikuyu land tenure tended to evolve . . . from individual to communal (i.e., *mbari*) ownership," while Njonjo (1977:46) pointed out that during Mau Mau, "attacks on the arisen large landowners . . . [were] often a family affair" (see also Njeru, 1976:20). During the interwar period, land accumulation in the Kikuyu Reserves was apparently neither ubiquitous nor irreversible.

Property Rights and Social Conflict

As we saw in chapter 3, by the 1930s and 1940s, colonial administrators voiced increasing concern over problems of soil erosion, deforestation, and overgrazing, all of which they attributed to African farmers' destructive methods of land use. In the context of ongoing struggles over the definition and control of rights to land, increasing state intervention into Africans' methods of cultivation and animal husbandry met with determined, even violent, resistance from the very farmers whose interests they were supposed to protect. In areas of northeastern Zambia, for example, where *citemene* cultivators were confined to Native Reserves, agricultural output began to suffer within a few years (Allan, 1965:446). New areas were opened for African settlement, but within them officials imposed elaborate controls on the practice of *citemene* cultivation. To their chagrin, "resistance to control assumed a political and emotional content," and the scheme accomplished little (Allan, 1965:135).

In West Africa agricultural officers mounted an aggressive campaign to arrest the spread of swollen-shoot disease, which was found in the late 1930s to have decimated much of the cocoa in Ghana's Eastern Province. Farmers were ordered to cut out diseased trees, often without compensation. Many refused to comply with official orders and demonstrated, sometimes violently, both against cutting out and against chiefs who tried to enforce it. Chiefs, in turn, abandoned the campaign, sometimes joining the opposition. The ensuing struggles served to dramatize a key fallacy of indirect rule—namely, the assumption that "traditional" rulers' interest in maintaining their own authority would lead them to side with the government rather than their subjects in times of crisis (Crook, 1986:96; see also Austin, 1964:59–66; Dunn and Robertson, 1973:317).

Rural resistance to government controls was even greater in Kenya, where it built on accumulated resentment over European settlers' appropriations of land. As we have seen, competition over land in the Kikuyu Reserve intensified in the late 1930s and 1940s, as Kikuyu squatters were pushed out of the Rift Valley. The government assumed that ex-squatters would be automatically reabsorbed by their kin or "the tribe." But most squatters had considered their move to the highlands to be permanent (Kanogo, 1987:26). Some had sold or relinquished their claims to land in the reserve, while others were simply unable to protect their claims to *mbari* land from a distance (Sorrenson, 1967:38–40). When they did return, many found themselves landless or reduced to the status of *ahoi* (Sorrenson, 1967:80; Kanogo, 1987:139).

Faced with a potentially explosive situation, the government cast about for a strategy which would accommodate the "repatriates" without undermining either social order or sound agricultural practices. In 1934, the Kenya Land Commission had recommended that the government move gradually to recognize individual titles in Kiambu "when people were ready for it" (quoted in Sorrenson, 1967:31 or 54), and a few agricultural officers argued that the time had come (Throup, 1988:206). Amid the tensions of the late 1940s, however, the Department of Agriculture came to the "conclusion that the policy of encouraging individual tenure was mistaken" (quoted in Sorrenson, 1967:60), and a majority of officials favored the restoration of communalism to avoid "chaos" and provide a "sound" basis for "planned farming" (Kenya, 1945:22; see also Sorrenson, 1967:58ff.; Throup, 1988:207).

As in Zambia, new areas were opened in Kenya for African settlement, but settlers were subjected to stringent restrictions on the size of holdings and the uses to which they could be put (Sorrenson, 1967:83; Kanogo, 1987:105–15; Throup, 1988:126). At Olenguruone, for example, only former *githaka* holders were accepted as settlers, and people expected to be treated as independent colonists in the new settlement area (Throup, 1988:124). Instead, they were bombarded with instructions on everything from what crops to plant to where and how to graze their livestock. When they protested—arguing that as *githaka* holders they were entitled to manage their land as they saw fit—officials replied curtly that the settlers were only "*ahoi* and would be dispossessed if they did not obey the settlement rules and the instructions of the Settlement Officer" (Throup, 1988:126; Furedi, 1989:81). Relations between the settlers and the government deteriorated quickly. By 1944, Olenguruone had become a "centre of militant opposition to the government's agricultural campaign" (Throup, 1988:120), and in 1948 the settlers were forcibly evicted from the scheme. Seething with resentment, they returned to the Kikuyu Reserve, where they have since been "credited with introducing the first Mau Mau oath" (Throup, 1988:120; see also Furedi, 1989:83).

Struggles over rural jurisdictions and associated claims on agricultural surplus also contributed to the rise of nationalist political movements in West Africa. In western Nigeria, parties recruited supporters by appealing to sectional and subethnic loyalties, and politicians frequently intervened in local disputes. In Ife, a dispute broke out in the late 1940s between families of Ife and Oyo descent over the latter's obligation to pay *isakole*. The Modakekes (as the Oyo descendants were known) had migrated to Ife during the wars of the nineteenth century, long before cocoa was even heard of. During the early years of the twentieth century, both Ife and Modakeke farmers moved into uncultivated forest areas outside to town to plant cocoa, establishing many villages south and southwest of Ile-Ife without paying *isakole* to anyone. In the late 1940s, a group of Ife families demanded *isakole* from Modakekes farming on "their" land, on the grounds that the Modakekes were strangers. The Modakekes refused, claiming that the land was theirs, and the dispute escalated. Local ethnic associations with ties to the emerging nationalist parties intervened, adding to the level of tension in the town. The case eventually found its way to the Native Court, where the Modakekes were ordered to pay *isakole* or face eviction from their farms (Berry, 1975:115). They complied, but the rift between the two groups deepened, contributing to a state of simmering tension which flared occasionally into violent confrontation (Oyediran, 1974:73–75; see also page 132 below).

In Ghana, the Convention People's Party faced serious opposition in the mid-1950s from the National Liberation Movement, which drew much of its support from the cocoa-farming areas of Asante. Both parties courted the support of Asante and Ahafo chiefs by promising to support them in their ongoing rivalries over, inter alia, the right to collect tribute from cocoa farmers (Dunn and Robertson, 1973:chap.8; Mikell, 1983:46; Konings, 1986:228). As in Nigeria, such strategies of political mobilization served to link debates over customary jurisdictions and land rights to emerging patterns of party conflict, ensuring that the politicization of rural property rights continued after the end of colonial rule.

LAND REFORM: POLICY AND PRACTICE IN THE POSTCOLONIAL ERA

Since independence, most African governments have adopted land-tenure policies based on the views of those who assume that property rights exercise a determining influence on the course of social and economic change (see p. 000 above). In all four of our cases, independent governments have undertaken programs of land reform, not to redistribute land to the poor or patriotic, but to rewrite the rules governing property rights and land transactions. The stated objective of these reforms is to promote economic development, but they also give officials greater leverage over land allocation. In Kenya, the colonial regime began to register freehold titles in Central Province in the mid-1950s under the Swynnerton Plan—a comprehensive program of agricultural reform designed as much to bring about political stabilization in the wake of Mau Mau as to promote agricultural development (Sorrenson, 1967:201). Land registration continued after independence, ostensibly to promote development outside the Kikuyu heartland. In Ghana, Zambia, and Nigeria, governments have nationalized control over land, also in the name of economic development.

Official efforts to rationalize property rights through legislation have added impetus to ongoing debates over the meaning of customary claims and their relevance to contemporary land-tenure practices. Although the ostensible purpose of nationalization was to permit African governments to allocate land to those most likely to develop it, in practice it has ensured that people's access to land depends on their political connections. If colonial regimes were partially paralyzed by their efforts to respect "traditional" jurisdictions, nationalist politicians became directly embroiled in sectional conflict among their constituents. Thus, nationalization of land tended to perpetuate the kinds of linkages among land rights, political influence, and social identity which were subject to so much debate during the colonial period.[9] Even in Kenya, where the land-reform program initiated in the late 1950s aimed to replace customary tenure with a system of private property, access to land has remained a function of patronage and political maneuvering (at local and national levels) as well as of the ability to pay. To illustrate the extent of continued linkages between access to land and social relations, I will discuss the Kenyan case in some detail and then compare it with the effects of nationalization in Nigeria, Ghana, and Zambia.

Under the Swynnerton Plan, African farmers were given title deeds which conveyed rights tantamount to freehold ownership. Before titles could be registered, however, the government had to identify the legitimate owners. Registration was, therefore, preceded by a process of adjudication in which the legitimacy of competing claims was to be established. Since colonial policy rested on the assumption that customary ownership was communal, Land Adjudication Boards recognized as legitimate claims based on social identity as well as on current use and previous transactions (Okoth-Ogendo, 1976:178, 182; Glazier, 1985:224; Haugerud, 1989:80–82). Accordingly, the Adjudication Boards had to determine the boundaries between clans or descent groups, as well as ascertain the basis for the claims of individual group members.

In Central Province, the initial phase of land registration was pushed through by colonial officials during the end of the emergency, before the Kikuyu were released from protected villages and detention camps, and the allocation of titles was caught up in the politics of Mau Mau. In drawing boundaries and allocating titles, British administrators relied heavily on the advice of Kikuyu "loyalists," who took the opportunity to accumulate land for themselves (Sorrenson, 1967:166–67; Mukaru Ng'ang'a, 1977:372). "Those who gained, at least in the initial stages of the consolidation program, were the rich, the powerful, and the loyal" (Sorrenson, 1967:212). When people were allowed to return to their villages, however, many "errors" were discovered, and boundaries were redrawn. "By 1960 former Mau Mau supporters or returned ex-detainees had gained control of some [Land Adjudication] committees and they did not hesitate to get their own back on the loyalists" (Sorrenson, 1967:180). But many former loyalists eventually assumed prominent positions in Kenya African National Union (KANU), gaining considerable leverage over land allocations and adjudication in the process. Some held on to their land in Central Province; others acquired even larger tracts in the Rift Valley (Mukaru Ng'ang'a, 1977:377; Wambaa and King, 1975:198–99; Njonjo, 1977:631).

Elsewhere, local descent groups played an important role in the process of adjudication. In Mbeere in the late 1940s, Land Adjudication Boards drew boundaries between clans and then left it to each clan to allocate land to its members (Njeru, 1976:12). In Embu, local officials had gone so far in the late 1940s as to require that immigrants into the district "take an oath in order 'to be born again' into a local clan" in order to obtain access to land (Glazier, 1985:208). Clans exercised jurisdiction over scattered pieces of land; boundaries were often unclear; and chiefs' assignments of plots to individuals sometimes led to open conflict (Haugerud, 1981a:7–8). In both areas, the actual allocation of plots involved complex negotiations which tended to create (or preserve) multiple interests in land. Writing of Embu, Haugerud commented that "individual success in the process of dispute settlement depended heavily on one's ties to influential persons as well as on payments of bribes and gifts to clan elders adjudicating cases" (Haugerud, 1981a:9).

Because of the influence that descent groups were able to exert in the process of adjudication, land registration provided an incentive for them to mobilize their members in defense of the interests of the group. For purposes of land adjudication, Mbeere clans organized themselves along more formal lines than they had in the past (Njeru, 1976:25). In some cases, new "descent coalitions" were formed among people who had previously paid scant attention to their possible common ancestry (Glazier, 1985:181ff.). In Kiambu, Nyeri, and Murang'a Districts, *mbari* also took an active role in adjudication, advancing claims to land in the name of customary rights and emerging from the registration process with a heightened awareness of their collective interests (Mackenzie, 1992:25; see also Njeru, 1976:22). Although the Native Lands Registration Ordinance (1959) stated explicitly that registration extinguished all "existing rights and interests under customary law" (Okoth-Ogendo, 1976:166), Land Boards usually refused to approve transactions which were challenged by the family of the title holder (Okoth-Ogendo, 1976). Many transactions were simply never recorded, making it difficult to monitor changing patterns of land control. As early as 1962, colonial officials complained that "the register is gradually ceasing to reflect the true state of affairs on the ground" (Homan, 1963:50), and they warned that holdings consolidated during the process of registration were likely to be refragmented (Homan, 1962:10).

Twenty years later, the situation had not changed (Okoth-Ogendo, 1976:182; Migot-Adholla et al., 1990a:8–9; Haugerud, 1989:66–67, 82–83).

Thus, social relations continued to play a significant role in determining actual patterns of access to land in Kenya, even after registration. In the late 1970s, it was still common for farmers to borrow rather than lease plots of land from relatives and neighbors (Haugerud, 1983:74; 1989:79–80; Glazier, 1985: 216; cf. Alila et al., 1985:28). *Mbari* elders supervised land sales and worked to preserve family rights to the land of deceased kinsmen (Okoth-Ogendo, 1976:166; Glazier, 1985:141). In particular, elders used their influence to prevent women from inheriting land, for fear that if a marriage ended in divorce, or a woman bequeathed land to her daughter(s), the land would be permanently removed from *mbari* control (Mackenzie, 1988:36ff., 1989:102ff.). The continued influence of *mbari* elders over matters of inheritance has been supported by the courts, who tend to treat registered owners of land as trustees, responsible for managing the land for the benefit of their kin (Coldham, 1978a:73–74; see also Migot-Adholla et al., 1990a:7–8).

The continued importance of group rights in land has shaped the socioeconomic consequences of land sales. Sales of registered land were fairly frequent during the 1960s and 1970s (Okoth-Ogendo, 1976:178–79; Collier and Lal, 1986:84; Njonjo, 1977; Haugerud, 1989:77–79; Njeru, 1976:18ff.). Some farmers sold land because they wanted to migrate, either to rural areas where land was more readily available or to the towns (Okoth-Ogendo, 1976:178). Others sold land to pay school fees, meet family expenses (extra food, medical expenses, bridewealth), pay off debts, or cover the costs of litigation (Njeru, 1976:19, 21; Okoth-Ogendo, 1976:179; Collier and Lal, 1980:29). Many buyers were civil servants or well-to-do farmers who could afford to pay in a lump sum, which met the sellers' financial needs (Okoth-Ogendo, 1976:178; Njeru, 1976:19, 21).

Scholars differ, however, over the extent to which registration and subsequent sales have led to a more concentrated pattern of landholdings. Sorrenson (1967:214) estimated that between 800 and 1000 people had been dispossessed in the process of registration in Kiambu, and as many as 4,000 in Fort Hall. Inequality in landholdings was acknowledged to be a problem in Kenya's Fourth Development Plan (Kenya, 1979:53) and has been described in a number of scholarly studies (Alila et al., 1985:24; Livingstone, 1986:165, 320; Mbithi and Barnes, 1975:27; House and Killick, 1981:163; Kitching, 1980:335; Bates, 1989:32; Migot-Adholla, 1984:272; Haugerud, 1983:77ff.; De Wilde, 1967:37). Data on the distribution of landholdings are not readily available, but evidence from the Agricultural Census of 1963 and the first Integrated Rural Survey in 1974 indicates a marked increase in inequality in Central Province during this period, which may be attributable to sales (Collier and Lal, 1986:84).

Table 3. Landholdings in Central Province

Landholding group	Percent of population	Percent acreage owned	
		1963	1974
Smallest	40	26	18
Middle	30	30	28
Largest	30	44	54

Source: Collier and Lal, 1986:84.

In general, it appears that the great majority of registered landholdings in Central Province are small. According to the second Integrated Rural Survey, 68 percent of the smallholdings in the "coffee zones east of the Rift Valley" were less than one hectare (Livingstone, 1986:163; see also Nyuguto, 1981:163ff.; Collier and Lal, 1986:83). Njonjo (1977:290) argued that land registration froze would-be African capitalists out of the reserves, "locking" most peasants in to holdings of five acres or less. To be sure, Kikuyu from Central Province have also acquired land in other parts of the country, so that data for Central Province don't give a complete picture of their holdings. In the mid-1970s, Okoth-Ogendo (1976:178) observed that "data from Kiambu suggests that many people were able either fraudulently or with the consent of the Land Control Boards to move into the Rift Valley," selling small parcels in Kiambu and buying larger, cheaper ones further west.

However, the fact that many—possibly the majority—of transactions in land are not recorded suggests caution in interpreting these figures. Within two or three years of land registration in Central Province, officials complained that consolidated holdings were being refragmented through unrecorded sales and bequests (Homan, 1962:10; De Wilde, 1967:60; Sorrenson, 1967:216). Fifteen years later, procedures for registering transactions had become so complicated that few people bothered to do so. "This means, of course that refragmentation or multiple use of land continues unabated" (Okoth-Ogendo, 1976:182). In other words, registration does not appear to have created exclusive rights in land: despite the letter of the law, ownership remains "heterogeneous and divisible" (Okoth-Ogendo, 1986:89).

In addition, it is not clear that land registration has led either to increased agricultural productivity or to the concentration of agricultural capital (Haugerud, 1989:76ff.; Okoth-Ogendo, 1976:175–76; Migot-Adholla et al., 1990a:20). Sales and other transfers of land may have operated to concentrate control of increasingly valuable rural land in the hands of a few and to dispossess a growing number of individuals. As in the colonial period, however, questions remain as to what rights in land are exchanged through inheritance, sale, or informal lending. Group interests still operate *de facto*, if not *de jure*, and effective control over land remains closely tied to political influence and negotiation. Successful competition for access to land requires "investment in social relations with kin, neighbors, bureaucrats and politicians" (Haugerud, 1989:76).

In Ghana, Zambia, and Nigeria, nationalization of land ownership has ensured that access to land remains subject to political maneuvering. In principle, control over land allocation has been centralized, but in practice the allocation of land rights and adjudication of rural land disputes is handled locally, by Land Allocation Boards, chiefs, headmen, and customary courts. In northeastern Zambia, where land was relatively abundant, land reform was not politically urgent at the time of independence. Indeed, nationalization of land was delayed until 1975 in deference to the few hundred European farmers in the south who produced a substantial share of the country's marketed agricultural output (Wood and Shula, 1987:290). In Northern Province, allocation of land rights and the settlement of land disputes continued to be carried out by chiefs and headmen after 1975, even though, at the time of independence, chiefs were stripped of most of their formal administrative functions (Van Donge, 1982:94). Accordingly, access to rural land continued to be linked to the negotiation of settlement rights and village allegiances.

Moreover, during the first decade of independence, the government pursued a policy of village regrouping which bore a close resemblance to colonial efforts to stabilize rural settlements. At first, villagers showed some enthusiasm for "village regrouping," but voluntary relocations declined as promised services and amenities failed to appear. People who were already well situated in terms of access to jobs and markets or who were loathe to give up established gardens for an uncertain future never participated at all (Bratton, 1980a: 143ff.; Bwalya, 1979:98–99; Pottier, 1988:chap. 8, passim).

Under village regrouping and subsequent programs of "integrated" rural development farmers negotiated land rights in the course of relocating their residences or seeking to participate in a rural development project (Milimo, 1983:318). With the creation of Village Productivity Committees (VPCs) in 1972, chiefs recovered some of their authority, as they were called upon to mediate relations between party cadres or local officials and VPCs (Bratton, 1980a:222ff.). VPC members and farmers who were already well-to-do usually managed to monopolize what services were provided, using them to increase their access to local productive resources—primarily labor. Pottier (1988:14, 22–23, 133) suggests that government restrictions on relocating villages created localized land shortages in some areas, but land scarcity was not a significant constraint on increased production, even in the 1980s (Stolen, 1983:350ff.).

Instead, access to land remained subject to negotiations over the interpretation of custom. When, for example, influential members of the VPC in the Mambwe village of Chele began to appropriate land, ostensibly to create "communal" gardens, the local courts ignored them rather than confront the leadership of the VPC. However, their acquisitions were halted by a couple of farmers in a neighboring village, who simply ploughed a strip of land across the advancing line of VPC acquisitions, thus creating a presumptive claim to the land by the customary right of first clearance (Potter, 1988:119–21).

In Ghana and Nigeria, rights to land and cocoa farms continued to proliferate after independence. In the fluid and competitive arena of electoral politics, jurisdictional struggles flourished. Because chiefs and politicians both found it advantageous to multiply their connections and keep their options open, jurisdictional disputes were rarely resolved (page 53). This contributed, in turn, to the indeterminacy of court rulings in land cases where claims to access or tribute turned on questions of chiefly jurisdiction (Dunn and Robertson, 1973:228, 346–51; Konings, 1986:69). In the 1970s, courts still recognized multiple rights in farms, and interpretations of previous transactions and "customary" rights remained contested and ambiguous (Okali, 1983a:123ff.).

In Nigeria, customary rights are expressly protected under the Land Use Act (1978).[10] To the extent that "customary rights" were already subject to proliferation and reinterpretation, the act appears to perpetuate the flexible, negotiable character of rural property rights. In fact, the law itself is ambiguous and has given rise to conflicting interpretations which have created new uncertainties and led, in one case at least, to violent conflict. For example, the Land Use Act vests ownership of all land in the Governors of the states, mandating that they allocate land to those most likely to develop it. Urban land is directly under the control of the Governor of each state, while land not in urban areas is under the control of local governments, which are empowered to appropriate land for public purposes. Since public purposes are broadly defined to include "control for . . . economic, industrial, or agricultural development," it has been suggested that the act gives government the power to dispossess customary right-holders (Francis, 1981:14).

Whether this interpretation has been borne out in practice is difficult to determine. Certainly some individuals and firms have acquired large tracts of rural land for purposes of agricultural development. The proposed developments have not always been successful, and it is not clear what happened to the land after they failed. The law deliberately sanctions political control over land access, which does not preclude commercialization. Thus, it has been suggested that obtaining the governor's consent to transfers of statutory rights to urban land has been "turned into a money making venture in some States" (Omotola, 1982:100). Far from making the process of land allocation more efficient, however, such commercialization "has resulted in unnecessary delay . . . thereby slowing down land development" (Omotola, 1982:100).

In the rural areas of southwestern Nigeria, promulgation of the act was followed not by any wholesale dispossession of local cultivators, but rather by heightened uncertainty over the status of existing rights. In principle, the act protects the rights of cultivators by providing that "any occupier or holder" of land being used for agricultural purposes (including fallow) could continue "in possession of the land for use for agricultural purposes as if a customary right of occupancy had been granted to the occupier or holder by the appropriate Local Government" (Section 36[2]). However, the language of the act is ambiguous. In particular, if "holder" is interpreted to mean anyone with customary rights of jurisdiction or "overlordship", while "occupier" means "cultivator," then the act appears not only to ratify the claims of both "landlords" and "tenants," but also to place them on an equal footing.

Previous practices had certainly not been free from ambiguity. Yoruba speakers, for example, often use the same expression—*olori oko*, or "owner of the farm"—to refer to both landlord and tenant (Berry, 1975:95). Such ambiguities could serve to complicate disputes over claims to *isakole*. However, it was common practice for cocoa farmers to acknowledge landowners' continued rights by paying *isakole*, and the customary courts tended to uphold that practice. The ambiguity of the Land Use Act served to undermine common practice and to "create a good deal of insecurity among tenants" (Francis, 1981:21).

Soon after the act was promulgated, both federal and state officials announced publicly that the act abrogated tenants' obligation to pay *isakole*, and many farmers stopped making payments to the families who claimed jurisdiction over the land on which they farmed. In the ensuing wave of litigation, courts' rulings tended to reflect rather than resolve the ambiguities of the act.[11] Some judges ruled that tenants could continue to use land which they were farming at the time of the decree without paying any more *isakole* to their customary "overlords" (*Akinloye* v. *Oyejide*, Ijero, 1981; *Ogunlusi* v. *Durodola*, Ondo, 1983). Others insisted that customary rights were unaltered by the act and that tenants must continue to pay *isakole* unless they were awarded customary rights of occupancy by the appropriate Local Government (*Owoeye* v. *Adedara*, Ikere-Ekiti, 1981). However, no one appeared very clear on what form such awards should take or how they were to be enforced.

In these unsettled conditions, some judges frankly sought to compromise. In *Akinloye* v. *Ogunbe* (Oyo State High Court, 1979), the judge affirmed the ownership rights of the plaintiff on the grounds that he had consistently harvested palm fruit on the disputed land—a right customarily reserved to the owner of the land. However, the plaintiff was denied the right to evict the defendants (although challenging the owner's title was grounds for eviction under customary law) because their right to continue to cultivate the land "as if they held customary rights of occupancy" was protected by the Land Use Act. In another, the tenants had been settled on the disputed land for decades: they had built a village, including schools and a dispensary, planted cocoa, and had unsuccessfully challenged the landlord's title in court five times between 1935 and 1960. In this case, the judge awarded customary rights of occupancy to *both* the plaintiff and the defendants, without offering any views on how to reconcile their claims (*Ogunola* v. *Eiyokole*, Ilaro HC, 1982).

On occasion, disputes over interpretation of the Land Use Act have become violent. In Ife, the Modakekes saw in the Land Use Act an opportunity to reassert their rights with the blessing of the federal government, and stopped paying *isakole* to Ife families. "This was resisted by the Ife[s] . . . resulting in the killing of many people" (Omotola, 1982:40). In the wake of this debacle, Omotola's conclusion that "the land struggle continues as if the Act had not come into effect" appears as something of an understatement.

CONCLUSION

Since precolonial times, access to rural property has been linked to social identity and status. Under indirect rule, such linkages were perpetuated, not in the sense that property rights were frozen into precolonial molds of communal ownership, but rather, through unresolved debates over the interpretation of customary rules and the right to enforce them. In the late colonial period and after independence, governments played an increasingly active role in trying to regulate patterns of land use, as part of a larger effort to direct the course of economic change. However, both the implementation and the effects of land-reform policies bear a striking resemblance to those of indirect rule.

African governments have displayed considerable ambivalence towards customary law and institutions, which helped to prolong debate over the meaning of custom and its role in contemporary systems of governance and adjudication. By simultaneously courting supporters in the name of customary social solidarities and disparaging ethnic loyalties as backward and politically disruptive, African governments have both intensified ethnic tension and political competition and rendered them more uncertain—thereby reinforcing people's propensity to invest in multiple social networks. With respect to land rights, the resulting proliferation of social networks has reinforced the multiplication of claims to land, making it difficult to enforce legislation designed to clarify and standardize tenure rules. It has also complicated efforts by governments and private individuals to consolidate control over land and other forms of property in the hands of individuals or corporate groups.

Thus, access to rural land remains contested and negotiable. Contests are fought with money and influence, in the name of customary rules and prerogatives. Some observers have concluded that, while land tenure in Africa is characterized by a murky superstructure of conflicting interpretations of customary and contemporary rules, at its base, commercialization and the centralization of power in colonial and postcolonial states have transformed land rights from a corollary of social identity to a marketable asset, control of which is becoming concentrated in the hands of wealthy and/or powerful people. Indeed, African governments *have* acquired large tracts of land for rural development schemes and sanctioned private acquisitions for the same purpose, but the significance of these transactions is not always clear.

In the previous pages, I have argued that despite (or perhaps because of) recent land-reform programs, access to land has remained contested and linked to social identity and status. In the past, networks based on kinship, common origin, residence, or political allegiance operated as arenas of negotiation, political maneuvering, and individual mobility. As Colson pointed out twenty years ago, commercialization provided an impetus for social networks to reconstitute themselves as corporate groups exercising exclusive control over economic resources. In recent years, however, this trend has been partially counteracted by increasingly unstable economic and political conditions. To cope with uncertainty, many people have multiplied their memberships, shifting attention from one network or relationship to another as circumstances change. As a result, networks themselves wax and wane in their capacity to act collectively or deliver services to their members, remaining "social arenas [which] permit the reopening and renegotiation of issues" (Moore, 1986:275) rather than being fully transformed into "economic corporations dealing in land" (Colson, 1971:211).

Diversification of memberships and the fluidity of social networks militate against the creation of large landed estates, whose owners hold a monopoly over rural labor and incomes by virtue of their control over land. Even in Kenya, "tenure reform . . . has not successfully institutionalized exclusive private control of land" (Haugerud, 1989:83), and most holdings, large and small, remain subject to multiple claims. People who have been excluded from access to land rights, by *mbari* or other established groups, sometimes form new ones to acquire land rights on their own. For example, as Kenyan men pressured Land Boards to protect *mbari* holdings by denying titles to women, Kenyan women began to form informal "self-help" groups to assist one another in acquiring land and other forms of rural property (Mackenzie, 1992:39; Stamp, 1975–76:33; 1986:40). Similarly, the state's continued vacillation over the appropriate judicial venue for land disputes suggests that even wealthy and powerful Kenyans continue to find local networks viable channels of accumulation.

In Ghana, Nigeria, and Zambia, rural land has remained subject to multiple interests and to a dynamic of litigation and struggle which both fosters investment in social relations and helps to keep them fluid and negotiable. Here, too, individuals and institutions have accumulated sizeable holdings of land, but it is not clear how far they have been able to "limit the ability of other persons to enjoy the benefits to be secured from the use and enjoyment" (Bates, 1989:29) of these estates. As Myers (1990:324) discovered in Iwo, Yoruba farmers with really large landholdings have not taken advantage of the Land Use Act to register them, apparently preferring to rely on their ability to play local networks in order to protect their claims. In general, the impact of land-reform programs on actual patterns of access and control has been, at most, tangential.

Chapter Six

Exploitation Without Dispossession

Markets, Networks, and Farmers' Access to Labor

IF RURAL PROPERTY RIGHTS remained contested and ambiguous during and after the colonial period, it is unlikely that African farmers were able to mobilize labor simply by hiring in dispossessed people at subsistence wages. On the whole, the evidence supports this hypothesis. While farmers' use of hired labor has certainly grown over time, in most African farming systems hired workers provide only a small part of the total labor devoted to agricultural production, even today. By and large, farm labor in Africa is still "family labor" (Cleave, 1974:27; Swindell, 1985:92ff.; Freund, 1988:70).[1] Despite the prevalence of family labor, however, most African farmers complain that they cannot mobilize enough labor to expand or even maintain output. On one level, this is consistent with evidence that most people in rural areas have access to land and are therefore able to cultivate on their own account. But this explains only why farmers are unable to *hire in* enough labor to meet their needs—not why they find it difficult to mobilize labor in general. If African farmers rely primarily on family labor, why has the shortage of hired labor acted as a significant constraint on agricultural growth?

In this chapter, I will argue that the availability of "family" labor has also declined over time, partly as a result of commercialization. This decline does not, however, fall neatly into standard conceptual frameworks such as peasantization or proletarianization. Rather, the changing availability of labor within families (and other social networks) reflects complex processes of struggle and negotiation over work and income, in which wider patterns of commercialization, political centralization, and social change have interacted with the dynamics of domestic groups and community relations in historically specific ways. Before describing these processes in detail, I will attempt briefly to locate the argument of this chapter in relation to the wider literature on African farm labor.

CONCEPTUAL ISSUES

Among neoclassical economists, emphasis has shifted over the last twenty years from the efficiency of small farms to the prevalence of imperfections in rural factor markets. Around the time of independence, economists and development planners discovered "economic man" in Africa, and decided that economic theories and policies developed in other parts of the world would also apply in Africa. During the 1960s, a spate of empirical studies purported to show that African peasants were "price responsive"—ready and able to expand output when it was profitable for them to do so. Policy analysts concluded that promoting agricultural development was largely a matter of "getting the prices right" (Eicher and Baker, 1982:59). Agricultural stagnation was blamed, accordingly, on government policies which discriminated against farmers (Bates, 1981:30ff.).

The argument that "proper" price incentives are sufficient to stimulate agricultural growth and efficient resource allocation rests, of course, on the assumption that both product and factor markets function smoothly and competitively. As agricultural prices rose in the late 1970s and early 1980s without leading to significant development,[2] economists began to reexamine the adequacy of supply response as a basis for policy making. Rather than question the economic rationality of African peasants or the efficacy of competition, however, they insisted that the fact of agricultural stagnation or decline must reflect the prevalence of market imperfections in rural economies.

Market imperfections were, in turn, attributed partly to government actions and partly to vaguely defined notions of "underdevelopment." Following the Berg Report (World Bank, 1981), numerous studies reiterated the theme that Africa's economic woes were due in large measure to bad policy (Eicher, 1982:163–64; Berg and Whitaker, 1986:10–12; Bates, 1981:chaps. 1, 2; see also Sender and Smith, 1986, for a partially sympathetic critique). African governments, they argued, had intervened excessively in both domestic markets and foreign trade and payments—getting the prices wrong, substituting cumbersome administrative structures for competitive markets, and wasting scarce resources. By the mid-1980s, as agricultural development continued to lag despite the fact that many African governments had adopted price and exchange-rate policies advocated by the World Bank, economists shifted their attention from politics to culture. In particular, it was suggested that, for historical and cultural reasons, rural factor markets were imperfect or "missing" in Africa, making it difficult if not impossible for farmers to expand output or use resources productively.

For example, in attempting to explain why Kenyan farmers do not use much hired labor, Collier and Lal (1986:138) resorted to a kind of cultural determinism. Absentee land ownership, they argued, together with Kenyans' "noncapitalist conception of land rights," blocked the emergence of "appropriate contracts" in rural factor markets, leading to misallocation of resources and stifling agricultural growth.[3] Why absentee landownership or noncapitalist forms of tenure should suppress or drive out "appropriate" contracts, such as wage labor or land rent, is never explained. Indeed, Collier and Lal's argument sometimes verges on the mystical—as when they insist on its power to "exorcise the analytical demons which have imprisoned thought on labor markets and poverty in Kenya" (Collier and Lal, 1986:113).

Another critique of the labor shortage argument comes from the left. Citing low levels of rural income and wages, some Marxist writers have argued that the problem is low productivity and limited opportunities, rather than a shortage of labor per se (Koopman, 1983:1044). However, it is not clear whether agricultural decline and rural poverty result from too much capitalist exploitation or too little (Meillassoux, 1981:117–19; Murray, 1981:98–99; Lawrence, 1986:passim). In the 1960s and 1970s, there was widespread agreement that capitalist accumulation had not really transformed the African countryside. Recently, however, some have argued that there is more proletarianization in rural Africa than meets the eye (Konings, 1986:71–72; Van Hear, 1982:chap. 1; see also Cowen and Murage, 1972:40ff.). In particular, several authors have suggested that many "traditional" forms of labor employment actually mask increasingly exploitative and/or commercialized relations between farmers and farm workers (Pottier, 1988:126–28; Nkadimeng and Relly, 1983:102–4).[4]

This view received considerable support from feminist writers, who point out that family labor is entirely consistent with patriarchy (Mackintosh, 1977:124; Folbre, 1986a:250–51, 1986b:27–30; Parpart and Stichter, 1988: introduction). Some argue that, over the course of the twentieth century, advancing commercialization combined with persistent patriarchy have worsened the economic position of rural women in Africa (Bukh, 1979:54–55, 64–65; Stichter, 1975–76:58–60). But Koopman (1988:49–51), Guyer (1980: 371–72), and others remind us that the historical record is mixed: in some cases, at least, commercial expansion has provided women with the means to earn and spend income independently of their husbands or male elders (Robertson, 1984:15–16:chap.4; Martin, 1988:47–48, 73). At Jahaly Pachar, an irrigated rice-farming project in the Gambia, some women hired themselves out rather than acquiesce in patriarchal exploitation of their labor on household plots (Carney, 1988:345). In general, these studies suggest that to understand access to labor on small farms, one must look not only at who works for whom, but also at how work is done, how terms are negotiated, and how the micropolitics of labor mobilization and control influences output, productivity, and distribution.[5]

In this chapter, I follow the approach of scholars who seek to understand labor relations in terms of changing historical circumstances and the dynamics of interaction within as well as between rural households and farms. In the case of land, although governments' efforts to regulate land tenure directly have rarely been successful, the growing presence of the state in rural areas did influence the conditions through which farmers gained access to land. In the case of labor, neither colonial nor independent African governments were especially interested in the conditions under which Africans worked for each other on small-scale farms. Colonial regimes were preoccupied with mobilizing labor for Europeans' use, and independent governments' development programs have emphasized technical change and the use of nonlabor inputs, rather than the reorganization of labor processes on small farms. To the extent that labor is provided by family members, however, conditions of employment may have been influenced by government efforts to codify or reform family law and adjudicate disputes over divorce and inheritance.

In practice, state policies toward family law have often been ambiguous or contradictory. Just as colonial policy on land tenure vacillated between recognition and suppression of individual as opposed to "communal" rights, so colonial policy on family law was beset by conflicting views over the importance of protecting individuals versus upholding the authority of "traditional" leaders, such as chiefs, elders, and household heads. Some historians argue that officials leaned in the latter direction, strengthening the power of men over women in the process (Chanock, 1985:186ff.; Ranger, 1983:257–59). However, the effects of colonial legislation and court rulings on actual practices were uneven. Colonial ordinances providing for the registration of (monogamous) marriages were, for example, honored mainly in the breach (Mann, 1985:55, 117ff.; Vellenga, 1983:146–47; Woodman, 1974:277–80; Chanock, 1985:211ff.). Independent African governments also displayed considerable ambivalence towards the respective rights of individuals and kin groups in matters of divorce and inheritance (Kamau, 1987:296ff.). On balance, it is not clear that marriage registration ordinances served to strengthen patriarchal hegemony any more than land registration laws acted to create private property.[6]

African farmers' access to labor and the conditions of agricultural employment were shaped less by legislation or administrative practice than by individuals' changing participation in wider markets and political arenas, and by culturally constructed understandings of authority and obligation within households, kin groups, communities, and other local networks. Access to farm labor, like access to arable land, was renegotiated in the course of agricultural commercialization and political centralization, and farmers mobilized and controlled labor through many of the same social arenas in which they debated conditions of access to land. However, negotiations over the terms of employment were affected differently by the growth and diversification of economic activity in colonial and national economies. Despite the continued prevalence of "family labor" on small-scale African farms, farmers' ability to mobilize labor through customary social institutions and relationships has declined over time—in contrast to land rights, which remain closely linked to membership in various social networks.

TRENDS IN AGRICULTURAL EMPLOYMENT

As predicted by the Leninist model of agricultural development, the commercialization of agricultural production did lead to an increase in the use of hired labor on African farms. However, the extent of wage employment varied a great deal from one rural economy to another.[7] On African farms hired labor was more common in the cocoa economies of Ghana and Nigeria than in either central Kenya or northeastern Zambia. In all four areas, however, labor mobilization and negotiations over terms of employment took place in the context of existing social relations and culturally constructed understandings of work, authority, and obligation. Agricultural commercialization gave rise to a series of partially overlapping arrangements and negotiations over conditions of agricultural employment, rather than a decisive transformation of family into market labor.

In the cocoa economies of Ghana and Nigeria, farmers did not begin to hire in labor until their first cocoa farms were well established and yielding a steady flow of income. Most sources concur with Polly Hill (1963:188) that

> During the first stage of the migration the farmer depended on family labour and his cash outlay on day-to-day operations was possibly negligible. . . . [T]he second stage . . . was reached when the farmer had successfully established a sufficient area of bearing cocoa *to support a labourer from its proceeds*.

However, some Ghanaian cocoa farmers were hiring labor as early as 1908 (Van Hear, 1982:66). In 1916, there were 12,000 northerners in Ashanti, the majority employed in agriculture (Sutton, 1983:479). Elsewhere, labor hiring did not begin until after the First World War (Austin, 1987:265). Thereafter, it grew steadily: by the end of the 1920s, "the employment of labour had become a regular feature of cocoa growing" (Great Britain, 1938:19–20; see also Austin, 1987:264; Hill, 1963:187ff.).

During the depression, cocoa farmers' incomes fell, and demand for hired labor declined, leading to unemployment and hardship, especially for migrants from the north who had few alternative sources of livelihood (Van Hear, 1982: 128ff.). As world markets for agricultural commodities recovered after the Second World War, however, demand for agricultural labor soared. In 1951–53, the Gold Coast Labour Department reported that 3,391 cocoa farmers in Ashanti employed over 30,000 laborers, exclusive of "family workers" (Killick, 1966:239).[8] In 1970, a survey carried out in mid-season found that 60 percent of 3,726 farmers who belonged to government Cooperative Societies employed an average of 3.3 "permanent laborers" each,[9] in addition to an unspecified number of casual laborers (Addo, 1974:207). Several smaller surveys confirmed that a majority of Ghanaian cocoa farmers employed some hired labor, even in the depressed conditions of the late 1970s (Konings, 1986:100ff.; Okali, 1974:11; Mikell, 1989:114).

In Nigeria, both cocoa cultivation and the use of hired labor expanded more slowly than they did in Ghana. Before the First World War, employment opportunities in Southern Nigeria were so limited that thousands of Nigerians emigrated to work in the Gold Coast, on cocoa farms as well as in gold mines and on the railway (Hopkins, 1966:148; Sutton, 1983:479–81). Cocoa farmers began to use hired labor in the 1920s, and some continued to do so during the depression (Forde and Scott, 1946:91–92). As in Ghana, demand for agricultural labor grew rapidly after 1945. In 1951–52, the Cocoa Marketing Board sponsored an exhaustive survey of cocoa farmers which found that 40 percent of the labor on all sample farms (and 60 percent on cocoa farms) was contributed by hired workers (Galletti et al., 1956:668). In 1970–71, half of the farmers I interviewed in four Nigerian villages were employing annual laborers, and nearly all used some labor hired on a casual basis (Berry, 1975:149). My informants concurred that labor hiring dated from the earliest years of cocoa cultivation and had increased as production expanded (Berry, 1975:130).

Beginning in the 1960s, when cocoa farmers' incomes were heavily taxed, cocoa production in both countries began to decline—absolutely in Ghana, relatively in Nigeria. In Ghana, overall economic decline together with government subsidies for mechanized production of rice and other food crops shifted the terms of trade in favor of food crops during the 1970s. These changes combined with booming economic conditions in Côte d'Ivoire and Nigeria to drain labor out of the Ghanaian cocoa economy at an unprecedented rate (Tabatabai, 1988:719–21; Konings, 1986:116).[10] In Nigeria, cocoa farmers faced acute labor shortages in the 1970s, as people left agriculture to seek quick profits in the oil-inflated trade and services sectors (Berry, 1985:88, 1987:206–7; Collier, 1983:212, 1988:773). In both countries, farmers found it difficult to make up for shortages of hired labor with the help of family members, since the latter were also seeking better opportunities outside of cocoa farming.

In central Kenya and northeastern Zambia, labor hiring on African farms has not developed to the same extent as in the cocoa economies of West Africa. In central Kenya, labor recruitment for European farms was a major source of tension among settlers, Kikuyu farmers, and the colonial regime in the early 1900s. By the 1920s, thousands of Kikuyu were working on European estates in Central Province, often under duress. During the decade, estate employment rose from 62,000 to 126,000 per annum (Collier and Lal, 1986:35), much of it supplied by women who also worked on their own fields. In 1925, 28,000 women and children worked on the coffee harvest in Kiambu alone (Presley, 1986:110; see also Cowen, 1978).

Some of the first Africans to use hired farm labor in Central Province were Christian teachers and artisans, who began to grow crops for sale in the early 1920s (Cowen and Murage, 1972:40; Mukaru Ng'ang'a, 1978:36). With encouragement from the government, some of these farmers planted wattle, using hired workers and relatively expensive processing methods copied from European farms to produce "green bark" for sale to tanning companies. In the mid-1930s, faced with increasing competition from Argentina, Forestal (the largest tanning company in Kenya) began to purchase dry bark, which was cheaper to produce and better suited to production on small farms. Cowen (1978:90) estimates that dry bark required only one-fifteenth the amount of labor needed to produce green bark, and could be harvested at slack times in the arable cropping calendar. In other words, dry bark wattle complemented rather than conflicted with other sources of household income, and entailed no financial costs.[11] Unlike cocoa growing in West Africa, the cultivation of wattle did not lead to the widespread use of hired labor on small farms.[12]

During the Second World War, the colonial government encouraged increased food-crop production to meet wartime needs, and African farmers' sales rose rapidly (Kitching, 1980:108ff.). However, the commercialization of food and other annual crops does not appear to have generated much increase in labor hiring on small farms. In rainfed agriculture, yields of annual crops vary substantially from season to season because of fluctuations in weather, pests, and crop diseases. In addition, on small farms, even "family" labor supplies may change suddenly for personal or domestic reasons. Illness, family quarrels, or other demands on people's time can cause substantial variations in labor inputs and output on a seasonal or even daily basis (Haugerud, 1988:170–71; Wolgin, 1975:623). Because returns to annual crop production are so unpredictable, cultivation for the market does not necessarily provide farmers the means to hire in labor on a regular basis.

In the 1950s, the colonial government lifted its ban on coffee growing by African farmers in the Kikuyu districts and began to encourage smallholder tea cultivation as well (Steeves, 1978:125). Coffee and tea require almost four times as much labor in a year as maize (Senga, 1976:98; Clayton, 1964:70), and because they are tree crops, they are more likely than annual crops to generate the means to finance hired labor. However, contrary to the expectations of the Swynnerton Plan (and the conclusions of some economists),[13] neither tree-crop cultivation nor land registration gave rise to the growth of a rural proletariat or the proliferation of small-scale capitalist farms relying on hired labor.

For one thing, tree crops were never grown by more than a minority of rural households in Central Province (Senga, 1976:81; Kitching, 1980:317;

Livingstone, 1986:170). In addition, the rapid subdivision of holdings after land registration meant that coffee and tea were often grown on very small holdings, by farmers who could not afford much hired labor (see p. 000 above). In practice, the households most likely to hire in labor for farm work have been the minority with access to regular sources of off-farm income (Lamb, 1974:59; Haugerud, 1984:306, 337; Kitching, 1980:359; Guyer, 1972). Overall, labor hiring on African farms in Central Province has remained limited. In 1969, hired labor was estimated to account for between 10 percent and 20 percent of total labor employed on small farms in Central Province (Senga, 1976:93), while according to the first Integrated Rural Survey (1974–75), only 10 percent of labor on small-scale farms was supplied by hired workers (Collier and Lal, 1986:118).[14]

In northeastern Zambia, there was little development of agricultural production for the market and no labor hiring to speak of until the 1950s. After 1945, the government abrogated chiefs' rights to demand tribute labor from their subjects, but raised their salaries, which permitted some chiefs to substitute hired for tribute labor (Richards, 1958:312). A few traders and "emergent" farmers, who had access to government credit, also hired laborers, but only a small number could compete with the then-plentiful supply of jobs in the Copperbelt (Hellen, 1968:207; Richards, 1958:309; Kay, 1962:43, 46).[15]

By the 1970s, labor hiring had become more common in the northeast (Pottier, 1988:15, 84–85, 113ff.; see also Hedlund and Lundahl, 1983:71). After 1974, declining employment opportunities in the Copperbelt meant that more young adults remained in rural areas—a situation which probably contributed to the rapid expansion of maize cultivation in the northeast during the 1980s (Milimo, 1983:321).[16] However, returns to farming were low, and few farmers had access to enough working capital to hire in labor on a regular basis. In one village near Mpika, 30 percent of the farmers interviewed in 1981 used hired labor, but only for a few days at harvest time (Milimo, 1983:320). The bulk of farm labor was provided by farmers' relatives or by traditional work groups, though the latter entailed increasingly unequal relations between farmers and workers, and labor scarcity remained a constraint on agricultural expansion (Marter and Honeybone, 1976:35, 47). The rapid increase in maize production after 1980 was accomplished primarily with family labor or by individuals working alone (Francis, 1988:41; see also Pottier, 1988:15).

SOCIAL NETWORKS AND ACCESS TO LABOR

The fact that farm workers were remunerated in cash or in kind did not mean that relations between farmers and hired farm workers were limited to impersonal cash transactions. In the early colonial period, increased agricultural production for the market was often associated with migration. In Ghana and

Nigeria, as farmers planted cocoa in uncultivated forest areas, they also established new communities, often moving together with members of their families or communities and drawing on existing social ties to mobilize labor for farming. In Kenya, Kikuyu "colonists" in Nyeri and the Rift Valley relied on the labor of their followers, wives, and children to farm and herd. In Zambia, where villages split periodically and people moved in different directions, access to labor often followed upon the successful negotiation of settlements and headmanships. Thus, access to labor for expanding agricultural production and sales was frequently negotiated in the process of establishing or reconstituting rural households and communities, and the terms of employment were shaped by prevailing practices with respect to the division of labor in conjugal and domestic relationships.

To the extent that labor was mobilized through existing social relations, farmers could undertake new agricultural ventures or invest in capital goods such as livestock and tree crops without prior access to working capital. This facilitated increased agricultural production for the market and also influenced the resulting development of labor relations. For example, in Ghana and Nigeria, farmers' wives, children, and junior kin did not receive direct compensation for helping to establish new cocoa farms. Instead, relatives worked in exchange for future claims (usually unspecified) on the assets or patronage of their "employers." In Ghana, farmers' wives and children often claimed that by investing labor in a farm, they had acquired rights to the farm itself—a practice analogous to the early system of *abusa* tenancy, whereby laborers who worked to establish new farms received one-third of the farm when the trees matured (Hill, 1963:213; Okali, 1983a:97, 103; Mikell, 1985:18–19; Vellenga, 1986:70–71). In Nigeria, wives and junior kin were more likely to expect assistance in establishing a farm or business of their own (Berry, 1985:69). In central Kenya, where marriage was virtually a precondition for establishing a farm and independent household, Kikuyu *ahoi* sometimes married the daughters of their patrons. Even in northeastern Zambia, where agricultural production for the market was virtually nonexistent, capital formation (mainly preparing new plots for *citemene* cultivation) was a labor-intensive process, requiring close cooperation among household members.

Rising returns to agricultural production led to increased demand for labor and frequent struggles over the division of tasks and income between farmers and farm workers, whether the latter were hired or recruited through existing social networks. In the process, farmers' wives, children, kin, and clients bargained over the terms of employment in increasingly commercial terms. In the Brong-Ahafo region of Ghana, the advent of cocoa around the turn of the century led to a "search for wives" so intense that men were negotiating for unborn females (Mikell, 1984:201). Later, Ghanaian farmers sometimes employed their children or other junior kin as *abusa* laborers (Okali, 1983a:117;

Hill, 1963:187; A. F. Robertson, 1987:73). Yoruba wives expect direct remuneration for some kinds of work on their husbands' farms, for example, harvesting *egusi* (melon seed) (Idowu and Guyer, 1991:12–13). In Zambia, as sales of maize, beans, and millet increased in the 1970s, debates over how much of the crops grown on household fields should be sold and by whom were a common source of domestic tension (Pottier, 1988:115–16, 128; Geisler et al., 1985:12; see also Colson and Scudder, 1988:37–38).

As agricultural commercialization led farmers to seek labor outside of their immediate social networks, they often attempted to reproduce patterns of social subordination—similar to those inherent in kin or other social networks—in their arrangements with hired workers. Annual laborers in the cocoa economies were treated in many respects like subordinate members of farmers' households. They worked for the same farmer all season, lived and ate with the farmer's household, and were treated as his or her dependents in any dealings with local authorities (Berry, 1975:134). As workers rejected annual contracts in Ghana, especially after 1945, farmers modified *abusa* contracts in an effort to gain the same degree of control over sharecroppers that they exercised over annual laborers. In the 1950s, "*abusa* labourers needed the consent of their land lords to supplement their incomes by hunting or by rearing livestock; [and] a convention grew up that no loans were offered to labourers without the knowledge of their 'overlords'" (Van Hear, 1982:222). Similarly, Kikuyu *ahoi* were often treated as clients by their "landlords" (Sorrenson, 1967:8–9; Leakey, vol. 1, 1977:115–16; Mukaru Ng'ang'a, 1978:11).

Agricultural laborers' ability to resist subordination depended on their access to alternative sources of income and security. In western Nigeria in the early 1970s, I found that the workers most likely to be engaged on annual rather than casual contracts were non-Yoruba migrants who had no resident kinsmen or compatriots in the cocoa belt to provide assistance or patronage in time of need. Annual contracts were less common among Hausa laborers, who lived with Hausa kola traders residing more or less permanently in Yoruba farming communities, than among Igbo laborers, who traveled alone or in small groups without ready access to local patrons (Berry, 1975:151–54).

During the depression, "labour's struggle with capital centered not on the level of wages, but on securing their actual payment" (Van Hear, 1982:163). Faced with declining cocoa sales and prices, Nigerian and Ghanaian farmers often failed to pay their hired laborers—treating them, in effect, like family members who could be expected to work in the hope of future assistance rather than current cash. As market conditions improved after 1945, however, migrant workers were increasingly able to demand not only better wages, but also casual contracts which gave them greater independence from their employers (Van Hear, 1982:214–16, 224ff.; Berry, 1975:138–39). The bargaining power of hired workers was further enhanced as farmers' children spent more time in school or off-farm employment.

In the long run, it has become increasingly difficult for farmers to mobilize labor by drawing on or creating relations of dependency. This has occurred not because social networks have disintegrated in the face of spreading commercial activity, but because members of rural households and communities have become involved in a growing number of income-seeking activities and social networks. In rural communities all over Africa, people's involvement in off-farm activities—schooling, wage employment, nonagricultural enterprises—has grown over time. This has occurred in periods of economic instability and decline as well as expansion, and in response to coercive pressures from colonial and postcolonial governments as well as through voluntary participation in new economic activities. Rural people have diversified their occupations and social networks—"straddling" rural and urban areas, agricultural and nonagricultural occupations, wages and self-employment—not only to take advantage of new opportunities, but also to cope with the effects of declining and/or increasingly unpredictable market conditions (see, e.g., Cowen, 1981:67; Kitching, 1980:403; Haugerud, 1989:73; Cooper, 1983:18; Pottier, 1988:32ff.; Berry, 1983:259ff.; 1985:80–81, 99ff.).

Economic and social diversification have, in turn, transformed the conditions under which farmers gain access to labor. Over time, both farmers and the people they seek to employ have become involved in a growing array of nonfarm activities, which have taken them away from farm work and often from the rural areas as well. The resulting decline in supplies of agricultural labor is a major source of the much-discussed problem of "labor scarcity" in African agriculture. In some cases, of course, hired farm labor is scarce and expensive because workers *can* earn more in other occupations. Often, however, farm labor is scarce not because workers can easily earn more in nonagricultural jobs, but because people are too busy trying to make ends meet by combining several marginal income-generating activities or investing in skills and social connections which might improve their future prospects. In addition, farmers find their own time and energy stretched as they struggle both to supplement inadequate farm output with other sources of income and to maintain their position in domestic and other social networks—whose importance as potential channels of access to income and opportunity is increasing as their ability to deliver declines. In short, a growing number of African farmers are finding it increasingly difficult to mobilize their own as well as other people's labor.

CHANGING PATTERNS OF LABOR CONTROL

In agriculture, the productivity of labor depends not only on how hard people work (and what they work with), but also on when they work. Agricultural production is a seasonal activity, whose work rhythms are determined, in part, by climate and by biological processes. Crop yields are affected by the timing of labor inputs—some far more so than others. High-yielding varieties of maize and rice are, for example, more sensitive to the timing of cultivation tasks than are most traditional varieties, and many grains and root crops are more sensitive than cassava (see p. 199 below). As farmers have experienced increasing difficulty in mobilizing labor because of rising rates of mobility and diversification of income sources, the control of labor timing has become increasingly problematic. This is especially true of labor mobilized through social networks.

In the past, labor arrangements which included elements of social subordination and dependency gave farmers considerable control over the timing of agricultural work. In Ghana and Nigeria, cocoa farmers reminisce about the advantages of annual laborers who, like family members, slaves, or pawns, were "always available" and could be called upon to perform many kinds of tasks (Konings, 1986:81, 101; Hill, 1963:188; Okali, 1974:11–12; Berry, 1975: 131–32). Casual laborers, on the other hand, were harder to control, since "labour is usually by piece work, and the labourer fixes his own hours and daily quota of work" (Cardinall, 1932:241, quoted in Van Hear, 1982:70). Like migrant farmers in West Africa, Kikuyu *ahoi* who moved to frontier areas during the early colonial period planned to settle there permanently (Kanogo, 1987:19, 26; Sorrenson, 1967:38, 83). In effect, they and their dependents constituted a full-time labor force. In northeast Zambia, labor relations were based on residential proximity, reinforced by social dependence. Brideservice gave Bemba parents full-time control over the labor of a new son-in-law, since the latter depended entirely on his mother-in-law for food (Richards, 1939:126). The position of social subordinates in all of these areas was summed up by the Yoruba woman who said she could be called on "at any time" to assist her husband on his farm (Berry, 1985:95).[17]

However, farmers' control over the timing of subordinates' labor was never absolute. Even the supply of family labor can be interrupted unexpectedly by illness or quarrels. In Embu, where a woman is likely to return to her parents' home in the event of a conjugal dispute, a husband's control over the timing of his wife's labor can be problematic. In 27 percent of Haugerud's sample of eighty-three households, domestic conflict had caused at least one major interruption to farm work during a period of twenty months (Haugerud, 1988: chap.5). For Bemba farmers in the 1930s, "the founding of a new village was a hazardous affair" (Richards, 1958:307), and village fission constituted a perennial threat to the stability of farm labor supplies. In general, the less secure a farmer's seniority, the more problematic his or her control over the labor of juniors. Over the course of the twentieth century, the increasing mobility of rural residents has further weakened farmers' ability to ensure that farm tasks are carried out at the right time, even when labor is supplied by members of their own households.

Control over the labor *effort* of subordinates is another matter. In many African societies, including all of those covered here, a person's ability to mobilize labor through social networks was directly related to his or her status or influence within them. Status depended, in turn, on frequent demonstrations of one's ability to command a following (Berry, 1989:48–49). Thus, while status conveyed privilege, including the right to demand various kinds of service from one's subordinates, the loyalty of subordinates was also necessary for maintaining status. In the past, people who were dissatisfied with their treatment at the hands of a chief, family head, spouse, or senior kinsman often moved, placing themselves under the protection of another relative or patron. Particular instances of divorce, emigration, village fission, or political defection were, of course, resisted, but the historical record suggests that such realignments were common in all of our case study areas and remain so today. In other words, the loyalty of subordinates was not assured: people had to work to retain it.

To the extent that status and influence depend on the size of one's following, social subordinates are constituents as well as workers. Relations of seniority or patronage may be used to exploit subordinates' labor, but there is little to be gained by dismissing them, even if, as workers, they are lazy or unproductive. On the contrary, "dismissing" one's clients or junior relatives could be counterproductive, reducing the following which constitutes the basis of one's ability to make claims on subordinates' labor. Thus, social networks which enable some members to draw on the services of others may serve as effective channels of access to labor for agricultural purposes, but they do not necessarily work very well as instruments of labor discipline. Cooperative work groups, for example, help to break labor bottlenecks, but there is some evidence that they cost more, in real terms, and are less productive than other forms of labor (Swindell, 1985:134–38; Richards, 1987:89).[18] In general, if subordinates are also constituents, the "sanction of the sack" is ineffective, since it is self-defeating to threaten them with dismissal for laziness or inefficiency (Berry, 1985:154–55). In addition, as we have seen, people often work for spouses, parents, chiefs, and so on in the expectation of future rewards—help with bridewealth, establishing a farm of one's own, or the right to invoke the patronage of one's employer as needed. Subordinates may not need to be paid for their services on a regular basis, but if followers are never rewarded, they are likely to seek other patrons, thus reducing the prestige as well as the labor force of the original one.

In such circumstances, labor control rests on the *partial* exclusion of subordinate categories of group members from certain prerogatives accorded to members of higher status, rather than the complete exclusion of some individuals from membership in the group at all.[19] In many rural economies in

Africa, the negotiability of property rights works to this effect. Subordinate members of rural households, kin groups, or communities are not excluded from access to land or capital goods which the group controls, but their rights are open to negotiation, and their ability to influence the outcomes of such negotiations may be compromised by their subordinate status. Thus, many Akan, Kikuyu, and Yoruba women have found it difficult to exercise claims to farms in which they have invested labor, or even to bequeath individually acquired farms to their daughters over the objections of their kin. In northeastern Zambia, property rights "are often the focus of unresolved struggles between the agnatic collectivity and the individual" (Bond, 1987:147), and both ownership of productive assets and control over others' labor depend on one's ability to exercise influence among kin and neighbors (Kapferer, 1967:46–47; Van Donge, 1985:69).

In one sense, then, reliance on social networks for mobilizing agricultural labor limits farmers' ability to raise or maintain productivity through effective labor discipline. However, the declining importance of network labor has not necessarily brought farmers greater control over labor effort.[20] Rather, because the decline has resulted from the increasing mobility of farmers as well as farm workers, supervision of labor effort has remained problematic. This is also true for farmers who rely primarily on hired labor and do not need to temper discipline in order to retain the loyalty of their worker/followers. In the 1980s, the minority of farmers who still made regular use of networks were likely to be influential members of rural communities who were fully occupied in local affairs and could mobilize labor among their local followers (Guyer, 1988:17). In Embu, farmers who regularly produced more foodstuffs than their families consumed were not necessarily those most likely to sell food crops. Instead, they used gifts or loans of foodstuffs to create networks of obligation among kin and neighbors, which they used to gain access to extra labor for their farms (Haugerud, 1988:175ff.). Because they are closely informed about their laborers' circumstances, such farmers are also better placed to monitor labor effort than are those who spend much of their time away from their farms on other business.

RURAL DIFFERENTIATION

So far, I have argued that the commercialization of agricultural production did not give rise to a progressive substitution of hired for network labor in the long run. Use of hired labor by African farmers has increased, but not enough to offset the declining availability of network labor. Moreover, changes in the use of both hired and network labor varied from one rural economy to another. On the whole, labor hiring grew more in the cocoa economies of West Africa than in the annual cropping systems of central Kenya or northeastern Zambia—

despite substantially different degrees of commercialization between the latter two. In all four areas, the distribution of rural income and wealth has become more unequal, but accompanying patterns of socioeconomic stratification have varied from one locality to another. Socioeconomic mobility was, if anything, greater in the cocoa economies of West Africa, where agricultural employment was more commercialized, than in either central Kenya or northeastern Zambia, where farmers' use of hired labor remains quite limited. In addition, where persistent patterns of differentiation have occurred, this has sometimes reflected the persistent exclusion of certain socially constructed categories of people from access to one or more resources, rather than the creation of social classes as a result of the unevenness of commercial expansion. I will elaborate these points in turn.

Income Inequality

In the cocoa economies of West Africa, conditions of access to agricultural labor favored socioeconomic mobility. Many of the people who worked on cocoa farms did so not because they had no alternative source of livelihood, but in order to acquire the means to establish farms or other enterprises of their own. The fact that farmers could mobilize labor from relatives and dependents enabled thousands of people to plant cocoa who could not have done so if they had had to hire in labor from the start. Once cocoa farms matured, however, they tended to become self-financing, enabling farmers to substitute the labor of hired workers or sharecroppers for that of family members. To the extent that family members or other dependents went on to establish independent farms or businesses of their own, the use of such labor in the early stages of cocoa cultivation contributed to the upward mobility of individuals within existing social networks. Sharecroppers and other hired workers also aspired to become independent farmers, and many succeeded (Hill, 1956:17; A. F. Robertson, 1987:73–74; Berry, 1975:144).

Not all farm laborers prospered, of course. Migrant workers were sometimes forcibly recruited, notably in northern Ghana during the early years of colonial rule, and later in periods of labor shortage (Thomas, 1973:passim; Van Hear, 1982:42, 136ff., 153ff.). During the depression, migrant workers who were unable to find work or pay for transport to their home areas endured hunger and sickness, while those who were employed received low wages and sometimes none at all. When cocoa prices and farm incomes rose after 1945, however, the mobility of migrant workers, combined with overall labor shortages, pushed agricultural wages up rapidly (see table 4). During this period, as we've seen, migrant workers successfully demanded *abusa* or casual rather than annual contracts (Van Hear, 1982:197–200, 224ff.; Konings, 1986:96ff.). They also organized. Groups of laborers were engaged to establish new farms under contracts which they negotiated jointly with individual farmers (Van

Table 4. Agricultural wages in Ghana

A. Nominal wages paid to cocoa farm laborers

	Annual			Daily		
	Asante	Brong-Ahafo	Ghana	Asante	Brong-Ahafo	Ghana
1910s (a)				1/6–2s		
1920s (a)	£8					
1946 (b)			£ 5–8			
1948 (b)			8–12			
1951–52 (b)			12–15			
1954–55 (b)			12*			
			25**			
1957 (b)	£25	£10–30				
1957–59 (c)	47¢	41		.32¢	.33	
1960–65 (c)	56	53		.41	.42	
1966–69 (c)	68	69		.47	.49	
1970 (c)	74	79		.54	.56	
1970 (d)	70	72			.50–.60 (.70–.80 incl. food)	
1972 (e)			99			

B. Average earnings of agricultural laborers (f)

Nominal (¢ per month)				Real (1970 = 100)			
1970	33	1977	155	1970	100.0	1977	65.2
1971	40	1978	72	1971	110.7	1978	41.4
1972	40	1979	186	1972	101.4	1979	28.1
1973	44	1980	329	1973	94.4	1980	30.9
1974	60	1981	503	1974	109.9	1981	22.5
1975	67	1982	559	1975	96.6	1982	20.5
1976	72	1983	886	1976	65.5	1983	14.1

Sources: (a) Sutton, 1983:479, 482; (b) Van Hear, 1982:198; (c) Addo, 1972:44; (d) Rourke and Sakyi-Gyinae, 1972:8; (e) Arhin, 1985:45; (f) Tabatabai, 1988:722. * Diseased farm; ** Healthy farm.

Hear, 1982:215–16, 241). Beginning in the 1960s, the growth of commercial food farming in Ejura and Atebubu, just north of the cocoa belt, began to bid labor away from the cocoa sector, further raising money wage rates (Van Hear, 1982:477; Addo, 1972:45–46; Rourke and Sakyi-Gyinae, 1972: 12). Similarly, in Nigeria, wages rose sharply during the postwar cocoa boom, and gangs of migrant workers negotiated piece-rate contracts with different farmers.[21]

Thus, although they were treated and paid poorly in times of declining farm incomes, in the long run farm workers in Ghana and Nigeria shared in the gains from expanding cocoa production, and many moved into self-employment. As world cocoa prices recovered after 1945, for example, farm workers successfully demanded higher wages, and in Ghana "there was a widespread changeover from annual to sharecropping contracts" (Van Hear, 1982:199; see also Berry, 1975:139–44; Robertson, 1987:73–74). In the annual crop economies of central Kenya and northeastern Zambia, there is evidence of a more persistent division of the rural population into those with and without the means of accumulation. Access to the means of accumulation has not, however, depended entirely or even primarily on access to land and tree crops. Migration to urban areas and, in Zambia, to the Copperbelt has been an important source of rural income and income differentials in both economies.

In Kenya, emerging inequality of landholdings in the Kikuyu districts was evident before 1920. "Big men" who cooperated with colonial authorities used their position to accumulate livestock and gain control over extensive areas of land (Sorrenson, 1967:44–45; Kenya Land Commission, 1934b: 260ff.). In the 1920s, Christian converts who took up commercial farming used hired labor and capital-intensive means of production (Cowen, 1972:40). As production for the market increased in the late 1920s, competition over land in the Kikuyu Reserve became intense and remained so in the 1930s as conditions worsened for squatters in the White Highlands. Squatters who left the White Highlands in the late 1930s rather than accept increasingly harsh terms of employment, or who were "repatriated" from reserves earmarked for other "tribes," found it difficult if not impossible to gain access to land in the Kikuyu Reserve (Sorrenson, 1967:250; Njonjo, 1977:45ff.; Mukaru Ng'ang'a, 1978:38ff.).

If there is evidence of growing accumulation and dispossession in the Kikuyu districts between 1910 and 1940, however, it also appears that the distribution of wealth and power was shifting and unstable. Some of the early accumulators later lost most of their land (Njonjo, 1977:54), and the profits of large farms in the Kikuyu Reserve were undercut during the depression by competition from peasant households (Cowen, 1978). In addition, ongoing debates over the interpretation of customary tenure left everyone's holdings open to multiple claims and periodic renegotiation of rights.

As we saw in chapter 5, rights to land remained negotiable even after registration. Some people lost access to land during registration in the late 1950s (Mukaru Ng'ang'a, 1978:151ff.; Njeru, 1976:20; see also Alila et al., 1985:10–12), and the distribution of holdings became more unequal between 1963 and 1974 (see table 3). However, most registered holdings were small to begin with, and were subdivided further in the 1960s and 1970s (Livingstone, 1986:161ff.). The second Integrated Rural Survey, which enumerated rural households rather than "small farms," found twice as many holdings under 0.5 hectare as were reported in the first survey (Livingstone, 1986:162, 164). Moreover, land boards, courts, and local officials continue to recognize multiple claims, so that many more people have access to land in practice than are listed as registered owners (Migot-Adholla et al., 1990a:15). In general, available evidence does not support the conclusion that land concentration and dispossession have operated as major sources of rural differentiation in Central Province.

Table 5. Income inequality among rural households in Kenya, 1974

A. Sources of smallholders' household income, by adult-equivalent income group, Kenya (Shillings)

	0–249	250–499	500–999	1000–1499	1500–2499	>2500
Farm operating surplus	30	193	451	740	1285	1449
(as percent of income)	(21)	(51)	(63)	(62)	(66)	(42)
Total income	141	379	716	1204	1943	3471

B. Distribution of household income, Central Province (%)

	Population (by income)	Income 1963	Income 1974
Poorest	40	24.4	18.2
Middle	30	25.3	27.7
Richest	30	50.3	54.1

Source: A. Livingstone, 1986:311; B. Collier and Lal, 1986:84.

Within the small-farm sector, persistent differences in household income appear to have been associated with access to nonfarm earnings rather than with the "agrarian revolution" often attributed to the spread of coffee, tea, and grade dairy cattle in the 1950s. In a study of two locations in Nyeri District, Cowen (1974:5) found that the interhousehold distribution of tea and milk sales became more equal between 1964 and 1971, and concluded that commercialization had strengthened the middle peasantry. Cowen's argument has been questioned, however, on the grounds that he looked only at the minority of farmers who own tea stumps and/or dairy cattle, ignoring the growing gap in income and wealth between those who owned such assets and those who did not (Kitching, 1980:365, 372).

It's true that less than half the farms in Central Province produced high-value tree crops: in 1974, coffee was grown on 45 percent of small farms in Central Province, and tea on 18 percent. However, tea and coffee were not the principal sources of cash income for most rural households. According to the first Integrated Rural Survey, sales of food crops accounted for 58 percent of the value of smallholders' agricultural output in the "coffee zone east of the Rift," and sales of export crops only 12.5 percent (Livingstone, 1986:179). In addition, cultivation of coffee and tea was not concentrated among the richest households. Over 30 percent of holdings between 0.5 and 5 hectares grew tea and coffee, compared to 10 percent of holdings of less than 0.5 hectare or more than 5 hectares in size. In addition, while households with annual incomes over 6,000 shillings owned more coffee bushes and tea stumps than those in lower income brackets, the disparity in trees owned was less than the difference in income levels (see table 6). This was also true for ownership of livestock units. In short, while the distribution of farm operating surpluses among all households became increasingly unequal between 1963 and 1974 (Livingstone, 1986:83,261), it does not appear that differential ownership of tree crops or dairy cattle was the primary source of this inequality.

Table 6. Smallholders' cultivation of export crops by size of farm, Kenya, 1974

	Percent of holdings with		
Farm size (ha)	Coffee	Tea	Pyrethrum
<0.5	10.2	8.3	6.2
0.5–1.9	32.9	26.9	8.8
2.0–4.9	30.7	32.1	8.6
>5.0	10.9	11.7	16.2

Source: Collier and Lal, 1986:133.

Rural inequality does appear to have been closely related to differential access of households and individuals to nonfarm income (Collier and Lal, 1984:1015; Haugerud, 1981a:22–24). According to the first Integrated Rural Survey, the poorest rural households derive over three-quarters of their income from off-farm sources (mainly remittances and wage earnings), and the proportion declines for higher income brackets (Livingstone, 1986:311–12). However, this does not belie the importance of nonfarm income as a source of savings for investment in education, as well as both agricultural and nonagricultural enterprises and assets (Haugerud, 1984:306, 337, 1989:73).

In northeastern Zambia, the benefits of increased agricultural sales have been unequally distributed, but differential access to off-farm income was also important, because the northeast became a major labor reserve for the Copperbelt. When the copper industry declined in the 1970s, many people were obliged to return to—or remain in—the rural areas. However, returns to farming were so low that most people continued to seek income from multiple sources. Both prosperous farmers and poor ones combined farming with trade and wage employment—if possible, in rural towns (Pottier, 1988:32ff.). Impoverishment has forced many, especially women, to "work for food," leading to increased wage employment and undermining the reciprocal character of traditional work groups (Pottier, 1988:84–85, 113ff.). In several Mambwe villages, poor people worked in groups on the fields of their prosperous neighbors in exchange for food, beer, cash, or access to a plough. In keeping with the rhetoric of "African humanism," such arrangements were often described as "cooperative." However, prosperous farmers did not reciprocate by working on the fields of their poorer neighbors. In effect, prosperous or influential farmers were exploiting the labor of their poorer neighbors in the name of traditional principles of collective cooperation (Pottier, 1988:126–37; see also Hedlund and Lundahl, 1983:71).

Agricultural wage employment reinforced as well as reflected differentiation between richer and poorer farmers in northeastern Zambia. Since most farmers grow the same crops, labor for others (whether remunerated in cash or in kind) often conflicts with work on one's own fields, and farmers who hire themselves out end up cultivating their own crops at less advantageous times. This has been a particular problem for farmers who grow hybrid maize, which tends to be sensitive to the timing of cultivation tasks (Gerhart, 1975:61; Pottier, 1988:125). The introduction of ox ploughs in the early 1980s also favored the relatively well-to-do. Larger farmers were the first to receive oxen, and were in turn able to cultivate larger areas, widening the gap between their holdings and those of the majority of their neighbors (Francis, 1988:38–39).

In all four cases, then, the distribution of income between farm owners and farm workers has fluctuated over time, as changing conditions in rural labor markets led to the renegotiation of wages and labor arrangements. In Ghana and Nigeria, as we have seen, agricultural wages rose in periods of expanding cocoa incomes, and laborers were able to negotiate better contracts. Thus, farm workers (family as well as hired) often shared in the gains from expanding cocoa production and sales. In central Kenya and northeastern Zambia, on the other hand, although the use of hired labor was more limited, differentiation among rural households appears to have been more pronounced in the long run.

Social Differentiation

Differentiation among rural households has occurred not only in response to the growth of agricultural production for the market, but also through the interplay of market forces and social relationships. Just as social networks and identities shaped struggles over access to land and labor and influenced patterns of labor control, so they have also played a role in processes of rural differentiation. To the extent that farmers mobilized labor through social networks, the terms of employment remained open-ended, subject to renegotiation in response to changes in social relations as well as market conditions. In practice, people of relatively low status and influence who lacked effective access to the means of negotiation might find that their share of rising agricultural proceeds lagged behind their contributions to increased output.[22] The point may be illustrated with reference to the positions of women and strangers.

The ambiguities of family and other network labor arrangements have often left room for considerable variation in "the degree of individual control" over farms (Hill, 1963:112). As we have seen, changes in patterns of household production for the market could lead to domestic tension. In Kenya, the division of labor between men and women "has become blurred" (Barnes, 1984:60), and the control of granaries and income from crop sales are often points of domestic contention (Fisher, 1954?:273–74; Stamp, 1975–76:32; see also Kitching, 1980:112; Mackenzie, 1986:124; Von Bulow and Sorenson, 1988: 176–77). Similar patterns of conflict have been noted in Zambia, Ghana, and Nigeria (Pottier, 1988:115–16; Geisler et al., 1985:12; Vellenga, 1983:147; Guyer and Idowu, 1991:266).

In struggles over the division of property, labor, and output, women frequently lost out relative to junior men, especially when returns to labor were tied to workers' ability to exercise influence within kin groups or other established social networks (Hill, 1963:116–17). In the cocoa economies of West Africa, women who worked on their husbands' farms without pay expected their husbands to contribute more to household expenses or give their wives money for trade when their cocoa farms began to bear. However, the extent to which wives were actually able to realize these expectations varied among women and over time (Vellenga, 1983:147; Abu, 1983:162ff.). Yoruba wives usually moved into trade or food processing rather than cocoa farming. Here, too, women were by no means assured of trading capital or other monetary rewards from their husbands, and often sought assistance from their own kin (Berry, 1985:95).

The open-endedness and negotiability of labor arrangements based on social relationships helped to make them as risky as taking part in an impersonal wage labor market: "all those assisting on farms who expected direct reciprocation *could* be disappointed" (Okali, 1983a:132; my italics). This was especially true when compensation for work done in the past became entwined with disputes over inheritance. In colonial times, matters of inheritance were left to the customary courts, where they were usually settled according to local interests rather than national statutes.[23] Even property which was individually acquired has tended to become family property in the long run and hence passes under the control of the individuals who wield the most influence within their family circles. Such influence is often concentrated in the hands of senior men. Over time, however, seniority has come to depend less on age, or success in farming, or local political affairs, and more on access to extra-local resources, through education, nonagricultural enterprises, or connections with the state.

In western Nigeria, for example, inheritance is patrilineal, with the children of each wife inheriting their share of their father's property jointly. Among siblings, authority customarily rests with the eldest brother, though practice varies from one family to another. In principle, daughters share equally in property inherited by a sibling group, but in practice, cocoa farms are usually controlled by men (Berry, 1988a:9). In Ghana, it has been argued that increasing numbers of farmers are transferring their farms to their children rather than their matrilineal heirs, in part because the former are more likely to have invested labor in the farm (Mikell, 1989:120ff.; Benneh, 1970:53). However, Okali (1983a:108) points out that individual sisters' sons are not assured of inheriting from their maternal uncles and may find it advantageous to work on their uncles' farms to strengthen their claims. After reviewing local court records in Asante and Ahafo, she concluded that most "conflicts did not arise from attempts to change the customary rules . . . but rather from the [existence of] multiple interests in farms" (Okali, 1983a:128).

Women who work on their husbands' farms are less likely than farmers' children or junior kin to retain access to them through inheritance. Neither Yoruba nor Akan wives customarily inherit from their husbands. In Ghana, women have sometimes claimed a share of their deceased husbands' cocoa farms on the grounds that they invested substantial amounts of labor in them, but have found it difficult to make their claims prevail over those of their children or their husbands' matrikin (Okali, 1983a:118ff., 136). For the most part, women's claims to inherited farms depend on their ability to exercise influence within their own kin groups. In some communities, cognatic ties were accorded considerable weight in court cases. In Ondo, for example, women appeared frequently in disputes over inherited farms and were by no means invariably the losers (Lloyd, 1962:298ff.).

Women have also encountered opposition when they tried to bequeath farms to their daughters, even when the farms in question were their personal property. Mikell (1984:203) has shown, for example, that although many Ghanaian women invested in cocoa farms, their farms were smaller on the average than men's farms and tended to pass into the control of men after their deaths, even when they specifically bequeathed them to their daughters (see also Okali and Mabey, 1975:17–18). In central Kenya, although women have provided a growing share of the labor on small farms, they have no claims to inherit land or farms which belong to their husbands. Some Kikuyu men have tried to prevent their wives from purchasing land on their own account (Mackenzie, 1986:392), and women who acquired land anyway—by purchase or from their own families—find that *mbari* elders oppose bequests to their daughters, fearing that the land will thereby be lost to the lineage as a whole (Mackenzie, 1986:401–3; see also Bukh, 1979:54).

There is some disagreement in the literature over whether or not strangers—migrants from other districts and/or ethnic groups—have also been systematically excluded from sharing in gains from agricultural commercialization. Migrant farmers have sometimes outdone locals in expanding production for the market (Hill, 1963:11, chap.7), and migrant workers have obtained better wages and working conditions in periods of expanding cocoa production and sales. What sets strangers apart from locals is not a systematic inability to gain access to land for permanent cultivation or find work on favorable terms when labor markets are tight. Rather it is that, like women, they often exercise less influence in local descent groups and other social networks and, accordingly, are vulnerable to demands for tribute or rent, or to threats of expropriation, based on their nonmembership in local descent groups. As we saw in chapter 5, such claims surfaced intermittently during the colonial period and afterwards in all of our case study areas.

In general, differentiation by social category served to reinforce the importance of networks as channels of access, encouraging members of disadvantaged categories to multiply their memberships and even to form their own groups. In all four of our case study areas, women maintain ties with their agnatic kin after marriage. They have also diversified their income sources, turning to wage labor or nonfarm employment in order to earn income independently of their husbands and other male relatives. In Ghana and Nigeria, the majority of rural wives engage in trade at some point in their careers (Galletti et al., 1956:558–59; Berry, 1985:91; Okali and Mabey, 1975:16), and it is becoming increasingly common for Kenyan and Zambian women to do so too (Pottier, 1988:147ff.; Mackenzie, 1986:515; see also Cowen, 1978).

Women also sought to create their own social networks, where they could enjoy the advantages of group membership without the disadvantages associated with their gender in kin groups and local polities. Women's traders' associations and savings clubs are ubiquitous in West Africa. In Kenya, women began to organize self-help groups in the 1960s, pooling their savings to buy fertilizer, cows, water tanks, improve their houses (Stamp, 1975–76:33ff., 1986:40; Thomas, 1985:174–76), and even to buy land, sometimes in direct defiance of their husbands (Mackenzie, 1986:402). In Zambia, Mambwe women sometimes joined nonreciprocal work groups on the farms of influential men, in order to get together with other women to exchange information on market conditions (Pottier, 1988:127).

CONCLUSION

Socioeconomic differentiation has not occurred uniformly across rural communities in Africa in the course of agricultural commercialization, but has varied from one locality to another. In the cocoa economies, the tendency for farms to become self-financing after a few years combined with prolonged periods of favorable market conditions to promote the use of hired labor and to permit large numbers of farm workers (family members as well as hired workers) to establish farms or other enterprises of their own. In other words, the spread of cocoa cultivation was associated with widespread, if modest, upward mobility—at least before the crises of the 1970s and 1980s. In Kenya and Zambia, on the other hand, where agricultural production for the market has been dominated by annual crops, farmers have made less use of hired labor. At the same time, however, the farming population has, over time, been increasingly divided into households (and/or individuals) with access to the means of accumulation and those without. Thus, in all four cases, processes of rural transformation diverged from the standard Leninist model, but they did so in different ways. In the cocoa economies of West Africa, extensive commercialization of agricultural labor relations was accompanied by considerable socioeconomic mobility—in contrast to the annual cropping systems of central Kenya and northeastern Zambia, where more pronounced differentiation was associated with more limited commercialization of agricultural employment.

Differentiation has occurred within households, kin groups, and communities as well as among them. Such differences may occur because of differential individual access to market opportunities or extra-local networks, or because some categories of people (women, strangers, matrilineal heirs) are unable to negotiate effectively for control over the fruits of their own labor. If such people are also less able to gain access to off-farm income and/or alternative networks, they tend to slide down the rural income scale over time (see, e.g., Sharp and Spiegel, 1985). At the same time, both processes of differentiation reflect the fact that social networks operate as arenas of individual mobility rather than closed corporate units of exclusive resource management and control, and that a person's economic status is not necessarily predetermined by his or her social identity.

Chapter Seven

Investing in Networks

Farmers' Uses of Income and Their Significance for Agrarian Change

OVER THE COURSE of the twentieth century, the growth of markets in rights to land, labor, and capital goods did not diminish the importance of social relationships for farmers' access to productive resources. Access to land and land-augmenting capital goods, in particular, has remained clearly linked to membership in descent groups, communities, and patron-client networks, and struggles over power or the delineation of network boundaries have contributed to the proliferation of claims on rural land. However, a growing number of farmers have found the same networks increasingly problematic as channels of access to labor. As the availability of labor through social networks declined, farmers who could not afford to hire in agricultural workers have often been obliged to farm alone.

In this chapter and the next, I discuss some of the implications of changing conditions of access for farmers' patterns of resource use and for the growth and structure of rural economy and society. Conditions of access have affected cropping patterns and methods of cultivation, as well as the organization of productive activity and farmers' uses of income. Partly because of the continued importance of social networks as channels of access to the means of production, many farmers have invested part of their income in maintaining or advancing their position within established networks and/or gaining entry into new ones. As a result, membership and status in social networks have influenced the organization of agricultural production, the level of agricultural output and sales, and the structure of social relations within rural communities.

In the present chapter, I describe patterns of investment in social networks and trace their implications for agricultural growth and rural differentiation. Investment in networks is taken to include all expenditures which influence people's social identity or status, whether or not farmers themselves label them as social investments. After considering the implications of such expenditures for the way networks are organized, I discuss how the changing roles of social networks as channels of access to the means of production have influenced processes of agrarian change in our four case study areas. Specifically, I argue that the effects of divergent trends in the significance of networks for farmers' access to land and to labor have varied from one rural economy to another, depending in part on variations in the way land, labor, and capital are combined in processes of agricultural production. In the following chapter, I turn to the implications of farmers' investments in social networks for changing methods of agricultural production and the impact of economic and political instability on agricultural performance.

INVESTING IN NETWORKS

In most African societies, social identity and status may be achieved as well as ascribed. Glazier's (1985:68) description of Mbeere, where "advancement through age grades occurred individually, depending . . . on particular events in the life cycle of individual age-set members as well as on distinctive individual capabilities" is widely applicable. "Particular events" include acts of expenditure. Funerals, marriages, naming ceremonies, and initiation rites create opportunities for individuals to gain respect and create obligations among their kin and neighbors by contributing food, drink, clothing, ritual offerings, and gifts. People's contributions to such ceremonies may serve, in turn, to reaffirm or advance their status within their families and communities and their ability to draw on the resources or support of the group in negotiating their own claims to productive resources.[1] This point was made in David Parkin's (1972) classic study of Kaloleni, a Giriama community near the coast of Kenya, where successful local accumulators spent lavishly on funerals and marriage ceremonies in order to demonstrate their commitment to local institutions of kinship and seniority. By doing so, they strengthened their ability to call on elders to testify on their behalf in disputes over rights to land and coconut palms (see also Berry, 1985:64–66, 78–79).

In addition to ceremonies, farmers have also invested in social networks by furthering the careers of kin and clients, and by contributing to community projects and organizations, such as cooperatives, home-town improvement unions, religious associations, and self-help groups. Outlays on the careers of dependents serve both to expand a person's following and to demonstrate his or her commitment to the networks which link them together. For example, by investing in schooling or apprenticeships for their children, farmers demonstrate their willingness and ability to provide for their dependents' future success. By doing so, they also strengthen their own claims to seniority and prestige (Berry, 1985:82).

Contributions to community groups and projects help to build networks as well as to enhance an individual's reputation for generosity and public mindedness. Self-help groups, cooperatives, and town improvement associations provide facilities in rural communities—schools, clinics, market stalls, warehouses, feeder roads—and may also serve as channels of access to opportunities and resources outside the local area. They also provide for the negotiation of local social and political relations. For example, rural self-help groups in Kenya (*harambee*) have mobilized both state and local resources to build hundreds of schools and clinics, but they also shape local politics. "People have different motives for contributing in *harambee* meetings, including dramatization of one's social status" (Njeru, 1976:34; see also Holmquist, 1984: passim; Lamb, 1974:60ff.). In both Kenya and Nigeria, farmers have even reorganized descent groups to serve as fund-raising or lobbying agencies for purposes of land registration or gaining access to extra-local markets and agencies, including the state (Glazier, 1985:183ff.; Haugerud, 1989:82; Coldham, 1978a:74; Berry, 1985:79–81).[2]

Even outlays on directly productive assets may influence people's standing in social networks. A particularly clear example is provided by the common practice in Ghana and Nigeria of building a house in one's ancestral community (Brokensha, 1966:58; Hill, 1963:190–91; Fortes et al., 1948:161; Berry, 1985:78). For farmers whose home towns are important urban centers, such houses may yield rental income, but many have been built in small towns or even villages where there is no rental market. In these cases, the role of houses as a form of symbolic capital is readily apparent. The houses may stand empty much of the time, but are always ready to receive their owners' dependents and guests—offering concrete testimony to the builders' commitment to kin and community and hence their right to make claims on the loyalty or resources of their relatives and compatriots (Berry, 1985:78, 181–82; Okali, 1983b:174).

If productive assets are owned or managed by a group of people, investment is likely to affect relations among them. In Bisa villages in Zambia, individual owners of cassava-pounding troughs organize groups of women who pound one another's cassava in turn in the same trough. Membership in a cassava-pounding group gives women access to others' labor and leverage over the men whose cassava they pounded. As manager of the group, the trough owner also plays a role in shaping social relations within the village. Village fission is common in Bisa, as in Bemba and Mambwe communities, and the viability of a rural settlement often depends on the headman's ability to keep his sisters in the village. Thus, a man may prefer to give a cassava trough to his wife, rather than run the risk that by forming a pounding group, a sister will gain enough independence to leave the village, thereby undermining his authority (Kapferer, 1967:39; see also Bond, 1987:174).

Similarly, in Ghana and western Nigeria, cocoa farms have typically become subject to multiple claims over time, thus serving as foci for the definition and renegotiation of social relations—as land has done since precolonial times. As Francis (1981:142) concludes in his study of land disputes in a small Yoruba town,

> debates about membership of kinship-based groups, the distribution of authority within families and lineages, the relationship of lineage segments to their shared resources and the relationship between lineages linked by marriage or cognatic kinship all frequently take place in the medium of disputes over land. Being the most concrete expression of such relationships of status and authority, control over land functions as a kind of coinage for more general and fluid social gains and losses.

Finally, expenditures on litigation may have a direct bearing on farmers' access to resources and can absorb substantial amounts of farmers' income.[3] In central Kenya, farmers have even sold land (or raised money by promising a share of the land they're awarded through adjudication) to pay the costs of land adjudication, including that of "feeding witnesses" (Njeru, 1976:21; see also Haugerud, 1981a:9; Glazier, 1985:256ff.; Mukaru Ng'ang'a, 1978:151). Where rural property disputes are settled outside of formal judicial proceedings, outcomes also hinge on relations among kin and neighbors, and increased competition over land and labor encourages investment in such relationships (Canter, 1978:262–66; Van Donge, 1985:71–72).

Farmers' investments have helped to maintain the salience of social networks as channels of access to productive resources, but neither networks nor their relationship to resource access and use have remained unchanged over time. Some scholars have argued that both the long-term commercialization of rural economic activity and the hierarchical structure of colonial and postcolonial governments (together with their penchant for governing according to written rules and formal administrative systems) have fundamentally altered the character of rural social networks in Africa. Thus, Colson (1971:211) has suggested that commercialization transformed Yoruba descent groups into "economic corporations dealing in land," while Chanock (1985:239) maintains that legalization brought an unprecedented degree of rigidity and hierarchy into African societies. Both tend to overlook the fact that with the growth and diversification of educational institutions, economic activities, and bureaucratic structures in colonial and postcolonial Africa, individual members of descent groups or communities have often participated differentially in wider spheres of exchange, influence, and social mobility. Differential participation has, in turn, created or widened social and economic differences within established social networks, as well as among them.

In Mbeere, for example, the rate at which individuals advance through age grades depends on their investment in seniority (Glazier, 1985:90ff.). Similarly, Yoruba farmers' investments in their children's education tends to enhance their own reputation as people who take care of their dependents and who therefore qualify as seniors who deserve respect (Berry, 1985:775ff.). However, education also gives farmers' children access to knowledge, income, and influence which often surpass those of their parents. Farmers' investments in education for their children thus tended to transform the meaning of seniority within established communities and descent groups. In both central Kenya and southwestern Nigeria, farmers' investments in culturally constructed values and social networks have served both to transform the meaning of social relations and to reinforce their importance for access to productive resources.

These processes are exemplified by the history of family rights to land in central Kenya. Both in the 1920s and again during the process of land registration, Kikuyu and Mbeere descent groups mobilized themselves to contest claims to land (see page 126 above). On the whole, courts and district officials have been sympathetic to people who claimed to be dispossessed by their own relatives, so that descent groups have continued to assert and defend their rights to "family land." However, the commercialization of transactions in land has altered the way descent groups define and organize themselves. Since the late 1920s, rights to family land have been allocated to those individuals who contributed to the costs of litigation. To raise money for litigation, descent groups have also defined their boundaries more widely, drawing in distant kin or even people who are not kin at all (Glazier, 1985:188–89). In effect, families sold shares in "descent coalitions" whose members were rewarded in terms of access to group resources according to their investment rather than their ancestry.

Internal mobility and permeable boundaries also leave room for considerable inequality within and among social networks. Such networks do not tend to redistribute resources equally among their members. Not only do individual members of networks gain or lose influence according to their individual successes or failures in mobilizing resources and followers, but culturally constructed categories of members may be systematically relegated to subordinate positions, which diminish their ability to contest rights of access vis-à-vis those of other network members. For example, in many rural areas, commercialization has been accompanied by the relative dispossession of women with respect to agricultural capital. Even in regions such as southern Ghana or central Kenya, where they play a major role in agricultural production, women have encountered difficulties in asserting claims to "family property," such as land or tree crops, which they have helped to acquire or create (Mikell, 1984:209–12; Okali, 1983a:118ff.; Vellenga, 1983:147; Mackenzie, 1989:102–4; Okoth-Ogendo, 1976:177–78).

Finally, as we have seen in previous chapters, the meaning of chiefly authority has been not only contested, but often redefined in the process of maintaining "community ownership" of land and other natural resources. In Ghana, chiefs who were too assiduous in collecting cocoa rents from strangers or levying their subjects to defray the costs of defending their own jurisdictional prerogatives in court sometimes lost their stools, while others parlayed such revenues into personal fortunes. In many areas, the basis for selecting chiefly successors also changed over time, with formal education and/or personal wealth taking on increased importance as qualifications for holding "traditional" offices (Dunn and Robertson, 1973:213; see also Berry, 1985:178–81, 1975:120–21).

But there have been counteracting pressures as well. While kin groups and communities have sometimes been inclined to close their "borders," limiting membership and narrowing the claims of subordinates in order to cope with growing scarcity, a person's ability to exercise influence through or within such groups has continued to depend on the size of his or her following. In the mid-1960s, Kay (1967:43) remarked that in northeastern Zambia, headmen's followings were rendered less stable by the growing availability of "new status symbols," such as education, church affiliation, and imported goods, which expanded "the means whereby a following can be acquired." In general, social networks have often been characterized by a tension between inclusive and exclusive strategies of recruitment and internal governance, which have helped to keep conditions of membership and status contested and negotiable. This, in turn, has contributed to the proliferation of rights in land and constrained farmers' ability to discipline family labor.

Differential participation in regional political and economic systems has also helped to keep network boundaries fluid and negotiable, and promoted individual mobility within them. Among Yoruba traders, for example, young men begin their careers by running errands and selling commodities for a senior kinsman. They receive no pay but may keep any profits they make over an agreed margin. As they gain experience and savings, however, they also begin to trade on their own account and, if successful, may eventually become completely independent traders, with clients and agents of their own (Eades, 1979:176–77; Peel, 1983:152–58; Berry, 1985:94). The mark of success, in this case, is to become an independent entrepreneur, rather than to contribute to the growth of a family firm.

In similar fashion, relatives or neighbors who pooled their savings to buy land for cocoa in southern Ghana subdivided it into individual plots for farming, rather than creating large, jointly managed plantations (Hill, 1963:47–48, 75–76). Communities may also encompass a great deal of internal movement. In northeastern Zambia, when households and villages split up, the inhabitants usually scatter, joining several new settlements, rather than moving as a group. In Kay's (1967:33) words, the Zambian "village is not a permanent social entity but rather an institution through which a large and varied company of people pass at different speeds." Much the same could be said both of the cocoa village where I worked in southwestern Nigeria, where turnover among the inhabitants was 60% between 1971 and 1978, and of the cocoa farmers' "ancestral" town, where every compound had a history of migration from somewhere else (Berry, 1985:46–47, 70–72). In short, many social networks resemble " 'life-term' social arenas" operating "in a mode which permits the reopening and renegotiation of issues after a period of time" (Moore, 1986: 275), rather than closed corporations which concentrate wealth and power by permanently excluding nonmembers and engaging in conclusive transactions.

The fluidity of social networks has made it possible for many people to multiply their social memberships over time. Social networks based on common educational backgrounds or occupational experiences, and shared religious beliefs or political interests have proliferated in colonial and postcolonial societies, but in joining them people have not abandoned their descent groups or communities of origin. In many areas, chiefs have retained power *de facto* in local political and judicial processes even when their authority has been abolished *de jure* (Van Donge, 1985:71–73; Pottier, 1988:100–1; Guyer, 1991:15–18). In western Nigeria, migrants maintained regular ties with their descent groups and home towns during absences of decades while at the same time becoming active in a wide array of occupational, community, and political groups in their communities of residence and employment (Berry, 1985:55–57). In the late 1960s, Kikuyu living on the outskirts of Nairobi were found to be more likely to spend recreational time with relatives, and to make them loans or gifts, than those living in a rural village on the opposite side of Kiambu. The great majority of the periurban residents were also active both in their *mbari* and in community organizations (Ferraro, 1970:12ff.).

To multiply their options in a rapidly changing world, Africans have created new networks as well as multiplied their memberships in existing ones. People often react to a worsening of their position in one social network by joining or creating others. In central Kenya, where their claims on descent group resources are extremely limited, women have made extensive use of the *harambee* movement to gain access to government resources, build local amenities, and undertake investment projects (Stamp, 1975–76:33–36, 1986:39–41; Thomas, 1985:174–76). In northeastern Zambia, women join work parties partly to gain access to other women's support and information about trading opportunities (Pottier, 1988:127). However, there are limits to individuals' energy and resources. Multiple memberships, like multiple enterprises, can be difficult to manage. Many local leaders devote prodigious amounts of time and energy to maintaining networks and assisting their followers (see, e.g., Barnes, 1984:82–85; Guyer, 1991:22). But even leaders' energies are finite, and most people's are largely taken up with struggling for a livelihood. Hence, most people shift their attention and resources from one network to another as circumstances demand.

Such diffusion of individual effort limits the degree to which any particular social network functions as an effective agent of collective action. Differential participation in extra-local political economies and the proliferation of memberships and networks have helped to keep networks operating as arenas of individual mobility and interaction, and to render social identities fluid and negotiable.[4] The fact that a group of people share, even cultivate, a strong sense of collective identity does not mean that they necessarily engage in collective action. In general, social networks through which people pursue access to resources and opportunities have not been consolidated into closed corporations, which act to exclude outsiders or stabilize their own internal hierarchies of authority, but instead continue to operate as arenas for individual mobility and accumulation.[5]

Contrasting Patterns of Agrarian Change

The significance of investment in social networks for patterns of agricultural production and rural differentiation has varied from one locality to another. In previous chapters, I argued that—despite historical differences in the way they were incorporated into wider processes of commercial expansion and political domination—the four rural economies discussed in this study experienced broadly similar patterns of change in the social organization of farmers' access to productive resources. However, while access to land and fixed capital goods remained closely linked to membership in social networks, access to labor has become increasingly individualized. Because land, labor, and capital are combined differently in different processes of production and exchange, the effects of farmers' investments in social networks have varied from one locality to another. In this section, I elaborate this argument by contrasting developments in the cocoa economies of West Africa with those which occurred in the predominantly annual cropping systems of central Kenya, northeastern Zambia, and (since the 1970s, when the terms of trade shifted in favor of food crops) in southern Ghana and western Nigeria as well. As we shall see, the differences between these two sets of cases may be traced not only to differences in cropping systems, but also to differences in regional economic histories and the way they framed debates over resource access and control.

The Dynamics of Cocoa Expansion in West Africa

In the cocoa economies of West Africa, family labor was especially important in the early stages of establishing a cocoa farm, before the trees began to yield enough income to cover the cost of hired labor. Once the trees had matured, cocoa farms became self-financing, and hired labor was substituted for the labor of farmers' wives, children, or other dependents. In both Ghana and Nigeria, the expansion of cocoa production gave rise to the growth of a rural labor market and widespread use of hired labor on cocoa farms (see p. 000 above). Family labor also remained important in the long run, but this did not occur as a consequence of farmers' investments in marriage, kin ties, and the accumulation of dependents. Rather it occurred because in both countries, market conditions were conducive to new planting over long periods of time, leading farmers to open up new areas for cultivation and drawing new groups of people into cocoa growing. During such periods of expansion, farmers relied on assistance from their wives and junior kin, and demand for family labor increased. In the early 1970s, for example, the areas in which Okali (1983a:52,57) found wives providing most of the labor on cocoa farms were also areas in which most of the cocoa trees were immature. In the older cocoa-growing areas, many farmers used hired labor, and women were much more likely to be engaged in trade (Okali and Mabey, 1975:16). Similarly, as their husbands' cocoa trees matured, Yoruba wives "graduated" from providing unpaid labor on their husbands' farms to self-employment in trade or processing (Berry, 1975:202).

More generally, although the expansion of cocoa production was largely dependent on farmers' access to family labor, it did not tend to reproduce a family labor supply. Between 1900 and the 1960s, market conditions for cocoa were relatively favorable, sustaining prolonged periods of increased planting. The sustained growth of cocoa output and income meant, in turn, that most farmers were able to assist the relatives who had worked on their farms to establish farms or other independent enterprises of their own. Even sharecroppers sometimes became farmers in their own right, and many hired workers were independent farmers who wanted to supplement their incomes by temporary wage employment (Berry, 1975:130–31; Robertson, 1987:70ff.). Thus, the growth of cocoa production was accompanied by considerable upward mobility: farm workers became farm owners, while farmers and their children diversified into nonagricultural occupations and forms of enterprise.

By the same token, while farmers invested in social networks both to gain access to land and labor for cocoa farming and to claim part of the resulting income or property, such investments did not reproduce traditional networks in unchanged form. Partly because of the occupational and socioeconomic mobility associated with cocoa production and the growth of income-earning opportunities outside of agriculture, and partly because of the fluidity and permeability of social boundaries and status, cocoa changed the ways in which people defined and participated in social networks. Changing patterns of participation, in turn, altered relations among members of social networks and, therefore, the significance of social memberships and identities.

I have already described how the significance of seniority in Yoruba descent groups changed as farmers' children surpassed their parents in education and income. In the literature on Ghana, discussion has focused on the issue of matrilineal versus patrilineal succession, rather than on the intergenerational effects of upward mobility among farmers' children. Specifically, several authors have argued that agricultural commercialization led farmers to bequeath property to their children rather than their matrikin (Adomako-Sarfoh, 1974:137–38; Okali, 1983a:8, 110; Benneh, 1970:53; Mikell, 1984:209ff.; Woodman, 1974:271–72; Migot-Adholla et al., 1990a:chaps.5, 7). However, a shift from matrilineal to patrilineal inheritance may also have generational implications. Since matrilineal heirs are frequently brothers rather than nephews of the deceased, a rising frequency of bequests to farmers' children may also betoken an intergenerational transfer of rural property. In other words, changing patterns of inheritance may also betoken changing relations of seniority within Ghanaian descent groups.

Gender relations also shaped and were affected by cocoa farmers' strategies of resource access and use. Yoruba women's advance from domestic/farm labor to self-employment in trade, processing, or handicrafts appears to have predated cocoa, but was certainly reinforced by the spread of cocoa cultivation. In Ghana, according to Mikell (1984:202ff., 1985:passim, 1989:121–22), many Brong women acquired cocoa farms during the 1920s and 1930s, but by the 1940s and 1950s, their farms had passed under the control of men through inheritance. Ghanaian wives also engaged in long, inconclusive struggles with their husbands or husbands' heirs over the farms they had helped to establish and, in the process, often lost control over income and property (Okali, 1983a: 118ff.; Bukh, 1979:65; Vellenga, 1983:147). After reviewing numerous court cases as well as informants' accounts, Okali pointed out that "all those assisting on farms who were expecting direct reciprocation could be disappointed" (1983a:132) and concluded that "overall . . . the economic rights of wives are not clear" (Okali, 1983a:136). In both Ghana and Nigeria, women's inability to assert claims to farms in the context of conjugal or lineal debate may help to explain their predilection for taking up nonfarm income-generating activities.

So far I have argued that while cocoa farmers invested in social networks to strengthen their access to productive resources, networks remained open, fluid arenas of individual maneuvering and negotiation. Although some people made quite a lot of money from cocoa growing and/or trade,[6] the expansion of cocoa cultivation did not lead to the formation of estates in which individuals (or corporate groups) exercised exclusive ownership rights over large, contiguous areas of cocoa trees. For one thing, most farmers lacked the capital to plant large tracts of cocoa at one time. Instead, they expanded their cocoa farms piecemeal, waiting until one became self-financing before starting another. Even in parts of southern Ghana, where companies of migrant farmers bought large tracts of land, these were subdivided into small plots or strips for cultivation. "Farmers with long 'land-sequences' spend much of their time travelling between their lands" (Hill, 1963:186), and many also diversified their portfolios by investing in nonagricultural enterprises (Hill, 1963:191–92; see also Berry, 1985:260–61).

In addition, because of the prolonged expansion of the cocoa economy and the openness of social networks through which people gained access to land and farms, the growth of cocoa farming hinged on the exploitation of upwardly mobile labor. Such exploitation depends on positive incentives, rather than the threat of dismissal. Farmers were able to exploit the labor of relatives and other subordinates not by threatening them with outright dismissal or dispossession, but by offering them future opportunities for independent accumulation. If conflict developed between a farmer and his or her laborers, the workers could usually find employment elsewhere, while the farmer was apt to be left with unweeded farms or unharvested crops. In such circumstances, the "sanction of the sack" was an empty threat. During the 1930s, when cocoa farmers' incomes fell sharply, laborers complained that farmers paid low wages or none at all (Austin, 1987:274; Grier, 1987:44). However, when market conditions improved again after 1945, demand for agricultural labor rose, and workers' bargaining power improved (Berry, 1975:138–39; Van Hear, 1982: 197ff.). Farmers continued to complain of labor scarcity and high costs into the 1970s and 1980s (Berry, 1985:88; Konings, 1986:202). In the long run, farmers' capacity to regulate or discipline their workers remained limited, in part because farm workers had other options.

These constraints on farmers' ability to control farm workers did not hold back the growth of cocoa production and income, however, because the productivity of a cocoa farm is not very sensitive to the precision or timing of cultivation tasks. For much of the year, a mature cocoa farm requires no labor at all, and there is little evidence that yields are especially sensitive to the timing of tasks such as clearing the undergrowth or spraying for pests. Harvesting is usually spread out over several weeks or even months, and leaves plenty of time in the day for other activities. Thus, cocoa farmers' profits did not depend on close supervision of farm workers' activities, apart from the perennial problem of monitoring labor at harvest time to guard against theft. To the extent that expansion of cocoa encouraged farmers to invest in family, community, or patronage networks in order to gain or preserve their access to land, labor and capital, these investments did not interfere with the effective management of cocoa farms.[7] At the same time, they probably facilitated accumulation and diversification by enabling farmers to delegate responsibility for individual farms and move from one enterprise to another (Berry, 1975:132–33; Hill, 1963:188–89).

Cocoa in Comparative Perspective

In rural economies where the principal cash crops did not become self-financing over time, and where farmers did not experience long periods in which market conditions and farmers' access to productive resources favored expanded crop production, the process of agricultural commercialization entailed different changes in patterns of resource mobilization, in relations of agricultural production, and in the distribution of gains from expanded peasant production for the market. In this section I will show how the significance of farmers' investments in social networks varied from one context to another by contrasting the process of expansion in the cocoa economies with (1) the history of farming systems in central Kenya and northeastern Zambia, and (2) developments which occurred in central Ghana and southwestern Nigeria in the late 1970s and 1980s, when farmers shifted from cocoa into food-crop production.

Central Kenya

Like Akan and Yoruba cocoa farmers in the twentieth century, Kikuyu who wanted to expand their farms and herds in the nineteenth century did so by opening up new land. Kikuyu pioneers recruited other men to follow them, as warriors and laborers, in exchange for access to land, protection, and sometimes wives. Young or propertyless men who followed such a "colonist" (Cowen and Murage, 1972:49–50; Cowen, 1978:13–14; Wambaa and King, 1975:202) contributed their labor for the provisioning and defense of a new settlement in exchange for the patronage of its head. Over time a successful follower might acquire wives, children, farms, and livestock of his own, thereby becoming increasingly independent and wealthy. In central Kenya, as in the cocoa farming areas of West Africa, junior men worked for their seniors in exchange for the opportunity to become socially and economically independent. In the process, new land was opened up for cultivation and grazing, and rural communities served as arenas through which people gained access to land and labor in order to engage in independent accumulation. In establishing new settlements, colonists often formed ties of affinity and kinship with their followers, although rural communities also contained many residents who were not related to the head. Settlement patterns were mobile (Ambler, 1988:32–43), and colonists and their followers did not necessarily retain close ties with the communities or kin they had left behind (Kanogo, 1987:26).

The first European settlers sought to co-opt Kikuyu colonization rather than curtail it. They encouraged Africans to settle on their land as squatters, offering them access to land for cultivation and grazing in exchange for labor just as African colonists had done in the past. In the Rift Valley, Europeans acquired such vast estates that Africans who followed them as squatters had virtually unrestricted access to land, and some accumulated even larger herds and followings than they had had in Central Province (Wambaa and King, 1975:2; Kitching, 1980:294–95; Kanogo, 1987:22, 26). As Europeans expanded their own farms and herds, however, they began to place restrictions on squatters, limiting their herds and demanding more labor from them as a condition for being allowed to remain on the land. With the onset of the depression in 1930, these pressures became acute, and squatters began leaving European farms, moving to other settler farms or to one of the African reserves in an attempt to escape increasingly onerous terms of employment (Bullock, 1974:38–42, 64–65; Kanogo, 1987:55; Furedi, 1989:54–55; Throup, 1988:110ff.).

During the late 1930s and the 1940s, increasing numbers of Kikuyu returned, more or less willingly, to Central Province, and tension over access to land in the Kikuyu Reserve became acute. The degree of tension was reflected in a sharp rise in land litigation (Cowen, 1972:62); the outpouring of Kikuyu testimony before the Kenya Land Commission (1934b:82–376); and growing tension between Kikuyu farmers and colonial officials over the extent of lands newly opened to Kikuyu settlement in the late 1930s and early 1940s, and over the terms on which farmers were permitted to use them (Throup, 1988:chap.6; Sorrenson, 1967:43, 82–84; Bullock, 1974:64–65, 83ff.).[8] Unlike migrant cocoa farmers in Ghana and Nigeria, who maintained close ties with their home towns even though they spent most of their adult lives on their farms, Kikuyu squatters who returned "home" in the late 1930s and 1940s were not always welcomed by relatives whom they had not seen for years, many of whom were short of land themselves. Far from providing channels of access to land and assistance to returning squatters, families were sometimes torn apart by conflict over rights to land (Njonjo, 1977:46).

The Swynnerton Plan, which was intended to forestall future rural rebellion and promote agricultural development by legalizing private land ownership, deliberately sought to create a rural proletariat through statutory and commercial dispossession. A number of Kikuyu were left landless after registration, but most of them left Central Province to seek land or employment elsewhere. Some acquired plots in resettlement schemes, which were set up at the time of independence to redistribute some former European estates to smallholders. Others moved to government-run squatter settlements (Mbithi and Barnes, 1975:34–36; Okoth-Ogendo, 1981:332), to semiarid lands, or to the cities. Thus, despite the dispossession of substantial numbers of people, the resident rural proletariat envisioned by Swynnerton did not emerge.

A further unintended effect of land registration was that it created new opportunities for descent groups to serve as channels of access to land. This occurred both through the process of adjudication which preceded land registration and through the way in which subsequent transactions in and disputes over registered land were actually handled. Adjudication was undertaken to determine who the legitimate owner(s) of a piece of land were, so that their "title" could be registered. Claims were based on customary law, which presumed that land within the reserves belonged to groups of people. Therefore, adjudication focused on ascertaining which group's claim to a piece of land was valid and, sometimes, which member(s) of a group were entitled to be registered as the owner(s) of the land (there was an arbitrary upper limit of five). Sales of land had taken place before registration, but were not clearly recognized under customary law, so even in the case of land which had already been purchased by individuals, the process of adjudication opened the door for the reassertion of group claims.

In attempting to make the most of this opportunity, many people resurrected ties of kinship or clientage which had long lain dormant, or even created them *ab novo*. As land adjudication proceeded in Mbeere, "genealogically unconnected [clan] segments [which Glazier calls "descent coalitions"] developed into kin-based corporations whose major *raison d'etre* is the control of land" (Glazier, 1985:181, 183). Because descent coalitions needed to raise money to pay the costs of litigation and to hire labor to demarcate boundaries and demonstrate effective land use, descent "alone will not guarantee to an individual member an award of land following successful litigation. Rather, a member's contributions of money and labor are essential if he is to secure land from the corporate group at the conclusion of the land reform program." (Glazier, 1985:183; see also Haugerud, 1989:79).

Despite the explicit language of the law, land boards and local courts continued to recognize family claims on land registered to individuals (Okoth-Ogendo, 1986:85). Official registration of land transactions, designed to allow the government to prevent "uneconomic" subdivision of holdings, was honored primarily in the breach, especially when land was transmitted to heirs (Coldham, 1979:617; Homan, 1962:10, 1963:50ff.; Okoth-Ogendo, 1976:82). Thus, rights to individual pieces of land proliferated through the very processes of registration and adjudication which were designed to consolidate them. Family rights were preserved in the name of privatization: descent groups, whose claims to land had been weakened by commercialization and growing land scarcity in the colonial period, reemerged after Mau Mau as important controllers of land access, and remained so despite the fact that land had been legally privatized.

However, in the face of continued increases in demand for agricultural land, the reconstitution of descent group control over land did not mean that everyone who belonged to a locally based family gained access to family land. During registration, customary tenants (*ahoi*) and people who were absent at the time of adjudication, or who lacked good contacts with members of the Land Adjudication Boards, often ended up with no land at all, whether or not they were related to those who became the registered owners (Njeru, 1976:18–19; Mukaru Ng'ang'a, 1978:163ff.; Sorrenson, 1967:213; Lamb, 1974:14; Kershaw,

1975–76:186; Haugerud, 1983:77). In 1976, 11.5 percent of the rural households in Central Province were landless (Collier and Lal, 1980:26).

Even after registration, *mbari* frequently invoked their collective interests in land in order to reduce or eliminate the rights of individuals who occupied subordinate positions within the family. This was especially the case for women. Traditionally, Kikuyu women did not own land, but married women were assured rights of access to land controlled by their husbands' *mbari* (Middleton and Kershaw, 1965:50; Leakey, 1977:170). By making land the property of individuals—usually men—registration made it legal for a man to sell his land, thereby depriving his wife of cultivation rights. Although women protested and the government took steps to protect their interests, in this—as in other matters pertaining to land—men have often been able to circumvent government regulations through political connections or control of their *mbari*. In the late 1970s, for example, after the government, at the behest of Charles Njonjo, enacted a measure requiring that family members assent in person to any sale of land by the head of the household, the number of land sales registered in Murang'a dropped from 1413 in 1979 to 923 in 1984. Mackenzie (1986:379, 1989:101) concludes that women's rights were strengthened by Njonjo's intervention, but it is also possible that men simply stopped registering sales in order to evade the new restrictions.

The relative dispossession of women, which was embodied in customary Kikuyu tenure and intensified by land registration, had different implications for the mobilization of agricultural labor in central Kenya than in West Africa. In the cocoa economies, as we have seen, women contributed labor to the establishment of men's cocoa farms in the expectation of a future return. In Ghana, many women sought to "cash in" their claims by establishing their own cocoa farms or claiming a portion of those they had helped to establish for their husbands. In practice, however, they were not very successful: as claims on farms multiplied over time, women had to defend their claims in social arenas (descent groups, customary courts) where men exercised more influence than women. As Mikell (1984:210–212) has shown, cocoa farms owned by women tended to fall under the control of men in the long run. In the older cocoa-farming areas, rural Akan women moved increasingly into trade and processing, as their Yoruba counterparts had done all along—profiting from the expansion of the cocoa economy by diversifying their economic activities rather than through investment in cocoa per se.

In central Kenya, the mobilization of labor for increased agricultural production for the market followed a different trajectory. Since early precolonial times, access to agricultural labor in central Kenya was organized primarily through conjugal and kinship ties. Women had no access to land except through their fathers or, after marriage, their husbands, so their labor on men's fields was assured. Unmarried girls helped their mothers with farming and domestic tasks; young men served as warriors and were mostly idle when not actually fighting (Leakey, 1977, vol.2:740–41). A crucial step in the process of Kikuyu colonization was for young men to marry, so that their wives could produce food supplies for the new community (Clark, 1980:362–63).

In the nineteenth century, married men cleared fields for their wives to cultivate, helped with some farm tasks, and often planted crops of their own on their wives' fields (Leakey, 1977, vol.1:172ff.). As the colonial economy expanded, both men and women spent increasing amounts of time working for Europeans. Many men migrated, voluntarily or under duress, to work for European employers in the White Highlands, in towns, or for the state. Large numbers of Kikuyu, especially women, also hired themselves out to work on coffee estates in Central Province (Cowen and Murage, 1972:42; Presley, 1986:107). However, most continued to cultivate their own farms as well.

As we saw in chapter 6, the growth of food-crop production for sale did not give rise to widespread demand for hired labor (as the expansion of cocoa production did in West Africa), partly because farmers' earnings from food-crop sales fluctuated too much from one season to another to enable them to hire in labor on a regular basis.[9] The only African farmers who were likely to be able to afford to hire labor regularly were those with large farms—such as the *athomi* described by Cowen (1978)—or those with regular sources of off-farm income. The majority relied on household labor, which was increasingly provided by women as growing numbers of men sought off-farm employment and children attended school. Most farm labor was provided by members of the farmer's household, and as more men sought off-farm employment in urban areas, a growing proportion of farm labor fell to their wives (Stichter, 1975–76:48–49; Fisher, 1954?:264–65).

The introduction of tree crops in the 1950s might have resulted in a pattern of agricultural expansion similar to that experienced in the cocoa economies of West Africa. When African farmers in Central Province were permitted to plant coffee and tea, demand for hired labor on smaller farms increased. However, the expansion of tree-crop cultivation in Central Province was limited by the scarcity of suitable land and, in the case of coffee, by planting restrictions which the government reinstated soon after independence, to comply with the quota set by the International Coffee Agreement in 1964 (Heyer and Waweru, 1976:342). By the late 1970s, hired labor still accounted for only about 10 percent of the total amount of labor performed on small farms (Collier and Lal, 1986:118). In addition, since the Cooperative Marketing Society purchased coffee from heads of households, most of whom were men, the women who actually managed most coffee farms did not control the proceeds, which may help to explain the limited use of hired labor on coffee farms.

Thus, as agricultural production for the market expanded, access to farm labor was negotiated primarily within rural households and, increasingly, between husbands and wives. To date, no researcher has attempted to trace in detail the history of debates over the division of labor between men and women on Kikuyu farms during the colonial period, although some contemporary observers noted that the issue was an ongoing source of domestic tension (Fisher, 1954?:273).[10] Land registration threatened to transform the basis for the exploitation of women's labor on household farms by making it legal for women to own land in their own right (Njeru, 1976:30; Mackenzie, 1989: 91). Whether or not the mobilization of descent coalitions to pursue land rights through adjudication was consciously designed to protect men's control of rural land, it usually had that effect. Few women were registered as land owners during the initial process of registration (Okoth-Ogendo, 1976:177–78). Moreover, continuing *de facto* control of registered land by the owners' *mbari* operated to prevent women from purchasing land and, often, from inheriting part of their fathers' subdivided holdings as well (Mackenzie, 1986:138, 380ff.). Some fathers have bequeathed land to their daughters (Mackenzie, 1986:403, 1989:102, 104), but evidently not in sufficient numbers to offset the growing tendency towards the dispossession of women through family control of land.[11]

In these circumstances, investment in descent-based and patronage networks has ensured continued access to rural land for many men, which they have used, in part, to perpetuate control over female labor. Through male outmigration, subdivision of land holdings, and rising rates of school attendance among farmers' children, the management of farms in Central Province has become increasingly individualized. For many rural women, the advantages of greater control over the organization of production have been offset by the increased burden of work (Abbott, 1974:63–64), and women face a continual struggle to muster the wherewithal to increase output and productivity on their farms. In the small-farm sector of central Kenya, investment in networks has not reduced the growing gap between those with access to stable incomes and assets and those who must rely primarily on their own labor in a lifelong struggle against poverty and insecurity.

Northeastern Zambia

Throughout the colonial period, opportunities for agricultural growth and commercialization were much more limited in northeastern Zambia than in either central Kenya or the West African cocoa economies, and the region remains poorer today. *Citemene* cultivation depended on access to flexible social networks. Preparation of a new field required substantial amounts of labor, which limited the amount of land that farmers could prepare at one time. Accordingly, it took several years for a husband and wife to accumulate a "full complement of gardens" (sufficient to maintain themselves and their dependents), during which time they relied on relatives for food and other necessities (Kay, 1964a:35ff.; see page 94 above). In addition, farmers needed access both to substantial areas of uncut woodland and to their established *citemene* fields, on which crops could be grown in rotation for several years.[12] Successful farming depended on the ability to locate fields so as to balance access to uncut woodland with continued access to established gardens, and to maintain a set of social relations through which labor and credit could be mobilized as needed.

Colonial administrators were more concerned with the administrative inconvenience of residential mobility and the environmental hazards of *citemene* cultivation than impressed with their agronomic advantages. Officials of both the British South Africa Company and the colonial administration spent a good deal of time trying to regroup the rural population into stable villages large enough to govern conveniently. Overall, village resettlement campaigns failed to create large, stable rural communities, but did prove highly disruptive to agricultural production. In effect, every time people were forced to abandon a *citemene* plot before the crop rotation was completed, capital was lost both to the farmer and to the agricultural economy. Thus, the colonial state undermined the traditional system of agricultural production and accumulation in northeastern Zambia just as thoroughly as in Kenya, although there were hardly any European settlers in the former colony. After the opening of the Zambian Copperbelt in the late 1920s, the destruction of agricultural capital brought about by efforts at village regroupment reinforced the region's growing dependence on labor migrancy as a source of income.

Access to land, labor, and credit continued to be negotiated through social networks, both kin- and nonkin-based, which were themselves reorganized (or newly constructed) as people's circumstances changed. Such networks were geared to individual mobility, both spatial and occupational, but by the same token, they left people vulnerable to aggregate fluctuations in income and employment opportunities, and to processes of economic and political differentiation. In the late 1930s, Richards (1939:269, chap. 15) noted the precariousness of people's livelihoods and the anxiety which attended decisions about agricultural production and investment in the Bemba villages where she worked. A new village was formed when people decided to follow (or join) an individual whom they judged able to mobilize a sufficient following to create a viable settlement—that is, one whose members could provide one another with the resources (principally labor and food supplies) to enable them all to farm successfully. Under both *citemene* and mound cultivation, farmers moved their field sites periodically, and people were continually reassessing the chances that a change of residence as well would improve their ability to increase or maintain production and to establish advantageous relationships.

Men who aspired to become village heads could do so only if they could attract sufficient followers to constitute a viable settlement. This placed a premium on establishing good relations with people who had followers of their own. A would-be headman might spend years living in temporary quarters while he tested various possible alliances, or move to an established village only to fail in his bid to become its headman (Harries-Jones and Chiwale, 1962:passim; Kay, 1964b:255–56). In such circumstances, women exercised considerable independence in choosing their own residential sites and could determine a man's ability to form a viable settlement (Watson, 1958:108; Harries-Jones and Chiwale, 1962:7–8). Since people lived in small, scattered settlements and moved fairly often, anyone contemplating a move usually had a number of options to choose from. This increased the tenuousness of any particular grouping or relationship of authority and encouraged people to invest time and resources in continually reaffirming or renegotiating a range of social relationships in order to keep their options open.

The tenuousness of rural settlements was associated with considerable uncertainty over farmers' access to labor. Colonial officials accepted as legitimate chiefs' rights to tribute labor (*umulasa*), but to collect it, chiefs had to keep their followers together, which was not always easy. Mobility and periodic renegotiation of settlement patterns militated against the consolidation of power over wealth and resources—whether by chiefs, headmen, husbands, households, descent groups, or communities—and also gave women leverage in domestic negotiations over control of labor and output (Richards, 1939: 110–11, 212–13; Harries-Jones and Chiwale, 1962:passim).

As in West Africa, claims on property tended to proliferate over time. In Yombe villages, "costly items such as grinding mills are often the focus of unresolved struggles between the agnatic collectivity and the individual" (Bond, 1987:174). By the same token, investments in social networks created (or reinforced) arenas of negotiation rather than corporate agencies of exclusive control. Disputes over property hinged on issues of seniority, and successful entrepreneurs avoided accusations of witchcraft by affirming their commitment to custom (Bond, 1987:175, 182ff.).

Richards did fieldwork in the mid-1930s, when employment opportunities in the mines and towns of the Copperbelt were limited (Parpart, 1983:47; Baldwin, 1966:84ff.), and the flow of cash into the northeast from migrants' remittances was correspondingly low. The revival of the mining industry in the 1940s ushered in a prolonged period of growth, leading to increased employment and flows of remittance income to the rural areas. Access to working capital, markets, and remittances continued to be negotiated through flexible networks. Challenging Watson's assertion that "Mambwe people adjusted to labour migration thanks to the permanency of their villages," Pottier (1988:70) concluded that "the majority of Mambwe villagers excel in their ability to move on from village to village" (1988:71) and that Mambwe villages are "continuously affected by processes of lineage dispersal and movement between villages" (1988:82). Hence, it is "unrealistic to want to assess rates of absenteeism for any particular village" (1988:82; see also Kapferer, 1967:7, 31ff.).

After independence, the Kaunda regime revived rural resettlement plans, arguing that stable villages were essential to rural development (Kay, 1967:1–3; Pottier, 1988:28), and also created a succession of new institutions for rural administration and development (see p. 000 above). The chief effect was to provide new nodes of network formation, which people adopted if they yielded new sources of wealth and opportunity or ignored if they proved ineffective—just as they activated or abandoned relationships with particular relatives, headmen, neighbors, and so forth as circumstances changed. Most villages ignored official exhortations to regroup, and although chiefs lost "all their formal powers" after independence, "unofficially they remained important arbitrators in the vital areas of land and headmanship" (Van Donge, 1985:70; see also Bwalya, 1979:97).

By the 1970s, rural commercialization was accompanied by increasing macroeconomic instability and, after the collapse of the world copper price in 1974, declining levels of income and employment outside of agriculture. Aggregate economic decline was compounded by Zambia's role as a frontline state in regional opposition to apartheid in South Africa and by increasingly chaotic management of the Zambian economy by the state (Wood and Shula, 1987:300–6). In this context, local social networks provided flexibility, but little gain. Though women were not necessarily left to farm alone, since more men were remaining in the rural areas (Pottier, 1988:44ff., 144), returns to farming were often so low that both men and women had to take time away from their own farms to trade or hire themselves out (Pottier, 1988:84). Increasingly, access to farm labor depended on access to regular sources of off-farm income. Such access enabled influential or prosperous farmers to exploit their poorer kin and neighbors through wage employment or under the rubric of "traditional" work groups (Pottier, 1988:122–23; Hedlund and Lundahl, 1983: 70–72; Cowie, 1979:62–66). Women's labor was also exploited within the context of household production. As Richards observed in the 1930s, women's exploitation often manifested itself in children's hunger. However, whereas in the 1930s, rural poverty was associated with the decline of migrants' remittances and the absence of opportunities for agricultural development, in the 1980s it was the children of commercial farmers who sometimes went hungry because their mothers were too busy working behind the plough to feed them (Geisler et al., 1985:104; Moore and Vaughan, 1987:536–38).

West Africa after Cocoa

The distinctiveness of the process of agricultural growth and commercialization which developed in the cocoa-farming economies of Ghana and Nigeria is underscored by the way the "cocoa dynamic" dissipated after the terms of trade shifted decisively in favor of food crops in the 1970s. As we have seen, cocoa did not leave a legacy of family estates or corporate farm enterprises which could be redirected towards other kinds of agricultural production and investment. In the 1970s and 1980s, when returns to cocoa declined and prices of food crops rose, most farmers were not able to mobilize family labor for food-crop farming as they had for the establishment of new cocoa farms in the past (Konings, 1986:117–20; Tabatabai, 1988:720–21). Instead, they had to rely on the market—which was possible only for people with large farms and/or a steady source of off-farm income—or on their own efforts.

In addition, most food crops require peak periods of labor input and/or more precise timing of cultivation tasks than does cocoa. (Cassava, which can remain in the ground for up to two years after maturation without deteriorating, is a major exception.) Farmers who rely on others' labor to cultivate food crops must therefore supervise them more closely than is necessary with cocoa. This means spending more time on the farm and, in the case of family or other "network" labor, more time in maintaining the relationships through which labor is recruited or controlled. Both are difficult to do in a declining economy. In a recent study of multicrop farms in Ibarapa Division of Oyo State, Guyer (personal communication) encountered some moderately prosperous male farmers who were heavily involved in local affairs and hence engaged full-time in maintaining networks of social relations in the rural community. These men were able to rely almost entirely on family and client labor to work their farms. However, they were in the minority. Women and men whose other income-earning or domestic activities interfered with their farming relied on hired labor or, if they could not afford it, cultivated their farms themselves. Large commercial farms used hired workers, although even chiefs found it difficult to control them, but the majority of farmers have been obliged to rely on their own labor.[13]

In short, while people continue to invest in networks as potential mechanisms of access to land, influence, and nonfarm income, these play less of a role in access to farm labor than they did when cocoa production was expanding. In the food-crop economies which have recently developed in Ghana and Nigeria, as in the older ones of central Kenya and northeastern Zambia, farmers' choices of crops, techniques, and investments have been shaped by the growing necessity of self-reliance.

CONCLUSION

Since early colonial times, African farmers have gained access to productive resources through social relationships as well as market transactions. The continued importance of social networks for resource access has led to the proliferation of claims on fixed assets such as land, tree crops, or cleared fields, and people's ability to exercise such claims has depended on their ability to wield influence in a variety of social arenas. Property rights have remained subject to renegotiation and multiple claims, rather than converging towards private ownership by individuals or by closed corporate groups.

The proliferation of claims on property and the negotiability of social identities reinforced the dynamic character of relations within social networks and the permeability of their boundaries. People could alter their positions within a particular network or shift their energies and attention from one to another as circumstances and their own resources changed. This gave farmers considerable flexibility to adjust their productive activities in response to changing opportunities and encouraged them to proliferate memberships in social networks. It also meant that membership in a particular network did not determine the way in which individuals participated in economic or political activities. Members of the same household, lineage, community, or status group often pursued economic opportunities independently of one another and experienced different patterns of changing income or wealth. Socioeconomic differentiation was as likely to occur within kin groups and communities as between them.

Although families remained the predominant source of labor on small farms, membership in a descent group, a community, or even a household did not guarantee farmers access to the labor of other members; it only influenced the terms on which such access might be negotiated. Differential status within a network conveyed different advantages in the negotiation of terms of employment, and members' relative positions were frequently altered by differential participation in the wider political economy. Husbands' access to the labor of their wives, parents' access to the labor of their children, and patrons' access to the labor of their clients all tended to vary with changing patterns of individuals' access to jobs, markets, contracts, education, and so on, and with their ability to use ties to one network to influence their position within another. Over time, farmers came to rely increasingly on their own and/or hired labor.

These divergent trends in the role of social networks as channels of access to land and labor had different implications for patterns of agricultural change in different local economies. In Ghana and Nigeria, the growth of cocoa production gave rise both to widespread use of hired farm labor and to a high incidence of modest upward mobility among both farmers and farm workers. In the predominantly food-crop producing economies of central Kenya and northeastern Zambia, agricultural employment has been both less commercialized and more differentiated along lines of gender and class. Both patterns diverge from the standard Leninist paradigm of the spread of capitalism to the countryside. In West Africa, commercialization of farm labor occurred without agricultural class formation; in central Kenya and northeastern Zambia, where the commercialization of agricultural employment has been more limited, rural differentiation has been more pronounced.

Chapter Eight

Time Is of the Essence

Intensification, Instability, and Appropriate Technology

THE LITERATURE on technical change and agricultural development in Africa poses something of a conundrum. On one hand, many of the classic studies of African farming systems argue that, in the long run, agricultural intensification is necessary and inevitable. While forms of intensification may vary among agroecological zones, sooner or later population growth, urbanization, and agricultural commercialization will lead farmers to cultivate land at more frequent intervals and/or for longer periods of time (see, e.g., Ruthenberg, 1980; Allan, 1965; De Schlippe, 1956; Kowal and Kassam, 1978; Mortimore, 1989). At the same time, as both economists and agronomists have pointed out, increased productivity requires that more labor and/or capital be applied to each unit of cultivated land. Constraints on farmers' ability to mobilize resources therefore limit their capacity to intensify farming methods.

In practice, as we have seen, most African farmers find it difficult to mobilize both capital and labor. Capital is scarce in rural areas of Africa: the majority of farmers are poor, government subsidies are limited, and those which are available are channeled to a minority of already prosperous farmers. Historically, labor has also been scarce relative to land. In the colonial period, both commercialization and government policies designed to "force out" cheap labor for Europeans' use drew people out of smallholder agriculture and raised the costs of agricultural intensification (Ruthenberg, 1980:365). In postcolonial times, labor scarcity remains one of the principal constraints on expanding agricultural output.[1] Many observers have concluded that agricultural intensification is necessary but unattainable for the great majority of African farmers.[2]

If the logic of agricultural intensification in Africa is problematic, so are its implications for development strategy. Since labor is the scarce factor of production, some economists have argued that sustained agricultural growth will require mechanization (Jahnke and Ruthenberg, 1985:84; see also K. Hart, 1982:158ff.; Eicher and Baker, 1982:146–50). Others point out that for the most part, neither African farmers nor their governments can afford to mechanize, and they suggest that Africa's best hope of agricultural progress lies in the transfer or adaptation of Green Revolution technology (Jahnke et al., 1987:105–6). In practice, however, governments' efforts to promote mechanization or Green Revolutions have not been very successful. From the well-known failures of the late colonial period—such as the Niger Agricultural Project, the Tanganyika Groundnut Scheme, or mechanized farming projects in the Gambia—to recent donor-financed schemes in northern Ghana, Nigeria, and Sudan, mechanization projects have contributed little to either aggregate output or rural living standards (Baldwin, 1957; Lawrence, 1986; Webb, 1984; Shepherd, 1981; Pearson et al., 1981; Haswell, 1975). Moreover, despite more than twenty years of internationally funded adaptive research, Africa has yet to experience a Green Revolution. The cost of irrigation, which is essential for successful cultivation of many high-yielding crop varieties, is higher in Africa than anywhere else in the world (FAO, 1986:42; Pearson et al., 1981:411, 414, 418–22; Von Braun et al., 1989:30). Farmers continue to grow traditional crops, ignore recommended combinations of inputs and cultivation practices, and leave irrigated perimeters undersubscribed, even when inputs and irrigation facilities are subsidized by outside donors of the state (Richards, 1985:39–40; Jones, 1983:1049; Carney, 1988:336; Carney and Watts, 1990:222).[3]

Since most mechanization and irrigation schemes have been managed and/or heavily subsidized by the state, African governments have received much of the blame for their failures. Projects and their managers have been taken to task for everything from poor engineering design and inappropriate technology to inadequate economic planning and failure to provide farmers with adequate incentives and support services to permit widespread adoption of improved techniques. In general, the literature argues repeatedly, if somewhat inconsistently, for less government interference in the workings of the market *and* for the funding of new programs of mechanization, water control, or planned technological improvement (Webb, 1984:127ff.; Binswanger et al., 1987:chap.8; Hart, 1982:72–73). Such inconsistencies belie claims for an official and scholarly consensus on the causes and remedies for Africa's economic problems (Berg and Whitaker, 1986:1; World Bank, 1981:chap.4) or suggest that, at best, it rests on a contradictory view of the state as both a condition for and an impediment to agricultural development.

In the preceding chapters, I have argued that changes in African agricultural production have been shaped, over the course of the twentieth century, by many-layered struggles over access to resources, in which neither direct producers nor governments have exercised a decisive influence on patterns of production and investment. Resource acquisition has been influenced by ongoing debates over the meaning of claims to resources and the legitimacy of rights to define and enforce them. Such debates have influenced not only the terms on which farmers gained access to land, labor, and capital, but also the structure and dynamics of rural social relationships in general and the organization of agricultural production in particular. Consequently, as I will argue in more detail below, issues of agricultural intensification and the design of "appropriate" technology cannot be reduced to a question of changes in relative factor proportions. Instead, changes in agricultural technology must be understood in relation to changes in the organization of agricultural production and specific regional configurations of economic, political, and social change.

RESOURCE ACCESS AND RESOURCE USE: REPRISE

Since the beginning of the colonial period, or before, African farmers' access to land and land-augmenting capital (such as cleared fields or tree crops) has been mediated, in part, through their membership in social institutions ranging from the family to the nation. However, definitions of social identities and their practical significance for resource access and use have been contested and ambiguous—partly because of colonial strategies of "indirect rule" and independent African governments' strategies of political mobilization. Beginning in the 1930s, colonial and postcolonial governments constructed increasingly elaborate legislative and administrative programs to restructure farmers' incentives, redefine property rights, and reorganize local structures of authority. In practice, such interventions served to create additional channels of institutional membership and access to resources, which were superimposed on existing ones rather than superseding them. Membership and status in descent groups, voluntary associations, and communities of origin have remained salient but contested grounds for claiming access to land and land-augmenting forms of capital, such as tree crops or cleared fields.

In these circumstances, farmers have invested in establishing or reinforcing social identities and status in order to maintain or increase their access to productive resources. Like increased government controls, such investments acted not to transform rural social networks into closed, corporate structures of exclusive control, but rather to maintain them as arenas of social mobility and interaction. Consequently, property rights have remained subject to multiple claims and periodic renegotiation.

Farmers have also mobilized agricultural labor through social relations such as marriage, parentage, seniority, and patronage, and divisions of labor and output have been continually renegotiated in the course of rural commercialization and political centralization. However, the outcomes of such negotiations have varied with changes in individuals' access to alternative sources of income and employment. Frequently, individual members of descent groups, communities, and other rural networks have participated differently in wider circuits of employment and exchange, and the results of struggles over agricultural labor have varied accordingly. Such variations served, in turn, to reinforce the fluidity of social institutions and limited the extent to which power over labor and output has crystallized in the hands of a single dominant class. Thus, the division of agricultural labor has been determined by myriad local and domestic struggles, whose outcomes were shaped both by culturally constructed idioms of authority and obligation, and by people's changing patterns of participation in wider processes of economic and social change. In the process, African farmers have been obliged to place increasing reliance on their own and/or hired labor.

However, access to hired labor requires working capital, which many farmers lack, and control over their own time may also be problematic. Attempting to strengthen their hand in ongoing negotiations over access to land, capital, and labor, many farmers have diversified their social and economic portfolios. But diversification places competing demands on farmers' own time and limits their access to the labor of dependent kin and other social subordinates, who also spend increasing amounts of time in school or off-farm employment. Thus diversification has reduced the access of poor farmers to other peoples' labor and intensified their struggles to stretch their own time and energy over a growing number of activities. Even for well-endowed farmers with ready access to credit or capital, money is not necessarily time: both African elites and foreign investors have found agricultural labor to be scarce, expensive, and difficult to control. Increasingly, therefore, farmers seek out patterns of production and social interaction which allow them additional flexibility in allocating their time among alternative undertakings.

The importance of flexibility in the management of agricultural production and other income-generating activities has been underscored in recent years by the increasing instability of the economic, political, and environmental conditions under which African farmers live and work. Like their choices of cropping patterns and methods of cultivation in the past, farmers' strategies for coping with recent increases in instability have been shaped by the ongoing dynamics of resource access and control. Instability places a premium on flexibility: to cope effectively with a volatile economy, farmers need to be able to make changes in their productive and income-earning activities on short notice. In poor countries, where working capital and purchased inputs are scarce or unobtainable, flexibility often boils down to a question of farmers' ability to control the use of their own and others' time. However, as I have argued in previous chapters, African farmers' ability to exercise such control appears to have declined over the course of the twentieth century.

In the following pages, I explore the implications of long-run changes in conditions of resource access and recent increases in economic and political instability for understanding trends in cropping patterns and methods of cultivation, and for the development of appropriate technology for African farmers. Section 2 argues that past trends in cultivation practices can be explained, in part, by taking account of how farmers gain access to productive resources and how conditions and strategies of access affect the organization of production. Section 3 relates changing conditions of resource access and control to the impact of economic and political instability in the 1970s and 1980s on African farmers and farming systems. Finally, section 4 discusses the growing importance of time as a constraint on agricultural production and argues that, in defining and developing appropriate technology for African farmers, it is important to take account of the sequences as well as the proportions in which inputs are combined in the process of cultivation.

THE VAGARIES OF AGRICULTURAL INTENSIFICATION: SOME HISTORICAL EXAMPLES

Generalizations about the importance of intensification in African agriculture have frequently been based on an uncritical use of synchronic evidence. Writing of upland rice, for example, Binswanger et al. (1987:28) assert that "the movement [sic] from forest fallow to annual cultivation is associated with an increase in total labor input per hectare from 770 hours in Liberia to 3300 hours in Cameroon." In reviewing evidence on agricultural production for forty-eight localities, Binswanger et al. did not encounter "any sparsely settled populated areas under annual cultivation or very densely populated areas under forest fallow or bush-fallow systems" (Binswanger et al., 1987:4,52), and they therefore conclude that population growth has been the principal cause of agricultural intensification.

The pitfalls of using synchronic evidence to make inferences about change over time may be illustrated by reference to Lagemann's classic study of farming systems in southeastern Nigeria. Through meticulous fieldwork in three villages, Lagemann documented the existence of three major field types and showed that within each village, the intensity of cultivation was lower the greater the distance between a field and the farmer's dwelling. Yields on intensively cultivated compound gardens were up to three times higher than yields on "distant" fields—largely because of differences in cropping patterns (Lagemann, 1977:93). He also found that average yields were lower in villages with higher levels of population density (Lagemann, 1977:59). Lagemann concluded that the "highly productive multi-storey cropping systems on the compounds" represented "emerging systems" which slowed but did not reverse the "degradation process" resulting from increased population density (Lagemann, 1977:117).

Lagemann did fieldwork in 1973–74, when the southeast was still recovering from the effects of the Nigerian civil war, and many people depended on farming for the bulk of their income. Ten years later, after a decade of massive oil revenues, a researcher from the International Institute of Tropical Agriculture in Ibadan found that the practice of intensive compound gardening had declined significantly (Latzke Begemann, 1985). Her results suggest that many compound gardens were established to cope with the extreme conditions of insecurity and food shortages which prevailed during the Nigerian civil war, rather than representing the latest stage in an evolutionary process of agricultural intensification.

Direct historical evidence also shows that agricultural intensification has been neither inevitable nor irreversible in sub-Saharan Africa. Archaeological findings at Engaruka (in northern Tanzania) and Inyanga (in eastern Zimbabwe) suggest that cultivation was more intensive in the seventeenth and eighteenth centuries than at any time during the twentieth (Sutton, 1984:35, 39). In central Nigeria, northern Cameroon, and northern Tanzania, farmers shifted from intensive to extensive farming when the end of wars or slave raids permitted them to descend from easily defended hilltop settlements to farm in the plains below (Netting, 1968:193ff.; Feierman, 1974:172; Boulet, 1975:23–24). In the lower Tchiri Valley of Malawi, cultivation methods increased and declined in intensity several times between 1860 and 1960, according to changes in the level of water in the river, variations in market opportunities for different crops, and shifts in government policies (Mandala, 1990:chaps.3–5 especially).

Variations in the pace and/or direction of agricultural intensification are occasioned not only by exogenous events, such as war or peace, drought or flood, but also by changes in the production dynamics of particular crops. Cultivation of tree crops, for example, has not automatically increased "whenever remunerative markets are available" (Binswanger et al., 1987:42n, citing Ruthenberg, 1980:45). As I argued in chapter 7, the prolonged expansion of cocoa cultivation in Ghana and Nigeria from the 1890s to the mid-1970s was probably facilitated by the fact that cocoa yields are not very sensitive to the timing of labor inputs, so that accumulation (in the form of additional bearing farms) did not depend on tight labor control. In other words, cocoa cultivation could expand over long periods of time *despite* the fact that agricultural labor was relatively mobile, spatially and socioeconomically. The flexibility which cocoa accorded farmers and farm workers was also conducive to diversification of farmers' own income-earning activities. Thus, the agronomic requirements of cocoa proved to be well suited to an expanding and diversifying rural economy in which farm owners and farm workers were both upwardly mobile.

Another crop whose spread in Africa is due in part to its inherent agronomic flexibility is cassava. Aggregate data on trends in cassava production are notoriously unreliable, but numerous local studies indicate that the production of cassava has expanded, both absolutely and in relation to other staple crops, over the course of the twentieth century (Phillips, 1983:84–86; Adam, 1980:5; Fresco, 1986:145; Martin, 1984:422–24; Newbury, 1984:37). In part, this is attributable to ecological factors: compared to other root crops and many cereals, cassava is more resistant to drought and tolerant of poor soils (Cock, 1985:18). Some authors have suggested that cassava is relatively labor-saving as well (Cock, 1985:56–57; Fresco, 1986:144–45). However, most cassava grown in Africa is toxic, as well as highly perishable, and must be processed before it is sold or consumed. When processing labor is taken into account, it is not clear that cassava requires significantly less labor than other staple food crops (Adam, 1980:20ff.; Oyewole et al., 1986:13).

However, the labor requirements of cassava cultivation *are* very flexible. Apart from planting, which must take place far enough in advance of the end of the rainy season for the stakes to sprout properly, variations in the timing of inputs have little effect on yield (Fresco, 1986:145). In particular, mature cassava roots can remain underground without deteriorating for long periods—up to twenty-four months for some varieties (Goering et al., 1979:19–20). Thus, farmers have a great deal of leeway in managing the harvest and sale of cassava. The crop may be harvested little by little, for immediate consumption or for sale to meet short-term needs for cash. Alternatively, farmers may wait for a favorable price, then harvest the crop all at once. In other words, cassava is well suited to both subsistence and commercial farming, on either a small or a large scale.

Because of its flexibility, cultivation of cassava has often increased when farmers' ability to mobilize labor or control the timing of their own activities declined (Berry, 1986:36). In northeastern Zambia, cultivation of cassava increased both in response to exogenous factors, such as labor migration and settlement controls, which disrupted farmers' access to land and labor, and as a consequence of increased demands on the labor of individual cultivators. Long-term changes in resource access and cultivation methods led women, in particular, to spend more time weeding and walking to distant fields (Geisler et al., 1985:13). Often they found that, compared to traditional cereal crops such as millet and sorghum, cassava gave them more flexibility to accommodate these other activities. Also, women who were obliged through poverty or lack of access to male labor to work for food may have found it easier to combine off-farm employment with cultivation of cassava than with more exacting crops such as millet or maize.

Farmers' search for flexibility has affected cultivation practices as well as cropping patterns. In Nigeria and Sierra Leone " 'traditional' intercropping strategies help flatten out the labour input profile" of individuals' farms (P. Richards, 1985:68; see also Olayemi, 1976). The same is true for farmers in Sierra Leone who cultivate both swamp and upland rice fields (P. Richards, 1985:68, 77).

The advantages of flexibility may also help to explain why, in some areas, farmers have intensified cultivation in the face of increasing labor scarcity. In the Kwango-Kwilu region of Zaire, for example, rates of male outmigration have been high for many years (Fresco, 1986:91). As adult men migrated out of the rural areas in search of employment, women were obliged to clear fields as well as cultivate them. To minimize the extra work, women cleared fields by burning them and also cultivated the same fields at more frequent intervals, thus reducing the length of fallow. Frequent burning promotes weed growth, however, so that women have had either to devote more labor to weeding or to settle for lower crop yields. To offset declining yields, women planted more cassava. They also cultivated larger fields and/or opened new ones on plateau lands where soils were poorer than on the slopes and valley bottoms (Fresco, 1986:121,208).

Labor inputs on the plateau fields were minimal: few women bothered to make ridges or dig in compost, and they rarely visited the fields between planting and harvest times. Plateau fields were cultivated partly to meet requirements of the government's compulsory cultivation program, partly as a fall back in case their other fields performed poorly.[4] As a result of these changes, formerly distinct forest and savannah fields have converged toward a common, amalgamated field type, in which savannah crops (cassava and groundnuts, but little or no maize) are combined with "forest methods of cultivation," which do not involve ridging or composting. In a further effort to gain flexibility, women farmers of the Kwango-Kwilu have also staggered both planting and harvesting times of cassava and other crops (see also Richards, 1987:86 ff.). Fresco (1986:107) concludes that "notwithstanding serious [economic] constraints at regional and national levels, . . . food production in the Kwango-Kwilu has increased considerably since the 1950s . . . because of the remarkable *flexibility* of present farming systems."

Similarly, the intensification of farming methods in northeastern Zambia may have occurred in response to increasing constraints on farmers' time, rather than growing scarcity of land. Intensification took several forms: shifts from small- to large-circle *citemene*, the substitution of mound cultivation for *citemene*, and increasing reliance on cassava (see, e.g., Peters, 1950:74–77; Trapnell, 1953:36–38).[5] *Citemene* fields can produce a variety of crops and relatively high yields, but are not very flexible. At any given time, farmers have a good deal of capital (literally, in this case, congealed labor) tied up in cultivated fields at different stages of one or more crop rotation cycles. A farmer who abandons a plot before the crop rotation cycle is finished stands to lose part of the returns to the investment in the farm. In the 1930s, although rural settlements split up and people relocated at frequent intervals, most farmers moved within a limited radius in order to retain access to established *citemene* fields (Richards, 1939:278). When a village split up for nonagricultural reasons, such as illness, quarrels, or the death of a headman, farmers often suffered economic losses. As people were relocated, through labor out-migration or village regroupment, the likelihood of such losses increased.

In contrast to *citemene*, mound cultivation, in which soil fertility is enhanced by composting, is easier to start and stop on short notice. Mound cultivation is more intensive than *citemene*, and can be carried out on grassland or on fields which have been left fallow for only a short time, as well as on established *citemene* fields. By curtailing people's ability to choose their own location, village regroupment and labor out-migration increased the difficulties of successful *citemene* cultivation and led farmers to rely more on composting, even though this resulted in lower yields, especially of millet.

Increased reliance on mound cultivation also altered agricultural labor patterns. Preparing a field of composted mounds is a laborious undertaking, though less so than the preparation of a *citemene* plot. However, in contrast to *citemene*, which suppresses the growth of weeds, composting promotes it (Svads, 1983:265). Since weeding is usually considered women's work, increased reliance on composting has meant an increase in the proportion as well as the amount of agricultural labor performed by women (Geisler et al., 1985:13; Pottier, 1988:170). In addition, the shift from *citemene* to composting was sometimes accompanied by the spread of cultivation patterns, such as millet monocropping, which further increased the amount of labor needed to weed a given field (Potter, 1988:22).

As these examples suggest, agricultural intensification has been neither inevitable nor continuous in African farming systems. In some areas, intensification was halted or reversed by changing environmental or political and economic conditions; in others, it has occurred not as an adaptive response to population growth or commercialization, but in the face of growing labor shortages and declining commercial activity. Such cases underscore the importance of studying farming as a dynamic social process. As farmers contend with shifting social as well as environmental conditions, changes occur not only in what is produced and how much, but also in when work is done and by whom. Thus, changes in cropping patterns and methods of cultivation are influenced by social factors which govern the timing as well as the amounts of labor devoted to farming, as well as the control of effort and output.

COPING WITH CONFUSION: FARMERS' RESPONSES TO ECONOMIC INSTABILITY IN THE 1970S AND 1980S

In the 1970s and 1980s, the economies of sub-Saharan Africa experienced a series of shocks—including severe drought, war, large fluctuations in world oil prices, global recession, and declining export prices. The combination of world recession, mounting external debt, and increasingly depressed conditions within African economies undermined investors' confidence, contributing to a vicious cycle of declining private foreign capital inflows which, together with stagnant or decreasing export earnings, forced African governments to borrow more from official sources and, at the same time, reduced lenders' willingness to meet their needs (Helleiner, 1986a:146; 1986b:87). By the mid-1980s, debt-service payments commonly exceeded net capital inflows, so that some of the world's poorest economies were exporting capital to the well-to-do (World Bank, 1986:11).

External shocks not only reduced aggregate levels of output, income, and investment, but also destabilized the conditions under which most Africans produced and earned income. After 1970, global commodity prices fluctuated more widely than before (Guillaumont, 1987:634), making it difficult for governments to predict, let alone offset, the impact of world price shocks on their domestic economies. In a study of fifty-eight developing economies, Guillaumont (1987:635) found that the impact of unstable export volumes (as well as prices) on savings and growth was negative for all developing economies, many of which are in sub-Saharan Africa. For African economies, the impact of global instability was frequently magnified by their heavy dependence on imports, which fell sharply in the early 1980s. In our four countries alone, total spending on imports fell by 48 percent in Ghana (1981–83), 49 percent in Kenya (1980–83) and Zambia (1980–85), and 78 percent in Nigeria (1981–86).[6]

African governments' efforts to cope with the deepening crisis frequently added to the instability of domestic markets and conditions of production. Price and exchange controls drove an increasing volume of transactions into parallel markets, subjecting traders to added risks and the expense of concealment or bribery (Lele and Candler, 1981:113–14; Lofchie, 1989:112–13; MacGaffey et al., 1991:passim; for a contrary view, see Ellis, 1982:266). Crash programs in agricultural development with catchy names, such as Operation Feed the Nation (Nigeria) or Operation Feed Yourself (Ghana), were undertaken in the mid-1970s, only to be abandoned within a few years for lack of funds or results. Cooperatives, planned villages, and local development committees were created and dismantled, or sidelined, with bewildering frequency (see pages 57–59 above).

By the 1980s, many African governments found it increasingly difficult to maintain, let alone expand, basic infrastructure and services in transportation, communications, education, and health (World Bank, 1986:9). Without money to maintain imports of crucial intermediate goods (petrol, tires, vehicle parts, medicine), basic services declined, crippling the production and the marketing of agricultural as well as industrial goods. In Zambia, foreign-exchange allocations were shifted unpredictably among commodities and enterprises as the government veered from one stopgap measure to another, in an effort to stave off pressures from foreign creditors, suppliers, and/or domestic interest groups. One observer estimates that as much as one-third of the maize purchased from Zambian farmers in 1985 was never collected, in part because foreign-exchange allotments for imports of diesel fuel, tires, and jute bags were inexplicably diverted at the last minute (Good, 1986:268).

In the face of global and national economic and political instability, the importance of flexibility increased just at the time that farmers were finding it more difficult to mobilize and control their own and others' labor. As we have seen in central Kenya and northeastern Zambia, uncertain returns to crop production make it difficult for farmers to finance hired labor. After 1970, unstable commodity prices aggravated farmers' difficulties in mobilizing labor through the market. In addition, farmers' efforts to protect themselves against fluctuations in crop output and sales by diversifying their income-earning activities both depended on their gaining greater control over labor time and reduced their ability to exercise it.

For example, several recent studies have argued convincingly that access to off-farm income increases households' food security. Using data on household income and consumption from two villages in Burkina Faso, Reardon et al. (1988:1069) found that in 1984 (a year of severe drought), the proportion of households with "consumption security" was higher in the sahelian than in the sudanic village, although agricultural productivity is lower in the Sahel.[7] The main reason was that, in the sahelian village, households earned a higher proportion of their income from off-farm sources. Consequently, they were able to maintain consumption in the face of abnormally low yields more effectively than households in the sudanic village, which derived a larger proportion of total real income from crop production and sales. Sahelian households relied more heavily on off-farm earnings because their environment was generally poor and subject to frequent severe shortfalls in yield than was the case further south. Farmers in the Sahel were accustomed to spend more time and travel greater distances in search of off-farm employment then were their counterparts in the Sudan.

Faced with increasing economic instability, African farmers have also expanded cultivation of crops which allow them more flexibility in the allocation of labor time, such as cassava and/or shorter-maturing varieties of maize and potatoes (Haugerud and Collinson, 1990:350–52). Farmers also continue to intercrop—despite frequent official injunctions or advice to the contrary—

not only because intercropping saves labor and raises total yield per unit of cultivated land, but also because it stretches out the time over which a cultivated plot and the labor invested in it yield some return (Norman, 1974:9–11; Kowal and Kassam, 1978:333; Fresco, 1986:165–67). However, instability does not always lead to intercropping. In the early 1980s, women in Kwango-Kwilu (Zaire) not only cultivated more cassava relative to other crops than in the past, but also staggered times of planting and harvest, reduced fallows, and engaged in "what could be named the 'monocropping' of cassava" (Fresco, 1986:166).

In other cases, farmers maintained or increased cultivation of local varieties of swamp rice in order to smooth the flow of output and income over time. In contrast to upland rice, which requires a variety of specialized skills and careful timing of cultivation tasks, traditional swamp rice is less specialized and sensitive to the timing of labor inputs (Johnny et al., 1981:606–8; P. Richards, 1987:22–24, 88ff.; Haswell, 1963:22; see also Linares, 1981:571–76). Swamp rice thus lends itself to cultivation by individuals working alone or by unskilled hired labor. In contrast, upland rice cultivation is better suited to larger farming units, which are capable of mobilizing and coordinating the activities of a number of people with different skills (Johnny et al., 1981:606–8; Linares, 1981:589). Also, yields are less dependent on the timing of labor inputs in swamp than in upland rice cultivation—another reason why swamp rice is easier to cultivate for individuals who lack access to others' labor (Johnny et al., 1981:606). These changes can be explained both in terms of the long-term individualization of farming (see chaps. 6 and 7) and as efforts to gain flexibility in the face of mounting economic instability.

In periods of economic instability, farmers may also attempt to increase their liquidity, converting assets to forms that are readily marketable and abandoning income-generating activities with relatively long gestation periods in favor of those with high rates of turnover. Trade, in which goods are bought and sold again in relatively short periods of time, is generally a more liquid activity than crop production, in which the rate of turnover depends on the biological growth cycle of the crops. Thus, contrary to the popular notion that risk aversion causes farmers to withdraw from markets and become self-sufficient,[8] crop sales sometimes increase when price fluctuations rise. In a recent study of the famine of 1949 in Malawi, Vaughan (1987:84–85) questioned the common view that increased tobacco cultivation by smallholders in the 1930s and 1940s occurred at the expense of maize. In fact, tobacco-growing households were better able to withstand the famine, since they could buy food when their own ran out. Similar points have been made in studies of households' strategies for coping with recent famines in Africa (see Shipton, 1990, for a review of this literature).

Similarly, Guyer and Idowu (1991:268) found in the late 1980s that Yoruba women were more likely than men to specialize completely in cassava. In their sample, women's farms were smaller than men's, but more commercialized. Women hired a larger proportion of their labor and sold a larger share of their output. They also found that the number of Yoruba women farming on their own account had increased markedly since 1969 (Guyer and Idowu, 1991:267). These observations are consistent with my argument that instability does not necessarily lead farmers either to withdraw from markets or to diversify crop production per se. On the contrary, economic instability may promote increased commercialization and specialization, even by very small scale farm enterprises.

In addition to selling off their crops in periods of increasing instability, farmers have also taken up trade. Diversification into trade has, of course, occurred partly as a result of agricultural growth. Many farmers who have made some money from cash-crop production invest part of their profits in local trade, either buying agricultural produce for sale to wholesalers or agents of marketing boards or purchasing consumption goods or agricultural inputs to retail in rural markets (Schwimmer, 1980:232–33; Colson and Scudder, 1988:31; Berry, 1975:186, 1985:72ff.; Hill, 1963:190–82; Southall, 1978:187; Clough, 1985:31; Saul, 1987:75; Boesen and Mohele, 1979:45). But trade may also offer better prospects for coping with unstable markets. Crops take weeks or months to mature, during which time prices of crops, labor, and other variable inputs may change dramatically, leaving the farmer exposed to considerable risk. Although traders do sometimes find themselves stuck with unsold inventories, they are not locked into biologically determined production periods of several weeks' or months' duration. A small stock of trade goods can usually be turned over fairly quickly, so that traders are in a better position than farmers to get out of declining markets and move into more buoyant ones on short notice.

The relative liquidity of trade compared to farming does not mean that trading profits are high: for many "petty traders" in both rural and urban areas in Africa, they are miserably low. But for people who must cope with unstable markets in addition to poverty, trade may appear preferable to farming because of its liquidity. The point may be illustrated with a brief comparison of farmers' strategies in northeastern Zambia and western Nigeria during the 1970s. In both countries, national economic conditions were increasingly unstable during this decade, but Zambia was involved in a prolonged recession brought on by the collapse of the world copper price, whereas Nigeria was in the midst of the oil boom.

In Zambia, the once-flourishing labor reserve of the northeast was badly hurt by the collapse of the world copper market in the early 1970s (Watson, 1958:135–36; Pottier, 1983:passim, 1988:21ff.). By 1978, the region was severely depressed: people suffered from "poor dietary variation and an unprecedented shortage of basic foodstuffs" (Pottier, 1983:2). While former miners and their relatives had little choice but to return to the rural areas, Pottier found that many returnees were not engaged in farming, but instead were eking out a precarious living from petty trade.[9] The preference for trade over farming was strikingly illustrated by the Mambwe response to high prices for beans. Although bean cropping was "warmly recommended by local politicians and town planners," and sales of beans increased, "bean fever has not resulted in land development and higher levels of local agricultural production. Rather the opposite is true, for the Zambian grassland Mambwe prefer to buy up cheap beans, and millet, in villages across the border" in Tanzania (Pottier, 1983:17). By trading in beans across the border rather than growing them, Mambwe attempted to shield themselves against the possibility that the government would change its mind and reduce the price again before a full cropping season had passed, leaving them with a harvest of worthless beans (see also Shepherd, 1981:184ff.; Chauveau et al., 1981:653).

Farmers in western Nigeria reacted similarly to destabilized markets in the 1970s, although in this case aggregate demand was growing rapidly, thanks to Nigeria's booming petroleum exports. The effect of the oil boom on low-income households in western Nigeria was, in many ways, a mirror image of the impact of the copper recession in northeastern Zambia. Soaring foreign-exchange earnings led to rapid growth in demand for imports and considerable domestic inflation. Prices of food crops and other agricultural staples rose even faster than the general price index, but this apparently did not lead to significant increases in agricultural production. Instead, people devoted their energy and working capital to acquiring imported goods and reselling them in local markets. In Nigeria's booming oil economy, anyone who could buy a sack of rice or wheat flour could resell it at a profit within a few weeks or even days. Hence, there was little incentive to invest money or labor in cultivating crops which would require months to mature, might yield poorly, and whose price might decline relative to prices of other goods between planting and harvest time.[10]

Aggregate economic and political instability has also reinforced farmers' propensity to invest in social networks. Recent studies of rural expenditure patterns have shown no tendency for farmers to abandon or even significantly reduce their outlays on social networks. In many rural areas, expenditures on ceremonies, bridewealth payments, construction of family houses, or the education of close and distant kin figure as prominently in rural budgets in the 1970s and 1980s as they did in earlier times (Weigel, 1982:79ff.; P. Richards, 1987:124ff.; Moore, 1986:129–30; Ross, 1986:233; Miller, 1975:9–11; Berry, 1985:75–78).

Nor have farmers relaxed their efforts to reorganize established institutions or create new ones in order to keep abreast of changing economic conditions and practices. In the late 1970s, Yoruba descent groups were electing or appointing officers, opening bank accounts, and issuing circulars to announce annual family meetings. Such meetings served not only as occasions for celebrating weddings, funerals, and naming ceremonies, or strategizing over traditional title disputes, but also as arenas for the allocation of scholarships, the management of family assets, or the launching of community development projects (Berry, 1985:106–7). In central Kenya, where descent groups continued to monitor land claims and pursue them in court, even after land registration (Migot-Adholla et al., 1990a:22–23), women and others whose claims have been ignored in the context of family relations have joined self-help groups or established alternative networks to gain independent access to land and capital goods (Mackenzie, 1986:505–11; Thomas, 1985:148ff., chap.7; Stamp, 1986:39–42).

The increased salience of social networks as a means of access to productive resources does not mean either that traditional institutions provide a reliable safety net for impoverished or crisis-stricken rural households, or that corporate groups are gaining in size or importance with respect to rural resource management. Impoverishment and instability often affect whole families and communities, undermining their ability to provide security for any—let alone all—of their members. In declining (or unstable) economies, the returns to investment in social memberships are likely to be low (for an extreme case, see Sharp and Spiegel 1985:passim). Also, because the meanings of social memberships are often contested or redefined as leaders compete for followers and people pursue resources and opportunities through social relationships, returns to investment in networks are uncertain, even in the best of times (Carney, 1988:340–42; Peters, 1984:40–41).

In short, instability tends to promote cropping patterns, methods of cultivation, and modes of organizing agricultural production which increase farmers' liquidity and/or permit them flexibility in the management of labor time. Cultivation of cassava and swamp rice has increased, and agricultural production has become more individualized. Farmers do not necessarily withdraw from unstable markets; on the contrary, they often increase crop sales or engage in more off-farm employment in order to increase their liquidity. However, crops and techniques of production which provide flexibility in the short run do not necessarily serve to enhance the sustainability of agricultural production in the long run. Under unstable economic and political conditions, farmers are reluctant to tie up land, labor, and capital in long-term projects, such as soil conservation, water control, or fixed capital formation, which may sustain soil fertility or augment available land and labor. Instead, they are likely to spend more time in off-farm employment or out-migration, both of which accentuate the trend toward smaller farming units and investment in liquid assets.

Recent instability has also reinforced long-term tendencies for social networks and membership in them to proliferate. Fluid, noncorporate networks have facilitated social diversification, but people cannot participate regularly and actively in an indefinite number of networks. Accordingly, as social memberships proliferate, people tend to shift their attention and energy from one group or institution to another, depending on immediate needs. The result is a high degree of mobility of people and resources, but little tendency for institutions to coalesce into stable frameworks for collective action, resource management, or the consolidation of capital and knowledge. Such processes help to explain why African agrarian economies have demonstrated great resilience in the face of environmental and economic instability, without experiencing sustained growth of agricultural outputs and incomes.

Appropriate Technology

Recent studies of African farmers' responses to some of the new crop varieties developed in the International Agricultural Research Centers indicate that farmers consistently prefer shorter-maturing over higher-yielding varieties, and continue to cultivate several varieties of the same crop, even when encouraged to specialize (Haugerud and Collinson, 1990:343–52). These findings reinforce the conclusions of Paul Richards, Louise Fresco, and others that African farmers are as concerned (if not more so) with the timing of agricultural inputs and outputs as with total productivity. When viewed in relation to changing conditions of access to resources and patterns of rural production and investment, these results suggest new perspectives on the limited impact, to date, of Green Revolution technology in Africa.

Green Revolution technology centers on the development and dissemination of high-yielding varieties of individual crops, together with packages of complementary inputs, such as fertilizer, pesticides, and water control. High-yielding varieties usually require more labor and/or capital than traditional varieties, and their yields are relatively sensitive to the timing of cultivation tasks. Consequently, the spread of high-yielding varieties in Africa has been limited not only by shortages of labor and/or farmers' lack of access to working capital, but also by constraints on farmers' ability to manage their own and others' labor time.

In many African countries, governments have tried since colonial times to promote cultivation of high-yielding varieties of rice on irrigated land. In general, gains from these schemes have been limited (Carney and Watts, 1990:209; Dey, 1982:390–92; Webb, 1984:126). In a review of irrigated rice-farming schemes in five West African countries, Pearson et al. (1981:412–13) concluded that except in Mali, costs of production exceeded real returns. More recently, researchers from the International Food Policy Research Institute found that, in Gambia, the domestic resource cost of rice grown under conditions of full or partial water control exceeded the world market price (Von Braun et al.,

1989:32–33). The high cost of irrigation systems has been a major obstacle to dissemination of high-yielding varieties of rice in Africa (FAO, 1986:42), but high labor requirements (compared to local swamp rice cultivation) add significantly to the total real cost of irrigated rice (Von Braun et al., 1989:41, 50–54).[11]

Hybrid maize, which has been much more widely adopted in Africa than high-yielding varieties of either wheat or rice, also requires more labor than traditional varieties, especially when combined with ploughing.[12] In addition, yields are very sensitive to the timing of cultivation tasks (Gerhart, 1975:61). In Zambia, where maize subsidies were extended from European to African farmers after independence, labor scarcity has emerged as the principal constraint on farmers' ability to expand the area under cultivation.[13] In Serenje, Chinsali, and Mpika Districts, increased prices and marketing services in the 1970s led to rapid increases in the cultivation and sale of maize. However, "with the technology available (98% hand cultivation), it is difficult for most farmers to pass through the 60 bags barrier" (IRDP, 1983:278; see also Stolen, 1983:336ff.; Wood and Shula, 1987:288–89, 292).

To break this constraint, oxen and ploughs were introduced into the northeast in the early 1980s (IRDP, 1983:283; Francis, 1988:37). Farmers who purchased oxen and ploughs planted more land in maize and therefore needed more labor to weed and harvest the crop (Francis, 1988:38). Insofar as the burden of extra labor fell disproportionately on women within farming households, the spread of hybrid maize may also have increased intrahousehold disparities in welfare. Studies conducted by the IRDP for Serenje, Mpika, and Chinsali found that malnutrition among young children was positively correlated with the amount of maize sold by households (quoted in Moore and Vaughan, 1986:536–37; see also Geisler, 1985:19). In other words, the introduction of oxen and ploughs seems to have recreated the conditions observed by Richards (1939) during the global depression of the 1930s, when rural household members often went hungry during the millet harvest because women were simply too tired to prepare meals (Moore and Vaughan, 1987:538).

Cultivating of hybrid maize also contributed to inequality among households as well as within them. Poorer farmers, who could not afford to buy oxen, had to pay for ploughing services, sometimes hiring themselves out to cover the cost. "As a consequence of taking up seasonal employment opportunities, lower income groups in Chiwale run into problems related to timing" (Pottier, 1985:125). Specifically, poorer farmers who hire out are likely to plant and weed their own fields at less than optimal times, thus losing much of the potential gain from hybrid maize (Pottier, 1988:136).

The development and dissemination of new agricultural technologies in Africa has also been affected by relations of authority and obligation among those engaged in agricultural production. Irrigated rice-farming projects, for example, have often been the setting for domestic conflict. In northern Cameroon, husbands and wives cultivated irrigated rice plots jointly, but husbands were in control, compensating their wives' labor (or not) as they saw fit. Christine Jones (1986:110–11) calculated in 1981 that average rates of compensation for married women's labor on conjugal rice fields was substantially lower than the prevailing wage rate for agricultural work. She also found that married women allocated less labor to rice and more to their own lower-yielding plots of sorghum, than did "independent" women (mostly widows) who cultivated both crops on their own. Overall, "married women's under-allocation of time to transplanting . . . cost their households a significant amount of income" (Jones, 1986:116). She concluded that "when new agricultural technologies are introduced, allocative efficiency is not instantaneously attained. Bargaining between husbands and wives over the division of effort and reward is likely to take place over many seasons of rice cultivation" (Jones, 1986:118).

In the Gambia, irrigated rice-production schemes have also given rise to intrahousehold struggles over the control of labor and output. In Jahaly Pachar, a site of state-sponsored rice schemes since 1948, the World Bank funded a project in the mid-1980s which was designed to make irrigated plots and improved inputs directly available to women, who play a major role in rice cultivation. However, project managers acceded to local requests that irrigated plots be classified as household fields (*maruo*). According to local practice, *maruo* fields were cultivated jointly by household members, and the output was used for household consumption under the management of the household head. By designating irrigated plots as *maruo* fields, male heads of household gained control over the increased output produced on irrigated fields (Carney, 1988: 340–41; Von Braun and Webb, 1989:524). To the extent that irrigated rice was sold rather than stored for home consumption, the proceeds tended to become the personal income of the household head, rather than a collective resource (Carney, 1988:341).

As in northern Cameroon, married women in Jahaly Pachar did not simply acquiesce in longer hours of work at lower rates of return. Those with access to individual (*kamanyango*) fields spent more time on them or successfully demanded compensation for their labor on *maruo* rice plots (Carney, 1988:343–44; Von Braun et al., 1989:68). Women without *kamanyango* fields found themselves in a weaker bargaining position and in some cases withdrew their labor from household rice plots altogether, preferring to join labor groups who worked on others' farms for pay (Carney, 1988:345). In short, cultivation of irrigated rice led some married women to become proletarians in order to escape domestic exploitation (Carney and Watts, 1990:228–29).

Problems of labor management have not been limited to resource-poor farmers. Even for holders of large farms with ready access to credit and other forms of working capital, money does not necessarily buy time. In western Nigeria, for example, as participation in farming increased, first in response to rising food-crop prices during the oil boom, and then in reaction to declining opportunities in trade and services during the oil recession of the 1980s, demand for hired labor rose in food-crop as well as cocoa production. Women provided the chief source of farm labor for periods of peak demand, such as at harvest time. However, women workers were by no means full-time proletarians: farmers sometimes found it difficult to mobilize as many as they needed or to retain them if they were dissatisfied with their terms of employment. As Idowu and Guyer (1991:23) have emphasized, "the process of 'disciplining' a cheap and efficient labor force" is especially difficult in "the context of a hard-working, self-employed, multi-occupational peasantry" and volatile market conditions (see also Shepherd, 1981:176).

More generally, the technical requirements of Green Revolution seed-water-fertilizer packages have often conflicted with African farmers' need for flexibility in managing their time. Many high-yielding varieties of seed have longer maturation periods than traditional varieties. They perform best when grown in sole stands rather than intercropped fields, and their yields are more sensitive to the timing of labor inputs than those of traditional varieties. Yields of hybrid maize decline for every day that planting is delayed after the start of the rainy season (Gerhart, 1975:61). High-yielding varieties of rice grown under irrigation require large amounts of labor inputs in concentrated periods of time (Richards, 1985:98), while improved varieties of maize, potatoes, and rice often take longer to mature than traditional varieties (Haugerud and Collinson, 1990:349ff.; Richards, 1985:79). In short, to benefit from high-yielding varieties, farmers not only need assured access to complementary inputs such as fertilizer, pesticides, and water, but they must also be able to mobilize labor in the amounts *and at the times* required to obtain the best results.

If, as I have argued above, African farmers' ability to mobilize labor and control labor time is declining, this has probably militated against the transfer of Green Revolution technology to Africa. In the long run, commercialization, the diversification of rural economic activity, and increased rates of migration and schooling have reduced farmers' access to labor through social networks and increased the proportion of farmers who must rely on their own or hired labor. Where income from agricultural production is low or uncertain, the hiring of labor on small farms has been limited. Thus, the number of people who farm alone has risen over time. Furthermore, the individualization of farming has been reinforced in the 1970s and 1980s, as both farmers and farm workers struggled to cope with instability by diversifying their sources of income and their social networks. Increasing involvement in trade, wage employment, or nonagricultural production takes time away from farming and can also compromise people's ability to control the timing of farm work.

Similarly, investment in social memberships takes time without necessarily enhancing farmers' access to or control over others' labor. In addition, the declining ability of farmers to control the timing of labor inputs reduces the likelihood that they will take up the cultivation of crops whose yields depend on proper timing of cultivation tasks—no matter how high those yields may be.[14]

CONCLUSION

Changes in patterns and methods of agricultural production in Africa have been affected not only by the logic of commercialization and population growth, but also by the changing social, economic, and political conditions under which farmers acquire and use productive resources. In Africa, over the course of the twentieth century, farmers have gained access to the means of production through exchange, negotiation, and struggle in a variety of social arenas, from the household to the nation. Outcomes in one arena have been shaped by contestants' changing and differential participation in others; by relations of power, social identities, and culturally constructed definitions of authority and obligation; and by relative scarcities of land, labor, and capital. In many parts of Africa, access to rural land and fixed agricultural capital continues to be negotiated through membership in descent groups and communities—despite commercialization and some government efforts to privatize or nationalize rights to land and other forms of property. Accordingly, farmers continue to invest in social identities and status in order to maintain or improve their access to property.

Investment in social networks has not, however, either reproduced "traditional" institutions intact or transformed them into corporate units of resource management and control. On the contrary, boundaries and structures of social networks have remained fluid and contested, and members' positions within them vary according to different individual patterns of participation in wider circuits of economic and social activity. Migration, education, and the diversification of income-earning activities have altered relations between elders and juniors, chiefs and subjects, husbands and wives, and reduced peoples' ability to count on any particular relationship as a stable basis for access to resources. In terms of agricultural production, this means that the ability to mobilize labor through "traditional" social relations has weakened over time, and farmers have come to rely increasingly on their own or hired labor.

Since the early 1970s, these long-term trends have been reinforced by the increasing volatility of African economic and political systems. Spontaneous agricultural intensification was not a foregone conclusion, and introduced improvements in crops or methods of agricultural production have often been problematic. In the context of ongoing debates over rights of access and the division of labor, government interventions have tended to create new spaces for maneuver and debate, rather than exerting a decisive influence on patterns of production or access to resources. The role of governments and donor agencies has been intrusive rather than hegemonic, often adding to the instability of farmers' circumstances rather than transforming farming practices per se. For African farmers, time is increasingly of the essence, and agricultural technologies which place a premium on the careful timing of cultivation tasks are not likely to lead to significant or sustained increases in agricultural output or rural outcomes.

Notes

Bibliography

Index

Notes

Chapter 1: Introduction

1. Deconstruction of accepted social typologies and historical accounts has been much influenced by postmodernist theory, which reminds us of the hegemonic power of language and ideas and questions the possibility that evidence can exist independently of its beholders. The work of Bourdieu and Foucault in particular is cited in the Africanist literature with increasing frequency.

2. See, for example, McCaskie, 1983 on Rattray; Prins, 1980 on Gluckman; Van Donge, 1985 on Marxist critiques of the Rhodes-Livingstone Institute; Mackintosh, 1977 on Meillassoux; Chauveau et al., 1981 on typologies of social, economic, and political systems.

3. Comprehensive discussions of the aims and methods of farm-management studies are provided in Collinson, 1972 and Upton, 1973. Some studies also amassed data on other economic and social variables, but used them primarily to analyze the profitability of farm-level production (see, e.g., Galletti et al., 1956).

4. This summary refers mainly to the anglophone farming-systems research, which is geared primarily towards the adaptation of technology to local farming conditions. There is a longer history of farming-systems research by francophone scholars, who have been more interested in accumulating large amounts of information on particular localities over long periods of time (see Fresco, 1984:26–27).

5. For reviews of the aims and methodologies of farming-systems research, see Collinson, 1982; P. Richards, 1983; Fresco, 1984; and articles by Norman, Gerhart, and Low in Moock, 1986.

6. In some areas, farmers produced for the market long before the colonial period (Meillassoux, 1971; Gray and Birmingham, 1970; Carney and Watts, 1990:220).

7. These included colonizers' debates over whether Africans' increasing involvement in commercial activity was progressive or corrupting; Africans' debates over the social and moral implications of different sources of wealth (see, e.g., Barber, 1982; Shipton, 1989:chap.4), and Africans' ambivalence over the political consequences of commercialization—elder men, for example, disparaged uppity women and kids but welcomed their earnings.

8. For examples and a review, see Bardhan, 1989. Such arguments retain strong overtones of Becker's (1962) ultimate neoclassical argument that economies can't be anything but perfectly competitive for any length of time.

9. In a recent essay, Stiglitz (1989:18–19) noted that "currently fashionable economic theories fail to address . . . the most central issue facing most of mankind today," namely, the persistence of "dramatically different standards of living" among countries and regions despite relatively free flows of labor and capital among them.

10. There is an extensive debate in the Marxist literature over the degree to which states exist independently of class structures or engage in actions which do not serve to reproduce the conditions for capital accumulation and the dominance of the accumulating classes. Marxists who argue that the state is a complex social phenomenon, incorporating as well as expressing class struggles, also view relations between economic and political forces as dialectical rather than hegemonic. For lucid and comprehensive discussions of this literature, see Jessop, 1982, 1990.

11. Contributors to both Marxist and neoclassical institutional economics have acknowledged the need to take account of specific historical circumstances in order to explain actual patterns of economic change. See Stiglitz, 1989:26; Jessop, 1982: 258–59.

12. See, for example, Hill, 1969, 1970; Geschiere, forthcoming; Udry, 1990.

13. To recognize the fact of negotiation is not to espouse a voluntaristic or instrumental theory of social causation. Outcomes of negotiations are influenced both by the power and resources which people bring to bear on them and by the process of negotiation itself. Culture and ideology are continually redefined through practice, which they also shape (Moore, 1986:passim; Feierman, 1990:27ff.). Negotiations can also lead to multiple, contradictory outcomes, which do not correspond to the intentions of any of the negotiators.

14. If rules and values are subject to multiple interpretations and transactions are not definitive, the concept of Pareto efficiency is not very useful for analyzing processes of resource allocation. Neoclassical economists have long acknowledged that Pareto efficiency can only be defined with reference to a given distribution of assets and income. If distribution changes, the same individuals will have different weights in determining the pattern of effective demand, and there is no theoretical basis for comparing the resulting value of output. If, in addition, the values used to compare alternative bundles of outputs are ambiguous, then it is not clear how to compare different patterns of resource allocation even if distribution is unchanged. To put it another way, if demand is not independent of supply, then allocating resources so as to maximize utility is not a meaningful concept.

CHAPTER 2: HEGEMONY ON A SHOESTRING

1. Killingray (1986:414–15) describes the weakness of security forces in most British colonies in Africa.

2. Ranger (1983:254–60) points out that some groups of people who were oppressed or subordinated as a result of the invention of tradition resisted, but argues that the outcome usually favored those groups (such as chiefs, elders, and men) who

claimed superiority under the rubric of tradition, rather than remaining fluid or indeterminate. See also Snyder, 1981:139ff.; W. MacGaffey, 1970:189ff.,302–3.

3. Phillips (1989:79, 88, 106, 118ff.) gives a cogent analysis of the contradictions of British colonial interests in West Africa, but tends to assume that Africans' interests vis-à-vis the colonial order were straightforwardly procapitalist.

4. In a recent paper, Sally Moore discusses British officials' understanding of Native Courts in Tanganyika in similar terms. The colonial "model" of customary courts as institutions which adjudicate cases in terms of consistent traditional rules is "predicated on the existence of some kind of authoritative hierarchy that ultimately determines what the rules are, who the judges are, who commands, who obeys, what is obeyed. . . . Such a design is not practical without a system of writing and record-keeping and without effective techniques of long distance communication. The catch-22 in Africa was that virtually none of the preconditions of this model obtained at the beginning of colonial rule. By the end much still had not been successfully instituted" (Moore, n.d.:25).

5. Organization and Re-organization Reports for both provinces and districts are in the CSO 26 series, Nigerian National Archives; see also Hailey, 1957:462.

6. Quoted in Hailey, 1957:446.

7. Berman and Lonsdale, 1980:71–75. Native Reserves were also instituted in Northern Rhodesia, as part of the Colonial Office's campaign to strengthen administration of the colony after they took it over from the British South Africa Company in 1924. The reserves quickly became too crowded to accommodate local methods of cultivation, leading to tension and protest (Allan, 1965:446; Ranger, 1971:17–19). However, there were so few European settlers in Northern Rhodesia that their claims to land never took on the political significance that they did in Kenya (Palmer, 1973:56).

8. Kitching (1980:286) points out the irrelevance of European concepts of ownership for understanding precolonial Kikuyu practice, but argues that "settler colonialism" effected a transition "from simultaneous to exclusive land use." I am arguing that simultaneous and overlapping claims on land and labor persisted under colonial rule, and that the nature of property rights was not transformed, but left unresolved.

CHAPTER 3: INCONCLUSIVE ENCOUNTERS

1. For illuminating recent discussions of this aspect of the "second colonial occupation" in eastern and southern Africa, see Beinart, 1984, 1989; Anderson, 1984. As Lonsdale and Berman (1979; Berman and Lonsdale, 1980) have argued for Kenya, coping with the contradictions of colonial rule led the government to adopt increasingly coercive and/or authoritarian approaches to solving the labor problem in Kenya. Compared to eastern and southern Africa, British colonial policy towards agriculture in West Africa was relatively noninterventionist, but a similar change occurred there, marked by such measures as the government takeover of the marketing of West African cocoa in 1939 and the campaign to cut out cocoa trees affected by swollen-shoot disease.

2. A similar attitude was expressed by the Northern Rhodesian Agricultural Advisory Board in a report on maize marketing in 1935. Among African farmers along the

line of rail, "traditional methods on traditional soils are being abandoned in favor of what is usually but a parody of European farming at its worst" (quoted in Makings, 1966:200).

3. As one Nigerian legislator told the Western Region House of Assembly in 1956: "I left St. Andrews College [Oyo] in 1928. I therefore know what I am saying" (quoted in Abernethy, 1969:138).

4. See Killick, 1978:24ff. for a lucid review of development theories of the 1950s and 1960s and their influence on the economic policies of the Nkrumah regime in Ghana.

5. Personal observation; personal communication from Jane Guyer.

6. Donor agencies replaced colonial regimes as the foreign institutions most directly involved in management of rural economic activity. Unlike colonial regimes, however, donor agencies do not have to pay their own way out of revenues raised from local economies. On the contrary, their performance is often judged by how much money they spend in a given accounting period. Also, donors do not have to govern the societies in which they are promoting development; they leave it to overburdened African states to cope with social tensions, environmental damage, and external costs occasioned by their development projects. See Morss, 1984, for a critique of donors' consumption of scarce managerial resources in African governments.

7. Such patterns were common in the management of River Basin Development Authorities in Nigeria (Palmer-Jones, 1981; Wallace, 1981; Forrest, 1981, forthcoming), mechanized rice-farming and irrigation schemes in Ghana (Shepherd, 1981; Konings, 1986), large-farm subsidies and maize-buying centers in parts of Kenya (Heyer, 1981; Bates, 1989), and Integrated Development Zones in Zambia (Tordoff, 1980; Bratton 1980a), among others.

8. Isaacman (1990:5–10) points out that peasant resistance in Africa was largely ignored by scholars until the 1980s. Since 1980, Africanist scholars have not only documented numerous episodes of both collective and individual peasant resistance to the state, but also pointed out that conflict with the state is only one form of social tension in rural communities. African farmers are involved in multiple interactive relationships with individuals and groups, both within rural communities and beyond them.

9. When the government addressed the problem of drought by banning the brewing of beer in order to conserve grain, Village Councils complied, but refrained from enforcing prohibition when local women protested the loss of an important source of income (Thiele, 1986:552–53). In contrast to Hyden (1980, 1983), Thiele's analysis suggests that Tanzanian peasants have not simply ignored or evaded the state, but have pursued their own interests by maneuvering within state institutions as well as around them.

CHAPTER 4: COMMERCIALIZATION, CULTIVATION, AND CAPITAL FORMATION

1. After Britain abolished the slave trade, traders put pressure on the British government to take military and political control of the West African coast, in order to prevent traders of other nationalities from taking over their markets (Robinson and Smith, 1979:176).

2. Egba refers to the territory and people under the jurisdiction of Abeokuta.

3. Food crops could be interplanted with young cocoa trees until they grew sufficiently to form a canopy, making the ground beneath them too shady. Most cocoa farmers continued to grow food crops, however, on bare spots within their cocoa farms and on fields not planted to cocoa (Okali, 1974:9–10). The extent of rural commercialization is reflected in the fact that farmers sold most of the food crops they grew and relied on the market for daily consumption needs (Berry, 1975:170–71; Jones, 1972:60).

4. Gammalin 20 is said to have accounted for between two-fifths and three-fifths of the 70 percent increase in Ghanaian output in 1959–61, but its effectiveness has probably declined over time (Birmingham et al., 1966:58). In Nigeria the effect on output of chemical spraying to control capsids is unclear (Berry, 1975:80, n46).

5. European control over the export trade was greatly facilitated by the West African Shipping Conference, formed in 1894 by Elder Dempster and Woermann, which controlled most of the shipping between Europe and West Africa (Leubuscher, 1963:15). Black Star was the first African-owned line to challenge this monopoly.

6. Cadbury's, Ltd. maintained numerous buying stations in the interior, but most expatriate firms confined their activity to ports and major towns, relying on African traders to collect produce in the rural areas and deliver it to commercial traders (Southall, 1978:192–93).

7. *Isakole* is a form of tribute paid by a person who uses land productively to the person or group who claims jurisdiction over the territory in question. With the spread of cocoa growing in western Nigeria, families demanded *isakole* from farmers who sought permission to grow cocoa on land over which they claimed jurisdiction. The amount of *isakole* was usually set at a fixed amount for each cultivator, regardless of the size of his or her cocoa farm. Thus, *isakole* remained a form of tribute, rather than developing into an economic rent, as cocoa cultivation expanded (Berry, 1975:108ff.).

8. Officials' qualms over combinations in restraint of trade were apparently overridden by the depression. Colonial authorities raised few objections when financially troubled European firms merged in the late 1920s and early 1930s, or when thirteen of the fourteen European firms trading in Ghana (who together handled 94 percent of the cocoa crop) formed a Buying Agreement in 1937, to set a common price for cocoa (Southall, 1978:197).

9. During the Second World War, the West African Produce Control Board purchased cocoa which it could not transport out of West Africa, thus subsidizing African farmers at the expense of British taxpayers (Green, 1960:138).

10. Tabatabai, 1988:715–16; cf. Berry, 1976:7.

11. Kikuyu seeking better access to land first moved west of the railway, but were cut off by the government's demarcation of Forest Reserves and land reserved to the Maasai (Cowen and Murage, 1972:51). Similarly, northward migration in Nyeri district was closed off by establishment of the Forest Reserve (Cowen, 1978:13–14).

12. Some illustrative data are presented in Kitching, 1980:36–38.

13. During the First World War, African sales of agricultural produce continued to increase, despite forced recruitment of thousands of Africans for the Carrier Corps, where many died of disease, aggravated by malnutrition and poor living conditions. After the war, European settlers again faced labor shortages, due to wartime mortality, Africans' increased involvement in agricultural production for the market, and their

reluctance to work for Europeans after bitter experience with the Carrier Corps (Clayton and Savage, 1974:85ff.).

14. The *athomi* were also hurt by the institution of government marketing controls, which they could not evade, being too conspicuous, but which were easily circumvented by women who simply headloaded their bark around official check points (Cowen, 1978).

15. Colonial officials' approach to agricultural policy after 1945 exemplified the contradictions of indirect rule. Convinced that technical improvements in African agriculture must draw on "customary" institutions, they extolled the virtues of "communalism" and ordered chiefs to mobilize labor for terracing in the name of traditional Kikuyu work parties (*ngwatio*) (Kenya, 1945:21–25; Throup, 1988:152).

16. For households in the poorest category, total earnings covered less than half of expenditures (House and Killick, 1981:40).

17. Describing resettlement schemes undertaken to relieve overcrowding in Eastern Province in the 1940s, Allan (1965:449) commented that "movement into these areas was largely voluntary, but in many cases a good deal of discussion and persuasion was needed to obtain the necessary numbers, since most villages preferred that their neighbors should do the moving and that they should take over the vacated land."

18. Seven chiefs and their followers were absorbed into the domains of neighboring chiefs, while two actually fled to the Congo Free State—hardly noted for enlightened colonial rule—rather than submit to the rigors of forced evacuation and resettlement in the Luapula Valley (Kay, 1964b:246).

19. To accommodate Africans who were moved to make room for European settlers, the colonial government convened three commissions to recommend where and how much land to "reserve" for African use. The reserves demarcated in 1929–30 proved inadequate to maintain production under the extensive forms of agriculture practiced in the northeast. Much of the land designated as Crown Land in 1930 (and therefore available for alienation to Europeans) was reclassified as Reserve Land in 1947 (Mvunga, 1980:35; Palmer, 1973:64).

20. To his credit, Trapnell (1953) described what he saw, whether or not it conformed to his theories of agricultural evolution. As a result, his work remains a classic, more useful to the student of agricultural change than some more recent classifications of land-use patterns in Zambia. Trapnell also respected indigenous agricultural knowledge—an attitude which anticipates recent work in this area by forty years.

21. Agronomists and ecologists devoted great care to estimating the amount of woodland that had to be cut to make *citemene* cultivation possible. In many parts of Bembaland, the ratio of wooded area to area cultivated was estimated in the late 1930s at between 5:1 and 10:1 (Allan, 1965: 131). Near Serenje, Peters gave a much higher figure of 30:1 (Peters, 1950:68–69).

22. Cassava cultivation requires less labor than either millet or maize. Many varieties are poisonous, however, and require fairly laborious processing. However, preparation of millet flour by hand is also laborious (ILO, 1981:85–86,89; Berry, 1986:3).

23. Schemes for "improved African farming" were confined to the south, where Africans were already producing for the market (Makings, 1966:225; Wood and Shula, 1987:283–84).

24. Integrated Development Zones, established in 1972 as centers for regionally concentrated rural development programs, had failed by 1974 (Gertzel, 1980:255–57). They were followed by a series of Integrated Rural Development Programs, which received considerable support from donor agencies and tended to be longer-lived (see, e.g., Svads, 1983:270ff.; Wood and Shula, 1987:290; Pottier, 1988:90–93).

CHAPTER 5: ACCESS TO LAND

1. See, for example, Adegboye, 1967:348–49; Famoriyo, 1973:3; Arhin, 1985: 35–37. Arhin points out, however, that in practice governments may not be willing or able to do this effectively. See also Migot-Adholla et al., 1990b:24–25.

2. The Aborigines' Rights Protection Society was a group of English-trained Ghanaian lawyers, clergymen, and merchants, who took an active role in speaking out against colonial policies which threatened Africans' rights.

3. Officials tried, unsuccessfully, to reduce the real burden of cocoa rents on farmers. In 1913, cocoa rents were fixed at a penny a tree, but falling prices soon made that amount more burdensome than the "customary" *abusa* payment (Austin, 1987:269).

4. Many Kikuyu told Beech (and later government commissions of enquiry) that they had purchased their land from the Dorobo, hunters who occupied much of Central Province before the Kikuyu (Sorrenson, 1967:20; Ambler, 1987:12; Coray, 1978:186).

5. Native Tribunals were the Kenyan equivalent of customary courts in West Africa.

6. Rights to other forms of rural property were also subject to shifting allegiances and conflicts among people with interests in the assets in question. In Yombe, as late as 1970, "costly items such as grinding mills are often the focus of unresolved struggles between the agnatic collectivity and the individual" (Bond, 1987:174). Kapferer (1967, 45ff.) describes the allocation of access to cassava-pounding troughs in southern Luapula as a complex process, linked to issues of kinship and village formation. Men preferred, for example, to give cassava troughs to their (politically neutral) wives, rather than to their sisters, who might move to another village if a quarrel occurred. A woman who owned troughs needed to exercise finesse in inviting other women to join her pounding group. If a group was too small, the labor was onerous, but too many members could mean that individuals were unable to have their cassava pounded often enough to keep their households supplied with food.

7. Mackenzie, 1986:390ff.; Bukh, 1979:52–55; Hill, 1963:116–17. Yoruba women could acquire land in their own right, though few engaged in farming before the 1970s. Under the Yoruba system of inheritance *per stirpes*, women inherit jointly with their male siblings (Lloyd, 1962:296). In Zambia, Mambwe women obtain cultivation rights through marriage (Watson, 1958:99).

8. Her conclusion contradicts those of Woodman (1966) and Brokensha (1966), who argued that over time, property rights had come to depend largely, if not exclusively, on the investment of labor rather than on claims of "customary" heirs.

9. In effect, independent governments, like colonial regimes, provoked debates over the interpretation of custom and its application to property rights which they were

in no position to resolve. The difference is that whereas colonial officials dithered because they were pursuing a chimera of stable, bounded "tribal" systems of law and social order, national governments hung fire because their power often depended, in part, on practicing methods of land allocation and political mobilization which they were committed to suppress.

10. The Land Use Decree, 1978, was renamed the Land Use Act under civilian rule. In effect, the Land Use Act applied the land-tenure system of colonial Northern Nigeria to the southern states. Note court debates over whether or not the act was void under the civilian constitution (Omotola, 1983:27).

11. The cases cited here are presented in Omotola, 1983. They are all High Court cases, heard between 1979 and 1983. High Court rulings are usually modeled on British legal procedures, in contrast to those of lower-level customary courts (Francis, 1984:19).

CHAPTER 6: EXPLOITATION WITHOUT DISPOSSESSION

1. In some areas, although cooperative work groups remained important during and after the colonial era, the distribution of responsibilities and rewards within them has changed dramatically (Pottier, 1988:127–28).

2. Agricultural prices rose for different reasons in different countries. In Ghana, for example, prices for food crops rose because of sharp declines in production associated with overall economic decline (Tabatabai, 1988:709ff.), while in Nigeria they rose because of oil-induced inflation and rising demand (Collier, 1988:766ff.; Berry, 1985:88–89).

3. Collier and Lal (1986:137) go so far as to calculate the loss in Kenyan national income resulting from rural factor market imperfections. Similar arguments have been advanced by Feder and Noronha, 1987; Von Braun et al., 1989; and Binswanger et al., 1987.

4. Murray (1981:173ff.) argues that in Lesotho the entire peasantry has been proletarianized, depending for their subsistence on wage employment in South Africa. See also Spiegel, 1980:160–61; Beinart, 1980:150–51.

5. For an incisive review of efforts to politicize the analysis of rural households' economic behavior, see Hart, 1992.

6. Official efforts to redesign rural class structures (such as the Swynnerton Plan in Kenya) have not been particularly successful either (Sorrenson, 1967:232–36).

7. I am using the term "hired labor" to refer to people paid for farm work on a piece- or time-rate basis, with cash or a share of the crop.

8. This figure is much higher than those given in other official sources. A survey carried out in Ashanti and Brong-Ahafo on the eve of independence reported an average of two hired laborers per farmer in a sample which was heavily weighted towards large farms (Ghana, 1960:61). In 1960, according to the Population Census, there were 312,000 cocoa farmers in Ghana employing 210,000 laborers, of whom 90,000 were described as "family workers" (cited in Killick, 1966:239). However, both the census and the survey of 1956 were conducted during months when there is little work

to be done on cocoa farms and may therefore understate the extent of labor hiring during the peak season.

9. In this study, "permanent" workers were defined to include both workers hired on annual contracts and *abusa* laborers who worked for one-third of the crop.

10. One author estimates that "the decline in the agricultural labor force would have been of the order of 15–20 percent between 1975 and the early 1980s" (Tabatabai, 1988:721).

11. Harvesting of dry bark did not conflict with the coffee harvest, when many women worked on European estates. Moreover, wattle trees provided logs and charcoal, which could be consumed or sold by producing households (Cowen, 1978:83–84; Kitching, 1980:66–67).

12. This is not inconsistent with Cowen's (1978:102) evidence that agricultural wages rose slightly during the depression. Much of the labor released by financially straitened European estates may have been absorbed in self-employment. A similar process occurred in western Nigeria during this time (Berry, 1975:84–85).

13. Accounts of the "agrarian revolution" brought about by Kenyan farmers cultivating coffee and tea appear, from hindsight, to have been somewhat exaggerated (see, e.g., Collier and Lal, 1984:1013; 1986:260).

14. In the first Integrated Rural Survey, smallholders were defined as households with farms of less than 20 hectares. The second IRS included an additional 200,000 rural households with small "back gardens" (Livingstone, 1986:161).

15. Of the taxable adult male residents of Northern Province, 50 percent were working outside the province in 1961 (Hellen, 1968:99).

16. As Pottier (1988:69) has pointed out, it is difficult to measure the impact of the copper recession on rural employment in the late 1970s, because returning migrants had several residential options, and many moved frequently from one village or rural town to another.

17. In a study of rice growing in Sierra Leone, Johnny et al. (1981:606–8) point out that large households and cooperative work groups have an advantage over smaller households and individual farmers in growing a crop, such as upland rice, which requires a variety of skills.

18. In a study of a Bamana village in southern Mali, Lewis (1981:61ff.) argued that members of small and/or politically marginal lineages worked harder and more consistently at grain production than farmers who belonged to large, politically central lineages. The latter were inclined to bursts of overproduction, for display, followed by periods of slacking off, when their harvests fell significantly below the consumption requirements of their immediate households. His findings suggest that agricultural labor was less effectively disciplined in large lineages, whose members were more preoccupied with status and prestige.

19. Hart (1986:194–95) has suggested that in southeast Asian economies, rural labor control often hinges on the threat of complete exclusion from jobs or tenancy contracts. By extending contracts to some workers or tenants and not others, landholders make the threat of exclusion credible and ensure high levels of effort from their tenants and laborers. The present argument suggests that such mechanisms are more likely to operate in densely populated rural areas, where withholding access to land is socially feasible.

20. In the case of people who work alone, this is presumably not a problem—constraints are competing demands on time or health. Studies of rural women's activities have described Kikuyu women who were so busy trying to support and care for their families that they had no time for friendships (Abbott, 1974:63-64; see also, Clark, 1975).

21. During the oil boom of the 1970s, the cost of agricultural labor was prohibitive for most small-scale farmers (Berry, 1985:88; Collier, 1983:212-14; 1988:773-74).

22. These processes are not necessarily reflected in data on inequality among rural households, since they often operate within households rather than between them.

23. After independence, several efforts were made to legislate firmer property rights and greater economic security for wives, especially in the event of divorce. Such laws were debated intensely: those that were not defeated left many areas of ambiguity and were, in any case, irregularly enforced (Vellenga, 1983:148-51; Woodman, 1974:277-80; Kamau, 1987:296ff.).

CHAPTER 7: INVESTING IN NETWORKS

1. Expenditures on ceremonies may also absorb a significant part of farmers' earnings. In 1951-52, a year of windfall gains due to high cocoa prices, Galletti et al. (156:707-8) found that the 187 cocoa-farming families for whom they collected budgets devoted 4 percent of their annual income, on average, to social and ceremonial expenses. See also Berry, 1985:75-78. In 1960, a survey of 350 adults in ten Ushi villages in northeastern Zambia found that outlays on ritual and ceremonial occasions and social memberships varied between 13 percent and 20 percent of total cash receipts for each village (Kay, 1964c:26). Sales of livestock or even land to raise money for marriage or funeral expenses were not uncommon in the 1970s (Njeru, 1976:21; Haugerud, 1981a:20; Cowen, 1974:40ff.). Pointing out the close association between "high social standing (*igweta*)" and the accumulation of livestock among early Kikuyu squatters in the Rift Valley, Kanogo (1987:22) notes that Leakey "identified 172 [ceremonies] between the birth and death of each average individual (Kikuyu), each of which demanded the slaughter of a beast."

2. Further examples are given for Ghana and Nigeria in Beckman, 1978:152ff.; Beer, 1976:chaps.3,8; Berry, 1985:171-72,183-88; Dunn and Robertson, 1973:57, 307ff.; Chazan, 1983:30-32; and for Kenya in Glazier, 1985:183ff.; Haugerud, 1989:82; Coldham, 1978a:74; Berry, 1985:79-81; Ferraro, 1970; and for Zambia in Rasmussen, 1974; Bratton, 1980a, b; Lamb, 1974; Holmquist, 1984.

3. For example, in a rural land dispute heard before a Nigerian court in 1982, the defendants—"customary tenants" on the land in question for over one hundred years—had unsuccessfully challenged the landholders' rights of ownership in court five times between 1935 and 1960 (Omotola, 1983:158). In Ghana, land cases sometimes dragged on for decades (Kyerematen, 1971:18ff.; see also Sutton, 1984:49).

4. Unlike proponents of the old pluralist paradigm (Epstein, 1958; Mitchell, 1956), I am not arguing that pluralism is either functional or stabilizing.

5. Sally Falk Moore (1986:304ff.) makes a similar point with respect to the Chagga.

6. In Ghana, some farmers owned as much as 50 or 100 acres of cocoa trees (Hill, 1956:87–88).

7. As used here, the term "patronage networks" includes long-term relations between migrant workers, sharecroppers, and farmers, as sometimes developed in Nigeria and Ghana (A. F. Robertson, 1987:73–74).

8. Tension over land between returning squatters and people who had remained in the Kikuyu Reserve was probably exacerbated by the fact that, when the squatters originally left the reserve area in the 1910s, they expected to establish themselves permanently in the Rift Valley (Kanogo, personal communication), continuing the nineteenth-century pattern of colonization. Since they did not plan to return, many squatters had not maintained close ties with their kin in the reserve. In addition, after 1920, their efforts to reproduce Kikuyu institutions in the highlands were suppressed by European settlers and colonial officials. "Since the *ciama* [councils of elders] made no attempt to curb . . . activities" such as illegal squatting or grazing, "the administration failed to see their utility" (Kanogo, 1987:76).

9. Insofar as small farms depended on family labor, their output was vulnerable to sudden fluctuations in labor supply due to family quarrels or illness. Between mid-1979 and early 1981, 27 percent of the households in Haugerud's sample in Embu experienced major changes in farm labor supply because of domestic conflict (Haugerud, 1984:chap.5). Also, women's access to credit and extension services tended to be limited, which further constrained their ability to raise farm output and productivity (Staudt, 1975–76:87–90).

10. Kitching's heroic attempt to generalize from Fisher's ahistorical account boils down to a lament that she didn't ask different questions. Presley (1986) provides valuable information on women's labor on European coffee estates, but not on African farms, while Mackenzie's (1986) account of this period is based entirely on secondary sources. Even Cowen (1978, 1981), whose thesis contains fascinating information on the ability of Kikuyu women to evade and ultimately vitiate government controls on wattle marketing, makes no effort to deconstruct the household as a unit of production.

11. In reaction to the perceived erosion of their land rights in the wake of registration, women have attempted to create their own networks to gain independent access to the market and/or the state. Self-help groups served as rotating savings clubs, enabling individual women to invest in fertilizer or other farm inputs, or to pool their resources for collective purchases of farms or buildings (Mackenzie, 1986:505–20; see also Stamp, 1975–76:25, 33–36; and see chap. 8 below).

12. To make a *citemene* plot of one acre required branches from between 10 and 20 acres of woodland (Peters, 1950:90). Trapnell (1953:45–50) describes crop rotations of between four and twelve years' duration.

13. Farm labor supplies were so tight in the late 1980s that, in a dramatic inversion of Yoruba notions of seniority, a group of laborers in Ibarapa, led by a thirteen-year-old girl, refused to work the field of an *oba* until he agreed to pay them more money (Guyer, personal communication).

CHAPTER 8: TIME IS OF THE ESSENCE

1. The scarcity of labor relative to land in African agriculture is commonplace in the literature. See, inter alia, Heyer, 1971; Clayton, 1964; Massell and Johnson, 1968; Upton, 1973; Collinson, 1972; Luning, 1967; Norman et al., 1981; Levi and Havinden, 1982; and Richards, 1983, 1987.

2. Others have criticized the overemphasis on evolutionary paradigms of agricultural change in many of these studies. Guyer, 1981, 1984; Berry, 1984; and Chauveau et al., 1981.

3. Even hybrid maize, widely adopted in some African countries, has not been an unqualified success (see page 197 below).

4. In 1976, the Zairean government revived the colonial system of *Cultures Imposées*, whereby regional officials could require farmers to cultivate minimum acreages of designated crops (Fresco, 1986:83–84).

5. Different forms of mound cultivation are practiced in northeastern Zambia, as described in chapter 4. Here the emphasis is on the general system of mound cultivation, as contrasted to *citemene*.

6. In a study of twenty-four African economies, Helleiner (1986a:146ff.) found significant negative relationships between (1) the annual rate of growth of GDP and instability of import volume, and (2) growth and the income terms of trade for the entire period from 1960 to 1980. He concluded that, by the 1980s, there was little African governments could do to reverse the decline without access to substantially larger flows of external resources than were currently available or projected. See also Wheeler, 1984:16–17; Green and Griffith-Jones, 1985:213–14; Helleiner, 1986b:86–88. Declines in imports for Ghana, Kenya, Zambia, and Nigeria were calculated from data in IMF, *International Financial Statistics*.

7. "Consumption security" is defined as a level of food consumption equal to or above 80 percent of FAO minimum calorie requirements for household members.

8. A particularly explicit statement of this misconception was the USDA's (1981:25) assertion that for most African farmers, "the reason for growing export crops is to sell them, while the reason for growing food crops is to eat them."

9. Return migrants often avoided returning to their previous villages of residence, since they had limited savings with which to reestablish themselves there and knew that what little they had would quickly be absorbed by relatives even poorer than themselves (Pottier 1983:9, 13; 1988:44–45).

10. Opportunities for self-employment grew rapidly in other tertiary activities. To cite one example, the motor-repair industry grew at a phenomenal pace during the 1970s, as oil revenues underwrote a flood of imported vehicles which wore down Nigeria's roads faster than the government could repair them or build new ones. Thus, not only did the volume of traffic double in the space of a few years, but vehicles also fell apart at an increasing rate. This, in turn, created a booming market for the services of mechanics, panel beaters, vulcanizers, battery charges, and a host of other specialists. The buoyancy of this market and the low barriers to entry attracted many farmers' sons (Berry, 1985:chap.6).

11. Cultivation of high-yielding varieties of wheat in Africa is severely limited by environmental conditions. Even where it is ecologically appropriate, as in the East

African highlands, wheat is grown primarily on large farms (Carter et al, 1990:13; Jones and Egli, 1984:13, 88). Elsewhere, wheat production depends on large subsidies (see, e.g., Andrae and Beckman, 1986:213–14).

12. Hybrid maize is cultivated by the majority of farmers in Kenya, Zimbabwe, and more recently Zambia, but by only 10 percent of farmers in Malawi (Jahnke et al., 1987:102).

13. Of course, failures of government marketing and input delivery have also seriously affected aggregate output. See Wood and Shula, 1987, for an overview.

14. In Nigeria, farmers intercrop local and high-yielding varieties of cassava, which mature at different times and have different "harvest life" periods, apparently for similar reasons (Berry, 1986:30).

Bibliography

Abalu, George. 1976. "A note on crop mixtures." *Journal of Development Studies* 12, 3:212–20.

Abbott, Susan. 1974. *Full-time farmers and weekend wives: Change and stress among rural Kikuyu women.* Ph.D. diss. University of North Carolina.

Abbott, Susan. 1976. "Full-time farmers and week-end wives." *Journal of Marriage and the Family* 38, 1:165–74.

Abernethy, David. 1969. *The political dilemma of popular education in southern Nigeria.* Stanford: Stanford University Press.

Aboyade, O., and A. Ayida. 1971. "The war economy in perspective." *Nigerian Journal of Economic and Social Studies* 13, 1:13–38.

Abu, Katherine. 1983. "The separateness of spouses: Conjugal resources in an Ashanti town." In C. Oppong, ed., *Female and male in West Africa.* London: George Allen & Unwin.

Adam, M. 1980. "Manioc, rente foncière et situation des femmes dans les environs de Brazzaville." *Cahiers d'Études Africaines* 77–78, XX, 1–2:5–48.

Addo, N. O. 1972. "Employment and labour supply on Ghana's cocoa farms in the pre- and post-Aliens Compliance Order era." *Economic Bulletin of Ghana* 2nd series, 2, 4:33–50.

Addo, N. O. 1974. "Some employment and labour conditions on Ghana's cocoa farms." In R. A. Kotey et al., *Economics of cocoa production and marketing.* Legon: Institute for Statistical, Social, and Economic Research.

Adegboye, Rufus A. 1967. "The need for land reform in Nigeria." *Nigerian Journal of Economics and Social Studies* 9, 4:339–50.

Adewoye, Omoniyi. 1977. *The judicial system of southern Nigeria, 1900–1950.* Atlantic Highlands, N.J.: Humanities Press.

Adeyeye, S. O. 1967. "The Western Nigeria Co-operative movement, 1935–64." Master's thesis. University of Ibadan.

Adomako-Sarfoh, J. 1974. "Migrant cocoa farmers and their families." In C. Oppong, ed., *Domestic rights and duties in southern Ghana.* Legon Family Research Papers, No. 1. Legon: Institute for African Studies, University of Ghana.

Afigbo, A. E. 1972. *The warrant chiefs: Indirect rule in southeastern Nigeria, 1891–1929.* London: Longman.

Afigbo, A. E. 1982. "The Native Revenue Ordinance in the Eastern Provinces: The adventures of a colonial legislative measure." In B. Obichere, ed., *Studies in southern Nigerian history.* London: Frank Cass.

Agiri, B. A. 1972. *Kola in western Nigeria, 1850–1950, a history of the cultivation of cola nitida in Egba-Owode, Ijebu-Remo, Iwo and Ota areas.* Ph.D. diss. University of Wisconsin.

Akintoye, S. A. 1971. *Revolution and power politics in Yorubaland, 1840–1893.* Ibadan History Series. London: Heinemann.

Alila, Patrick et al. 1985. "The rural landlessness situation in Kenya." Institute for Development Studies, University of Nairobi.

Allan, William. 1965. *The African husbandman.* New York: Barnes & Noble.

Alvis, V., and P. Temu. 1966. *The marketing of selected food crops in Kenya.* Nairobi: Institute for Development Studies.

Ambler, Charles. 1988. *Kenyan communities in the age of imperialism.* New Haven: Yale University Press.

Anderson, David. 1984. "Depression, dust bowl, demography, and drought." *African Affairs* 83, 332:321–44.

Andrae, Gunilla, and Bjorn Beckman. 1986. "The Nigerian wheat trap." In Peter Lawrence, ed., *World recession and the food crisis in Africa.* London: James Currey.

Anthony, K., et al. 1979. *Agricultural change in tropical Africa.* Ithaca: Cornell University Press.

Anyang' Nyang'o, Peter. 1987. "Agrarian capitalist classes in the Ivory Coast." In Paul Lubeck, ed., *The African bourgeoisie: Capitalist development in Nigeria, Kenya, and the Ivory Coast.* Boulder, Colo.: Lynne Rienner.

Apter, David. 1963. *Ghana in transition.* New York: Athenaeum.

Arhin, Kwame. 1972. "The Ashanti rubber trade with the Gold Coast in the 1890s." *Africa* 42, 1:32–43.

Arhin, Kwame. 1979. *West African traders in the nineteenth and twentieth centuries.* London: Longman.

Arhin, K. 1985. *The expansion of cocoa production in Ghana: The working conditions of migrant cocoa farmers in Central and Western Regions.* Mimeographed.

Arhin, K., P. Hesp, and L. van der Laan. 1985. *Marketing boards in tropical Africa.* London: Routledge & Kegan Paul.

Arntzen, J. W., et al. 1986. *Land policy and agriculture in eastern and southern Africa.* Tokyo: United Nations University.

Aronson, Dan. 1978. *The city is our farm.* Cambridge, Mass.: Schenkman.

Asante, S. K. B. 1975. *Property law and social goals in Ghana, 1844–1966.* Accra: Ghana Universities Press.

Asiegbu, A. J. 1984. *Nigeria and its British invaders.* New York: Nok.

Atanda, J. 1973. *The new Oyo empire: Indirect rule and change in Western Nigeria, 1894–1934.* London: Longman.

Austin, Dennis. 1964. *Politics in Ghana.* London: Oxford University Press.

Austin, Gareth. 1987. "The emergence of capitalist relations in south Asante cocoa-farming, c. 1916–33." *Journal of African History* 28, 4:259–79.

Austin, Gareth. 1988. "Capitalists and chiefs in the cocoa hold-ups in south Asante, 1927–1938." *International Journal of African Historical Studies* 21, 1:63–96.

Ayako, Aloys et al. 1989. "Contract farming and outgrower schemes in Kenya: Comparative analysis." *Eastern Africa Economic Review* Special Issue, August.

Baldwin, K. D. S. 1957. *The Niger Agricultural Project.* Oxford: Basil Blackwell.

Baldwin, Robert E. 1966. *Export growth and economic development in Northern Rhodesia.* Berkeley and Los Angeles: University of California Press.

Barber, Karin. 1982. "Popular reactions to the petro-naira." *Journal of Modern African Studies* 20, 3:431–50.

Bardhan, Pranab. 1980. "Interlocking factor markets and agrarian development: A review of issues." *Oxford Economic Papers* 32:82–98.

Bardhan, Pranab. 1989. "Alternative approaches to the theory of institutions in economic development." In P. Bardhan, ed., *The economic theory of agrarian institutions.* Oxford: Clarendon Press.

Barkan, Joel, ed. 1984. *Politics and public policy in Kenya and Tanzania*. Rev. ed. New York: Praeger.

Barker, Jonathan. 1984. *The politics of agriculture in tropical Africa.* Beverly Hills, Calif.: Sage.

Barnes, Carolyn. 1984. "Differentiation by sex among small-scale farming households in Kenya." *Rural Africana* 15/16:41–63.

Barnes, Sandra. 1986. *Patrons and power: Creating a political community in metropolitan Lagos.* Bloomington, Ind.: Indiana University Press.

Bassett, Thomas. 1993. "Land use conflicts in pastoral development in northern Ivory Coast." In Thomas Bassett and Donald Crummey, eds., *Land in African agrarian systems.* Madison: University of Wisconsin Press.

Bassett, Thomas, and Donald Crummey, eds. 1993. *Land in African agrarian systems.* Madison: University of Wisconsin Press.

Bateman, Merrill. 1969. "Supply relations for perennial crops in the less developed areas." In C. Wharton, ed., *Subsistence agriculture and economic development.* Chicago: Aldine.

Bates, Robert. 1976. *Rural responses to industrialization.* New Haven, Conn.: Yale University Press.

Bates, Robert. 1981. *Markets and states in tropical Africa.* Berkeley and Los Angeles: University of California Press.

Bates, Robert. 1983. *Essays on the political economy of rural Africa.* Cambridge: Cambridge University Press.

Bates, Robert. 1989. *Beyond the miracle of the market: The political economy of agrarian development in Kenya.* Cambridge: Cambridge University Press.

Bauer, Peter. 1963. *West African trade.* London: Routledge & Kegan Paul.

Baylies, Carolyn, and Morris Szeftel. 1984. "The rise to political prominence of the Zambian business class." In Gertzel et al., eds., *The dynamics of the one-party state in Zambia.* Manchester: Manchester University Press.

Becker, Gary S. 1962. "Irrational behavior and economic theory." *Journal of Political Economy* 70, 1:1–13.

Beckett, W. H. 1944. *Akokoaso.* London: Percy, Lund Humphries for the London School of Economics.

Beckman, Bjorn. 1978. *Organizing the farmers: cocoa politics and national development in Ghana.* Uppsala: Scandinavian Institute of African Studies.

Beckman, Bjorn. 1981. "Ghana, 1951–78: The agrarian basis of the post-colonial state." In J. Heyer et al., eds., *Rural development in tropical Africa.* New York: St. Martin's.

Beer, C. E. F. 1976. *The politics of peasant groups in western Nigeria.* Ibadan: Ibadan University Press.

Beinart, William. 1980. *The political economy of Pondoland, 1860–1930.* Cambridge: Cambridge University Press.

Beinart, William. 1984. "Soil erosion, conservationism and ideas about development: A southern African exploration, 1900–1960." *Journal of Southern African Studies* 11, 1:52–83.

Beinart, William. 1989. "Introduction: The politics of colonial conservation." *Journal of Southern African Studies* 15, 2. Special issue on the politics of conservation in southern Africa.

Beinart, William, Peter Delius, and Stanley Trapido, eds. 1986. *Putting a plough to the ground.* Johannesburg: Ravan.

Beinart, William, and Colin Bundy. 1987. *Hidden struggles in rural South Africa.* London: James Currey.

Benneh, George. 1970. "The impact of cocoa cultivation on the traditional land tenure system of the Akan of Ghana." *Ghana Journal of Sociology* 6, 1:43–60.

Benneh, George. 1973. "Small-scale farming systems in Ghana." *Africa*, 43,2:134–46.

Bequele, Assefa. 1983. "Stagnation and inequality in Ghana." In D. Ghai and S. Radwan, eds., *Agrarian policies and rural poverty in Africa.* Geneva: ILO.

Berg, Robert, and Jennifer Whitaker, eds. 1986. *Strategies for African development.* Berkeley and Los Angeles: University of California Press.

Berman, Bruce. 1990. *Control and crisis in colonial Kenya.* London, Nairobi, and Athens, Ohio: James Currey, Heinemann, and Ohio University Press.

Berman, Bruce, and John Lonsdale. 1980. "Crises of accumulation, coercion, and the colonial state: The development of the labor control system in Kenya, 1919–1929." *Canadian Journal of African Studies* 14, 1:37–54.

Bernstein, Henry, and Bonnie Campbell, eds. 1985. *Contradictions of accumulation in Africa.* Beverly Hills: Sage.

Berry, Sara. 1975. *Cocoa, custom and socio-economic change in rural western Nigeria.* Oxford: Clarendon Press.

Berry, Sara. 1976. "Supply response reconsidered: Cocoa in western Nigeria, 1909–44." *Journal of Development Studies* 13, 1:4–17.

Berry, Sara. 1983. "Work, migration and class in western Nigeria: A reinterpretation." In Fred Cooper, ed., *Struggle for the city: Migrant labor, capital and the state in urban Africa.* Beverly Hills: Sage.

Berry, Sara. 1984. "The food crisis and agrarian change in Africa." *African Studies Review* 27, 2:59–112.

Berry, Sara. 1985. *Fathers work for their sons.* Berkeley and Los Angeles: University of California Press.

Berry, Sara. 1986. "Socio-economic aspects of cassava cultivation and use in Africa: Implications for the development of appropriate technology." Unpublished paper.

Berry, Sara. 1987. "Oil and the disappearing peasantry: Accumulation, differentiation, and underdevelopment in western Nigeria." In M. Watts, ed., *State, oil, and agriculture in Nigeria.* Berkeley, Calif.: Institute of International Studies, University of California, Berkeley.

Berry, Sara. 1988a. "Property rights and rural resource management: The case of tree crops in West Africa." *Cahiers des Sciences Humaines* 24, 1:3–17.

Berry, Sara. 1988b. "Concentration without privatization? Some consequences of changing patterns of rural land control in Africa." In R. E. Downs and S. P. Reyna, eds., *Land and society in contemporary Africa.* Durham, N.H.: University Press of New England.

Berry, Sara. 1989. "Social institutions and access to resources in African agriculture." *Africa* 59, 1:41–55.

Berry, Sara. 1990. "Migrant farmers and land tenure in the Nigerian cocoa belt." In O. Otite and C. Okali, eds., *Readings in Nigerian rural society and rural economy.* Ibadan: Heinemann.

Binswanger, Hans, et al. 1987. *Agricultural mechanization and the evolution of farming systems in sub-Saharan Africa.* Baltimore: Johns Hopkins University Press.

Birmingham, Walter, et al., 1966. *The economy of Ghana.* Vol. 2 of *A study of contemporary Ghana.* Evanston, Ill.: Northwestern University Press.

Boesen, Jannik, and A. T. Mohele, 1979. *The 'success story' of tobacco farming in Tanzania.* Uppsala: Scandinavian Institute of African Studies.

Bond, George. 1987. "Religion, ideology and property in northern Zambia." In Irving Markovitz, ed., *Studies in class and power in Africa.* New York and Oxford: Oxford University Press.

Boulet, J. 1975. *Magoumaz: Pays Mafa (nord Cameroun) (Étude d'un territoire montagne).* ORSTOM, Atlas des Structures Agraires au Sud du Sahara, 11. Paris: Mouton.

Bratton, Michael. 1980a. *The local politics of rural development: Peasant and party-state in Zambia.* Hanover, N.H.: University Press of New England.

Bratton, Michael. 1980b. "The social context of political penetration." In Tordoff, ed., *Administration in Zambia.* Manchester: Manchester University Press.

Brokensha, David. 1966. *Social change in Larteh, Ghana.* Oxford: Clarendon Press.

Brokensha, David, and Jack Glazier. 1973. "Land reform among the Mbeere of central Kenya." *Africa* 43, 3:182–206.

Brown, C. V. 1966. *The Nigerian banking system.* London: Allen and Unwin.

Bruce, John. 1986. "Land tenure issues in project design and strategies for agricultural development in sub-Saharan Africa." Madison, Wis.: Land Tenure Center.

Bruce, John. 1988. "A perspective on indigenous land-tenure systems and land concentration." In R. E. Downs and S. P. Reyna, eds., *Land and society in contemporary Africa.* Durham, N.H.: University Press of New England.

Bukh, Jette. 1979. *The village woman in Ghana.* Uppsala: Scandinavian Institute of African Studies.

Bullock, R. A. 1974. *Ndeiya: Kikuyu frontier.* Waterloo, Ontario: University of Waterloo, Dept. of Geography.

Bury, Barbara. 1983. *The human ecology and political economy of agricultural production on the Ufipa Plateau, Tanzania, 1945–81.* Ph.D. diss. Columbia University.

Busia, K. A. 1951. *The position of the chief in the modern political system of Ashanti.* London: Oxford University Press.

Bwalya, M. C. 1979. "Problems of village regrouping: The case of Serenje District." In D. Honeybone and A. Marter, eds., *Poverty and wealth in rural Zambia.* Lusaka: Institute for African Studies, University of Zambia.

Bwalya, M. C. 1980. "Rural differentiation and poverty reproduction in northern Zambia. The case of Mpika District." In R. Finch and J. Markakis, eds., *The evolving structure of Zambian society.* Edinburgh: Centre for African Studies, University of Edinburgh.

Caldwell, Jack C. 1969. *African rural-urban migration: The movement to Ghana's towns.* New York: Columbia University Press.

Callaghy, Thomas. 1987. "The state as lame leviathan: The patrimonial administrative state in Africa." In Zaki Ergas, ed., *The African state in transition.* New York: St. Martin's.

Callaghy, Thomas. 1988. "The state and the development of capitalism in Africa." In Chazan and Rothchild, eds., *The precarious balance: State and society in Africa.* Boulder, Colo.: Westview.

Canter, Richard. 1978. "Dispute settlement and dispute processing in Zambia." In L. Nader and H. Todd, eds., *The disputing process.* New York: Columbia University Press.

Carney, Judith. 1988. "Struggles over crop rights and labor within contract farming households in a Gambian irrigated rice project." *Journal of Peasant Studies* 15, 3:334–49.

Carney, Judith, and Michael Watts. 1990. "Manufacturing dissent: Work, gender and the politics of meaning in a peasant society." *Africa* 60, 2:207–41.

Carter, Michael, et al. 1990. "Tenure security for whom? An econometric analysis of the differential impacts of land policy in Kenya." Paper prepared for a conference on Rural Land Tenure, Credit, Agricultural Investment & Farm Productivity in Sub-Saharan Africa, Nairobi, June 4–8.

Chanock, Martin. 1985. *Law, custom and social order.* Cambridge: Cambridge University Press.

Chanock, Martin. 1991. "Paradigms, policies and property: A review of the customary law of land tenure." In K. Mann and R. Roberts, eds., *Law in colonial Africa.* Portsmouth, N.H. and London: Heinemann and James Currey.

Chauveau, Jean-Pierre, et al. 1981. "Histoires de riz, histoires d'igname: Le cas de la moyenne Côte d'Ivoire." *Africa* 51, 2:621–58.

Chazan, Naomi. 1983. *Anatomy of Ghanaian politics: Managing political recession, 1968–1982.* Boulder, Colo.: Westview.

Chazan, Naomi, and D. Pellow. 1986. *Ghana: coping with uncertainty.* Boulder, Colo.: Westview.

Chazan, Naomi, and Donald Rothchild, eds. 1988. *The precarious balance: State and society in Africa.* Boulder, Colo.: Westview.

Chazan, Naomi, et al. 1988. *Politics and society in contemporary Africa.* Boulder, Colo.: Lynne Rienner.

Cheater, Angela. 1981. "Women and their participation in commercial agricultural production: The case of medium-scale freehold in Zimbabwe." *Development and Change* 12:349–77.

Clark, Carolyn, 1975. *Kinship morality in the interaction pattern of some Kikuyu families.* Ph.D. diss. Michigan State University.

Clark, Carolyn. 1980. "Land and food, women and power in 19th century Kikuyu." *Africa* 50, 1:357–70.

Clark, Gracia, ed. 1988. *Traders versus the state: Anthropological approaches to unofficial economies.* Boulder, Colo.: Westview.

Clayton, A., and D. Savage. 1974. *Government and labour in Kenya, 1895–1963.* London: Frank Cass.

Clayton, Eric. 1964. *Agrarian development in peasant economies.* New York: Macmillan.

Cleave, John. 1974. *African farmers.* New York: Praeger.

Cliffe, Lionel. 1978. "Labour migration and peasant differentiation: The Zambian case." *Journal of Peasant Studies* 5, 3:326–46.

Clough, Paul, 1985. "The social relations of grain marketing in northern Nigeria." *Review of African Political Economy* 34:16–34.

Clough, Marshall. 1990. *Fighting two sides: Kenyan chiefs and politicians, 1918–1940.* Boulder, Colo.: University Press of Colorado.

Cobbing, Julian. 1988. "The mfecane as alibi: Thoughts on Dithakong and Mbolompo." *Journal of African History* 29:487–519.

Cock, James. 1985. *Cassava: New potential for a neglected crop.* Boulder, Colo.: Westview.

Coker Commission. 1962. *Report of the Commission of Inquiry into certain statutory corporations in Western Nigeria.* Ibadan: Government Printer.

Colclough, C. 1985. "Competing paradigms—and lack of evidence—in the analysis of African development." In Tore Rose, ed., *Crisis and recovery in sub-Saharan Africa.* Paris: OECD.

Coldham, Simon. 1978a. "Land control in Kenya." *Journal of African Law* 22, 1:63–77.

Coldham, Simon. 1978b. "The effect of registration of title upon customary land rights in Kenya." *Journal of African Law* 22, 2:91–111.

Coldham, Simon. 1979. "Land tenure reform in Kenya: The limits of law." *Journal of Modern African Studies* 17, 4:615–27.

Coleman, James S. 1960. *Nigeria: Background to nationalism.* Berkeley and Los Angeles: University of California Press.

Collier, Paul. 1983. "Malfunctioning of African rural factor markets: Theory and a Kenyan example." *Oxford Bulletin of Economics and Statistics* 45, 2:141–72.

Collier, Paul. 1988. "Oil shocks and food security in Nigeria." *International Labour Review* 127, 6:761–82.

Collier, Paul, and Deepak Lal. 1979. *Poverty and growth in Kenya*. Studies in Employment and Rural Development, No. 55. Washington, D.C.: IBRD.

Collier, Paul, and Deepak Lal. 1980. "Poverty and growth in Kenya." World Bank Staff Working Paper No. 389.

Collier, Paul, and Deepak Lal. 1984. "Why poor people get rich: Kenya, 1960–74." *World Development* 12, 10:1007–18.

Collier, Paul, and Deepak Lal. 1986. *Labour and poverty in Kenya, 1900–1980.* London: Oxford University Press.

Collinson, Michael. 1982. *Farming systems research in Eastern Africa.* East Lansing, Mich.: Department of Agricultural Economics, Michigan State University.

Colson, Elizabeth. 1971. "The impact of the colonial period on the definition of land rights." In Victor Turner, ed., *Profiles of change: African society and colonial rule.* Vol. 3 of L. Gann and P. Duignan, eds., *Colonialism in Africa.* Cambridge: Cambridge University Press.

Colson, Elizabeth, and Thayer Scudder. 1988. *For prayer and profit.* Stanford: Stanford University Press.

Comaroff, John. 1980. *The meaning of marriage payments.* London: Academic Press.

Comaroff, John, and Jean Comaroff. 1987. "The madman and the migrant: Work and labor in the historical consciousness of a South African people." *American Ethnologist* 14, 2:191–209.

Comaroff, John, and Jean Comaroff. 1991. *Of revelation and revolution: Christianity, colonialism and consciousness in South Africa.* Vol. 1. Chicago: University of Chicago Press.

Commins, Stephen, et al. 1986. *Africa's agrarian crisis: the roots of famine.* Boulder, Colo.: Lynne Rienner.

Cooper, Frederick, ed. 1983. *Struggle for the city: Migrant labor, capital, and the state in urban Africa.* Beverly Hills: Sage.

Cooper, Frederick. 1990. "Mau Mau and the discourses of decolonization." *Journal of African History* 29:313–20.

Coquery-Vidrovitch, Catherine. 1969. "Recherche sur un mode de production africain." *La pensée* 144:61–78.

Coray, Michael. 1978. "The Kenya Land Commission and the Kikuyu of Kiambu." *Agricultural History* 52, 1:179–93.

Cowen, Michael. 1972. "Differentiation in a Kenya location." East Africa Universities Social Science Council. Eighth Annual Conference Proceedings. Vol. I.

Cowen, Michael. 1974. "Concentration of sales and assets: Dairy cattle and tea in Magutu, 1964–71." Nairobi: Institute for Development Studies Working Paper No. 146.

Cowen, Michael. 1978. "Capital and household production: The case of wattle in Kenya's Central Province, 1903–64." Ph.D. diss. Cambridge University.

Cowen, Michael. 1981. "Commodity production in Kenya's Central Province." In J. Heyer et al., eds., *Rural development in tropical Africa.* New York: St. Martin's.

Cowen, Michael. 1982. "The British state and agrarian accumulation in Kenya." In Martin Fransman, ed., *Industry and accumulation in Africa.* New York: St. Martin's.

Cowen, Michael. 1984. "Early years of the Colonial Development Corporation: British state enterprise overseas during late colonialism." *African Affairs* 83, 332:63–75.

Cowen, Michael, with Fred Murage. 1972. "Notes on agricultural wage labour in a Kenya location." In *Developmental trends in Kenya*. Edinburgh: Centre for African Studies, University of Edinburgh.

Cowen, Michael, and Kabiru Kinyanjui. 1977. "Some problems of capital and class in Kenya." Occasional Paper No. 26. Nairobi: Institute for Development Studies, University of Nairobi.

Cowie, W. J. 1979. "Aspects of resource access among villagers and farmers in Kanyanja Parish, Chipata District." In D. Honeybone and A. Marter, eds., *Poverty and wealth in rural Zambia.* Lusaka: Institute for African Studies, University of Zambia.

Crook, Richard. 1986. "Decolonization, the colonial state, and chieftaincy in the Gold Coast." *African Affairs*, 85:75–105.

Crook, Richard. 1988. "Farmers and the state." In Douglas Rimmer, ed., *Rural transformation in tropical Africa.* Athens, Ohio: Ohio University Press.

Cruise O'Brien, Donal. 1971. *The Mourides of Senegal.* Oxford: Clarendon Press.

Cutshall, Charles. 1982. "Culprits, culpability and crime: Stocktheft and other cattle manoeuvers among the Ila of Zambia." *African Studies Review* 25, 1:1–26.

Daniel, Philip. 1979. *Africanization, nationalization and inequality.* Cambridge: Cambridge University Press.

Delgado, Christopher, and John Mellor. 1984. "A structural view of policy issues in African agricultural development." *American Journal of Agricultural Economics* 66, 5:665–70.

Derrick, Jonathan. 1984. "West Africa's worst year of famine." *African Affairs* 83, 332:281–99.

De Schlippe, P. 1956. *Shifting cultivation: The Zande system of agriculture.* London: Routledge and Kegan Paul.

Dewey, Clive, and A. G. Hopkins, eds. 1978. *The imperial impact.* London: Institute of Commonwealth Studies.

De Wilde, John. 1967. *Experiences with agricultural development in tropical Africa.* Vol. 2. Baltimore: Johns Hopkins University Press.

De Wilde, John. 1984. *Agricultural marketing and pricing in sub-Saharan Africa.* Los Angeles: African Studies Center, University of California at Los Angeles.

Dey, Jennie. 1982. "Development planning in the Gambia: The gap between planners' and farmers' perceptions, expectations and objectives." *World Development* 10, 5:377–96.

Dodge, Doris. 1977. *Agricultural policy and performance in Zambia.* Berkeley, Calif.: Institute for International Studies.

Douglas, Mary. 1969. "Is matriliny doomed in Africa?" In M. Douglas and P. Kaberry, eds., *Man in Africa*. London: Tavistock.

Downs, Richard E., and Stephen P. Reyna, eds. 1988. *Land and society in contemporary Africa*. Durham, N.H.: University Press of New England.

Dozon, Jean-Pierre. 1979. "Impasses et contradictions d'une société de développement: l'exemple de l'opération 'riziculture irriguée' en Côte d'Ivoire." *Cahiers ORSTOM*, série Science Humaine, 16,1–2:37–58.

Dudley, Billy. 1973. *Instability and political order: politics and crisis in Nigeria.* Ibadan: Ibadan University Press.

Dudley, Billy. 1982. *An introduction to Nigerian government and politics.* Bloomington, Ind.: Indiana University Press.

Dumett, Raymond. 1971. "The rubber trade of the Gold Coast and Asante in the nineteenth century: African innovation and market responsiveness." *Journal of African History* 12, 1:79–101.

Dunn, John, and A. F. Robertson. 1973. *Dependence and opportunity: Political change in Brong Ahafo.* Cambridge: Cambridge University Press.

Dunn, John, ed. 1978. *West African states: Failure and promise.* Cambridge: Cambridge University Press.

Eades, Jeremy. 1979. "Kinship and entrepreneurship among Yoruba in northern Ghana." In William Shack and Elliott Skinner, eds., *Strangers in Africa.* Berkeley and Los Angeles: University of California Press.

Edsman, Bjorn. 1979. *Lawyers in Gold Coast politics.* Ph.D. diss. Uppsala University. Stockholm: Almqvist & Wiksell.

Eele, G. 1989. "The organization and management of statistical services in Africa: Why do they fail?" *World Development* 17, 3:431–38.

Eicher, Carl K. 1982. "Facing up to Africa's food crisis." *Foreign Affairs* 61:151–74.

Eicher, Carl K., and Doyle Baker. 1982. *Research on agricultural development in sub-Saharan Africa.* East Lansing, Mich.: Department of Agricultural Economics, Michigan State University.

Elias, T. O. 1951. *Nigerian land law and custom.* London: Routledge & Kegan Paul.

Elliot, Charles. 1971. *Constraints on economic development in Zambia.* London and Nairobi: Oxford University Press.

Elliot, Charles. 1983. "Equity and growth: An unresolved conflict in Zambian development." In Ghai and Radwan, eds., *Agrarian policies and rural poverty in Africa.* Geneva: ILO.

Ellis, Frank. 1982. "Agricultural price policy in Tanzania." *World Development* 10, 4:263–83.

Epstein, A. L. 1958. *Politics in an African urban community.* Manchester: Manchester University Press, for the Rhodes-Livingstone Institute.

Ergas, Zaki, ed. 1987. *The African state in transition.* New York: St. Martin's.

Essang, Sunday M. 1970. *The distribution of earnings in the cocoa economy of Western Nigeria.* Ph.D. diss. Michigan State University.

Fallers, Lloyd A. 1950. *Bantu bureaucracy.* Cambridge: Heffer.

Fallers, Lloyd A. 1961. "Are African cultivators to be called 'peasants'?" *Current Anthropology* 2:108–10.

Falola, Toyin, and Julius Ihonvbere. 1985. *The rise and fall of Nigeria's Second Republic, 1979–84.* London: Zed Press.

Famoriyo, Segun. 1973. "Some problems of customary land tenure system in Nigeria." *Land Reform, Land Settlement and Cooperatives* 2:1–11.

FAO, 1986. *Irrigation in Africa south of the Sahara.* Investment Centre Technical Paper 5. Rome: FAO.

Feder, Gershon, and R. Noronha. 1987. "Land rights systems and agricultural development in sub-Saharan Africa." *World Bank Research Observer* 2, 1:143–69.

Feierman, Steven. 1974. *The Shambaa kingdom: A history.* Madison: University of Wisconsin Press.

Feierman, Steven. 1990. *Peasant intellectuals: Anthropology and history in Tanzania.* Madison: University of Wisconsin Press.

Ferraro, Gary. 1970. "Kikuyu kinship interaction in Nairobi and rural Kiambu." Discussion Paper 12. Nairobi: Institute for Development Studies, Cultural Division, University of Nairobi.

Ferraro, Gary. 1976. "Changing patterns of bridewealth among the Kikuyu of East Africa." In W. Arens, ed., *A century of change in East and Central Africa.* The Hague: Mouton.

Fisher, Humphrey. 1982. "Early Arabic sources and the Almoravid conquest of Ghana." *Journal of African History* 23:549–60.

Fisher, Jeanne. 1954? *The anatomy of Kikuyu domesticity and husbandry.* London: Department of Technical Cooperation.

Fitch, Bob, and Mary Oppenheimer. 1966. *Ghana: End of an illusion.* New York: Monthly Review Press.

Folbre, Nancy. 1986a. "Cleaning house: New perspectives on households and economic development." *Journal of Development Economics* 22:5–40.

Folbre, Nancy. 1986b. "Hearts and spades: Paradigms of household economics." *World Development* 14, 2:245–55.

Forde, C. Daryll, and R. Scott. 1946. *The native economies of Nigeria.* Vol. 1 of M. Perham, ed., *The economics of a tropical dependency.* London: Faber & Faber.

Forrest, Tom. 1981. "Agricultural policies in Nigeria, 1900–78." In Heyer, Roberts, and Williams, eds., *Rural development in tropical Africa.* New York: St. Martin's.

Forrest, Tom. Forthcoming. *Politics, policy and capitalist development in Nigeria, 1970–88.* Boulder, Colo.: Westview.

Fortes, Meyer. 1948. "The Ashanti social survey: A preliminary report." *Rhodes-Livingstone Journal, Human Problems in British Central Africa* 6:1–36.

Fortes, Meyer. 1975. "Strangers." In M. Fortes and S. Patterson, eds., *Studies in African social anthropology.* London: Academic Press.

Fortes, Meyer, et al. 1948. "The Ashanti survey, 1945–46: An experiment in social research." *The Geographical Journal* 110, 4–6:149–79.

Foster, Philip. 1965. *Education and social change in Ghana.* Chicago: University of Chicago Press.

Francis, Paul. 1981. *Power and order: A study of litigation in a Yoruba community.* Ph.D. diss. University of Liverpool.

Francis, Paul. 1984. " 'For the use and common benefit of all Nigerians': The Land Use Decree of 1978." *Africa*, 54, 3:5–28.

Francis, Paul. 1988. "Ox draught power and agricultural transformation in northern Zambia." *Agricultural Systems* 27:35–49.

Frankel, S. H. 1938. *Capital investment in Africa.* London: Oxford University Press.

Fransman, Martin, ed. 1982. *Industry and accumulation in Africa.* New York: St. Martin's.

Fresco, Louise. 1984. "Comparing anglophone and francophone approaches to farming systems research and extension." Farming Systems Support Project Networking Paper 1. Gainesville: University of Florida.

Fresco, Louise. 1986. *Cassava in shifting cultivation.* Wageningen: Netherlands, Royal Tropical Institute.

Freund, William. 1988. *The African worker.* Cambridge: Cambridge University Press.

Fry, James. 1979. *Employment and income distribution in the African economy.* London: Croom Helm.

Furedi, Frank. 1989. *The Mau Mau war in perspective.* London, Nairobi, and Athens, Ohio: James Curry, Heinemann, and Ohio University Press.

Galletti, R., et al. 1956. *Nigerian cocoa farmers.* London: Oxford University Press.

Gann, Lewis. 1963. *A history of Northern Rhodesia to 1953.* London: Chatto & Windus.

Gaury, C. 1977. "Agricultural mechanization." In C. Leakey and J. Wills, eds., *Food crops of the lowland tropics.* Oxford: Oxford University Press.

Geisler, Gisela, et al. 1985. *Needs of rural women in the Northern Province.* Lusaka: Report prepared for NCDP/NORAD.

Gerhart, John. 1975. *The diffusion of hybrid maize in western Kenya.* Mexico City: CIMMYT.

Gerhart, John. 1986. "Farming systems research, productivity and equity." In Joyce Moock, ed., *Understanding Africa's rural households and farming systems.* Boulder, Colo.: Westview.

Gertzel, Cherry. 1980. "Two case studies in rural development." In William Tordoff, ed., *Administration in Zambia.* Manchester: Manchester University Press.

Gertzel, Cherry, et al. 1984. *The dynamics of the one-party state in Zambia.* Manchester: Manchester University Press.

Geschiere, Peter. 1993. "Kinship, witchcraft and 'the market': Different articulations in southern and western Cameroonian societies." In Roy Dilley, ed., *Contesting markets: the anthropology of ideology, discourse and practice.* Edinburgh: Edinburgh University Press.

Ghai, Dharam, and Lawrence Smith. 1987. *Agricultural prices, policy, and equity in sub-Saharan Africa.* Boulder, Colo.: Lynne Rienner.

Ghai, Dharam, and Samir Radwan. 1983. *Agrarian policies and rural poverty in Africa.* Geneva: International Labor Organization.

Ghana. 1960. *Survey of cocoa producing families in Ashanti, 1956–57.* Statistical and Economic Papers No. 7. Accra: Government Statistician.

Glantz, Michael, ed. 1987. *Drought and hunger in East Africa: Denying famine a future.* Cambridge: Cambridge University Press.

Glazier, Jack. 1985. *Land and the uses of tradition among the Mbeere of Kenya.* New York: University Press of America.

Gluckman, Max. 1941. *The economy of the central Barotse plain.* Livingstone, Northern Rhodesia: The Rhodes-Livingstone Institute.

Gluckman, Max. 1965. *The ideas in Barotse jurisprudence.* Manchester: Manchester University Press.

Goering, T., et al. 1979. *Tropical root crops and rural development.* World Bank Staff Working Paper No. 324. Washington, D.C.: World Bank.

Good, Kenneth. 1986. "Systematic agricultural mismanagement: The 1985 'bumper' harvest in Zambia." *Journal of Modern African Studies* 24, 1:257–84.

Goody, Jack. 1971. *Technology, tradition and the state.* Cambridge: Cambridge University Press.

Goody, Jack. 1980. "Rice burning and the Green Revolution in northern Ghana." *Journal of Development Studies* 16, 2:136–55.

Gray, Richard, and David Birmingham, eds. 1970. *Pre-colonial African trade.* London and New York: Oxford University Press.

Great Britain. 1914. "Correspondence concerning palm oil grants in West Africa." Colonial Office Confidential Print No. 1023.

Great Britain. 1938. *Report of the Commission on the Marketing of West African Cocoa.* House of Commons, Cmd. 5845. London: His Majesty's Stationery Office.

Green, Reginald. 1960. "Ghana cocoa marketing policy, 1958–60." *NISER Conference Proceedings* 132–60.

Green, Reginald, and Stephen Hymer. 1966. "Cocoa in the Gold Coast: A study of the relations between African farmers and agricultural experts." *Journal of Economic History* 26, 3:299–319.

Green, Reginald, and Stephanie Griffith-Jones. 1985. "Africa's external debt." In Tore Rose, ed., *Crisis and recovery in sub-Saharan Africa.* Paris: OECD.

Grier, Beverly. 1987. "Contradictions, crises and class conflict: The state and capitalist development in Ghana prior to 1948." In I. Markovitz, ed., *Studies in class and power in Africa.* New York and London: Oxford University Press.

Guillaumont, Patrick. 1987. "From export instability effects to international stabilization policies." *World Development* 15, 5:633–42.

Guyer, Jane. 1978. "The food economy and French colonial rule in Central Cameroon." *Journal of African History* 19, 4:577–98.

Guyer, Jane. 1980. "Female farming and the evolution of food production patterns amongst the Beti of south-central Cameroon." *Africa* 50, 4:341–56.

Guyer, Jane. 1981. "Household and community in African Studies." *African Studies Review* 24, 2–3:87–137.

Guyer, Jane. 1983. "Women's work and production systems: A review of two reports on the agricultural crisis." *Review of African Political Economy* 27–28:186–92.

Guyer, Jane. 1984. *Family and farm in southern Cameroon.* Boston: Boston University African Studies Center.

Guyer, Jane. 1988. "Everybody's farming now." Paper prepared for the annual meeting of the African Studies Association.

Guyer, Jane. 1991. "Representation without taxation." Boston: Boston University African Studies Center Working Paper 152.

Guyer, Jane, with Olukemi Idowu. 1991. "Women's agricultural work in a multimodal rural economy: Ibarapa District, Oyo State, Nigeria." In Christina Gladwin, ed., *Structural adjustment and African women farmers.* Gainesville: University of Florida Press.

Gwyer, G. D. 1972. "Labour in small-scale agriculture: analysis of the 1970/71 farm enterprise cost survey, labour and wage data." Working Paper 62. Nairobi: Institute for Development Studies, University of Nairobi.

Hailey, William. 1950–53. *Native administration in the British African territories.* 5 vols. London: Her Majesty's Stationery Office.

Hailey, William. 1957. *An African survey.* Rev. ed. London: Oxford University Press.

Hancock, William Keith. 1942. *A survey of commonwealth affairs.* Vol. 2, Pt. 2. London: Oxford University Press.

Hansen, Emmanuel, and Kwame Ninsin, eds. 1989. *State, development and politics in Ghana.* Dakar: CODESRIA.

Hansen, M., and H. Marcussen. 1982. "Contract farming and the peasantry: Case studies from Kenya." *Review of African Political Economy* 23:9–36.

Harries-Jones, Peter, and Jacques Chiwale. 1962. "Kasaka. A case study in succession and dynamics of a Bemba village." *Rhodes-Livingstone Journal, Human Problems in British Central Africa* 33:1–67.

Hart, Gillian. 1986. "Interlocking transactions: Obstacles, precursors or instruments of agrarian capitalism?" *Journal of Development Economics* 23:177–203.

Hart, Gillian. 1991. "Engendering everyday resistance: Politics, gender and class formation in rural Malaysia." *Journal of Peasant Studies* 19, 1:93–121.

Hart, Gillian. 1992. "Household production reconsidered: Gender, labor conflict, and technological change in Malaysia's Muda region." *World Development* 20, 6:809–24.

Hart, Keith. 1973. "Informal income opportunities and urban employment in Africa." *Journal of Modern African Studies* 11, 1:61–90.

Hart, Keith. 1978. "The economic basis of Tallensi social history." In G. Dalton, ed., *Research in Economic Anthropology* 1:185–216.

Hart, Keith. 1982. *The political economy of West African agriculture.* Cambridge: Cambridge University Press.

Harvey, Charles, ed. 1984. *Agricultural pricing policy in Africa: Four case studies.* London: Macmillan.

Haswell, Margaret. 1963. *The changing pattern of economic activity in a Gambian village.* London: Her Majesty's Stationery Office.

Haswell, Margaret. 1975. *The nature of poverty.* London: Macmillan.

Haugerud, Angelique. 1981a. "Development and household economy in two eco-zones of Embu District." Working Paper No. 382. Nairobi: Institute for Development Studies, University of Nairobi.

Haugerud, Angelique. 1981b. "Economic differentiation among peasant households: A comparison of Embu coffee and cotton zones." Working Paper No. 383. Nairobi: Institute for Development Studies, University of Nairobi.

Haugerud, Angelique. 1983. "The consequences of land tenure reform among smallholders in the Kenya highlands." *Rural Africana*, 15–16:65–90.

Haugerud, Angelique. 1984. "Household dynamics and rural political economy among smallholders in the Kenya highlands." Ph.D. diss. Northwestern University.

Haugerud, Angelique. 1988. "Food surplus production, wealth, and farmers' strategies in Kenya." In R. Cohen, ed., *Satisfying Africa's food needs.* Boulder, Colo.: Lynne Rienner.

Haugerud, Angelique. 1989. "Land tenure and agrarian change in Kenya." *Africa* 59, 1:61–90.

Haugerud, Angelique, and Michael Collinson. 1990. "Plants, genes and people: Improving the relevance of plant breeding in Africa." *Experimental Agriculture* 26:341–62.

Havenik, Kjell, ed. 1987. *The IMF and the World Bank in Africa*. Uppsala: Scandinavian Institute of African Studies.

Hayford, J. Casely. 1969. *The truth about the West African land question.* Rev. ed. New York: Negro Universities Press.

Hedlund, Hans, and Mats Lundahl. 1983. *Migration and change in rural Zambia.* Uppsala: Scandinavian Institute of African Studies.

Helleiner, Gerald. 1964. "The fiscal role of the marketing boards in Nigerian economic development, 1947–61." *Economic Journal* 74, 295:582–610.

Helleiner, Gerald. 1966. *Peasant agriculture, government and economic growth in Nigeria.* Homewood, Ill.: R. D. Irwin.

Helleiner, Gerald. 1986a. "Outward orientation, import instability and African economic growth: An empirical investigation." In S. Lall and F. Stewart, eds., *Theory and reality in development: Essays in honor of Paul Streeten.* New York: St. Martin's.

Helleiner, Gerald. 1986b. "The question of conditionality." In Carol Lancaster and John Williamson, eds., *African debt and financing.* Washington, D.C.: Institute for International Economics.

Helleiner, Gerald. 1986c. "Balance of payments experiences and growth prospects of developing countries: A synthesis." *World Development* 14, 8:877–908.

Hellen, John. 1968. *Rural economic development in Zambia, 1890–1964.* Munich: Weltforum Verlag.

Henn, Jeanne. *See* Jeanne Koopman.

Heyer, Judith. 1971. "Linear programming analysis of constraints on peasant farms in Kenya." *Food Research Institute Studies* 10, 1:55–67.

Heyer, Judith. 1981. "Agricultural development policy in Kenya from the colonial period to 1975." In J. Heyer et al., eds., *Rural development in tropical Africa.* New York: St. Martin's.

Heyer, Judith, and J. Waweru. 1976. "The development of the small farm areas." In J. Heyer et al., eds., *Agricultural development in Kenya.* Nairobi: Oxford University Press.

Heyer, Judith, Pepe Roberts, and Gavin Williams, eds. 1981. *Rural development in tropical Africa.* New York: St. Martin's.

Hill, Polly. 1956. *The Gold Coast cocoa farmer.* Oxford: Oxford University Press.

Hill, Polly. 1963. *Migrant cocoa farmers of southern Ghana.* Cambridge: Cambridge University Press.

Hill, Polly. 1968. "The myth of the 'amorphous peasantry': A northern Nigerian case study." *Nigerian Journal of Economics and Social Studies* 10:239–60.

Hill, Polly. 1969. "Hidden trade in Hausaland." *Man* 4, 1:392–409.

Hill, Polly. 1970. *Studies in rural capitalism.* Cambridge: Cambridge University Press.

Hinga, S. N., and J. Heyer. 1976. "The development of large farms." In Heyer et al., eds., *Agricultural development in Kenya.* Nairobi: Oxford University Press.

Hogendorn, Jan. 1975. "Economic initiative and African cash farming." In vol. 4 of P. Duignan and L. Gann, eds., *Colonialism in Africa*. Cambridge: Cambridge University Press.

Hogendorn, Jan. 1978. *Nigerian groundnut exports: Origins and early development*. Zaria and Ibadan: Ahmadu Bello University Press and Oxford University Press.

Holmquist, Frank. 1970. "Implementing rural development policies." In Goran Hyden et al., eds., *Development administration in Kenya*. Berkeley and Los Angeles: University of California Press.

Holmquist, Frank. 1984. "Class structure, peasant participation and rural self help." In Joel Barkan, ed., *Politics and public policy in Kenya and Tanzania*. New York: Praeger.

Homan, F. D. 1962. "Consolidation, enclosure and registration of title in Kenya." *Journal of Local Administration Overseas* 1, 1:4–14.

Homan, F. D. 1963. "Succession to registered land in African areas in Kenya." *Journal of Local Administration Overseas* 2, 1:49–54.

Honeybone, David, and Alan Marter, eds. 1979. *Poverty and wealth in rural Zambia*. Lusaka: Institute for African Studies, University of Zambia.

Hopkins, A. G. 1966. "Economic aspects of political movements in Nigeria and the Gold Coast, 1918–1939." *Journal of African History* 7:133–52.

Hopkins, A. G. 1969. "A report on the Yoruba, 1910." *Journal of the Historical Society of Nigeria* 5, 1:67–100.

Hopkins, A. G. 1973. *An economic history of West Africa*. London: Longman.

Hountoundji, Paulin. 1976. *African philosophy: Myth and reality*. Bloomington, Ind.: Indiana University Press.

House, William, and Tony Killick. 1981. "Inequality and poverty in the rural economy, and the influence of some aspects of policy." In Tony Killick, ed., *Papers on the Kenyan economy*. Nairobi: Heinemann.

Howard, Rhoda. 1976. "Differential class participation in an African protest movement: The Ghana cocoa boycott of 1937–38." *Canadian Journal of African Studies* 10, 3:469–80.

Hunter, John. 1963. "Cocoa migration and patterns of land ownership in the Densu valley near Suhum, Ghana." *Transactions and Papers. Institute of British Geographers*, 31:61–87.

Hyden, Goran. 1980. *Beyond ujamaa in Tanzania*. Berkeley and Los Angeles: University of California Press.

Hyden, Goran. 1983. *No shortcuts to progress: African development management in perspective*. Berkeley and Los Angeles: University of California Press.

Hyden, Goran et al. 1970. *Development administration: The Kenyan experience*. Nairobi: Oxford University Press.

Idowu, Olukemi, and Jane Guyer. 1991. "Commercialization and the harvest work of women, Ibarapa, Oyo State, Nigeria." Women's Research and Documentation Center Working Paper 1. Ibadan: University of Ibadan.

Ikiara, G. K., and T. Killick. 1981. "The performance of the economy since independence." In Tony Killick, ed., *Papers on the Kenyan economy*. Nairobi: Heinemann.

Iliffe, John. 1979. *A modern history of Tanganyika*. Cambridge: Cambridge University Press.

ILO. 1981. *Basic needs in an economy under pressure.* Addis Ababa: ILO.

IDRP. 1983. "Dynamics of cropping patterns and maize production in Serenje, Mpika and Chinsali Districts." In H. Svads, ed., *Proceedings of the seminar on soil productivity in the high rainfall areas of Zambia*. Oslo: Agricultural University of Norway.

Isaacman, Allen. 1990. "Peasants and rural social protest in Africa." *African Studies Review* 33, 2:1–120.

Jabara, Cathy. 1985. "Agricultural pricing policy in Kenya." *World Development* 13, 5:611–26.

Jahnke, Hans, and Hans Ruthenberg. 1985. *Innovation policy for small farmers in the tropics.* Oxford: Clarendon Press.

Jahnke, Hans, et al. 1987. *The impact of agricultural research in tropical Africa.* Washington, D.C.: World Bank.

Jeffries, R. 1982. "Rawlings and the political economy of underdevelopment in Ghana." *African Affairs* 81, 324:307–17.

Jenkins, George D. 1965. *Politics in Ibadan*. Ph.D. diss. Northwestern University.

Jessop, Bob. 1977. "Recent theories of the capitalist state." *Cambridge Journal of Economics* 1, 4:353–74.

Jessop, Bob. 1982. *The capitalist state: Marxist theories and methods.* New York: New York University Press.

Jessop, Bob. 1990. "Regulation theories in retrospect and prospect." *Economy and Society* 19, 2:153–216.

Johnny, Michael, et al. 1981. "Upland and swamp rice farming systems in Sierra Leone: The social context of technological change." *Africa*, 51, 2:596–620.

Johns, Sheridan. 1980. "The parastatal sector." In William Tordoff, ed., *Administration in Zambia*. Manchester: Manchester University Press.

Johnson, Douglas, and David Anderson. 1988. *The ecology of survival: Case studies from northeast African history.* London and Boulder, Colo.: L. Crook and Westview.

Johnson, G. E., and W. E. Whitelaw. 1974. "Urban-rural income transfers in Kenya: An estimated remittances function." *Economic Development and Cultural Change* 22, 3:473–79.

Johnson, Samuel O. 1921. *A history of the Yorubas*. Lagos: Church Missionary Society.

Jones, Christine. 1983. "The mobilization of women's labor for cash crop production: A game theoretic approach." *American Journal of Agricultural Economics* 65, 5:1049–54.

Jones, Christine. 1986. "Intra-household bargaining in response to the introduction of new crops: A case study from northern Cameroon." In Moock, 1986.

Jones, Christine. 1988. "The mobilization of resources for agricultural development in sub-Saharan Africa: An economic perspective." Mimeographed.

Jones, William I., and Roberto Egli. 1984. *Farming systems in Africa: The great lakes highlands of Zaire, Rwanda and Burundi.* Washington, D.C.: World Bank.

Jones, William O. 1959. *Manioc in Africa*. Stanford: Stanford University Press.

Jones, William O. 1972. *Marketing staple food crops in tropical Africa.* Ithaca, N.Y.: Cornell University Press.

Joseph, Richard. 1984. "Class, state and prebendal politics in Nigeria." In Nelson Kasfir, ed., *State and class in Africa*. London: Frank Cass.

Joseph, Richard. 1987. *Democracy and prebendal politics in Nigeria: The rise and fall of the second republic.* Cambridge: Cambridge University Press.

Kamau, G. K. 1987. "The African or customary marriage in Kenyan law today." In David Parkin and David Nyamwira, eds., *Transformations of African marriage.* Manchester: Manchester University Press for the International African Institute.

Kanoga, E. M. 1978. "Informal credits in Mathira Division, Nyeri District." Master's thesis. University of Nairobi.

Kanogo, Tabitha. 1987. *Squatters and the roots of Mau Mau.* London, Nairobi, and Athens, Ohio: James Currey, Heinemann, and Ohio University Press.

Kapferer, Bruce, 1967. *Cooperation, leadership and village structure.* Zambian Paper No. 1. Lusaka: Institute for Social Research, University of Zambia.

Kay, Geoffrey. 1972. *The political economy of colonialism in Ghana.* Cambridge: Cambridge University Press.

Kay, George. 1962. "Agricultural change in the Luitikila Basin Development Area." *Rhodes-Livingstone Journal, Human Problems in British Central Africa* 31:21–50.

Kay, George. 1964a. *Chief Kalaba's village.* Rhodes-Livingstone Institute Papers No. 35. Manchester: Manchester University Press.

Kay, George. 1964b. "Aspects of Ushi settlement history." In R. W. Steele and R. M. Prothero, eds., *Geographers and the tropics.* London: Longman.

Kay, George. 1964c. "Sources and uses of cash in some Ushi villages, Fort Rosebery District, Northern Rhodesia." *Rhodes-Livingstone Journal, Human Problems in British Central Africa* 35:14–28.

Kay, George. 1967. *Social aspects of village regrouping in Zambia.* Lusaka: Institute for Social Research, University of Zambia.

Kayser, B., et al. 1981. "Cherte du manioc et pauvrété paysanne dans le bas-Zaire." *Les Cahiers d'Outre Mer,* 34, 134:97–110.

Keegan, Tim. 1985. "Crisis and catharsis in the development of capitalism in South African agriculture." *African Affairs* 84, 336:371–98.

Kenya. 1945. *The Kikuyu lands.* Nairobi: Government Printer.

Kenya. 1968. *Economic survey of Central Province, 1963–64.* Nairobi: Central Bureau of Statistics.

Kenya. 1979. *Development Plan, 1979–83.* Nairobi: Government Printer.

Kenya, 1982. *The integrated rural surveys, 1976–79. Basic report.* Nairobi: Central Bureau of Statistics.

Kenya Land Commission. 1934a. *Report.* Great Britain, Parliamentary Command Paper No. 4556. London: His Majesty's Stationery Office.

Kenya Land Commission. 1934b. *Evidence and memoranda.* Vol. 1. London: His Majesty's Stationery Office.

Kenyatta, Jomo. 1938. *Facing Mt. Kenya.* London: Faber & Faber.

Kershaw, Gretha. 1975–76. "Changing roles of men and women in the Kikuyu family structure by socioeconomic strata." *Rural Africana* 29:173–94.

Killick, Tony. 1966. "Labour: A general survey." In Walter Birmingham et al., eds., *A study of contemporary Ghana.* Vol. 1. Evanston, Ill.: Northwestern University Press.

Killick, Tony. 1973. "Price controls in Africa: The Ghanaian experience." *Journal of Modern African Studies* 11, 3:405–26.

Killick, Tony. 1978. *Development economics in action: A study of economic policies in Ghana.* New York: St. Martin's.

Killick, Tony, ed. 1981. *Papers on the Kenyan economy.* Nairobi: Heinemann.

Killick, Tony, and William House. 1983. "Social justice and development policy in Kenya's rural economy." In Dharam Ghai and Samir Radwan, eds., *Agrarian policies and rural poverty in Africa.* Geneva: International Labor Organization.

Killingray, David. 1986. "Maintenance of law and order in British colonial Africa." *African Affairs* 85:411–37.

Kimble, David. 1963. *A political history of Ghana.* Oxford: Clarendon Press.

King, Kenneth. 1977. *The African artisan.* London: Heinemann.

Kitching, Gavin. 1980. *Class and economic change in Kenya.* New Haven, Conn.: Yale University Press.

Kitching, Gavin. 1985. "Politics, method and evidence in the 'Kenya debate.' In H. Bernstein and B. Campbell, eds., *Contradictions of accumulation in Africa.* Beverly Hills: Sage.

Klein, Martin. 1967. *Islam and imperialism in Senegal.* Stanford: Stanford University Press.

Klein, Martin, ed. 1980. *Peasants in Africa.* Beverly Hills: Sage.

Klepper, R. 1980. "State and peasantry in Zambia." In R. Finch and J. Markakis, eds., *Evolving structure of Zambian society.* Edinburgh: Centre for African Studies, University of Edinburgh.

Konings, Piet. 1986. *The state and rural class formation in Ghana: A comparative analysis.* London: Kegan Paul.

Koopman, Jeanne. 1983. "Feeding the cities and feeding the peasants: What role for Africa's women farmers?" *World Development* 11, 12:1043–55.

Koopman, Jeanne. 1988. "The material basis of sexism: A mode of production analysis." In Jane Parpart and Sharon Stichter, eds., *Patriarchy and class in Africa.* Boulder, Colo.: Westview.

Kopytoff, Igor. 1987. *The African frontier: The reproduction of traditional African societies.* Bloomington, Ind.: Indiana University Press.

Kotey, R. A., C. Okali, and B. E. Rourke, eds. 1974. *The economics of cocoa production and marketing.* Legon: Institute for Statistical, Social and Economic Research.

Kowal, J. M., and A. H. Kassam. 1978. *Agricultural ecology of savannah: A study of West Africa.* Oxford: Clarendon Press.

Kuklick, Henrika. 1979. *The imperial bureaucrat: The colonial administrative service in the Gold Coast, 1920–39.* Stanford: Hoover Institution Press.

Kydd, Jonathan. 1988. "Zambia." In Charles Harvey, ed., *Agricultural pricing policy in Africa.* London: Macmillan.

Kyerematen, A. A. Y. 1971. *Inter-state boundary litigation in Ashanti.* African Social Research Documents 4. Cambridge: African Studies Center, Cambridge University.

Lagemann, Johannes. 1977. *Traditional farming systems in eastern Nigeria.* Munich: IFO Institut für Wirtschaftsforschung.

Lamb, Geoffrey. 1974. *Peasant politics: Conflict and development in Murang'a.* New York: St. Martin's.

Lamb, Geoffrey, and Linda Muller. 1982. *Control, accountability and incentives in a successful development institution: The Kenya Tea Development Authority.* Washington, D.C.: World Bank.

Lancaster, Carol. 1990. "Governance in Africa: Should foreign aid be linked to political reform?" In *African Governance in the 1990s.* Working Papers from the Second Annual Seminar of the African Governance Program. Atlanta: The Carter Center of Emory University.

Lancaster, Carol, and John Williamson, eds. 1986. *African debt and financing.* Washington, D.C.: Institute for International Economics.

LaRue, George Michael. 1989. *The hakura system: Land and social stratification in the social and economic history of the sultanate of Dar Fur (Sudan), ca. 1785–1875.* Ph.D. diss. Boston University.

Latzke Begemann, U. 1985. "Compound gardening in southeastern Nigeria." Ibadan: International Institute for Tropical Agriculture.

Lawrence, Peter, ed. 1986. *World recession and the African food crisis.* London: James Currey.

Lawson, Rowena. 1977. *Agricultural entrepreneurship of upper income Africans.* London: Ministry of Overseas Development.

Leakey, Louis. 1977. *The southern Kikuyu before 1903.* 3 vols. London: Academic Press.

Lele, Uma, and Douglas Candler. 1981. "Food security: Some East African considerations." In A. Valdes, ed., *Food security in East and Central Africa.* Boulder, Colo.: Westview.

Leonard, David. 1977. *Reaching the peasant farmers: Organization theory and practice in Kenya.* Chicago: University of Chicago Press.

Leonard, David. 1991. *African successes: Four public managers of Kenyan rural development.* Berkeley and Los Angeles: University of California Press.

Leubuscher, Charlotte. 1963. *The West African shipping trade, 1909–59.* Leyden: A. W. Sythoff.

Levi, J., and M. A. Havinden. 1982. *Economics of African agriculture.* Harlow: Longman.

Lewin, Thomas. 1978. *Asante before the British: The Prempean years, 1885–1900.* Lawrence: Regents Press of Kansas.

Lewis, John van Dusen. 1981. "Domestic labor intensity and the incorporation of Malian peasant farmers into localized descent groups." *American Ethnologist* 8, 1:53–73.

Leys, Colin. 1974. *Underdevelopment in Kenya.* Berkeley and Los Angeles: University of California Press.

Leys, Colin. 1978. "Capital accumulation, class formation, and dependency: The significance of the Kenya case." In R. Miliband and J. Saville, eds., *Socialist Register* 241–66.

Linares, Olga. 1981. "From tidal swamp to inland valley: On the social organization of wet rice cultivation among the Diola of Senegal." *Africa* 51, 2:557–95.

Livingstone, Ian. 1986. *Rural development, employment and incomes in Kenya.* Geneva: International Labour Organization.

Lloyd, Peter C. 1962. *Yoruba land law.* Ibadan: Oxford University Press.

Lofchie, Michael. 1989. *The policy factor: Agricultural performance in Kenya and Tanzania.* Boulder, Colo.: Lynne Rienner.

Long, Norman. 1968. *Social change and the individual.* Manchester: Manchester University Press.

Lonsdale, John. 1981. "States and social processes in Africa: A historiographical survey." *African Studies Review* 24, 2/3:139–225.

Lonsdale, John, and Bruce Berman. 1979. "Coping with the contradictions: The colonial state in Kenya, 1895–1914." *Journal of African History* 20, 4:487–506.

Low, Allan. 1986. "On farm research and household economics." In J. Moock, ed., *Undestanding Africa's rural households and farming systems.* Boulder, Colo.: Westview.

Lubeck, Paul, ed. 1987. *The African bourgeoisie: Capitalist development in Nigeria, Kenya and the Ivory Coast.* Boulder, Colo.: Lynne Rienner.

Lugard, Frederick D. 1923. *The dual mandate in tropical Africa.* 2d ed. Edinburgh: Blackwell.

Luning, H. 1967. "Economic aspects of low labour-income farming." Research Report 699. Wageningen: Center for Agricultural Publications and Documentation.

McCaskie, Thomas. 1980. "Office, land and subjects in the history of Manwere *fekuo*." *Journal of African History* 21, 2:189–208.

McCaskie, Thomas. 1983. "R. S. Rattray and the construction of Asante history." *History in Africa* 10:187–206.

McCaskie, Thomas. 1984. "*Ahyiamu*—'a place of meeting': An essay on process and event in the history of the Asante state." *Journal of African History* 25, 2:169–88.

MacGaffey, Janet. 1987. *Entrepreneurs and parasites: Struggles for indigenous capitalism in Zaire.* Cambridge: Cambridge University Press.

MacGaffey, Janet, et al. 1991. *The real economy of Zaire.* London and Philadelphia: James Currey and University of Pennsylvania Press.

MacGaffey, Wyatt. 1970. *Custom and law in the lower Congo.* Berkeley and Los Angeles: University of California Press.

Mackenzie, Fiona. 1986. *Land and labour: Women and men in agricultural change, Murang'a District, Kenya, 1880–1980.* Ph.D. diss. University of Ottawa.

Mackenzie, Fiona. 1988. "Land and territory: The interface between two systems of land tenure, Murang'a District, Kenya." *Africa* 59, 1:91–109.

Mackenzie, Fiona. 1993. "Perspectives on land tenure: Social relations and the definition of territory in a smallholding district, Kenya." In T. Bassett and D. Crummey, eds., *Land and agrarian systems in Africa.* Madison: University of Wisconsin Press.

Mackintosh, John, et al. 1966. *Nigerian government and politics.* London: Allen & Unwin.

Mackintosh, Maureen. 1977. "Reproduction and patriarchy: A critique of Claude Meillassoux, 'Femmes, greniers et capitaux'". *Capital and Class* 2:119–27.

Maizels, Alfred. 1987. "Primary commodities in the world economy: Problems and policies." *World Development* 15, 5:537–50.

Makings, S. M. 1966. "Agricultural change in Northern Rhodesia/Zambia." *Food Research Institute Studies* 6, 2:195–247.

Mandala, Elias. 1982. "Peasant cotton agriculture, gender and intergenerational relationships: The Lower Tchiri Valley of Malawi, 1906–1940." *African Studies Review* 25:27–44.

Mandala, Elias. 1990. *Work and control in a peasant economy: A history of the Lower Tchiri Valley in Malawi, 1859–1960.* Madison: University of Wisconsin Press.

Mann, Kristin, and Richard Roberts, eds. 1991. *Law in colonial Africa.* London and Portsmouth, N.H.: James Currey and Heinemann.

Markovitz, Irving, ed. 1987. *Studies in class and power in Africa.* New York: Oxford University Press.

Marris, Peter, and Anthony Somerset. 1971. *African businessmen.* London: Routledge & Kegan Paul.

Marter, Alan, and David Honeybone. 1976. *The economic resources of rural households and the distribution of agricultural development.* Lusaka: Rural Development Studies Bureau, University of Zambia.

Martin, Susan. 1984. "Gender and innovation: Farming, cooking, and palm processing in the Ngwa region, southeastern Nigeria, 1900–1930." *Journal of African History* 25:411–27.

Martin, Susan. 1988. *Palm oil and protest: An economic history of the Ngwa region, south-eastern Nigeria, 1800–1980.* Cambridge: Cambridge University Press.

Massell, B., and R. Johnson. 1968. "Economics of smallholder farming in Rhodesia." *Food Research Institute Studies* Supplement to vol. 8.

Matingu, Mary. 1974. "Rural to rural migration and employment: A case study in a selected area of Kenya." Master's thesis. University of Nairobi.

Maxwell, Simon. 1986. "Farming systems research: Hitting a moving target." *World Development* 14, 1:65–77.

Mbithi, Philip, and Carolyn Barnes. 1975. *Spontaneous settlement problems in Kenya.* Nairobi: East Africa Literature Bureau.

Meebelo, Henry S. 1971. *Reaction to colonialism.* Manchester: Manchester University Press.

Meebelo, Henry S. 1986. *African proletarians and colonial capitalism: Origins, growth and struggles of the Zambian labour movement to 1964.* Lusaka: Kenneth Kaunda Foundation.

Meek, Charles K. 1946. *Land law and custom in the colonies.* London and New York: Oxford University Press.

Meek, Charles K. 1957. *Land tenure and land administration in Nigeria and the Cameroons.* London: Her Majesty's Stationery Office.

Meillassoux, Claude. 1981. *Maidens, meal and money.* Cambridge: Cambridge University Press.

Meillassoux, Claude, ed. 1971. *Development of indigenous trade and markets in West Africa.* London: Oxford University Press.

Middleton, John, and Gretha Kershaw, 1965. *The central tribes of the northeastern Bantu.* London: International African Institute.

Migot-Adholla, Shem. 1984. "Rural development policy and inequality." In Joel Barkan, ed., *Politics and public policy in Kenya and Tanzania.* New York: Praeger.

Migot-Adholla, Shem, et al. 1990a. "Security of tenure and land productivity in Kenya." Paper prepared for a conference on Rural Land Tenure, Credit, Agricultural Investment and Farm Productivity in sub-Saharan Africa, Nairobi.

Migot-Adholla, Shem, et al. 1990b. "Land, security of tenure and productivity in Ghana." (See 1990a, above.)

Mikell, Gwendolyn. 1983. "Ghanaian chiefs, social strivers, and politics in a global economy." *Rural Africana* 17:31–55.

Mikell, Gwendolyn. 1984. "Filiation, economic crisis and the status of women in rural Ghana." *Canadian Journal of African Studies* 18, 1:195–218.

Mikell, Gwendolyn. 1985. "Expansion and contraction in economic access for rural women in Ghana." *Rural Africana* 21:13–30.

Mikell, Gwendolyn. 1989. *Cocoa and chaos in Ghana.* New York: Paragon House.

Miles, John. 1978. "Rural protest in the Gold Coast: The cocoa hold-ups." In C. Dewey and A. G. Hopkins, eds., *The imperial impact.* London: Athlone Press for the Institute of Commonwealth Studies.

Milimo, J. T. 1983. "Socio-economic aspects of small-scale farmers in the Northern Province of Zambia." In H. Svads, ed., *Proceedings of the seminar on soil productivity in the high rainfall areas of Zambia.* Oslo: Agricultural University of Norway.

Miller, Leonard. 1975. "Present and potential uses of credit by small maize and rice farmers in Western and Kwara States, Nigeria." Ibadan: Department of Agricultural Economics and Extension, University of Ibadan.

Mitchell, J. Clyde. 1956. *The Kalela dance.* Rhodes-Livingstone Institute Paper No. 27. Manchester: Manchester University Press.

Mkandawire, Thandika. 1989. "Structural adjustment and the agrarian crisis in Africa: A research agenda." Working Paper No. 2/89. Dakar: CODESRIA.

Moffat, U. J. 1932. "Native agriculture in the Abercorn District." Second Annual Bulletin of the Department of Agriculture, Northern Rhodesia.

Moock, Joyce L. 1986. *Understanding Africa's rural households and farming systems.* Boulder, Colo.: Westview.

Moore, Henrietta, and Megan Vaughan. 1987. "Cutting down trees: Women, nutrition and agricultural change in the Northern Province of Zambia, 1920–86." *African Affairs* 86, 345:523–40.

Moore, Sally Falk. 1975. *Law as social process.* Berkeley and Los Angeles: University of California Press.

Moore, Sally Falk. 1986. *Social facts and fabrications.* Cambridge: Cambridge University Press.

Moore, Sally Falk. n.d. "A double transfer of legal knowledge: Telling colonial officers what to say to Africans about running 'their own' Native Courts." Unpublished paper.

Morris, H. F., and J. S. Read, eds. 1972. *Indirect rule and the search for justice.* Oxford: Clarendon Press.

Morss, Elliot. 1984. "Institutional destruction resulting from donor and project proliferation in sub-Saharan Africa." *World Development* 12, 4:465–70.

Mortimore, Michael. 1989. *Adapting to drought: Farmers, famines and desertification in West Africa.* Cambridge: Cambridge University Press.

Moseley, Paul. 1983. *The settler economies.* Cambridge: Cambridge University Press.

Mudimbe, Valentin Y. 1988. *The invention of Africa.* Bloomington, Ind.: Indiana University Press.

Mukaru Ng'ang'a, D. 1977. "Mau Mau, loyalists and politics in Murang'a, 1952–70." *Kenya Historical Review* 5, 2:365–84.

Mukaru Ng'ang'a, D. 1978. *A political history of Murang'a District, 1900–1970.* Ph.D. diss. University of Nairobi.

Mulasa, Thomas. 1970. "Central government and local authorities." In G. Hyden et al., eds., *Development administration in Kenya.* Berkeley and Los Angeles: University of California Press.

Mungeam, G. H. 1966. *British rule in Kenya, 1895–1912.* Oxford: Clarendon Press.

Munro, J. Forbes. 1975. *Colonial rule and the Kamba.* Oxford: Clarendon Press.

Muriuki, Godfrey. 1974. *A history of the Kikuyu, 1500–1900.* Nairobi: Oxford University Press.

Murray, Colin. 1981. *Families divided.* Cambridge: Cambridge University Press.

Mvunga, M. P. 1980. *The colonial foundations of Zambia's land tenure system.* Lusaka: National Educational Company of Zambia.

Myers, Gregory. 1990. *This is not your land: An analysis of the impact of the Land Use Act in southwest Nigeria.* Ph.D. diss. University of Wisconsin.

Nader, Laura, and Henry Todd, eds. 1978. *The disputing process.* New York: Columbia University Press.

Netting, Robert. 1968. *Hill farmers of Nigeria.* Seattle: University of Washington Press.

Newbury, Catherine. 1984. "*Ebutumwa bw'emiogo*: The tyranny of cassava." *Canadian Journal of African Studies* 18:35–54.

Nixson, Fred. 1982. "Import substituting industrialization." In Martin Fransman, ed., *Industry and accumulation in Africa.* New York: St. Martin's.

Njeru, Enos. 1978. *Land adjudication and its implications for the social organization of the Mbeere.* Madison, Wis.: Land Tenure Center.

Njonjo, Apollo. 1977. *The Africanisation of the 'White Highlands': A study in agrarian class struggles in Kenya, 1950–74.* Ph.D. diss. Princeton University.

Nkadimeng, M., and G. Relly, 1983. "Kas Maine." In B. Bozzoli, ed., *Town and countryside in the Transvaal.* Johannesburg: Ravan.

Norman, David. 1974. "Rationalising mixed cropping under indigenous conditions: The example of northern Nigeria." *Journal of Development Studies* 11, 1:3–21.

Norman, David, et al. 1981. *Farm and village production systems in the semi-arid tropics of West Africa.* Patancheru, India: International Crop Research Institute for the Semi-Arid Tropics.

Norman, David, and D. C. Baker. 1986. "Components of farming systems research, FSR credibility, and experiences in Botswana." In J. Moock, ed., *Understanding Africa's rural households and farming systems.* Boulder, Colo.: Westview.

Nyuguto, P. M. 1981. "Settlement patterns in Nyeri District." Master's thesis. University of Nairobi.

Ogot, Bethwell A., ed. 1975. *Hadith 5: Economic and social change in East Africa.* Nairobi: East Africa Literature Bureau.

Okali, Christine. 1974. "Costs and returns for the cocoa farmer." In R. A. Kotey et al., eds., *The economics of cocoa production and marketing*. Legon: Institute for Statistical, Social and Economic Research.

Okali, Christine. 1983a. *Cocoa and kinship: The matrilineal Akan*. London: Kegan Paul.

Okali, Christine. 1983b. "Kinship and cocoa farming in Ghana." In C. Oppong, ed., *Female and male in West Africa*. London: George Allen & Unwin.

Okali, Christine, and Susan Mabey. 1975. "Women in agriculture in southern Ghana." *Manpower and Unemployment Research* 8, 2:13–40.

Okali, Christine, and James Sumberg. 1985. "Sheep and goats, men and women: Household relations and small ruminant development in southwestern Nigeria." *Agricultural Systems* 18:39–59.

Okoth-Ogendo, H. W. O. 1976. "African land tenure reform." In J. Heyer et al., eds., *Agricultural development in Kenya*. Oxford: Oxford University Press.

Okoth-Ogendo, H. W. O. 1981. "Land ownership and land distribution in Kenya's large farm areas." In Tony Killick, ed., *Papers on the Kenyan economy*. Nairobi: Oxford University Press.

Okoth-Ogendo, H. W. O. 1986. "The perils of land tenure reform: The case of Kenya." In J. W. Arntzen et al., eds., *Land policy and agriculture in eastern and southern Africa*. Tokyo: United Nations University.

Olayemi, J. K. 1976. "Swamp rice production in Kwara State." *Sierra Leone Agricultural Journal* 3:9–17.

Ollenu, N. A. 1962. *Principles of customary land law in Ghana*. London: Sweet & Maxwell.

Olson, Mancur. 1971. *The logic of collective action*. Rev. ed. New York: Schocken.

Olusanya, P. O., et al. 1978. *Migrant farmers of the eastern cocoa zone of southwestern Nigeria: A study in forest-savannah relationships*. Ile-Ife: Department of Demography, University of Ife.

Omotola, J. A., ed. 1982. *The Land Use Act: Report of a national workshop*. Lagos: Lagos University Press.

Omotola, J. A. 1983. *Cases on the Land Use Act*. Lagos: Lagos University Press.

Onwueme, I. 1978. *The tropical tuber crops*. Chichester: John Wiley & Sons.

Overton, John. 1988. "Origins of the Kikuyu land problem." *African Studies Review* 31, 2:109–26.

Oyediran, O. O. 1973. "Local influence and traditional leadership: The politics of the Ife Forest Reserve." *Odu*, n.s. 7:68–82.

Oyediran, O. O. 1974. "Modakeke in Ife," *Odu*, n.s. 10:63–78.

Oyemakinde, W. 1974. "Railway construction and operation in Nigeria, 1895–1911: Labour problems and socio-economic impact." *Journal of the Historical Society of Nigeria* 7, 2:303–24.

Oyewole, Tunde, et al. 1986. "Cassava processing in Ibadan area." Ibadan: International Institute of Tropical Agriculture.

Oyo Province. 1922. *Annual Report*. Nigerian National Archives.

Oyo Province. 1925. *Annual Report*. Nigerian National Archives.

Palmer, Robin, ed. 1973. *Zambian land and labour studies.* 3 vols. Lusaka: National Archives.

Palmer-Jones, R. W. 1981. "How not to learn from pilot irrigation projects." *Water Supply Management* 5, 1:81–105.

Panter-Brick, S. Keith, ed. 1978. *Soldiers and oil: The political transformation of Nigeria.* London: Frank Cass.

Parkin, David. 1972. *Palms, wine and witnesses.* San Francisco: Chandler.

Parpart, Jane. 1983. *Labor and capital on the African Copperbelt.* Philadelphia: Temple University Press.

Parpart, Jane, and Sharon Stichter, eds. 1988. *Patriarchy and class: African women in the home and the workforce.* Boulder, Colo.: Westview.

Pearson, Scott, et al. 1981. *Rice in West Africa: Policy and economics.* Stanford: Stanford University Press.

Peel, J. D. Y. 1983. *Ijeshas and Nigerians.* Cambridge: Cambridge University Press.

Perham, Margery. 1938. *Native administration in Nigeria.* London: Oxford University Press.

Perham, Margery, ed. 1936. *Ten Africans.* London: Faber & Faber.

Peters, D. U. 1950. *Land usage in Serenje District.* Rhodes-Livingstone Paper 19. Manchester: Manchester University Press.

Peters, Pauline. 1984. "Struggles over water, struggles over meaning." *Africa* 54, 3:29–49.

Peters, Pauline. 1987. "Embedded systems and rooted models: The grazing lands of Botswana and the 'commons' debate." In Bonnie McCay and James Acheson, eds., *The question of the commons.* Austin: University of Texas Press.

Peters, Pauline. 1988. "Understanding resource mobilization in arable agriculture in sub-Saharan Africa." Mimeographed.

Phillips, Anne. 1989. *The enigma of colonialism: British policy in West Africa.* London: James Currey.

Phillips, Arthur. 1944. *Report on Native Tribunals.* Nairobi: Colony and Protectorate of Kenya.

Phillips, Truman. 1983. "An overview of cassava consumption and production." In F. Delange and R. Ahluwalia, eds., *Cassava toxicity and thyroid: Research on public health issues.* Ottawa: IDRC.

Pim, Alan. 1940. *The financial and economic history of the African tropical territories.* Oxford: Clarendon Press.

Pim, Alan. 1948. "Mining, commerce and finance." In Margery Perham, ed., *The economics of a tropical dependency.* Vol. 2. London: Faber & Faber.

Pletcher, James. 1986. "The political uses of agricultural markets in Zambia." *Journal of Modern African Studies* 24, 4:603–17.

Post, Ken. 1963. *The Nigerian federal election of 1959.* London: Oxford University Press.

Post, Ken, and Michael Vickers. 1973. *Structure and conflict in Nigeria, 1960–65.* London: Heinemann.

Pottier, Johan. 1983. "Defunct labour reserve? Mambwe villages in the post-migration economy." *Africa* 53, 2:2–23.

Pottier, Johan. 1985. "Reciprocity and the beer pot: The changing pattern of Mambwe food production." In J. Pottier, ed., *Food systems in central and southern Africa.* 2 vols. London: SOAS.

Pottier, Johan. 1988. *Migrants no more: Settlement and survival in Mambwe villages, Zambia.* Bloomington, Ind.: Indiana University Press.

Presley, Cora. 1986. *The transformation of Kikuyu women and their nationalism.* Ph.D. diss. Stanford University.

Prins, Gwyn. 1980. *The hidden hippopotamus.* Cambridge: Cambridge University Press.

Quick, James. 1978. *Humanism or technocracy: Zambia's farming cooperatives, 1965–1972.* Lusaka: Institute for African Studies, University of Zambia.

Ranger, Terence O. 1971. *The agricultural history of Zambia.* Historical Association of Zambia. Pamphlet No. 1. Lusaka: National Educational Company of Zambia.

Ranger, Terence O. 1983. "The invention of tradition in colonial Africa." In E. Hobsbawm and T. Ranger, eds., *The invention of tradition.* Cambridge: Cambridge University Press.

Rasmussen, Thomas. 1974. "The popular basis of anti-colonial protest." In W. Tordoff, ed., *Politics in Zambia.* Manchester: Manchester University Press.

Rathbone, Richard. 1978. "Ghana." In John Dunn, ed., *West African states: Failure and promise.* Cambridge: Cambridge University Press.

Reardon, Thomas, et al. 1988. "Coping with household level food insecurity in drought-affected areas of Burkina Faso." *World Development* 16, 4:1065–74.

Richards, Audrey. 1939. *Land, labour and diet in Northern Rhodesia.* London: Oxford University Press.

Richards, Audrey. 1958. "A changing pattern of agriculture in East Africa: The Bemba of Northern Rhodesia." *Geographical Journal* 124, 3:302–14.

Richards, Audrey. 1959. "The Bemba of Northeastern Rhodesia." In E. Colson and M. Gluckman, eds., *Seven tribes of British Central Africa.* Manchester: Manchester University Press.

Richards, Audrey. 1971. "The conciliar system of the Bemba." In A. I. Richards and A. Kuper, eds., *Councils in action.* Cambridge: Cambridge University Press.

Richards, Paul. 1983. "Ecological change and the politics of African land use." *African Studies Review* 26, 2:1–72.

Richards, Paul. 1987. *Coping with hunger.* London: Allen & Unwin.

Rimmer, Douglas. 1978. "Elements of the political economy." In S. K. Panter-Brick, ed., *Soldiers and oil: The political transformation of Nigeria.* London: Frank Cass.

Rimmer, Douglas, ed. 1988. *Rural transformation in tropical Africa.* Athens, Ohio: Ohio University Press.

Roberts, Andrew. 1973. *A history of the Bemba.* London: Longman.

Roberts, Andrew. 1976. *A history of Zambia.* New York: Africana.

Robertson, A. F. 1983. "*Abusa*: the structural history of an economic contract." *Journal of Development Studies* 18, 4:447–78.

Robertson, A. F. 1984. *People and the state: An anthropology of planned development.* Cambridge: Cambridge University Press.

Robertson, A. F. 1987. *The dynamics of productive relationships: African share contracts in comparative perspective.* Cambridge: Cambridge University Press.

Robertson, Claire. 1983. *Sharing the same bowl.* Bloomington, Ind.: Indiana University Press.

Robertson, Claire, and Iris Berger, eds. 1986. *Women and class in Africa.* New York: Holmes & Meier.

Robinson, David, and Douglas Smith. 1979. *Sources of the African past.* New York: Africana.

Roider, Werner. 1968. *Nigerian farm settlement schemes.* Berlin: Institut für Ausländische Landwirtschaft an der Technischen Universität Berlin.

Rosberg, Carl, and John Nottingham. 1967. *The myth of Mau Mau: Nationalism in Kenya.* New York: Praeger, for the Hoover Institute, Stanford University.

Rose, Tore. 1985. *Crisis and recovery in sub-Saharan Africa.* Paris: OECD.

Ross, Paul. 1986. "Land as a right to membership: Land tenure dynamics in a peripheral area of the Kano close settled zone." In M. Watts, ed., *State, oil, and agriculture in Nigeria.* Berkeley, Calif.: Institute for International Studies.

Rotberg, Robert. 1965. *The rise of nationalism in Central Africa.* Cambridge, Mass.: Harvard University Press.

Rourke, B. E., and S. K. Sakyi-Gyinae. 1972. "Agricultural and urban wage rates in Ghana." *Economic Bulletin of Ghana* 2d series, 2, 1:3–13.

Rowling, C. W. 1952. *Report on land tenure in Ondo.* Ibadan: Government Printer.

Rowling, C. W. 1956. *Report on land tenure in Ijebu.* Ibadan: Government Printer.

Runge, Carlisle Ford. 1981. "Common property externalities." *American Journal of Agricultural Economics* 63:595–606.

Ruthenberg, Hans. 1980. *Farming systems in the tropics.* 3d ed. London: Oxford University Press.

Sandbrook, Richard. 1985. *The politics of Africa's economic stagnation.* Cambridge: Cambridge University Press.

Sandbrook, Richard. 1986. "State and economic stagnation in tropical Africa." *World Development* 14, 3:319–32.

Saul, Mahir. 1986. "Development of the grain market and merchants in Burkina Faso." *Journal of Modern African Studies* 24, 1:127–53.

Saul, Mahir. 1987. "The organization of a West African grain market." *American Anthropologist* 89, 1:74–95.

Schultz, Jurgen. 1976. *Land use in Zambia.* Munich: IFO Institut für Wirtschaftsforschung.

Schwimmer, Brian. 1976. "Periodic markets and urban development in southern Ghana." In C. Smith, ed., *Regional analysis.* Vol. 1. New York: Academic Press.

Schwimmer, Brian. 1980. "The organization of migrant farmer communities in southern Ghana." *Canadian Journal of African Studies* 14, 2:221–38.

Seers, Dudley. 1963. "The stages of growth of a primary producer in the middle of the twentieth century." *Economic Bulletin of Ghana* 7, 4:57–69.

Seidman, Ann. 1974. "The distorted growth of import-substituting industry: The Zambian case." *Journal of Modern African Studies* 12, 4:601–32.

Sender, John, and Sheila Smith. 1986. "What's right with the Berg Report and what's left of its criticisms." In Peter Lawrence, ed., *World recession and the food crisis in Africa.* London: James Currey, for Review of African Political Economy.

Senga, W. M. 1976. "Kenya's agricultural sector." In J. Heyer et al., eds., *Agricultural development in Kenya.* Nairobi: Oxford University Press.

Sharp, John, and Andrew Spiegel. 1985. "Vulnerability to impoverishment in South African rural areas: The erosion of kinship and neighborhood as social resources." *Africa* 55, 2:133–52.

Shepherd, Andrew. 1981. "Agrarian change in northern Ghana: Public investment, capitalist farming and famine." In Heyer, Roberts, and Williams, eds., *Rural development in tropical Africa.* New York: St. Martin's.

Shipton, Parker. 1985. "Land, credit and crop transitions in Kenya: The Luo response to directed development in Nyanza Province." Ph.D. diss. Cambridge University.

Shipton, Parker. 1988. "The Kenyan land tenure reform: Misunderstandings in the public creation of private property." In R. E. Downs and S. P. Reyna, eds. *Land and society in contemporary Africa.* Durham, N.H. University Press of New England.

Shipton, Parker. 1989. *Bitter money: Cultural economy and some African meanings of forbidden commodities.* American Ethnological Society Monograph Series 1. Washington, D.C.: American Anthropological Association.

Shipton, Parker. 1990. "African famines and food security: Anthropological perspectives." *Annual Review of Anthropology* 19:353–94.

Sklar, Richard. 1963. *Nigerian political parties.* Princeton: Princeton University Press.

Smith, L. D. 1976. "An overview of agricultural development policy." In J. Heyer et al., eds., *Agricultural development in Kenya.* Nairobi: Oxford University Press.

Snyder, Francis G. 1981. *Capitalism and legal change: An African transformation.* New York: Academic Press.

Sorrenson, M. P. K. 1967. *Land reform in the Kikuyu country.* Nairobi: Oxford University Press.

Sorrenson, M. P. K. 1968. *Origins of European settlement in Kenya.* Nairobi: Oxford University Press.

Southall, Roger. 1978. "Farmers, traders and brokers in the Gold Coast cocoa economy." *Canadian Journal of African Studies* 12:185–211.

Spiegel, Andrew. 1980. "Rural differentiation and the diffusion of migrant labour remittances in Lesotho." In Philip Mayer, ed., *Black villagers in an industrial society: Anthropological perspectives on labour migration in southern Africa.* Cape Town: Oxford University Press.

Stamp, Patricia. 1975–76. "Perceptions of change and economic strategy among Kikuyu women of Mitero, Kenya." *Rural Africana* 29:19–44.

Stamp, Patricia. 1986. "Kikuyu women's self-help groups." In C. Robertson and I. Berger, eds., *Women and class in Africa.* New York: Holmes & Meier.

Staudt, Kathleen. 1975–76. "Women farmers and inequities in agricultural services." *Rural Africana* 29:81–94.

Steeves, Jeffrey. 1976. "Farmers, stratification and tea development in Kenya." *The African Review* 6, 4:46–64.

Steeves, Jeffrey. 1978. "Class analysis and rural Africa: The Kenya Tea Development Authority." *Journal of Modern African Studies* 16, 1:123–32.

Stichter, Sharon. 1975–76. "Women and the labor force in Kenya." *Rural Africana* 29:45–68.

Stiglitz, Joseph. 1989. "Rational peasants, efficient institutions, and a theory of rural organization: Methodological remarks for development economics." In P. Bardhan, ed., *The economic theory of agrarian institutions.* Oxford: Clarendon Press.

Stolen, Kristi. 1983. "Socio-economic constraints on changes in peasant agriculture in the Northern Province of Zambia." In H. Svads, eds., *Proceedings of the seminar on soil productivity in the high rainfall areas of Zambia.* Oslo: Agricultural University of Norway.

Stromgaard, Peter. 1985. "A subsistence society under pressure: The Bemba of northern Zambia." *Africa* 55, 1:39–59.

Sudarkasa, Niara. 1979. "From stranger to alien: The socio-political history of the Nigerian Yoruba in Ghana, 1900–1970." In William Shack and Elliott Skinner, eds., *Strangers in Africa.* Berkeley and Los Angeles: University of California Press.

Suret Canale, Jean. 1971. *French colonialism in tropical Africa, 1900–45*, tr. T. Gottheiner. London: Hurst.

Sutton, Inez. 1983. "Labour and commercial agricultural in Ghana in the late nineteenth and early twentieth centuries." *Journal of African History* 24:461–83.

Sutton, Inez. 1984. "Law, chieftaincy and conflict in colonial Ghana: The Ada case." *African Affairs* 83, 330:41–62.

Svads, Henning. 1983. "Existing cultivation systems in the high rainfall areas of Zambia." In H. Svads, ed., *Proceedings of the seminar on soil productivity in the high rainfall areas of Zambia.* Oslo: Agricultural University of Norway.

Swainson, Nicola. 1980. *The development of corporate capitalism in Kenya, 1918–1977.* Berkeley and Los Angeles: University of California Press.

Swainson, Nicola. 1987. "Indigenous capitalism in Kenya." In Paul Lubeck, ed., *African bourgeoisie: Capitalist development in Nigeria, Kenya and Ivory Coast.* Boulder, Colo.: Lynne Rienner.

Swindell, Ken. 1985. *African farm labour.* Cambridge: Cambridge University Press.

Tabatabai, H. 1988. "Agricultural decline and access to food in Ghana." *International Labour Review* 127, 6:703–34.

Teriba, O., and M. O. Kayode, eds. 1972. *Industrial development in Nigeria.* Ibadan: Ibadan University Press.

Thiele, Graham. 1986. "The state and rural development in Tanzania: The village administration as a political field." *Journal of Development Studies* 22, 3:540–57.

Thomas, Barbara. 1985. *Politics, participation and poverty: Development through self-help in Kenya.* Boulder, Colo.: Westview.

Thomas, R. G. 1973. "Forced labour in British West Africa: The case of the northern territories of the Gold Coast." *Journal of African History* 14, 1:79–103.

Throup, David. 1988. *Economic and social origins of Mau Mau.* London, Nairobi, and Athens, Ohio: James Currey, Heinemann, and Ohio University Press.

Tignor, Robert. 1976. *The colonial transformation of Kenya.* Princeton: Princeton University Press.

Tordoff, William. 1965. *Ashanti under the Prempehs, 1888–1935.* London: Oxford University Press.

Tordoff, William. 1980. "Rural administration." In Tordoff, ed., *Administration in Zambia.* Manchester: Manchester University Press.

Tordoff, William, and Ian Scott. 1974. "Political parties: Structures and policies." In William Tordoff, ed., *Politics in Zambia.* Manchester: Manchester University Press.

Trapnell, Colin G. 1953. *The soils, vegetation and agriculture of North Eastern Rhodesia.* Lusaka: Government Printer.

Turner, Teresa. 1978. "Commercial capitalism and the 1975 coup." In K. Panter-Brick, ed., *Soldiers and oil: The political transformation of Nigeria.* London: Frank Cass.

Turok, Ben, ed. 1979. *Development in Zambia.* London: Zed Press.

Udry, Christopher. 1990. "Credit markets in northern Nigeria: Credit as insurance in a rural economy." *The World Bank Economic Review* 4, 3:251–69.

Upton, Martin. 1973. *Farm management in Africa.* London: Oxford University Press.

USDA. 1981. *Food problems and prospects in sub-Saharan Africa.* Washington, D.C.: USDA.

Vail, Leroy. 1976. "Ecology and history: The example of eastern Zambia." *Journal of Southern African Studies* 3, 2:129–55.

Vail, Leroy. 1983. "Political economy of East-Central Africa." In David Birmingham and Phyllis Martin, eds., *A history of Central Africa.* Vol. 2. London: Longman.

Vail, Leroy, ed. 1989. *The creation of tribalism in southern Africa.* Berkeley and Los Angeles: University of California Press.

Van den Driesen, I. R. 1971. "Patterns of land holding and land distribution in the Ife Division of Western Nigeria." *Africa* 41:42–53.

Van Donge, Jan Kees. 1982. "Politicians, bureaucrats and farmers: A Zambian case study." *Journal of Development Studies* 19, 1:88–107.

Van Donge, Jan Kees. 1985. "Understanding rural Zambia: The Rhodes-Livingstone Institute revisited." *Africa* 55, 1:60–75.

Van Hear, Nicholas. 1982. *Northern labour and development of capitalist agriculture in Ghana.* Ph.D. diss. University of Birmingham.

Van Onselen, Charles. 1976. *Chibaro: African mine labour in Southern Rhodesia, 1900–1933.* London: Pluto.

Vaughan, Megan. 1987. *The story of an African famine.* Cambridge: Cambridge University Press.

Vellenga, Dorothy. 1977. "Differentiation among women farmers in two rural areas of Ghana." *Labour and Society* 2, 2:197–208.

Vellenga, Dorothy. 1983. "Who is a wife: Legal expressions of heterosexual conflict in Ghana." In C. Oppong, ed., *Female and male in West Africa.* London: Allen & Unwin.

Vellenga, Dorothy. 1986. "Matriliny, patriliny and class formation among women cocoa farmers in two rural areas of Ghana." In C. Robertson and I. Berger, eds., *Women and class in Africa.* New York: Holmes & Meier.

Von Braun, Joachim, et al. 1989. *Irrigation technology and commercialization of rice in the Gambia: Effects on income and nutrition.* Research Report 75. Washington, D.C.: International Food Policy Research Institute.

Von Braun, Joachim, and Patrick Webb. 1989. "Impact of new crop technology on the agricultural division of labor in West Africa." *Economic Development and Cultural Change* 37:513–34.

Von Bulow, Dorthe, and Anne Sorenson. 1988. *Gender dynamics in contract farming: Women's role in smallholder tea production in Kericho District.* Copenhagen: Center for Development Research.

Wallace, Tina. 1981. "The Kano River Project, Nigeria." In Heyer, Roberts, and Williams, eds., *Rural development in tropical Africa.* New York: St. Martin's.

Wambaa, Rebman, and Kenneth King. 1975. "The political economy of the Rift Valley: A squatter perspective." In B. A. Ogot, ed., *Hadith 5: Economic and Social Change in East Africa.* Nairobi: East African Literature Bureau.

Wangari, Esther. 1990. *Effects of land registration on small-scale farming in Kenya: The case of Mbeere in Embu District.* Ph.D. diss. The New School for Social Research.

Ward Price, H. L. 1939. *Land tenure in the Yoruba provinces.* Lagos: Government Printer.

Wasserman, Gary. 1976. *Politics of decolonization: Kenya Europeans and the land issue, 1960–65.* Cambridge: Cambridge University Press.

Watson, William. 1958. *Tribal cohesion in a money economy.* Manchester: Manchester University Press.

Watson, William. 1976. "British colonial policy and tribal political organization." In W. Arens, ed., *A century of change.* The Hague: Mouton.

Watts, Michael, ed. 1986. *State, oil and agriculture in Nigeria.* Berkeley, Calif.: Institute of International Studies.

Webb, Patrick. 1984. "Of rice and men: The story behind The Gambia's decision to dam its river." In E. Goldsmith and Hilyard, eds., *Social and environmental effects of large dams.* Vol. 2. Britain: Wadebridge Ecological Centre.

Weber, Jacques. 1977. "Structures agraires et évolution des milieux ruraux: le cas de la région cacaoyère du centre-sud Cameroun." *Cahiers ORSTOM,* série Science Humaine, 14, 4:361–81.

Weigel, Jean Yves. 1982. *Migration et production domestique des Soninké de Sénégal.* Paris: ORSTOM Travaux et Documents.

Weiskel, Timothy. 1975. *French colonial rule and the Baule peoples.* Oxford: Clarendon Press.

Wells, Jerome C. 1974. *Agricultural policy and economic growth in Nigeria, 1962–68.* Ibadan: Oxford University Press, for the Nigerian Institute of Social and Economic Research.

Werbner, Richard. 1967. "Federal administration, rank, and civil strife among Bemba royals and nobles." *Africa* 37, 1:22–48.

West African Lands Committee. 1916a. *Minutes of evidence.* London: Printed for the Colonial Office.

West African Lands Committee. 1916b. *Papers and correspondence.* London: Printed for the Colonial Office.

West, Henry. 1972. *Land policy in Buganda.* Cambridge: Cambridge University Press.

Wheeler, David. 1984. "Sources of stagnation in sub-Saharan Africa." *World Development* 12, 1:1–23.

Wilks, Ivor. 1975. *Asante in the nineteenth century.* Cambridge: Cambridge University Press.

Williams, Gavin, ed. 1976. *Nigeria: economy and society.* London: Collings.

Williams, Gavin, ed., 1980. *State and Society in Nigeria.* Idanre: Afrografika.

Wolgin, Jerome. 1975. "Resource allocation and risk: A case study of smallholder agriculture in Kenya." *American Journal of Agricultural Economics* 57, 4:622–30.

Wood, Adrian, and Eric Shula. 1987. "The state and agriculture in Zambia." In Naceur Bourenane and Thandika Mkandawire, ed., *The state and agriculture in Africa.* Dakar: CODESRIA.

Woodman, Gordon. 1966. *The development of customary land law in Ghana.* Cambridge: Cambridge University Press.

Woodman, Gordon. 1974. "The rights of wives, sons and daughters in the estates of their deceased husbands and fathers." In C. Oppong, ed., *Domestic rights and duties in southern Ghana.* Legon Family Research Papers No. 1. Legon: Institute for African Studies, University of Ghana.

World Bank. 1981. *Towards accelerated development in sub-Saharan Africa.* Washington, D.C.: World Bank.

World Bank. 1984. *Towards sustained development in sub-Saharan Africa.* Washington, D.C.: World Bank.

World Bank. 1986. *Financing adjustment with growth in sub-Saharan Africa, 1986–90.* Washington, D.C.: World Bank.

World Bank. 1989. *Successful development in Africa.* Washington, D.C.: World Bank.

Yahaya, A. D. 1978. "Creation of states." In S. K. Panter-Brick, ed., *Soldiers and oil: The political transformation of Nigeria.* London: Frank Cass.

Young, Crawford. 1988. "The African colonial state and its political legacy." In Chazan and Rothchild, eds., *The precarious balance.* Boulder, Colo.: Westview.

Young, Crawford, N. Sherman, and T. Rose. 1981. *Cooperatives and development: Agricultural politics in Ghana and Uganda.* Madison: University of Wisconsin Press.

Index

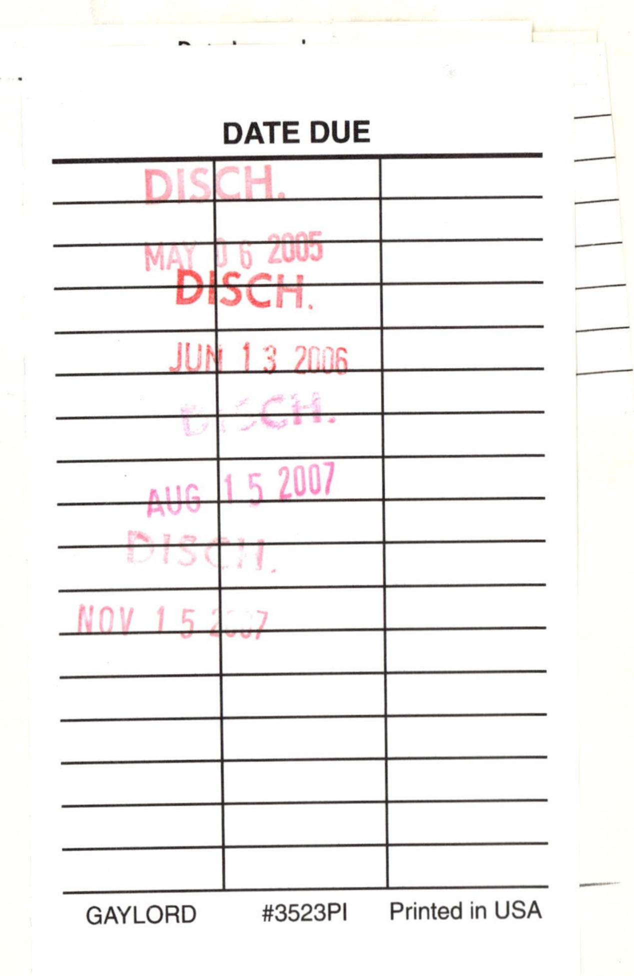